100 Mountain &

GUIDI

California Backroads & 4-Wheel-Drive Trails

Charles A.Wells & Matt Peterson

Chloride Cliff above Chloride City Trail #42, rated moderate

Published by FunTreks, Inc.
P.O. Box 3127, Monument, CO 80132-3127
Phone: Toll free 877-222-7623
Fax: (719) 277-7411
E-mail: books@funtreks.com
Website: www.funtreks.com

Writing, design, photography and production by Charles A. Wells & Matt Peterson.

Edited by Shelley Mayer

First Edition

Printed in China

Library of Congress
Control Number: 2013920902
ISBN: 978-1-934838-07-5
FREE trail updates and GPS downloads available at www.funtreks.com.

To order additional books, call toll-free 1-877-222-7623 or order online at www.funtreks.com.

ACKNOWLEDGEMENTS

Our thanks to: everyone we met on the trails for giving us their time and allowing us to use their pictures; active 4-wheel-drive clubs across California who have adopted trails and work hard to keep trails open; staffers and rangers at the U.S. Forest Service, BLM and other government land agencies for their time and patience answering our many questions; 4 wheelers and clubs who, 10 years ago, showed us most of the trails in this book.

We would also like to thank our dedicated trail scouts Carl Lea and Rob Harmon. Carl drives a 2003 gold TJ (page 36) and Rob a 1988 black Range Rover (page 7).

GUARANTEE OF SATISFACTION
We guarantee you will enjoy the trails in this book. If not, or if you are dissatisfied with the book in any other way, return it to us for a full refund. Or, call our toll-free number during business hours at 1-877-222-7623. We promise to do whatever it takes to make you happy.

DISCLAIMER

Travel in California's backcountry is, by its very nature, potentially dangerous and could result in property damage, injury or even death. The scope of this book cannot predict every possible hazard you may encounter. If you drive any of the trails in this book, you acknowledge these risks and assume full responsibility. You are the final judge as to whether a trail is safe to drive on any given day, whether your vehicle is capable of the journey and what supplies you should carry. The information contained herein cannot replace good judgment and proper preparation on your part. The publisher and authors of this book disclaim any and all liability for bodily injury, death or property damage that could occur to you or any of your passengers.

We have made every effort to update trails to match U.S. Forest Service Motor Vehicle Use Maps (MVUMs) that were available at the time of this writing. We cannot match maps that have not yet been issued or keep up with annual changes to existing maps. We will attempt to report changes on our website, but make no guarantee of accuracy. You are ultimately responsible for following the latest and correct MVUM. In addition, OHV laws described in this book change constantly. We do our best to keep up with them; however, you are ultimately responsible to know the correct and latest laws. The publisher and authors of this book disclaim any and all liability for fines or other punishment that could result from being on the wrong trail or breaking the law.

Note: Telephone numbers and websites that appear in this book were verified Jan. 1, 2014.

CONTENTS

TRAIL LIST

Green = Easy, Blue = Moderate, Red = Difficult

To find a trail, use list at left and map below to determine in which area a trail is located, then turn to the page indicated. Detailed area maps will direct you to individual trails.

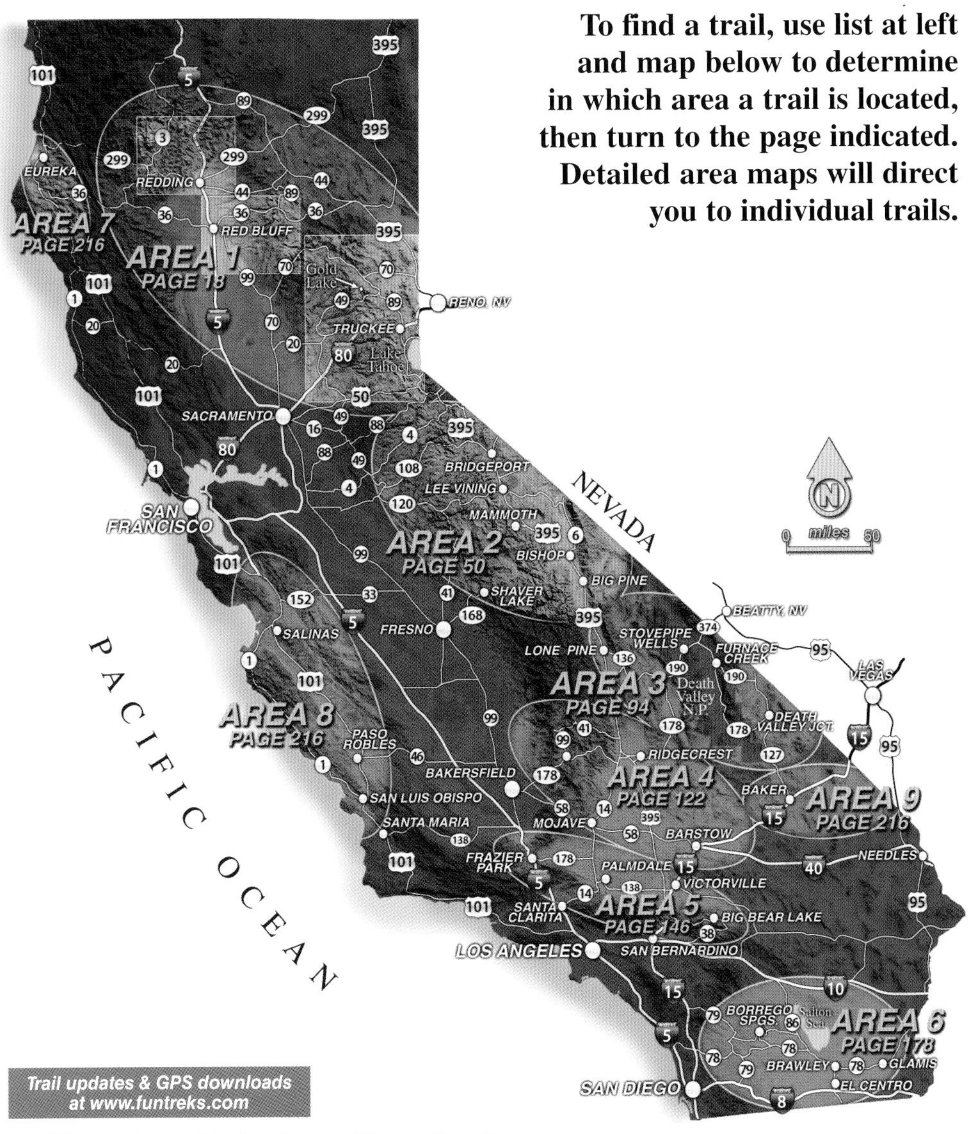

Trail updates & GPS downloads at www.funtreks.com

Throughout this book, you'll see the above gray box. It's a reminder that our website has trail updates that come from customers just like you. We invite you to send updates to us through our website, email to *books@funtreks.com*, or call toll-free at 877-222-7623.

In addition, all waypoints in this book are available as free .gpx downloads for your mobile device, GPS unit or computer. Simply go to our website and click on *Guidebooks*, then scroll down to *FREE Waypoint Downloads*.

TRAIL RATINGS DEFINED

Trail ratings are very subjective. Conditions change for many reasons, including weather and time of year. An easy trail can quickly become difficult when washed out by a rainstorm or blocked by a fallen rock. You must be the final judge of a trail's condition on the day you drive it. In this book, if any part of a trail is difficult, the entire trail is rated difficult. You may be able to drive a significant portion of a trail before reaching the difficult spot. Read each trail description carefully for specific information.

Easy

Gravel, dirt, clay, sand, or mildly rocky road. Gentle grades. Water levels low except during periods of heavy runoff. Full-width single lane or wider with adequate room to pass most of the time. Where shelf conditions exist, road is wide with minor sideways tilt. Clay roads, when wet, can significantly increase difficulty. Some trails can be driven in 2WD under ideal conditions. Others will need 4WD and, in some cases, low-range gearing.

Our Vehicles: (See above photos)

A. 1988 Range Rover SWB (scout owned): Mostly stock, Old Man Emu suspension added, 1.5″ lift, 29″ BFG AT tires, brush guard & roof rack. (See photo A above and opposite page.)

B. 2012 Jeep® Rubicon 4-DR: Standard equipment includes lockers front and rear and push-button, quick-disconnect sway bar. Added CB radio and front steel bumper with brackets to tow vehicle behind motorhome.

C. 2012 Jeep® Rubicon 2-DR: Standard equipment includes lockers F&R and quick-disconnect sway bar. Added 3-inch lift, steel bumpers, winch and CB radio.

Moderate

Rutted dirt or rocky road. Careful tire placement may be necessary. Some grades fairly steep but manageable if dry. Soft sand possible. Sideways tilt will require caution. Narrow shelf roads possible. Backing may be necessary to pass. Water depths passable for stock high-clearance vehicles except during periods of heavy runoff. Mud holes may be present especially in the spring. Undercarriage may scrape occasionally depending on ground clearance. Rock-stacking may be necessary in some cases. Brush may touch vehicle. Four-wheel drive, low range, and higher ground clearance required in most cases. Standard factory skid plates and tow hooks recommended on many trails.

Difficult

Grades can be very steep with severe ground undulation and large boulders. Sideways tilt can be extreme. Sand hills very steep with soft downslopes. Deep water crossings possible. Shelf roads extremely narrow; use caution in full-size vehicle. Passing may be difficult with backing required for long distances. Brush may scratch sides of vehicle. Body damage possible. Some trails suitable for more aggressive stock vehicles but most trails require vehicle modification. Lifts, differential lockers, aggressive articulation, and/or winches recommended in many cases. Skid plates and tow hooks required.

Introduction

Sierra Pelona Ridge/Rowher OHV, Trail #64

Fun Trails – Our Promise to You

We all look forward to getting out in the backcountry and having fun in our 4-wheel drives. It's so disappointing to come back from a trip that turned out to be a big waste of time. After three decades of exploring the West, we've learned the difference between "yawner" trails and real adventures.

When we're in our SUV, we want the drive to be interesting with curves and dips and something real to see. We expect the same pleasures driving our hard-core Jeep, but with an obstacle or two along the way. If we're riding our ATVs, in addition to trail details, we need to know if we're legal and where to unload and camp.

This book replaces two previous black-and-white books that were written over a decade ago. In that time, some of the trails were closed. Of the ones still open, we whittled our list down to the best 100. We think these trails are, collectively, the best batch of California trails ever put together in one place. We are so sure, we've guaranteed it. (Really! See our guarantee at the top of page 2.)

So go forth, have fun, but remember to be responsible and always stay on designated trails.

What's New in This Edition

This book features a new color format that is simpler and easier to use. A separate mileage log has numbered locations that graphically jump off the page. Our new maps now include detailed relief backgrounds. Referencing the numbered locations between the mileage log and map makes it easy to sense your location. In addition, exact GPS coordinates are provided for each numbered location.

Every detail about a trail appears on a handy two-page spread. Vehicle symbols identify types of vehicles allowed on each trail. Reverse mileages are now included for all trails, and more historical highlights have been added.

Website Updates and Downloads

Go to www.funtreks.com and click on Trail Updates. While there, check out our free GPS downloads. Learn about our other great books and related products. The site is very simple to use and includes inspiring photographs to get you off the couch and into the backcountry.

Explanation of Vehicle Symbols

Please read carefully before attempting any trail in this book.

SUV or Pickup Truck
This symbol represents a street-licensed stock sport utility vehicle or pickup truck with 4-wheel drive. Minimum ground clearance should be 7" to 8" at low point of vehicle and about a foot at rocker panel. Low range is recommended for rocky, steep and high elevation trails. More aggressive models will have higher clearance and factory off-road enhancements such as skid plates, tow points and differential lockers. Longer and wider vehicles require more ground clearance.

In addition to vehicle capability and size, other factors such as driver's skill, tires and tolerance for damage greatly affect which trails can be driven. Every vehicle is different and every trail is different. Judgment as to whether a vehicle is capable of traversing a specific trail lies solely with the owner of the vehicle. Read each trail description carefully.

Hard-core Modified. This symbol represents street-licensed vehicles that have been significantly modified for difficult hard-core situations. Most modifications are custom, but there are specific factory models that meet hard-core standards. Minimal tire size starts at 32", but 33" to 35" is more typical. Lifts of 3" or more, heavy-duty skid plates and accessories, increased articulation and differential lockers are the norm. Many additional modifications are possible.

These vehicles should be able to handle all trails in this book, with the possible exception of trails #13, #14, #32, #34, #35 and #71. These trails are at the top end of the difficult range with portions of the trail, at certain times of the year, possibly falling into the extreme category. Vehicle modifications and a very experienced driver may be necessary to complete the trail.

60"-Wide Side-by-Sides. This symbol represents what are commonly called UTVs, or Utility Terrain Vehicles. They are generally considered unlicensed vehicles; however, some states, like Arizona and Montana, allow licensing if modified for street use. For the purposes of this book, this symbol represents unlicensed vehicles.

Capability of these vehicles ranges from simple utility uses on ranches and farms to extreme modifications for hard-core trail use. Their width prohibits its use on 50"-ATV trails. For this book, 4-wheel-drive capability is assumed.

When you see this symbol at the top of the page, it primarily indicates the trail allows unlicensed vehicles (or in California, green-sticker vehicles). The ratings of easy, moderate and difficult are open to far greater interpretation. Only the operator can determine the appropriateness of the trail.

50"-Wide ATVs and Side-by-Sides. This symbol represents ATVs, or All Terrain Vehicles, not wider than 50". It also represents the newest craze—50"-wide side-by-sides (e.g., the "RZR"). Both are generally considered unlicensed vehicles; however, some states, like Arizona and Montana, allow licensing if modified for street use. For the purposes of this book, they are considered unlicensed vehicles.

These vehicles range in size from tiny 2WD machines for kids to large 4WD machines for adults. Generally, trails in this book are for 4-wheel-drive ATVs, but we know some 2-wheel-drive units can be equally capable.

When you see this symbol at the top of the page, it primarily indicates the trail allows unlicensed vehicles (or in California, green-sticker vehicles). The ratings of easy, moderate and difficult are open to far greater interpretation. Only the operator can determine the appropriateness of the trail.

Dirt Bikes (Unlicensed). This symbol represents unlicensed dirt bikes only. Licensed, dual-purpose bikes can ride any trail in this book.

The symbol does not mean the trail is a single-track trail; it only means unlicensed dirt bikes are allowed. All trails in this book are wide enough for SUVs and Jeeps, but most are still great rides for dirt bikes. Some trails in this book connect to 50"-wide and single-track trails. These narrower trails are specified on Motor Vehicle Use Maps. (See page 11.)

Easy, moderate and difficult ratings do not apply to dirt bikes, but they do provide general information on what to expect. Generally, a dirt bike can complete a trail in far less time than a Jeep or SUV, so take this into consideration.

About California

When to go. Plan to drive northern trails in the spring, summer and fall. These trails are at higher elevations and many are closed in the winter due to snow. Low-elevation areas in southern California, especially Death Valley National Park, are desert. June, July and August can be dangerously hot, and we recommend avoiding these months unless you are very experienced in desert travel. Monsoon rains and flash floods occur most often in late summer. December and January are usually pleasant, but spurts of cool, damp weather are not uncommon.

Contact with illegal aliens. Although unlikely, it is possible you could come into contact with illegal aliens, especially on the southernmost trails in this book. We encountered several illegal aliens on Mortero Wash, Trail #87. Fortunately, they were friendly and we had no problems. Still, you may not be so lucky. We recommend you travel in a group on trails close to the border.

Self-reliance. Most of us live in populated areas and are accustomed to having other people around when things go wrong. In California's remote backcountry, you must be self-reliant. Don't count on help from passersby.

Take plenty of water. We can't stress enough the importance of carrying and drinking plenty of water. Carry at least one gallon per person per day.

Avoid hottest part of day. On long summer days, try to travel in the morning and evening to avoid the hottest part of the day, or head to the high country.

First aid. Always carry a good first-aid kit. Take a first-aid course and learn the basics. Make sure the kit contains a thorough instruction booklet.

What to do if you have mechanical problems or you get lost. Stay with your vehicle. There's always a chance that someone will come along if you stay near the road. Your vehicle is easier to see than you are. Seek shade. Don't sit on the hot ground. Dig down to cooler sand below. Create your own shade with blankets or a tarp. Drink plenty of water; don't wait until you get thirsty. Wear light-colored, loose-fitting clothing that covers as much of your skin as possible. Wear a hat and use sunscreen. Collect firewood before dark. Build a fire before you need it. If you get lost or separated from your group, stay in one place.

If you're familiar with the area and know exactly how far it is to hike out and are absolutely sure you can make it, consider walking out.

Try to draw attention to yourself using a whistle or signal mirror. Creating a smoky fire is a difficult thing to do in the desert, but this method could be used as a last resort. Just make sure to keep the fire under control.

If you have a cell phone, try to find a point where you can get a signal and call for help. Carry a satellite phone if you can afford one. Carry a GPS unit to avoid getting lost in the first place.

Hyperthermia. When your body overheats it's called hyperthermia. Symptoms include dry, flushed skin, inability to sweat, rapid heartbeat, and a rising body temperature. Hyperthermia is often preceded by cramps. They may not go away by drinking water alone. You may need food or salt. If hyperthermia is allowed to progress, you could collapse from heatstroke, which can be fatal if not treated quickly.

To prevent hyperthermia, stay in the shade, don't overexert yourself and drink plenty of water. If work is required, conserve your energy as best as possible.

Hypothermia. It gets cold in the desert after the sun goes down. If it rains and gets windy, you could find yourself shivering in no time, especially if you've worked up a sweat during the day. Your hands and feet will become stiff. You may not be able to hold a match and start a fire. Prevention is the key. Put on a jacket before you begin to get cold. Stay dry. Change clothes if necessary. If you get too cold, blankets may not be enough to warm you. Build a fire, drink hot liquids, or cuddle up with someone else.

Dehydration. As your body sweats to cool itself, it dehydrates. You may be drinking water but not enough. Eating may make you nauseous. You won't want to eat or drink. As symptoms get worse, your mouth will become dry, you may become dizzy, develop a headache, and become short of breath. At some point, you may not be able to walk or care for yourself.

You must prevent dehydration before it happens. Drink more than just to quench your thirst. If you must conserve water, rest as much as possible, try not to sweat, and don't eat a lot. Digestion requires body fluids. If you have plenty of water, drink it.

Trail Rules and Etiquette

- Stay on existing trails at all times. Don't shortcut switchbacks, widen existing routes or make new trails.
- Vehicles going uphill have the right-of-way over downhill vehicles.
- Carry proper paperwork for your vehicle. Items may include driver's license, proof of insurance, vehicle registration and special permits.
- Don't drive or ride while under the influence of alcohol or drugs.
- Never drive or ride a motor vehicle in a wilderness area.
- Drive cautiously at all times, especially around blind curves.
- Cross streams at designated crossings only.
- Pull over at existing wide spots when you are out of your vehicle, not moving, or when overtaken by a faster vehicle. Be extra careful around hikers, bikers, horses and pack animals.
- Leave gates the way you find them unless posted otherwise.
- Public roads often cross or parallel private land. Respect rights of private property owners.
- Don't blast your radio or gun your engine. Don't blow your horn unless it is absolutely necessary.
- Pack out your trash, except in fee areas that have approved receptacles.

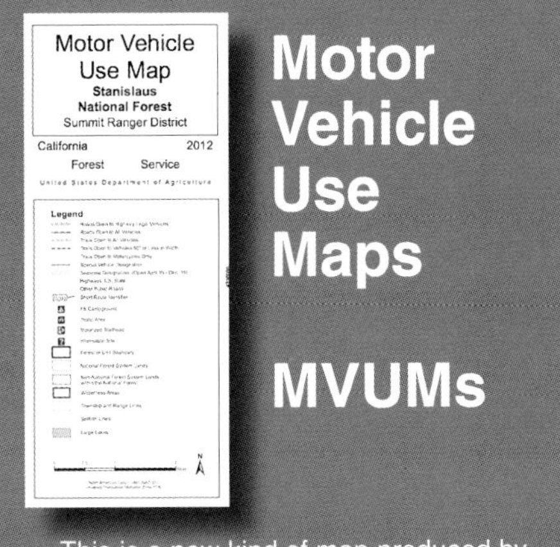

Motor Vehicle Use Maps

MVUMs

This is a new kind of map produced by the U.S. Forest Service, and everyone who travels in the backcountry needs to know what they are. These black-and-white maps are free and available at ranger districts and other forest offices. Many can be downloaded as PDFs from forest service websites. Some maps have already been published and more are still in the pipeline. The maps are intended to be legal documents to assist law enforcement and are not necessarily easy to use. Several maps are often needed to cover an area, since roads stop at forest or ranger district boundaries. The maps identify road usage by vehicle type. If a road is not shown on the map it is considered closed. Presence or absence of signs in the field is no longer relevant. Violations are subject to fines up to $5,000 and/or imprisonment up to 6 months.

FunTreks has made every effort to update trails based on the maps that were issued at the time of this writing. New MVUMs are nearing publication and existing maps are updated every year. It is impractical for any published guidebook to keep up with the changes. Published MVUMs supersede anything in this book. Get a copy of your local MVUM and follow it carefully. For a list of published MVUMs, go to: www.fs.fed.us/recreation/programs/ohv/ohv_maps.shtml.

• Don't pick wildflowers, walk on delicate tundra or remove anything from historical sites.

• Control your pets when allowed.

Safety Tips:

• Wear your seat belt and use child restraints. Your vehicle can unexpectedly slide, lurch or stop abruptly. Serious injuries can occur even at slow speeds.

• Keep heads, arms and legs inside moving vehicle. Many trails are narrow. Brush, tree limbs and rock overhangs may come very close or even touch your vehicle. Enforce this rule with your children. Don't let your dog stick its head out the window when moving.

• Stay away from mines and mine structures. Besides the fact that most are on private land, these areas are extremely dangerous. Don't enter mine adits or shafts. They can collapse, contain poisonous gases, or have open shafts in the floor. Be especially careful with children and pets.

• Carry detailed paper topographic maps regardless of whether you have a GPS unit or laptop computer. Electronic devices can fail at any time. This book will direct you along a specific route, but if you get lost, you'll want a map. We recommend map atlases, like the DeLorme Gazetteer or Benchmark Road & Recreation Atlas. They are very handy and inexpensive given that they cover the entire state in great detail. Don't rely much on MVUMs to help with navigation.

• Travel with another vehicle whenever possible. If you must go alone, stay on easier, more traveled routes. Never travel alone on difficult trails. Make sure you tell someone where you are going and when you plan to return. Report to them when you return.

• Join a 4-wheel-drive club. It's fun and you'll learn a great deal. Pick a club with similar interests and vehicles.

• If you get lost or stuck, stay with your vehicle unless you are very close to help. Your vehicle will provide shelter and is easier to see by search parties.

• Inspect your vehicle and maintain it properly. Pay particular attention to fluids, hoses, belts, battery, brakes, steering linkage, suspension system, driveline, and anything exposed under the vehicle. Tighten anything that may be loose. Inspect your tires carefully for potential weak spots and tread wear. If you have a mechanic do the work, make sure he understands 4-wheeling.

Don't let dogs bark or chase wildlife.

• Bury human waste 6 to 8 inches deep at least 200 feet from any water source, campsite, or trail. When possible, bring your own portable toilet. Some trails, like the Rubicon, require it.

• Avoid using soap around lakes or streams. Heat water to clean utensils.

• Finally, be courteous to everyone regardless of how they treat you. To save our trails, we must all be good ambassadors for motorized recreation.

Campfires

• In California, a campfire permit is required on all federally controlled lands, including the U.S. Forest Service, National Park Service, and the Bureau of Land Management. Permits are required for open fires, barbecues and portable stoves. The permits are free and easy to obtain. There are also times when fires are not allowed at all depending on weather and location. This can also affect state lands. We suggest you call the specific land agency in which you will be traveling for latest fire status. A phone number is provided for each trail under "Current Conditions."

• When fires are allowed, always camp close to the trail and use existing campsites whenever possible. Camp away from streams, lakes, hiking trails and historical sites. To avoid wildfires caused by catalytic converter, don't park in tall grass.

• Use existing fire rings for campfires when possible, or bring your own camp stove. Completely douse fires and leave campsite cleaner than you found it, which includes removing fire waste. Bring your own firewood if possible, even if it is not required.

GPS Settings

All GPS coordinates in this book are displayed using datum WGS84. Lat./Long. format is: hh/mm.mm (not hours/minutes/seconds). Make sure your GPS unit is set the same way or you'll get different readings.

Backcountry Driving Tips

The basics. Practice on easy trails first to learn how to operate your off-road features. As your confidence builds, you'll want to try harder trails.

Low and slow. Shift into 4-wheel drive or low range before it is needed. When going slow, stay in low gear as much as possible for maximum power. With standard transmissions, minimize use of your clutch. As you encounter resistance on an obstacle or an uphill grade, apply a little gas. As you start downhill, allow the engine's resistance to act as a brake. If the engine alone will not slow you enough, help with light brake pressure. When you need more power but not more speed, press on the gas and feather the brake a little at the same time.

Rocks and other high points. Don't straddle rocks. Instead, drive over the highest point with your tire. This will help lift your undercarriage. If the point is too high, stack rocks on either side to create a ramp. Remove rocks when done. As you enter a rocky area, look ahead to identify the high points. Learn the low and vulnerable spots of your undercarriage. In difficult situations it may be necessary to get out of your vehicle for a better look or use a "spotter" outside the vehicle to direct you.

If high centered. If you get lodged on an object, first have passengers get out to lighten the load. Reinflate your tires if aired down. Try rocking the vehicle. If this doesn't work, jack up your vehicle and place something under the tires. Try going forwards and backwards. Repeat if necessary.

Scout ahead. When unsure of what's ahead, get out of your vehicle and walk the trail ahead of you. This gives you an opportunity to turn around at a wide spot of your choosing. Back up if necessary. Don't try to turn in a narrow confined area.

Blind curves. When approaching blind curves, assume that there is a speeding vehicle in your lane coming from the opposite direction. This will prepare you for the worst.

Driving uphill. Use extreme caution when attempting to climb a steep hill. Shift into low range first. Air down your tires to improve traction. Four factors determine difficulty:

Length of the hill. Momentum will help carry you over short hills, but not necessarily long hills.

Traction. A rock surface is usually easier to climb than soft dirt.

Bumpiness. Big bumps on steep grades may lift your tires off the ground and stop your progress, especially if your vehicle has poor articulation. Temporarily disconnecting your front sway bar will improve your articulation; however, this is difficult to do on some vehicles.

Steepness. This can be difficult to judge, so examine the hill carefully by walking up it first. Abort if you are not sure. If you proceed, approach it straight on and stay that way all the way to the top. Do not turn sideways or try to drive across the hill. Keep moving at a steady pace. Make sure no one is coming up the other side. Try not to spin your tires. If you lose traction, jiggle your steering wheel back and forth. This may give you additional grip in soft soil. If you stall, use your foot brake, and if necessary, your emergency brake, while you restart your engine. If you start to slide backwards even with your brake on, you may have to ease up on the brake enough to regain steering control. Don't allow your wheels to lock up. If you don't make it to the top of the hill, shift into reverse and back down slowly in a straight line. Try the hill again, but only if you think you learned enough to make a difference. Ease off the gas as you approach top of hill.

Driving downhill. Make sure you are in 4-wheel drive. Air down your tires to improve traction. Go straight down the hill; do not turn sideways. In low gear, allow the engine's compression to hold you back. Do not ride the clutch. Feather the brakes slightly if additional slowing is needed. Do not allow the wheels to lock up. If you start to slide sideways, ease up on the brake and accelerate slightly to maintain steering control. Turn in the direction of the slide as you would on ice or snow.

Parking on a steep hill. Put your vehicle in low-range reverse gear if pointing downhill or in low-range forward gear if pointing uphill. For automatic transmissions, shift to park. Set your emergency brake hard, but don't depend on it holding. Always block your wheels to avoid vehicle creep.

Side hills and tippy situations. Side hills can be very dangerous, so try to avoid them if possible. No one can tell you how far your vehicle can safely lean. Travel in a group and watch similar vehicles. Although SUVs have a high center of gravity, don't get paranoid; your vehicle will likely lean more than you think. Drive slowly to avoid bouncing. Use extreme caution if the road surface is slippery. Turn around if necessary.

Passing on narrow shelf roads. When possible, wait for road to clear. If surprised by an oncoming vehicle, don't panic. By law, the vehicle going uphill has the right-of-way, but in the real world common sense should apply. It might make more sense for the uphill vehicle to back up if a wide spot is closer. Often one vehicle can back up easier than a large group. Don't be forced too close to the outer edge or to tip your vehicle excessively on a high inside bank. Both situations are dangerous. If necessary, talk to the other driver.

Crossing streams and water holes. You must know the depth of the water and what your vehicle can go through. Fast flowing deep water can float you downstream. You don't want water in your air intake or to cover your engine

Checklist

Things to consider taking depending on vehicle and space available:

- Plenty of food and drinking water. Consider water purification tablets or a water filter.
- Rain gear plus loose-fitting, light-colored clothing, large-brim hat.
- Sleeping bags in case you get stuck overnight even if you are not planning to camp.
- A good first aid kit including sunscreen and insect repellent.
- Candle, matches, lighter, fire starter.
- An extra set of keys, glasses, watch.
- Toilet paper, paper towels, wet wipes and trash bags.
- A large plastic sheet or tarp.
- Detailed topographic maps, map atlas.
- GPS unit and/or compass.
- Sharp knife or Leatherman.
- If you plan to make a fire, consider carrying your own firewood. Propane stoves are better.
- Work gloves.
- A heavy duty tow strap.
- Fire extinguisher.
- Jumper cables.
- Fuses and electrical tape.
- Flashlight and extra batteries.
- A full tank of gas. Extra gas for long trips.
- A good set of tools including specialized tools for UTVs, ATVs and dirt bikes.
- Baling wire and duct tape.
- An assortment of hose clamps, nuts, bolts and washers.
- A full-size spare tire.
- Tire repair kit.
- A tire pressure gauge, electric tire pump that will plug into your cigarette lighter, and a can of nonflammable tire sealant.
- A jack that will lift your vehicle fairly high off the ground. Carry a high lift jack if possible, especially on more difficult trails. Test your jack before you leave.
- Shovel, tree saw, axe. Folding shovels work great.
- CB radio, cellular phone or satellite phone.
- Portable toilet.
- Tent.

Store items in tote bags or large plastic containers so they can be easily loaded when it is time to go.

computer module. If you don't know where these things are, consult your owner's manual or talk to your dealer. You can learn much by traveling with vehicles similar to yours. Low cooling fans can throw water on your engine and cause it to stall. I've seen people cover their grill with cardboard or canvas to push water to the side. This only works if you keep moving at a steady pace. Check differentials later for possible water contamination. Fluids will look milky if water gets in.

Always cross streams at designated water crossings. Don't drive upstream or downstream except in areas where it is allowed.

Mud. Plan ahead, equip your vehicle with proper tires. Install tow points and, if possible, differential lockers. Air down your tires to improve traction. Go around mud if it doesn't widen the trail. Make sure you are in 4-wheel-drive. Low range may or may not help. If you enter mud, use momentum and keep moving at a steady pace. Try not to spin your tires. Follow existing ruts. If you get stuck, try backing out. If that doesn't work, dig around tires to break the suction. If tire is spinning on one side only, try feathering your brakes while accelerating gently. If all else fails, ask a friend or passerby to strap you out.

Ruts or washouts. If a rut runs parallel to the road, you might be able to straddle it or drive in the bottom. The goal is to center your vehicle to remain level. Cross ruts at a 30-degree angle using momentum. However, without differential lockers or good articulation, one wheel may spin in the air while the other does nothing.

Sand. Dry sand is more difficult to cross than wet sand. Make sure you are in 4-wheel drive. Airing down will improve traction. Keep moving straight using momentum as much as possible. Stay in high gear and try to power through without spinning your tires.

Sand dunes. Limit yourself to smaller dunes. Stay off the soft side of dune where wind is depositing the sand. Soft sand will not support your vehicle. Worse than getting stuck, you could roll over. To avoid digging in, don't accelerate quickly or slam on your brakes.

Washboard roads. These are annoying to everyone and can't be avoided in the California backcountry. Air down your tires to improve traction and soften the ride. Experiment with different speeds to find the smoothest ride. Slowing down is usually best, but some conditions may be improved by speeding up a little. Be careful around curves where you could lose traction and slide. Check your tires to make sure they are not over-inflated.

Airing down. A typical SUV can usually be aired down to 18 to 20 lbs. without noticeable handling difficulties at slow speeds. The tire should bulge slightly. At minimum, carry a small air pump that plugs into your cigarette lighter to reinflate. I've seen large tires on hard-core rigs aired down to as little as 3 to 5 lbs.

Winching

Winches are helpful but not always necessary unless you travel by yourself or drive hard-core trails on a regular basis. If you go with another vehicle you can strap each other. However, make sure you have tow points. If you get a winch, also carry work gloves, a tree strap, a snatch block and a clevis.

Winching Tips

• Your winch cable should be lined up straight with the pulling vehicle. If you can't pull straight, attach a snatch block to a tree or rock.

• Attach your winch line to the largest tree possible using a tree strap and clevis. If no tree is large enough, wrap several smaller trees. The strap should

be as low as possible.
• Keep your engine running while winching to maximize electrical power.
• Help the winch by driving the stuck vehicle slowly in low gear. Don't allow slack in the winch cable.
• To double your pulling power, attach a snatch block to the stuck vehicle and run the cable back to the starting point.
• Set the emergency brake on the anchor vehicle and block the wheels if necessary. You may have to strap to another vehicle or tree.
• Throw a blanket or heavy coat over the winch cable while pulling. If the cable breaks, it is less likely to snap back and injure someone.
• Make sure there are at least 5 wraps of the winch cable left on the spool.
• Never hook the winch cable to itself or allow kinks in the cable.
• Never straddle or stand close to the winch cable while it is under stress.
• If tow points are not available on the stuck vehicle, attach the winch cable to the frame not the bumper.
• When finished winching, don't let the end of the cable wind into the spool. Hook end to sturdy part nearby like a tow point or brush guard.

OHV Requirements

Your best source of up-to-date OHV laws is the California State Parks website at www.ohv.parks.ca.gov. They have a full 165-page version and a shorter 40-page "Quickbook" version. Here is a very brief summary:

Street-legal vehicles include SUVs, Jeeps and dual-purpose motorcycles. They must display standard highway license plate. No OHV sticker required. Operator must have driver's license and proof of insurance.

Green-sticker vehicles include ATVs, UTVs, unlicensed rock buggies, dune buggies, sand rails and unlicensed dirt bikes. These vehicles are allowed in OHV areas, on most BLM dirt roads, and forest roads as specified on Motor Vehicle Use Maps. These vehicles require green OHV sticker.

Red-sticker vehicles are same as green-sticker vehicles, but use is restricted on specified dates during high air-pollution periods. Dates vary by area or land designation. These vehicles require red OHV sticker.

Additionally:

• All riders must wear helmets.

• ATVs cannot carry two passengers unless the ATV is designed for two.

• A safety course is required for all riders under age 18.

• A safety certification is required along with parental supervision for riders under age 14.

• Vehicles must have muffler, spark arrester and brakes plus lights if used at night.

• No riding under the influence of alcohol or drugs.

Additional rules in OHV areas:
• Safety flags usually required.
• No glass containers are allowed.
• No open alcoholic beverage containers allowed.
• In most areas, pack out your trash.
Other local rules, permits and fees may be applicable. For details, call phone number provided for each trail.

Out-of-state requirements: Rules vary by state. You may need to purchase a 60-day non-resident permit. See the State Park website for details.

Important Websites:

U.S. Forest Service...........www.fs.fed.us
National Parks..................www.nps.gov
Bur. of Land Mgt. ....www.blm.gov
Cal. State Parks...www.ohv.parks.ca.gov
California Association of 4-Wheel-Drive Clubs...........www.cal4wheel.com
California Off-Road Vehicle Association....................www.corva.org
Blue Ribbon Coalition.................www.sharetrails.org
Tread Lightly.........www.treadlightly.org

The Trails

Bronco Peak, Trail #91

Redding, Red Bluff, Gold Lake, Lake Tahoe

We've broken down Area 1 into three parts. This allows us to show better detail on each trail location.

Take note that Area 1 includes the mighty *Rubicon,* perhaps the most publicized trail of its time. This trail lives up to all the hype and should be at the top of every 4-wheelers bucket list. We've split this trail into a 2-day unforgettable adventure. As we were completing the Rubicon, we noticed a side trail that wasn't included in the first edition of this book, *Buck Lake*. It gives you a taste of the Rubicon, but requires far less time to drive. It climbs higher than the Rubicon and has outstanding mountain views. After the Rubicon, head north from Lake Tahoe to smaller Gold Lake, around which you'll find three extremely beautiful trails: easy Sierrra Buttes (one of our favorites), moderate *Deer Lake/Gold Valley* and difficult *Snake Lake*. There's something in this area for all skill levels.

We round out Area 1 with mix of trails not far from Redding and Red Bluff. Two are near lakes in tourist areas, and two are in remote areas, known mostly to hunters, fisherman and 4-wheelers.

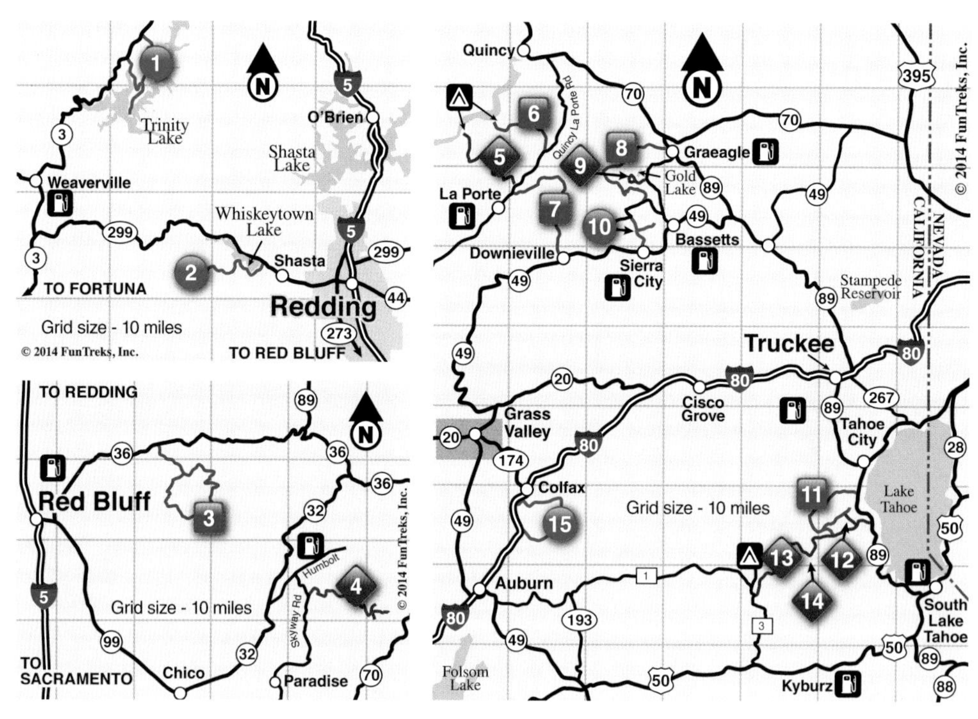

Rubicon Trail #13 and #14, rated difficult. Leaving camp below Buck Island Lake to start day two.

Bowerman Ridge

AREA 1 map on page 18

Setting up camp for the night at the end of Bowerman Ridge.

Great views of Trinity Lake from the high ridge.

Historical Highlight: *Bowerman Ridge is named after Jacob Bowerman, who came to northern California in 1856 to look for gold. Finding none, he became a successful rancher. The last part of this route passes the Bowerman Barn, the only remaining structure of historic Bowerman Ranch, now owned and maintained by the Forest Service.*

Trinity Lake is one of the largest man-made lakes in California. Its many remote coves make it ideal for fishing and water skiing. This lake sees far less traffic than nearby Shasta Lake, which is conveniently adjacent to Redding and Interstate 5.

Overview: We start the book off with an easy cruiser in a remote but beautiful part of California. After a long scenic drive to the start, you'll follow a winding forest road along a high ridge that looks down on gorgeous, sprawling Trinity Lake. There's a little 4 wheeling at the end as you descend a narrow road to reach a great camp spot at the water's edge. Return route passes historic Bowerman Ranch. Street-legal vehicles only except at the end.

Rating: Easy. Most of route is a wide gravel road that winds through dense forest. Four-wheel drive needed south of Waypoint 02, where it's narrow and steep with tight brush. Muddy when wet. Suitable for stock 4x4 SUVs.

Stats: Length: 21.7 miles. Time: 2 to 3 hours. Elevation: 2,400 to 4,024 ft. Best time: June-Sept.

Current Conditions: Shasta Trinity National Forest, Weaverville R.D. Call (530) 623-2121.

Getting There: From Redding, take Hwy. 299 west to Weaverville. Then follow Hwy. 3 north 25.5 miles to well-marked Bowerman Ridge Rd. on right.

START MILEAGE LOG:

0.0 Zero trip odometer **[Rev. Miles]**
From Highway 3 head southeast on Bowerman Ridge Rd. 36N35. **[10.5]**
01 **N40 56.683 W122 44.796**

0.8 Stay right. **[9.7]**

1.9 Bear right as many private roads branch off the main road. **[8.6]**

4.5 Continue straight where road joins on right then branches off left. **[6.0]**

5.3 Bear left. **[5.2]**

6.1 Continue straight where 35N24 goes right. **[4.4]**

6.3 Stay right. **[4.2]**

6.4 Continue straight where 35N31Y goes right. **[4.1]**
02 **N40 52.793 W122 44.649**

7.9 Stay right as road narrows and becomes steeper following the ridge. **[2.6]**

9.4 Driver's choice, we went right. **[1.1]**

10.5 Arrive at small secluded campsite on ridge. **[0.0]**
03 **N40 49.840 W122 46.065**

0.0 Zero trip odometer at Wpt. 03
Return to Wpt. 02 **[11.2]**

4.1 Turn left on gated road 35N31Y (sign number was nearly illegible.) **[7.1]**
02 **N40 52.793 W122 44.649**

5.8 Stay right downhill. **[5.4]**

8.4 Continue straight where lesser road joins on right. **[2.8]**

8.8 Alpine View Campground on left. **[2.4]**

9.6 Continue straight where 35N24 joins on right. **[1.6]**
04 **N40 53.637 W122 46.089**

10.0 Historic Bowerman Barn on left. **[1.2]**

11.2 Trail ends at Hwy. 3. **[0.0]**
05 **N40 54.875 W122 46.319**

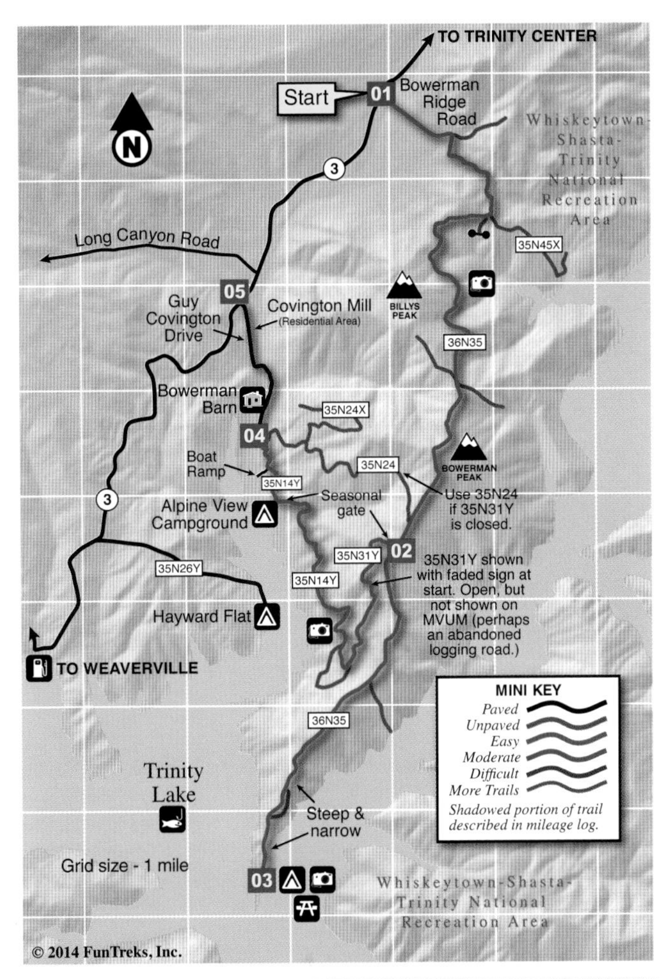

Historic Bowerman Barn.

Trail is narrow with tight brush in a few places.

Shasta Bally Peak

AREA 1 map on page 18

Trees change to manzanita brush at the top.

Drive across 282-ft.-high Whiskeytown Dam.

Road is sandy and steep in places.

Historical Highlight: *In 1963 the Whiskeytown Dam was dedicated by John F. Kennedy along with a crowd of 10,000. It is part of the Central Valley Project, which was created to move water from abundant sources in the north to drier areas in the south. The Whiskeytown Project included blasting a 10-mile-long, 17-ft.-diameter tunnel through solid granite, connecting the Trinity River to the Sacramento River system. The dam provides a dependable water supply and hydroelectric power.*

Overview: A steep, sandy road climbs nearly 4,000 feet to the top of Shasta Bally Peak. Great views of Whiskeytown Lake below and, on a clear day, you can see Mount Shasta 60 miles to the northeast. Sheep Camp, along the route, has picnic tables, grills and a vault toilet. Street-legal vehicles only. A small fee is charged to use the park. Pay at the visitor center at start of trail. While at the visitor center learn about the history of the area and the many activities available, including swimming, canoeing, sailing, hiking, horseback riding and gold panning.

Rating: Easy: Wide washboard road, rutted and very steep in places. Use low-range gearing coming down rather than your brakes. Road closed in winter or if too wet and muddy.

Stats: Length: 12.7 miles. Time: 3 to 4 hours. Elevation: 1,231 to 6,168 ft. Best time to go: Mid June-Sept.

Current Conditions: Trinity N.F., Whiskeytown N.R.A.Visitor Center: Call (530) 246-1225.

Getting There: From Redding take Highway 299 west. At 7.7 miles turn left onto well-marked road. Parking lot for the visitor center is on the right.

START **MILEAGE LOG:**

0.0 Zero trip odometer **[Rev. Miles]**
Pay entry fee at visitor center then follow paved road south around Whiskeytown Lake. **[12.7]**
01 N40 36.903 W122 31.177

1.6 Bear right at the glory hole and cross dam. **[11.1]**

4.6 Continue straight. Road on right goes to Brandy Creek Picnic Area. **[8.1]**

4.7 Turn left following signs for Brandy Creek Rd. **[8.0]**
02 N40 36.771 W122 34.488

4.8 Bear left uphill. **[7.9]**

6.0 Continue straight at 3-way intersection. **[6.7]**
03 N40 36.079 W122 34.911

6.9 Bear right following signs to Shasta Bally. **[5.8]**
04 N40 35.774 W122 35.463

7.2 Cross small bridge just before passing Sheep Camp on right. **[5.5]**

12.7 After passing gated radio towers, trail ends in tight manzanita brush. **[0.0]**
05 N40 36.043 W122 39.108

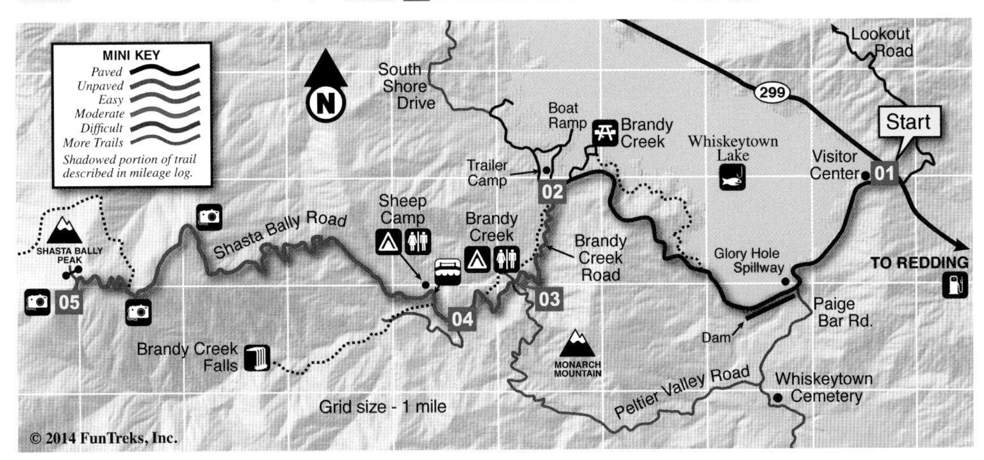

View of Whiskeytown Lake as you near the top.

Looking northwest from summit at 6,168 feet.

Shaded campsites at Sheep Camp.

3 Peligreen Jeepway

AREA 1 map on page 18

Remote area with stark scenic views throughout most of the trail.

Rougher parts require good ground clearance.

This hill is quite steep.

Overview: Trail starts with an easy scenic drive through pine trees as it crosses several small creeks. The real fun starts when the road becomes a rough narrow one-lane drive over long volcanic ridges. Scenic views throughout until you reach Ishi Road, where you once again reach wide gravel roads. Forest campgrounds along Hogsback Road plus dry camping. Green-sticker vehicles on side roads only, not main route shown here.

Rating: Moderate: Easy, wide gravel road then changes to rough rocky terrain after Wpt. 03. High-clearance SUV recommended. One steep incline and several rocky sections along ridge are tricky to navigate. Grapevine Jeepway can be tight with brush. Optional shortcut can be difficult to impassible due to numerous fallen trees.

Stats: Length: 37.3 miles as described. Time: 4-5 hours. Elevation: 1,264 to 3,619 ft. Best driven in spring or fall when temperatures are cooler.

Current Conditions: Lassen National Forest, Almanor Ranger District. Call (530) 258-2141.

Getting There: From Highways 99 and 36 east of Red Bluff, take Highway 36 east in the direction of Lassen Volcanic National Park. After 20 miles, turn right on Paynes Creek Loop at mile post 64. Go 0.4 miles and turn right on Plum Creek Road. Follow paved road 8.3 miles to Ponderosa Way (F.S. Road 28N29, also County Road 707B).

START *MILEAGE LOG:*

0.0 Zero trip odometer [Rev. Miles]
Head south on Ponderosa Way 28N29. [17.1]
01 N40 17.860 W121 48.086

3.0 Stay right following more-traveled Ponderosa Way as lesser roads go left and right. [14.1]

7.5 Continue straight where 28N71 goes left. [9.6]

9.5 Cross wooden bridge just after small hidden campground on right. [7.6]

11.5 Stay on main road as it curves slightly to the right through intersection. [5.6]

12.4 Turn right on 28N57 following sign to Peligreen Jeepway. [4.7]
02 N40 14.068 W121 46.558

13.1 Bear left. [4.0]

13.9 Continue straight. Optional shortcut goes right and can be difficult. [3.2]
03 N40 13.307 W121 46.287

16.1 Trail turns right and follows ridge. [1.0]

17.0 Bear right where Rancheria Hiking Trail goes left. [0.1]

17.1 Turn left at intersection. The shortcut starting at Waypoint 03 rejoins main trail here. [0.0]
04 N40 12.515 W121 46.832

0.0 Zero trip odometer at Wpt. 04
Continue east following sign to Peligreen. [20.2]

0.4 Continue straight past site of Peligreen Place. [19.8]

1.3 Turn left. Faint trail goes right uphill along Indian Ridge. [18.9]

4.6 Turn hard right following Grapevine Jeepway. [15.6]
05 N40 11.412 W121 50.857

8.9 Turn sharp right on easy Ishi Road. [11.3]
06 N40 13.339 W121 53.889

15.6 Turn right on Hogsback Road at intersection. [4.6]
07 N40 16.177 W121 52.567

17.5 Turn left on 28N23 [2.7]
08 N40 16.622 W121 50.754

20.2 End trail at paved Plum Creek Road. [0.0]
09 N40 18.031 W121 51.438

Tree blocked optional short-cut.

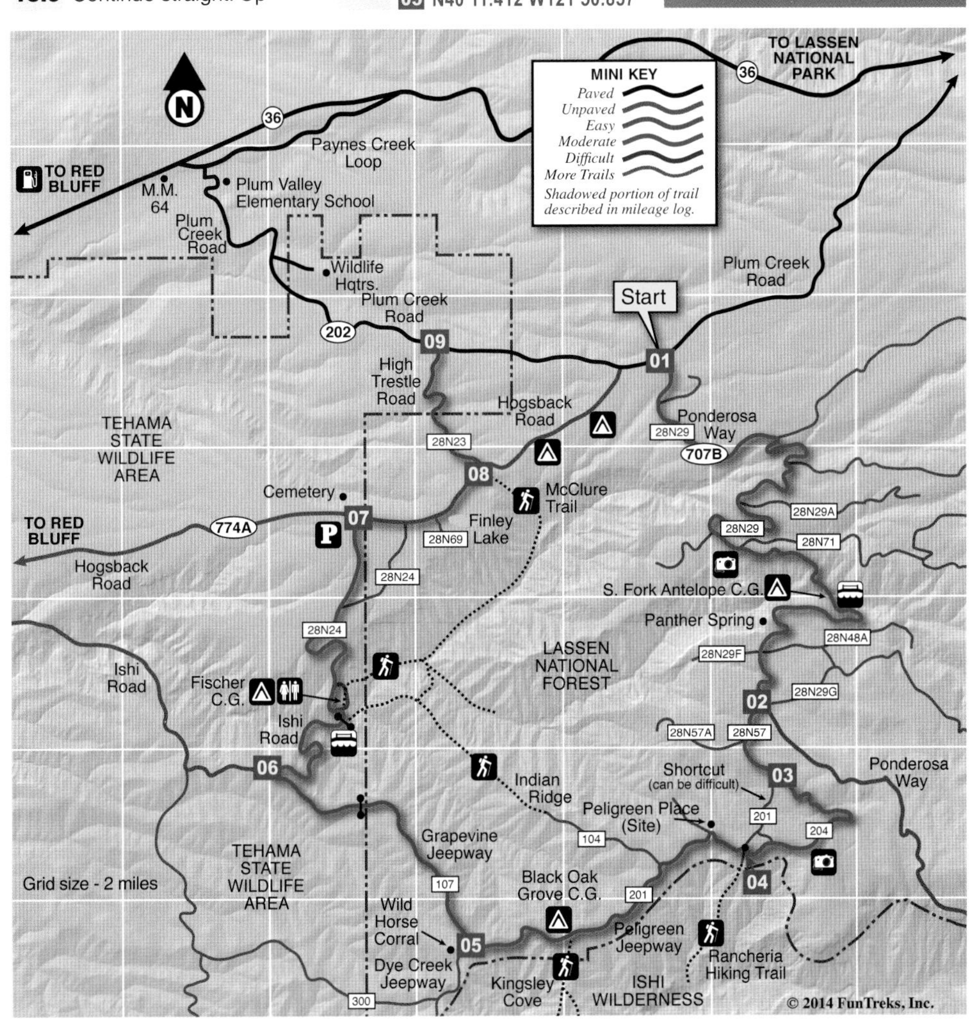

4 High Lakes

AREA 1 map on page 18

Looking down at Campbell Lake and Long Lake from Forest Road 611.

Challenging rock ledges before Waypoint 05.

Trail to Morris Lake is extremely difficult.

Historical Highlight: *This area, known as the Kimshew Mining District, has a long history starting with prospecting in the mid 1800s and continuing as late as 1980 with modern hydraulic mining. Source: Friends of the High Lakes, www.friendsofhighlakes.com.*

Overview: Camp, fish and relax in remote seclusion after a day of challenging rock crawling. Despite damage from recent fires, this is a great place to spend a weekend exploring a gorgeous high plateau with numerous glacier-carved lakes. The trail is part of the High Lakes OHV Area, which is open to green-sticker vehicles. Staging begins at Waypoint 04. Please stay on designated routes and pack out your trash.

Rating: Difficult: Although much of this trail is moderate, one difficult spot before Waypoint 05 will stop most stock vehicles. We managed to get through with our stock 4-door Rubicon, but just barely. You'll find tight spots between trees with large tree roots. F.S. 608 to Morris Lake is extreme rock crawling.

Stats: Length: About 18 miles one way. Time: Allow 4-5 hours for round trip. Elevation: 5,028 to 6,603 ft. Best time: May-September.

Current Conditions: Lassen National Forest, Almanor Ranger District. Call (530) 258-2141.

Getting There: From Chico, take Highway 32 north about 27 miles from Highway 99. Turn right on paved Humboldt Road just before mile marker 37. Continue another 5.3 miles on Humboldt to Skyway (Road) at Butte Meadows. This intersection is about 0.3 miles after Butte Meadows Campground. Follow Skyway 5.9 miles to large intersection for Humbug Summit Road on left.

START **MILEAGE LOG:**

0.0 Zero trip odometer **[Rev. Miles]**
Head northeast on Humbug Summit Road, a wide dirt road. [11.2]
01 N40 01.947 W121 31.671

1.2 Stay left. [10.0]

1.8 Turn right on paved Philbrook Road. [9.4]
02 N40 02.657 W121 30.283

4.9 Turn left uphill on Forest Road 25N05. [6.3]

6.7 Bear right. [4.5]

8.8 Bear right. [2.4]

11.2 Arrive at T intersection marked with kiosk. [0.0]
03 N40 01.349 W121 24.331

0.0 Zero trip odometer at Wpt. 03
Turn right at Waypoint 03. After a few hundred feet, bear left on F.S. 611. [6.4]

1.0 Reach staging area and kiosk. Stay right and go downhill. [5.4]
04 N40 00.791 W121 23.519

1.5 Stay right on F.S. 611. Left goes to camp spots at Spring Valley Lake. [4.9]

3.4 Stay left on F.S. 611 [3.0]
05 N39 59.828 W121 22.118

3.8 Stay left where F.S. 613 goes right to Campbell Lake and Long Lake.
06 N40 00.020 W121 21.811
Then, in 100 ft, stay right where extremely difficult F.S. 608 goes left to Morris Lake. [2.6]

4.1 Stay right. [2.3]

4.5 Stay right where lesser road goes left. [1.9]

5.8 Continue straight as lesser road on right heads south towards Mud Lake. [0.6]

5.9 Turn left downhill towards Chips Lake. (For Ben Lomond Mountain, continue straight on F.S. 611.) [0.5]
07 N40 00.080 W121 20.026

6.3 Bear left. (To reach Chips Lake, hike right here about 0.3 miles.) [0.1]

6.4 Reach camp spot at edge of unnamed lake. [0.0]
08 N40 00.357 W121 19.902

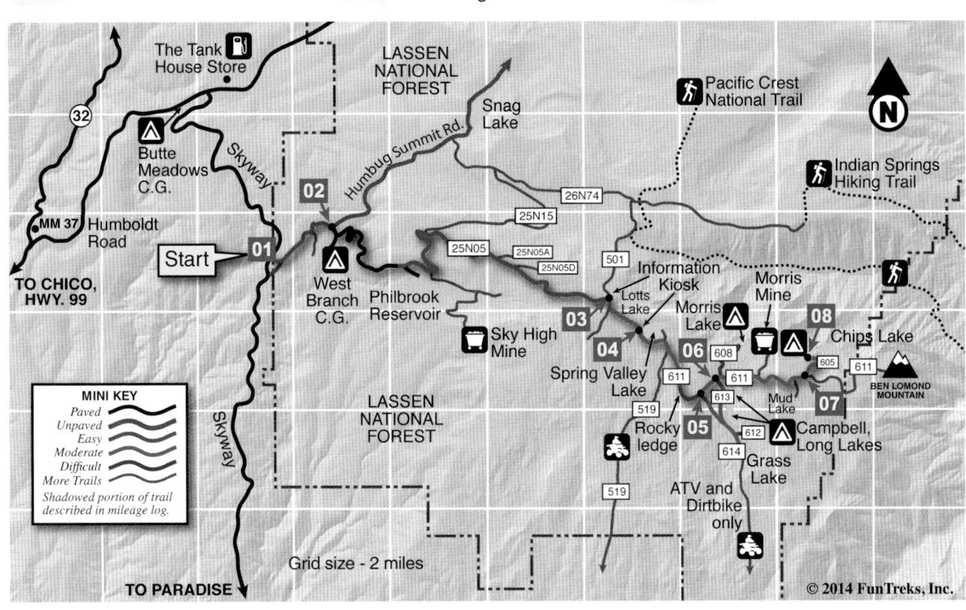

Gas and supplies at Tank House Store (see map).

Camp spot at end of trail, Waypoint 08.

5 Stag Point

AREA 1 map on page 18

Very narrow and steep after Waypoint 05.

Unique shoreline slightly upstream from C.G.

Stag Point OHV Campground—lots of shade and a short walk to river.

Overview: A heart-pounding descent to remote camping and fishing along the banks of the Feather River. One of few points where river access is allowed in this designated "Wild and Scenic" river valley. Not a great route for green-sticker vehicles since they are not allowed on the main paved roads.

Rating: Difficult: We've chosen to include the first 13.5 miles of paved road as part of the trail to better describe how to get to the 4-wheel-drive portion. After Waypoint 05, there are no hard-core obstacles, but steep, narrow switchbacks, we think, push the rating of this trail a bit beyond moderate. Backing up to get around an oncoming vehicle can be very tricky.

Stats: Length: 17.7 miles as described. Four-wheel-drive portion is just 2.6 miles. Time: About 2 hours one way. Elevation: 2,764 to 5,824 ft. Best time of year: July-September.

Current Conditions: Plumas National Forest, Feather River Ranger District. Call (530) 534-6500.

Getting There: From La Porte, drive 1.5 miles northeast on paved Quincy La Porte Road, where a paved road goes right. You continue straight.

START **MILEAGE LOG:**

0.0 Zero trip odometer **[Rev. Miles]**
Continue straight. Follow signs to Little Grass Valley Recreation Site. **[17.7]**
01 N39 41.896 W120 57.966

6.1 Continue on paved road passing Black Rock C.G. on right. **[11.6]**
02 N39 43.791 W121 00.897

6.6 Continue left up switch-back road. **[11.1]**

8.2 Turn left on F.S. 22N27 at major intersection. **[9.5]**

8.3 Turn right on F.S. 22N94 following signs to Tamarack Flat. Road will be gravel for short time. **[9.4]**
03 N39 44.346 W121 01.594

10.9 Stay right where F.S. 22N24 goes left. **[6.8]**

11.7 Stay right, continuing on paved road, ignoring side roads. **[6.0]**

13.5 Turn right on F.S. 22N72, dirt road. **[4.2]**
04 N39 45.482 W121 04.521

14.0 Continue straight **[3.7]**

14.3 Bear left. **[3.4]**

15.1 Reach Stag Point Parking and Trailhead. The next 2.6 miles are steep and narrow with no room to turn around. **[2.6]**
05 N39 46.538 W121 04.086

17.7 Arrive at Stag Point OHV C.G. Take short hike over ridge to get to river. **[0.0]**
06 N39 47.549 W121 04.855

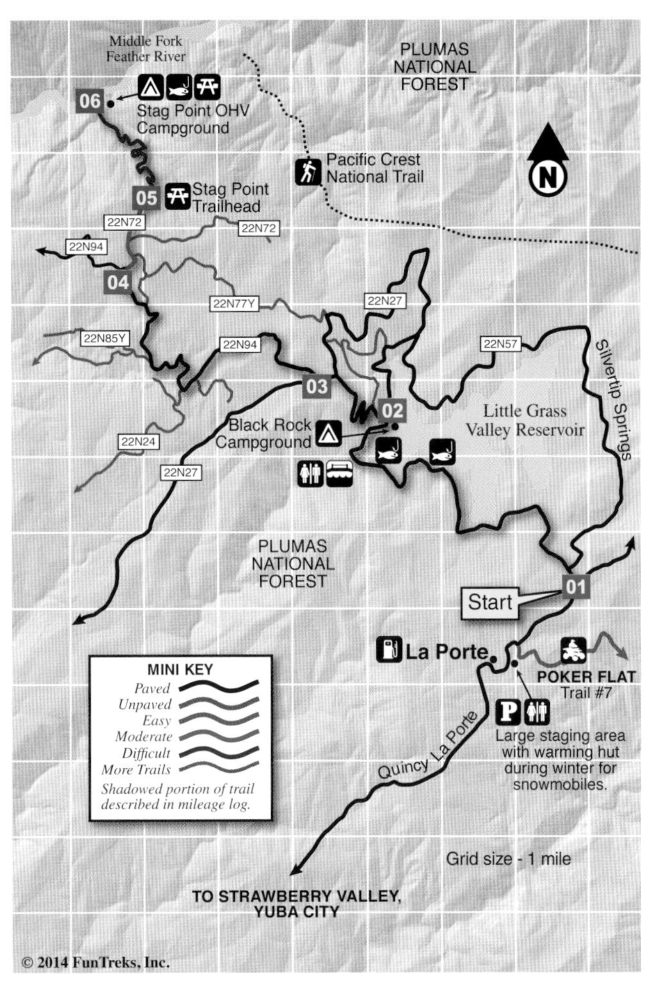

Tight brush and very tricky to pass.

Popular Little Grass Valley Reservoir.

Cleghorn Bar

AREA 1 map on page 18

Last mile of trail is steep and narrow as it drops downhill to Cleghorn Bar OHV Campground.

Look for this sign at the beginning of the trail.

Easy fishing access to Feather River.

Overview: A fun drive through scenic valleys and over ridges, ending with a steep one-mile descent to the Middle Fork of the Feather River. Similar to Stag Point without the pavement, and final descent is not as long. Easy fishing access to river from OHV campground. Green-sticker vehicles allowed. Stage at Waypoint 03.

Rating: Moderate: Most of the trail is easy gravel road. Last mile has steep switchbacks. Four-wheel-drive and low-range gearing are recommended.

Stats: Length: 11.9 miles. Time: About 1 hour to Cleghorn Bar. Elevation: 3,086 to 6,478 ft. Best time to go: Late June-September.

Current Conditions: Plumas National Forest, Feather Ranger District. Call (530) 534-6500.

Getting There: From La Porte OHV Recreation Staging Area on north side of La Porte, head northeast 11.8 miles on La Porte/Quincy Road. Turn left on F.S. 23N24 at sign for Cleghorn Bar.

START **MILEAGE LOG:**

0.0 Zero trip odometer [Rev. Miles]
Head west on gravel road F.S. 23N24. [11.1]
01 N39 47.911 W120 52.942

3.8 Bear left downhill. [8.1]

5.6 Stay right. [6.3]
02 N39 48.824 W120 56.905

7.6 Bear right and continue on more traveled road. [4.3]

8.4 Continue straight as road narrows. [3.5]

8.7 Reach parking area with sign identifying start of the 4WD trail. [3.2]
03 N39 48.173 W120 59.075

10.9 Begin steep switchbacks. [1.0]

11.9 Reach wide area with several camp spots by river. [0.0]
04 N39 49.137 W121 00.813

Trail updates & GPS downloads at www.funtreks.com

Trail along ridge opens up to scenic views.

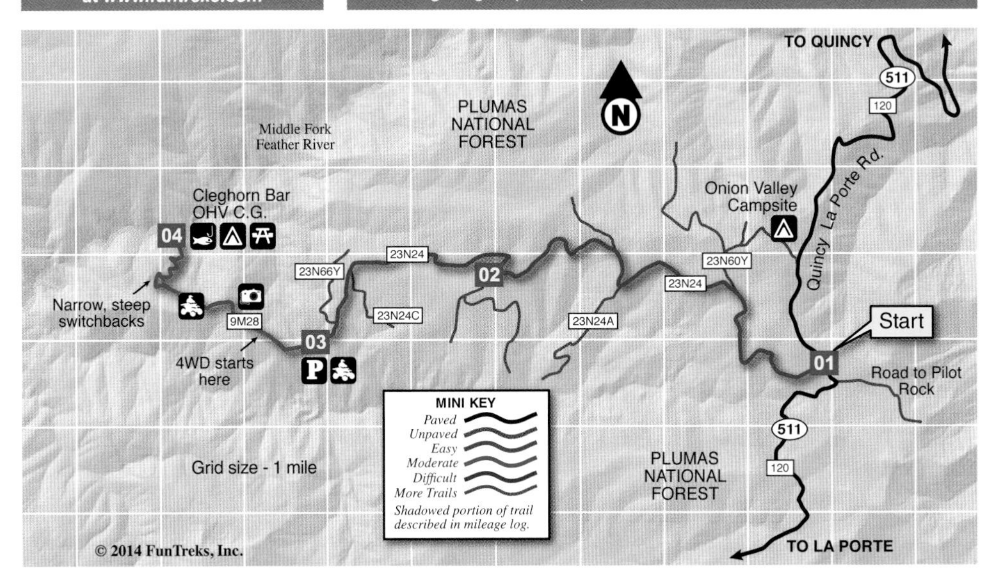

Stock vehicles should have low-range gearing.

Mostly easy gravel road.

7 Poker Flat

AREA 1 map on page 18

1886 home at Poker Flat has collapsed since last visit.

Water crossing just before Poker Flat.

Gas and food in Downieville.

Scenic views at many points along the trail.

Take time to visit interesting Potosi Cemetery.

Historical Highlight: *In 1850, Poker Flat produced $700,000 in gold every month. Nearly 2,000 people occupied the town at its peak. The town developed its notoriety largely from a fictional tale by Bret Harte entitled "Outcasts of Poker Flat." Howland Flat produced an estimated $14 million in gold over its lifetime.*

Overview: A challenging drive that passes through two historic gold mining towns: Poker Flat and Howland Flat. The trail can be used as a shortcut between Downieville and La Porte. Trip to Saddleback Mountain Lookout Tower has rewarding views. Green-sticker vehicles can stage on the La Porte side at the large warming hut. We enjoyed our stop in rustic Downieville.

Rating: Moderate: Mostly a wide, easy, dirt road. One narrow, steep, rocky climb with banks on each side between Waypoints 06 and 07. Stock SUVs should have high ground clearance and skid plates.

Stats: Length: Almost 29 miles. Time: 3-4 hours. Elevation: 3,000 to 6,608 ft. Best time to go: Late June-September.

Current Conditions: Plumas N. F., Feather R. D. Call (530) 534-6500. Tahoe N. F., Yuba R. D. Call (530) 288-3231.

Getting There: From Downieville, head west 0.3 miles and turn right on a graded dirt road marked to Poker Flat.

START **MILEAGE LOG:**

0.0 Zero trip odometer **[Rev. Miles]**
Follow dirt road uphill heading northwest. [8.7]
01 N39 33.477 W120 50.043
2.0 Stay right. [6.7]
2.9 Bear right on more traveled road. [5.8]
4.5 Continue straight where Fir Cap OHV Trail goes right. [4.2]
7.7 Continue straight through large intersection where Fir Cap OHV Trail reconnects on right. [1.0]
8.1 Turn right uphill following rocky road. [0.6]
02 N39 38.018 W120 52.060
8.7 Reach parking spot below lookout tower (Only place to turn around.) Return to Waypoint 02. [0.0]
0.0 Zero trip odometer at Wpt. 02
Continue north on Saddleback Road. [5.9]
0.9 Stay right. [5.0]
2.0 Bear left for Poker Flat. Chimney Rock Trail goes right. [3.9]
03 N39 39.330 W120 51.831
2.7 Turn right on more traveled road. [3.2]
04 N39 39.825 W120 51.660
3.8 Good road ends at loop. Follow Poker Flat OHV Trail north downhill. [2.1]
05 N39 40.444 W120 51.438
4.3 Follow more traveled road to the right. [1.6]
5.6 Bear left at bottom of steep hill. [0.3]
5.7 Stay right after crossing Canyon Creek. [0.2]
5.9 Reach Poker Flat. [0.0]
06 N39 41.667 W120 50.602
0.0 Zero trip odometer at Wpt. 06
Head northwest up steep, rocky trail with banks on each side. [13.6]
1.9 Stay straight and join wide dirt road. [11.7]
3.2 Bear left towards Howland Flat. [10.4]
07 N39 43.015 W120 52.731
3.3 Stay left towards cemetery. [10.3]
6.9 Turn right following more traveled road. [6.7]
08 N39 42.121 W120 54.713
8.3 Turn right. [5.3]
09 N39 41.692 W120 55.848
13.6 Reach Highway 120. Turn left to reach La Porte. [0.0]
10 N39 41.481 W120 58.549

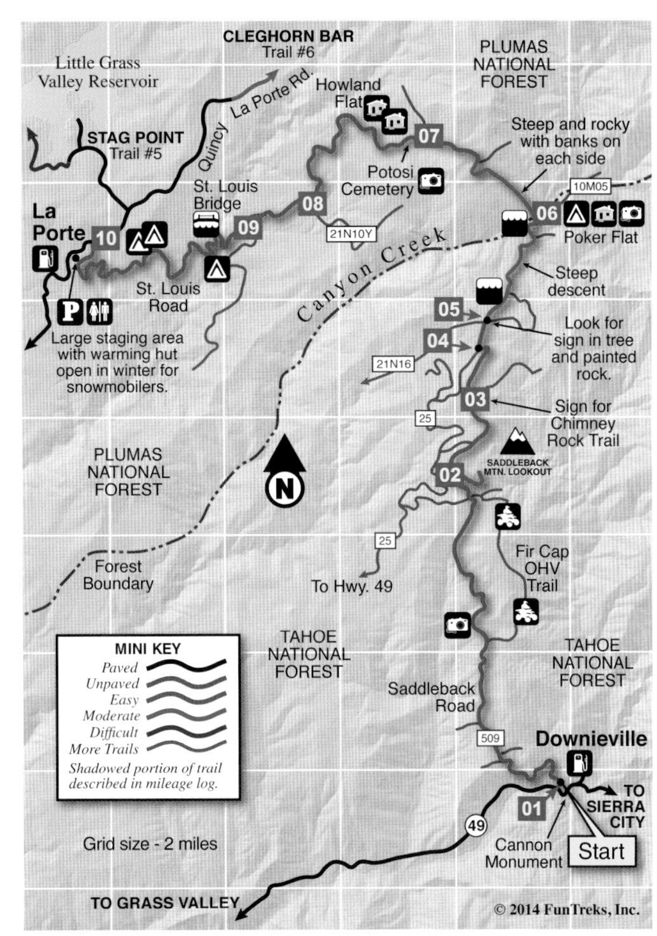

Toughest part of trail is after Wpt. 6.

Saddleback Mtn. Lookout.

A few buildings still stand at Howland Flat.

Deer Lake, Gold Valley

AREA 1 map on page 18

Looking down from trail above Deer Lake. Sierra Buttes can be seen in distance.

You'll cross this high ridge after Four Hills Mines.

Historical Highlight: *Sierra County was an extremely active gold mining area starting with the gold rush in the 1850s. Many mines are located between Sierra City and Johnsville, including the Four Hills Mine on this route. Nearly a half million dollars in gold was extracted here from a high-grade surface deposit. To learn more, take time to visit the excellent Plumas Eureka State Park Museum at the end of the route.*

Overview: Trail begins with an easy climb to a high scenic ridge above beautiful Deer Lake. The route then descends into rugged Gold Valley and heads north past mines and lakes. To modify the trip, you can head north from Waypoint 02 to a scenic campground above Gold Lake or just exit back to Gold Lake Highway. Another option is to head north from Waypoint 02 and immediately turn left to run difficult Snake Lake, Trail #9. Unlicensed vehicles must stop at Waypoint 06.

Rating: Moderate: Deer Lake trail is mostly easy except at the north end. After Waypoint 03, the trail drops steeply into Gold Valley and wanders back-and-forth across a narrow, rocky creek bed. Okay for stock 4x4 SUVs with high clearance and skid plates. Novice drivers use caution.

Stats: Length: 4x4 portion is 15.7 miles. Time: Allow 4 to 5 hours to Waypoint 07. Elevation: 4,380 to 7,483 ft. Best time: May-September.

Current Conditions: Tahoe N.F., Yuba River R.D. (530) 288-3231. Plumas N.F., Beckwourth R.D. (530) 836-2575.

Getting There: Take Highway 89 north from Truckee about 30 miles, then head west on Highway 49 about 14 miles to Bassetts Station Country Store. From store, head north on Gold Lake Highway 1.3 miles and turn left on Packer Lake Road across bridge. Stay on this paved road 4.4 miles until you reach the top of steep hill at Packer Saddle. Deer Lake Trail is on right.

START *MILEAGE LOG:*

0.0 Zero trip odometer **[Rev. Miles]**
From paved road at Packer Saddle, head north uphill following sign to Deer Lake. **[3.6]**
01 N39 37.174 W120 40.039

0.8 Bear left. **[2.8]**

1.8 Continue north along ridge. Great views of Deer Lake on right. Watch for hikers on the Pacific Crest Hiking Trail. **[1.8]**

2.1 Bear right to take side trip down to parking area above Deer Lake. **[1.5]**

2.4 After visiting lake, return to top of hill, bear right and continue north. Rougher road winds through trees. **[1.2]**

3.6 At intersection near Summit Lake (on right), make hard left almost reversing direction. (If you continue north here, you run into Snake Lake Trail #9 and Gold Lake OHV Campground.) **[0.0]**
02 N39 39.661 W120 40.571

0.0 Zero trip odometer at Wpt. 02
You head south then southeast downhill on good road. **[21.8]**

0.5 Continue downhill to left. Road on right goes uphill and connects to Snake Lake Trail #9. **[21.3]**

1.1 Bear right. You are now on Gold Valley Trail. **[20.7]**
03 N39 39.012 W120 41.190

1.9 Stay right past gated road on left. Trail gets steeper and rougher with possible water crossings. **[19.9]**

2.7 Continue straight. Left goes to Smith Lake. **[19.1]**
04 N39 39.190 W120 42.483

2.9 Ignore lesser road on left. Trail swings right with rocky creek crossings. Most are dry. **[18.9]**

5.0 Stay left through complex intersection. Right goes to Snake Lake. **[16.8]**
05 N39 40.625 W120 42.002

5.6 Continue straight. Left goes to private youth camp at Hawley Lk. **[16.2]**

7.0 Follow road as it curves right past Four Hills Mine (on left). After mine, make a hard left and head north again. **[14.8]**

7.8 Nice views as you climb to ridge and continue north. **[14.0]**

8.1 Watch for hikers as road is shared with Pacific Crest Hiking Trail. **[13.7]**

10.1 Bear right at "T" intersection called A-Tree. **[11.7]**

12.1 Turn right on Johnsville-McCrea Road and head downhill along Jamison Creek past several campgrounds. (Street-legal vehicles only after Waypoint 06.) **[9.7]**
06 N39 44.087 W120 45.419

15.4 Pavement. **[6.4]**

16.6 Bear right after State Park Museum. **[5.2]**

21.8 Follow Graeagle-Johnsville Road east until you reach Highway 89 at town of Graeagle. **[0.0]**
07 N39 46.287 W120 37.201
To return to Bassetts Station, head south 1.7 miles on Hwy. 89 and turn right on Gold Lake Highway. It's a scenic 16-mile drive with places to picnic, hike and camp.

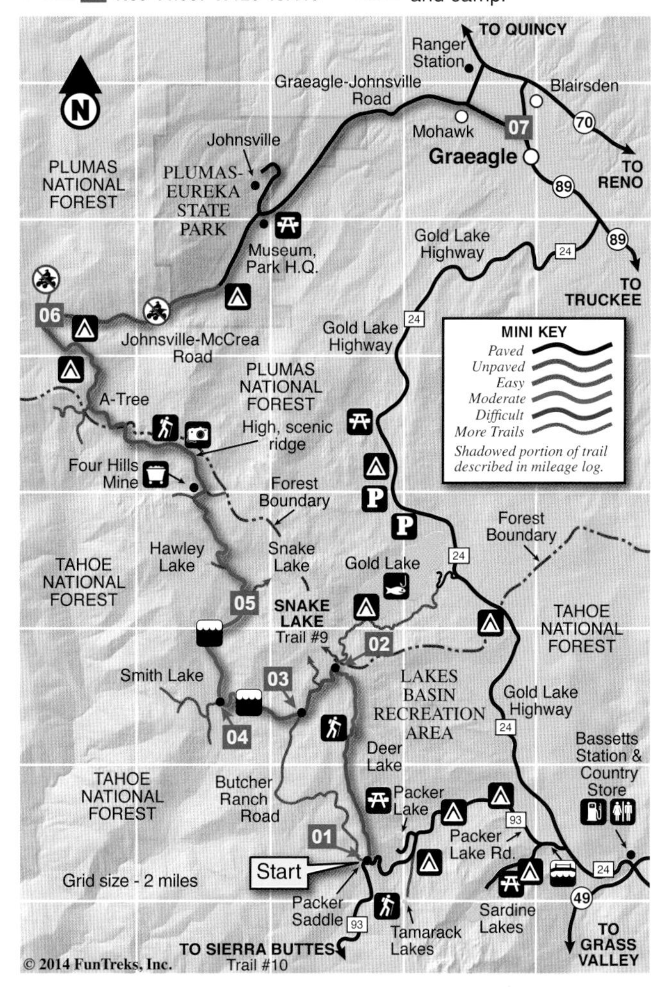

Rough spot on Gold Valley Trail.

Boiler marks Four Hills Mine.

Snake Lake

AREA 1 map on page 18

Gold Lake OHV Campground.

View of Gold Lake after Waypoint 02.

Good ground clearance needed.

Bottom of hill nearing Snake Lake.

Rocky, steep and tippy going down.

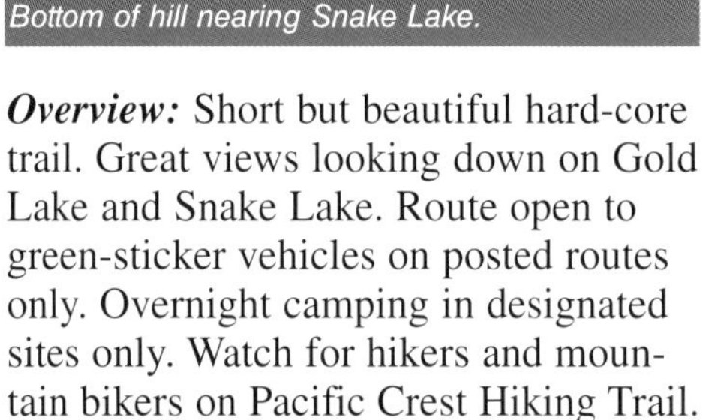

Overview: Short but beautiful hard-core trail. Great views looking down on Gold Lake and Snake Lake. Route open to green-sticker vehicles on posted routes only. Overnight camping in designated sites only. Watch for hikers and mountain bikers on Pacific Crest Hiking Trail.

Rating: Difficult: Very steep and rocky descending to Snake Lake with more obstacles coming back up alongside Little Deer Lake. For modified vehicles and experienced drivers only.

Stats: Length: Round trip returning to start is 10.1 miles. Time: 3 to 4 hours. Elevation: 6,421 to 7,419 ft. Best time: May-September.

Current Conditions: Tahoe N.F., Yuba River R.D. (530) 288-3231. Plumas N.F., Beckwourth R.D. (530) 836-2575.

Getting There: Follow directions to Bassetts Station as described in Trail #8. From there, head north 6.3 miles on paved Gold Lake Highway. Turn left on Gold Lake Road following signs to boat ramp. Continue straight after 0.45 miles when pavement turns north to boat ramp. Parking and start of trail are just ahead. Adequate room for staging.

START **MILEAGE LOG:**

0.0 Zero trip odometer [Rev. Miles] Head south on well-marked OHV trail. No camping allowed along road. [7.3]
01 N39 40.627 W120 38.810

0.4 Continue straight. Road that joins on left goes to Squaw Lake. [6.9]

1.3 Continue straight. Gold Lake OHV Campground on right. Camp in designated sites only. [6.0]

1.5 Continue straight. Left is Little Gold Lake. [5.8]

1.6 Follow trail left away from lake. [5.7]

2.0 Continue straight. [5.3]

2.2 Stay left uphill [5.1]

2.6 Follow trail as it curves to right. [4.7]

2.8 Turn right following sign to Snake Lake. Road heads NW and climbs along ridge with great views of Gold Lake below. [4.5]
02 N39 39.696 W120 40.544

3.5 Continue straight. You'll loop back to this point later. [3.8]
03 N39 40.086 W120 41.022

4.1 Trail descends past Oakland Pond (on left). [3.2]

4.4 Descend very steep rocky section. [2.9]

4.7 Trail passes along north edge of Snake Lake. [2.6]

5.0 Turn hard left through trees on lesser road. Easy to miss this turn as better road continues straight and connects to Gold Valley, Trail #8. [2.3]
04 N39 40.713 W120 41.647

5.4 First of several difficult spots as you climb past Little Deer Lake. Great views looking back down the hill. [1.9]

6.0 Enter trees again as trail turns left and continues to climb. [1.3]

6.3 Stay left. Right is shortcut if you plan to drive Gold Valley Trail #8 next. [1.0]

6.6 Return to Waypoint 03 where loop started. Bear right. [0.7]

7.3 Return to Waypoint 02. Left goes out the way you came in. Right connects to Deer Lake, Gold Valley, Trail #8. [0.0]

Trail updates & GPS downloads at www.funtreks.com

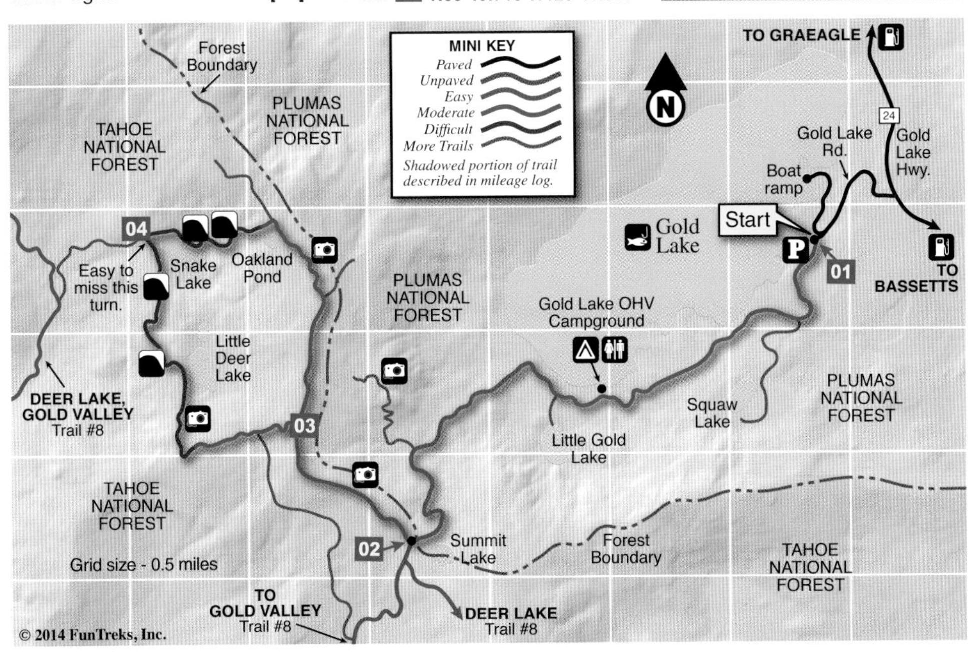

Easy to miss this left turn at Waypoint 04.

Don't forget your fishing pole (and license).

Sierra Buttes

AREA 1 map on page 18

Narrow shelf road hugs mountain as it climbs.

Park below gate at Waypoint 05 and hike to top.

Sierra City has a few shops and 24-hr. gas.

Loose boulder partially blocked the trail.

Historical Highlight: *Sierra City served as an important mining town starting in the 1850s. Today, the quaint town consists of many turn-of-the-century buildings complete with boardwalks. Don't miss the Kentucky Mine Stampmill and Museum east of town.*

Overview: Perhaps the most enjoyable easy trail in this book when driven, as described here, from Sierra City. The drive is fun, exhilarating and very beautiful. The view from Sierra Buttes Lookout is dizzying. A steep 3/4-mile hike is required to reach the lookout. Take plenty of water, your camera and binoculars. Green-sticker vehicles may wish to start at the top where there is more room to park. Follow directions at right starting from Bassetts.

Rating: Easy: A narrow shelf road that climbs steeply up the mountainside. Minor loose rocks in a few places and quite steep towards the top. Suitable for stock, high-clearance 4WD SUVs.

Stats: Length: 10 miles. Time: 3-4 hours. Elevation: 4,200 to 7,950 ft. Best time: May-September.

Current Conditions: Tahoe National Forest, Yuba River Ranger District. (530) 288-3231.

Getting There: **From Grass Valley:** Take Hwy. 49 past Downieville to Sierra City. **From Truckee:** Take Hwy. 89 north then turn west on Hwy. 49 to Sierra City. **From Bassetts to start at top:** Head north on Gold Lake Hwy. 1.3 miles and turn left on Packer Lake Road across bridge. Stay on this paved road 4.8 miles until you reach a parking area on left for Sierra Buttes Hiking Trail.

START **MILEAGE LOG:**

0.0 Zero trip odometer **[Rev. Miles]**
Head north uphill on paved Butte St. & bear left on Sierra Buttes Rd. [6.3]
01 N39 33.952 W120 38.126

1.1 Turn right on dirt road and start to climb. [5.2]

2.5 Make a hard right on lesser road. Next 2 miles are a narrow shelf road with very little room to pass. [3.8]
02 N39 34.572 W120 39.686

4.8 Bear right following sign for Sierra Buttes. [1.5]
03 N39 35.051 W120 40.454

5.2 Turn right following sign to Sierra Buttes Lookout, then stay to left as you climb sandy road. [1.1]
04 N39 35.276 W120 40.083

5.6 Bear left. [0.7]

6.1 Bear left. [0.2]

6.3 Reach major parking area with hiking trail to lookout tower. You may continue another 0.2 miles to gate to avoid some of the hiking. After visiting tower return to Waypoint 4. [0.0]
05 N39 35.703 W120 39.254

0.0 Zero trip odometer at Wpt. 04
From Wpt. 04 head north on much flatter road. [2.6]

0.6 Stay right. (Left goes to Monarch Mine.) [2.0]
06 N39 35.643 W120 40.300

0.8 Stay right. [1.8]

1.9 Stay right where good road cuts over to 93. [0.7]

2.6 Trail ends at large parking area. To reach town of Bassetts, turn right and follow paved 93 east downhill. [0.0]
07 N39 36.852 W120 39.983

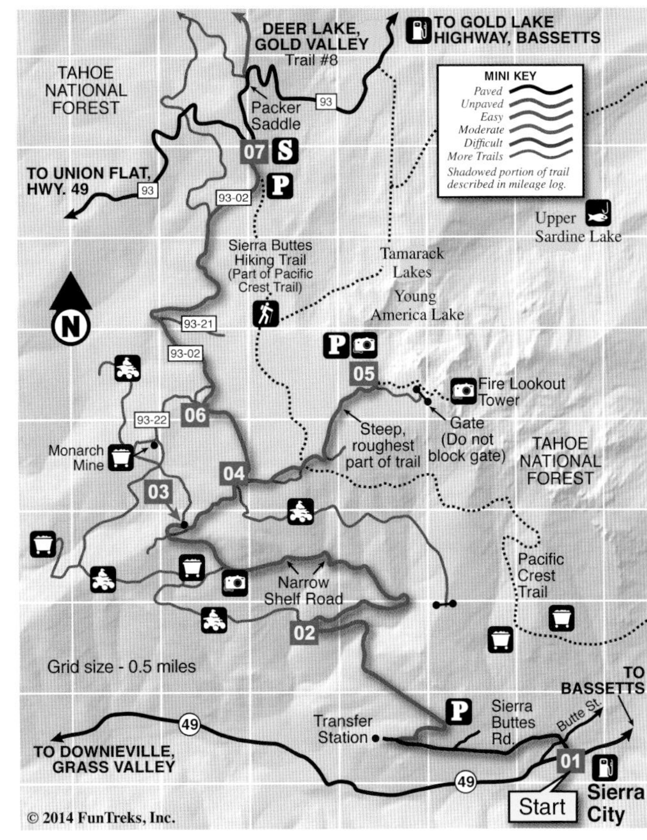

Steep staircase to tower.

Views from lookout tower are outstanding on a clear day.

Ellis Peak

AREA 1 map on page 18

Views of Lake Tahoe from Ellis Peak.

Great views as you climb.

We made a quick stop at Bear Lake.

Side trip to Ellis Lake is worth the extra time.

Overview: Beautiful, high mountain area west of Lake Tahoe. Route passes several beautiful lakes with outstanding views of Lake Tahoe from top of Ellis Peak. Open to green-sticker vehicles with large staging area at start.

Rating: Moderate: Narrow, steep and rough in places. Suitable for stock high-clearance 4x4 SUVs. Some tight brush.

Stats: Length: 21.2 miles as described. Time: At least 4 hours. Elevation: 6,284 to 8,539 ft. Best time to go: June-October.

Current Conditions: Tahoe N.F., Truckee R.D. (530) 587-3558. Lake Tahoe Basin Mgt. Unit (530) 543-2600.

Getting There: Head south from Tahoe City on Hwy. 89. Turn right after 4.3 miles on Barker Pass Road. After 2.2 miles, continue straight on dirt road where pavement turns left. Staging area is hidden in trees on right in 0.45 miles.

START *MILEAGE LOG:*

0.0 Zero trip odometer **[Rev. Miles]** From staging area, head west on dirt road. **[10.9]**
01 N39 06.191 W120 12.241

3.1 Pass through gate, then continue straight across large circular area. Stay right of white tanks. **[7.8]**

3.2 Cross major Barker Pass Road and continue downhill on lesser road. **[7.7]**
02 N39 04.603 W120 14.128

3.5 Stay right. **[7.4]**

5.1 Turn left on more traveled road where F.S. 03 04 09 goes straight. **[5.8]**
03 N39 03.535 W120 15.120

5.5 Continue straight. **[5.4]**

7.4 Continue straight where small road on right goes to Bear Lake. **[3.5]**

7.9 Turn left on F.S. 03 04 12 for Ellis Peak. **[3.0]**
04 N39 02.747 W120 13.622

8.6 Turn right. **[2.3]**

9.1 Turn hard left. **[1.8]**

9.4 Stay right. **[1.5]**

10.2 Stay left where Buck Lake (Trail #12) goes right. **[0.7]**

10.5 Stay right. Trail on left goes to Ellis Lake. **[0.4]**

10.9 Park just below Ellis Peak. Short climb to top for views of Lake Tahoe. Return to Wpt. 04. **[0.0]**
05 N39 03.948 W120 11.847

0.0 Zero trip odometer at Wpt. 04
Head south at Waypoint 4. (You may also exit the way you came in.) **[7.3]**

1.3 Turn left. Road from Rubicon, East Side, Trail # 14, joins on right. **[6.0]**
06 N39 02.233 W120 13.351

1.7 Continue straight. You'll pass several lakes. **[5.6]**

4.5 Continue straight where Buck Lake (Trail #12) goes left. **[2.8]**

4.8 Continue straight past staging area. **[2.5]**
07 N39 02.749 W120 10.065

6.6 Turn right on road marked Springs Ct. following signs for Hwy. 89. **[0.7]**

6.9 Turn left on Bellevue. **[0.4]**

7.0 Turn right on McKinney Rubicon Springs Rd. **[0.3]**

7.3 Arrive at Hwy. 89. **[0.0]**
08 N39 04.219 W120 08.411

Fun area for ATVs.

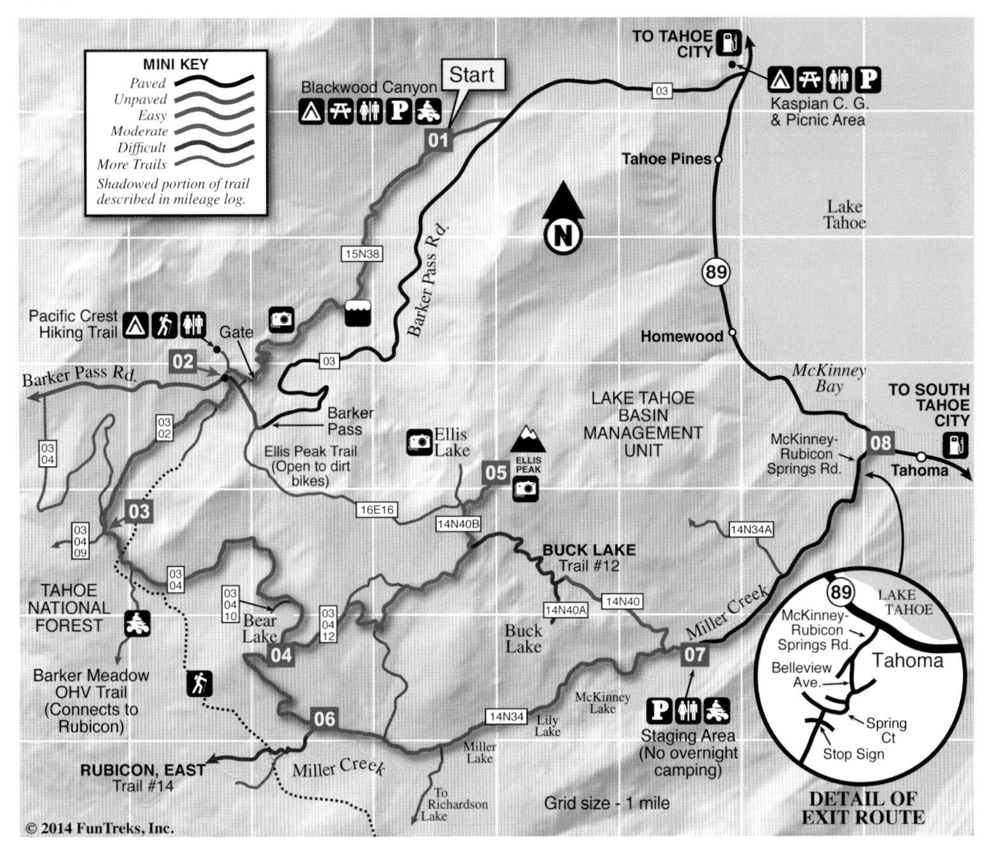

Buck Lake

AREA 1 map on page 18

Climbing past Buck Lake. Lake Tahoe can be seen in the distance upper left.

Several good campsites at Buck Lake.

Tight brush in places.

Overview: Add this trail to the Rubicon or drive as stand-alone. Alternate route to top of Ellis Peak is both challenging and beautiful. Quickly reached from west shore of Lake Tahoe. Difficult access to Buck Lake means good campsites are often available. Trail is open to green-sticker vehicles with large staging area just east of Waypoint 02. Thanks to the North Tahoe Trail Dusters for adopting this trail.

Rating: Difficult: Moderate to Waypoint 03. Large, loose rocks above Buck Lake. Fallen trees and large rocks make side trip to Buck Lake very challenging. Steep with tight brush in places.

Stats: Length: Four-wheel-drive portion with side trip to Buck Lake is 2.8 miles. About 6 miles to Ellis Peak from start. Time: About 2 hours one-way. Elevation: 6,284 to 8,048 ft. Open seasonally from June - November.

Current Conditions: Tahoe National Forest, Lake Tahoe Basin Management Unit. Call (530) 543-2600.

Getting There: **From Tahoe City:** Drive 8 miles south on Highway 89 to McKinney-Rubicon Springs Road on right. **From Tahoe Valley:** Drive 19.4 miles north on Highway 89 to McKinney-Rubicon Sprgs. Road on left.

START *MILEAGE LOG:*

0.0 Zero trip odometer **[Rev. Miles]**
Head west on paved McKinney-Rubicon Springs Road. **[2.8]**
01 N39 04.219 W120 08.411

0.2 Turn left on Bellevue. **[2.6]**

0.4 At stop sign turn right on Springs Court. **[2.4]**

0.7 Turn left at sign for Rubicon Trail and Miller Lake access. **[2.1]**

2.5 Continue straight past staging area on left. **[0.3]**

2.8 Turn right at start of Buck Lake trail. **[0.0]**
02 N39 02.737 W120 10.376

0.0 Zero trip odometer at Wpt. 02
Head north up narrow F.S. 14N40. **[1.7]**

1.5 Turn left for Buck Lake. The trail narrows as you get closer to lake. **[0.2]**
03 N39 03.272 W120 11.427

1.7 Arrive at campsite area. Return to Waypoint 03 when done. **[0.0]**
04 N39 03.087 W120 11.431

Zero trip odometer at Wpt. 03

0.0 Turn left uphill. **[0.9]**

0.9 Join Ellis Peak (Trail #11) described on previous pages. Turn right to reach top of Ellis Peak or left to exit. **[0.0]**
05 N39 03.464 W120 12.005

Trail updates & GPS downloads at www.funtreks.com

Trip to Buck Lake is difficult with downed trees and large rocks.

Quiet moment at edge of Buck Lake, Waypoint 04.

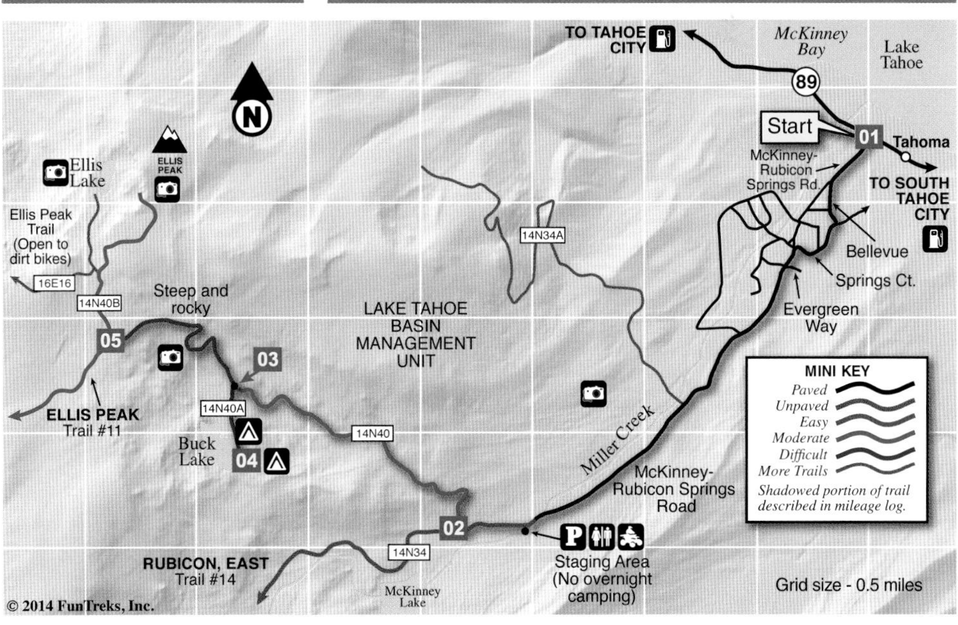

Rubicon, West Side

AREA 1 map on page 18

Looking down from dam at start of trail.

Author (right front) listens in on driver's meeting.

Entire first half of trail is above 6,000 feet.

Follow yellow trail markers across Granite Bowl.

Historical Highlight: *The Rubicon Trail has a long history dating back to 1844. Rubicon Springs once had a hotel, but in 1908 it was destroyed by 8-ft.-deep flood waters. Even today, Rubicon Springs is closed much of the winter due to flooding. The first Georgetown Jeepers Jamboree occurred in 1952 and still continues today, the last weekend of July. More history at www.rubicontrailfoundation.org.*

Overview: The Rubicon is our all-time favorite. It's a mix of gorgeous scenery and very challenging terrain. Our group camped overnight at the halfway point below Buck Island Dam. Trail is under constant scrutiny by environmental groups; stay on designated route at all times. ATVs, UTVs and dirt bikes are allowed. U.S.F.S. fire permit and portable toilet required. Official map and accurate trail information available free at www.rubicontrailfoundation.org.

Rating: Difficult: West Side is dominated by open granite tracts interspersed with tight boulder fields and tall ledges. Lockers, lifts, 33" minimum tire size and skilled driver recommended. Optional *Little Sluice* and *Old Big Sluice* significantly increase difficulty.

Stats: Length: This half is 5.8 miles. Allow 6 to 8 hours or more. Elevation: 6,270 to 6,764 ft. Best time to go: Mid June-Sept. except during Jeep Jamborees late July to early August. Check weather forecast; freak snowstorms have closed trail even in July.

Current Conditions: Eldorado N.F., Pacific R.D. Call (530) 644-2349

Getting There: From U.S. Hwy. 50, between Placerville and South Lake Tahoe, head north on paved, well-marked Icehouse Road. Turn right after 23 miles (left here goes to Wentworth Springs, an alternate way to drive to the trail). Stay on Icehouse Road another 9 miles until you cross Loon Lake Dam. Bear left downhill after dam to reach start. Gas available on Hwy. 50 at Kyburz, 8 miles east of Icehouse Road (Credit-card pumps open 24 hours).

START MILEAGE LOG:

0.0 Zero trip odometer [Rev. Miles]
Climb well-marked trail to right and cross large granite dome. [5.8]
01 N39 00.192 W120 18.691

0.2 Drop down other side and swing right at trees. [5.6]

0.6 Climb obstacle out of trees and bear left following markers across Granite Bowl. [5.2]
02 N39 00.465 W120 18.410

1.6 Continue north as Wentworth Springs Road joins on left. [4.2]
03 N39 00.465 W120 18.410

1.9 Vault toilet on left. [3.9]

2.7 Log bridge. [3.1]

3.9 Driver's choice. Main route, described here, goes left up granite slope to bypass difficult "Little Sluice," which is to the right. [1.9]
04 N39 01.251 W120 16.555

3.9 As you head up granite, bear LEFT in 100 yards and go around east side of granite dome. [1.9]

4.2 Trails rejoin at "T" above Little Sluice. Turn left downhill. (Note: To see Spider Lake, turn right and go about 70 yards, then hike south following white stone line.) [1.6]
05 N39 01.172 W120 16.352

4.9 Stay left downhill. (Entrance to Old Big Sluice is in trees on right.) [0.9]
06 N39 00.821 W120 16.000

5.3 Stay left. Trail appears to go straight. [0.5]

5.5 Stay left downhill through trees. Old Big Sluice rejoins on right. [0.3]
07 N39 00.421 W120 15.697

5.8 Pass through narrow, tippy section and twist downhill. Soon you'll approach several camp spots in trees around a granite clearing. We camped on right before creek at a point below the dam. [0.0]
08 N39 00.345 W120 15.429

Beware: We were inundated with bears throughout the night. Car horns scare them away. Be careful.

Trail updates & GPS downloads at www.funtreks.com

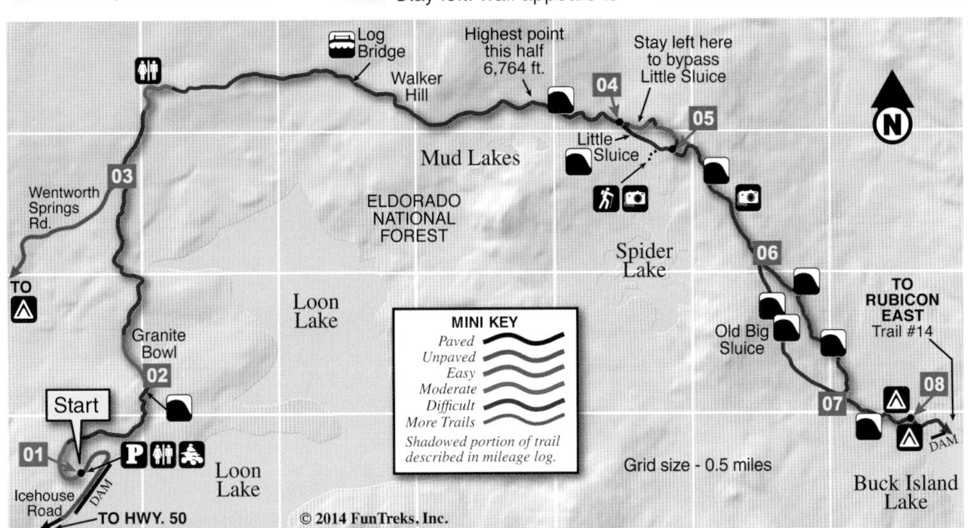

Slow going most of the way. Stay on the official trail at all times.

Optional Old Big Sluice.

Our camp below Buck Island Lake Dam. Expect bears at night.

Rubicon, East Side

AREA 1 map on page 18

Leaving Waypoint 01.

Our 2012 Rubicon just barely squeezed through Big Sluice.

Camping at Buck Island Lake.

Toyota FJ with 35-inch tires climbs daunting Cadillac Hill.

Overview: The east side of the Rubicon provides nonstop challenges and extreme fun. Water can play a bigger role where trail meanders along the volatile Rubicon River. You'll pass through Rubicon Springs Campground at no charge unless you stop to camp or use facilities. Just when you think everything is over, you're confronted by daunting Cadillac Hill and many more miles of rough road.

Rating: Difficult: Named obstacles include Big Sluice and Cadillac Hill. These boulder obstacle courses are extremely difficult and have no bypasses. Wider vehicles beware. High water can make conditions impassable along the Rubicon River during all but the driest times. Best when trail is dusty.

Stats: Lengths: This half is 10.6 miles. Time: 8 hours or more. Elevation: 5,984 to 7,205 ft.

Current Conditions: Eldorado N. F. Pacific R.D., (530) 644-2349 and Tahoe N.F., Truckee R.D., (530) 587-3558.

Getting There: Follow directions for Trail #13 on previous page. To run trail in opposite direction, start at east side staging area (Waypoint 07). Refer to Area map on page 18 and detail of exit route on opposite page. Or, just follow directions to Buck Lake, Trail #12.

START **MILEAGE LOG:**

0.0 Zero trip odometer [Rev. Miles] This description is a continuation of Trail #13. From camp spot below dam, cross creek and follow tire marks uphill. Trail crosses east end of dam and swings left. Many obstacles follow as trail weaves along north end of Buck Island Lake. [10.6]
01 N39 00.345 W120 15.429

0.3 Stay right downhill. [10.3]

0.9 After long descent, trail swings hard left as you enter difficult Big Sluice. (no bypass). [9.7]
02 N39 00.239 W120 14.644

1.4 Enter private land. No fees to pass through. [9.2]

1.7 Cross Rubicon Brdg. [8.9]

1.9 Driver's choice. Narrow opening on left is easier unless flooded. Right has obstacle, but is drier. [8.7]
03 N39 00.878 W120 14.621

2.1 Caretaker's Cabin marks entry into Rubicon Springs C.G. Note posted fees to use facilities. [8.5]
04 N39 01.007 W120 14.769

2.2 Swing left after going past helipads. [8.4]

2.8 Leave private land. [7.8]

3.2 Stay right. (Trail TKS-11 goes left.) [7.4]

3.4 Trail zigzags to right and starts up Cadillac Hill.
05 N39 01.845 W120 15.160
Check ahead to make sure no one is coming down. It is extremely difficult to pass. [7.2]

4.2 Large overlook on left. Great spot for group photo. You still have a long way to go and trail gets rough again. [6.4]

5.0 Stay right past Barker Meadow OHV Trail. [5.6]

6.1 Trail gets easier. [4.5]

7.1 Continue straight. Trail #11 joins on left. [3.5]
06 N39 02.229 W120 13.346

8.1 Continue straight. Right goes to Richardson Lake. You'll pass several more lakes. [2.5]

10.3 Continue straight. Buck Lake Trail on left. [0.3]

10.6 Arrive at Rubicon East Staging Area. [0.0]
07 N39 02.749 W120 10.065
See map detail below for directions to Highway 89 and Lake Tahoe.

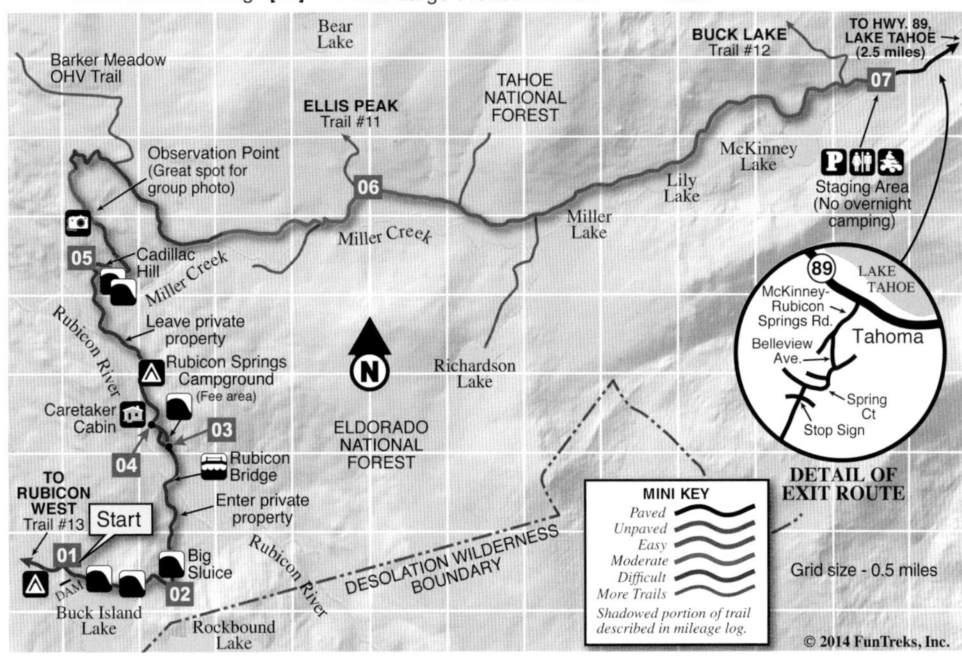

Observation Point. We thank the Mile High Jeep Club, Patrol #2, for allowing us to join them.

Shirttail Canyon

AREA 1 map on page 18

Families enjoy the crystal-clear water below the suspension bridge. Great spot on a hot summer day.

Only original building left in Iowa Hill.

Tight parking on east side of suspension bridge.

Historical Highlight: *Gold was first discovered in Iowa Hill in 1853 and mining continued off and on into the 1930s. A few mines have been intermittently worked in recent years. Most mining has been hydraulic, scars of which you'll see along the route. One spot along Iowa Hill Road has sheer cliffs on each side of the road due to hydraulic undercutting.*

Overview: The main attraction of this route is a popular swimming hole below Colfax-Foresthill Suspension Bridge. Our round-about way of getting there follows a paved road through historic Iowa Hill, then continues on a narrow, winding dirt road through the forest. Take a picnic lunch and inner tube to enjoy the crystal-clear water of the American River inside Auburn State Recreation Area (fee area). Street-legal vehicles only. To go direct to swimming hole, use reverse directions.

Rating: Easy: First half is a twisting paved road, narrow in spots. Watch for bikers. Second half is an easy dirt road. Four-wheel drive recommended.

Stats: Length: 24.6 miles. Time: 2-3 hours plus stop time. Elevation: 980 to 2985 ft. Best time: Hot summer days.

Current Conditions: Auburn State Recreation Area. Call (530) 885-4527.

Getting There: Take I-80 to town of Colfax. Take exit for Highway 174. Westbound exiters must cross over freeway. Follow Canyon Way south along east side of freeway 0.3 miles to paved Iowa Hill Road on left.

START **MILEAGE LOG:**

0.0 Zero trip odometer [Rev. Miles]
Head east on paved Iowa Hill Road. [24.6]
01 N39 05.457 W120 57.039

2.6 Tight switchback at Stevens Creek Falls. [22.0]

2.9 Cross concrete bridge alongside Iowa Hill Suspension Bridge. [21.7]

3.0 Mineral Bar C.G. on left. Great place to camp with many activities. [21.6]

8.9 Sign for Iowa Hill. Caution: Sheer cliffs on each side of road. [15.7]

9.1 Cabin on right is the only original structure built after the town's last fire in 1920. [15.5]

9.2 Iowa Hill Store on left still in operation. [15.4]

9.3 Bear right on Big Dipper Road. [15.3]
02 N39 06.531 W120 51.521

9.5 Stay right downhill. [15.1]

10.4 Mine on left. [14.2]

11.4 Bear right following signs to Shirttail Canyon and Yankee Jims Road. [13.2]

11.8 Bear left on Shirttail Canyon Road (dirt). [12.8]
03 N39 05.584 W120 51.459

17.7 Single-lane bridge. [6.9]

17.9 Turn right on Yankee Jims Road. [6.7]
04 N39 02.440 W120 53.167

18.4 As you pass through Devil's Canyon, we noticed orange paint on boulders near the boundary to Auburn State Recreation Area. [6.2]

18.7 Devil's Falls on right. Best water flow in spring. [5.9]

19.2 Cross suspension bridge. Small parking area with portable toilet on other side. Fee area. Steep hike down to swimming. [5.4]
05 N39 02.409 W120 54.184

20.9 Mine adit on right. [3.7]

22.8 Pavement starts. [1.8]

23.9 Bear right on Canyon Way. [0.7]
06 N39 04.118 W120 57.348

24.6 E.B. entrance to I-80 on left. Cross over just ahead for W.B. [0.0]

Trail updates & GPS downloads at www.funtreks.com

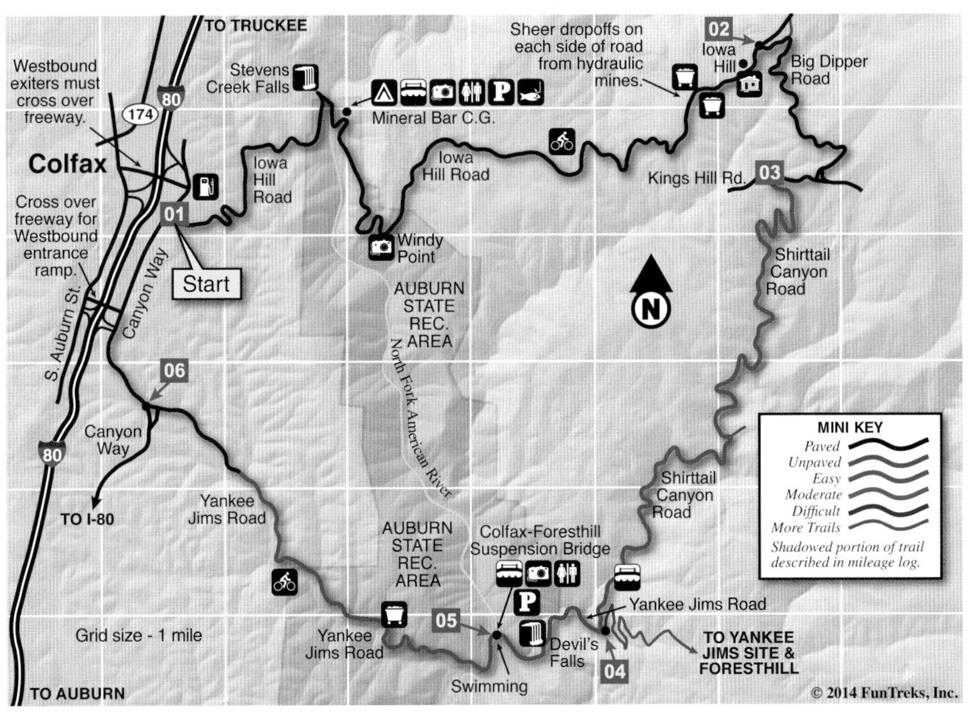

Shelf road through Shirttail Canyon is dusty in the summer.

Suspension bridge built in 1930.

Lake Alpine, Bridgeport, Mammoth Lakes, Big Pine, Shaver Lake

All the trails in this area surround world-renowned Yosemite National Park and most traverse the slopes of the majestic Sierra Nevada. Trails are a perfect blend of beauty and adventure. One example is *Laurel Lakes, Trail #24* (pictured on opposite page). This trail, located not too far from Mammoth Mountain Ski Area, can be driven in any stock high-clearance 4x4 sport utility vehicle. Novice drivers may be a bit intimidated at first, but will certainly go home with a smile on their face. There are 11 easy or moderate routes and three difficult routes on the eastern side of the Sierras. Most are accessed from Highway 395.

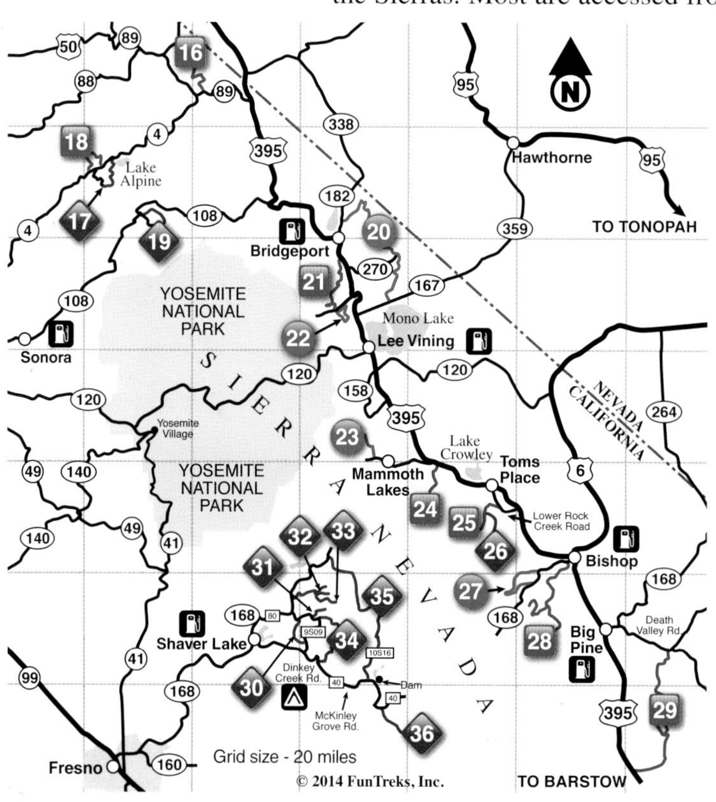

On the western side, surrounding the mountain town of Shaver Lake northeast of Fresno, you'll find seven of the best hard-core trails anywhere in California. This includes the long, grueling and spectacular *Dusy/Ershim Trail*.

Barney Riley is a new trail we discovered. Just north of Bridgeport, it features two hot springs with stone pools free to anyone with a vehicle that can reach their remote location (see photo on page 52).

Laurel Lakes, Trail #24, rated moderate. Popular SUV trail just outside Mammoth Lakes.

16 Barney Riley

AREA 2 map on page 50

Great views from many high points along the route. Highest point of trail is about 8,000 feet.

Camp spot is ½ mile downstream from springs.

One of two hand-built pools. Water was hot!

Historical Highlight: *The cemented stone pools at the hot springs were built by the general public over a long period of time. The Forest Service has attempted to knock them down, but people just rebuild them. The pools are very popular with river rafters when the river is high and 4-wheelers when the river is low. During our visit in early September, we found the river ankle deep at the hot springs.*

Overview: Very scenic with great mountain views from high points along the route. Mix of open and wooded terrain with aspen trees that provide fall color. Great camping along East Fork of Carson River at the end. Unique stone hot spring pools on north side of river must be accessed by foot, raft or canoe depending on depth of river. Trail open to green-sticker vehicles, but no motorized vehicles are allowed to cross river.

Rating: Moderate: Most of this trail is easy, but several steep, rocky sections will test novice drivers. Stock SUVs can do it, but skid plates and moderate ground clearance are recommended.

Stats: Length: 11 miles one way. Time: 2-3 hours to end at river. Great weekend campout. Elevation: 6,123 to 8,008 ft. Best time: May-September. Water levels generally lower in the fall.

Current Conditions: Humboldt-Toiyabe N.F., Carson R.D. Call (775) 882-2766.

Getting There: From South Lake Tahoe, take Highway 50 south to Hwy. 89. Then follow 89 southeast about 28 miles. When Hwy. 4 continues south, bear left and stay on 89 another 1.7 miles. Loope Canyon Road is a wide dirt road and comes downhill on the left. We saw no signs, so it was easy to miss. Look for a wide spot to pull over on the south side of Hwy. 89 opposite the start.

START **MILEAGE LOG:**

0.0 Zero trip odometer **[Rev. Miles]**
Head north on Loope Canyon Road 190. Ignore lesser side roads. **[11.0]**
01 N38 39.942 W119 41.856

1.1 Stay right on 190. **[9.9]**

1.5 Follow 190 as it curves right past camp spot with view on left. **[9.5]**

1.7 Continue straight on 190. (On left is the south end of 190B.) **[9.3]**

3.3 Turn left uphill on 190B (This is the north end of 190B.) **[7.7]**
02 N38 41.900 W119 41.763

3.7 Stay right. Left goes to camp spot in trees. **[7.3]**

4.0 Stay left on 190B. (Lesser 314 goes right.) **[7.0]**

4.2 Stay right on 310, then trail curves right. **[6.8]**

4.6 Continue straight. Road 310B joins on right. **[6.4]**

5.0 Stay right. (306 goes left.) **[6.0]**
03 N38 42.325 W119 42.867

5.7 Continue straight. **[5.3]**

7.0 Steep rocky climb with rubber water bars. **[4.0]**

7.1 Top of high ridge, great views. Steep descent down other side. **[3.9]**

8.0 Stay right. Old Barney Riley trail joins on left. **[3.0]**
04 N38 44.106 W119 43.536

10.1 Continue north. Road on right goes to Carson River at a point directly across from hot springs. Road looked well traveled, but is not shown on Motor Vehicle Use Map. **[0.9]**
05 N38 45.436 W119 43.386

10.7 Stay right as you drop down to river. Road joins on left. **[0.3]**

11.0 Great shaded camp spot with picnic table and fire ring next to river. **[0.0]**
06 N38 46.093 W119 43.427
This camp spot is about a half-mile west of the hot springs. You are NOT allowed to drive across the river. When river is low, there are spots shallow enough to wade across. Bring a raft or canoe if you have one. Only you can determine if it is safe to cross.

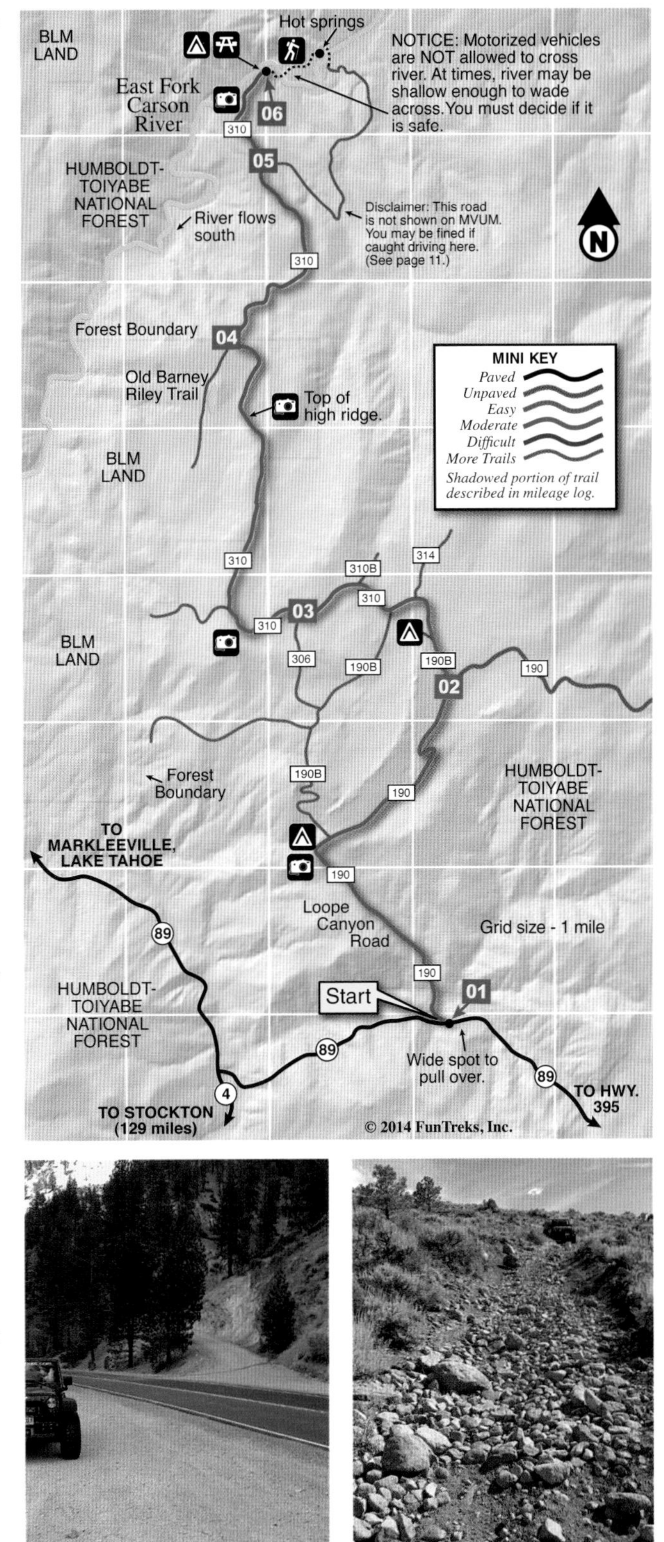

Start not marked at Hwy. 89.

Rough, bone-jarring in spots.

Slickrock Trail

AREA 2 map on page 50

Trail runs alongside crystal-clear Silver Creek.

Difficult part begins here at steep-walled canyon.

Steep descent down granite ledge.

Continue straight at Wpt. 03 up this tight spot.

Overview: This short route is a rare combination of difficult obstacles and great scenery. Passes through popular Union/Utica recreation area. Lots of hiking, biking and water activities at each end of the route. Street-legal vehicles only. Great camping along the trail after Waypoint 02. We recommend you camp over the weekend and explore area on foot.

Rating: Difficult: Awkward, tight turns through large boulders and solid rock. Body damage possible. Not for stock SUVs. Experienced drivers only.

Stats: Length: 6.5 miles as described. Just 1.5 miles is difficult. Time: 2-3 hours. Elevation: 6,698 to 7447 ft. Open April 15-Dec. 15. Best May-Sept.

Current Conditions: Stanislaus N.F., Calaveras R.D. Call (209) 795-1381.

Getting There: From Stockton, take Route 4 northeast about 97 miles to Bear Valley where gas is available. Continue another 3.4 miles and turn right at sign for Lake Alpine West Shore. Follow paved road south just one-tenth mile. Avoid left turn for Alpine Lake Campground. Bear right where road swings left to main parking area. Road immediately changes to gravel. Trail starts on left where Bear Valley Biking Trail goes right.

START *MILEAGE LOG:*

0.0 Zero trip odometer **[Rev. Miles]** Bear left on dirt road 7N17 (not marked) where Bear Valley Bike Trail goes right. [6.5]
01 N38 28.591 W120 00.471

0.2 Follow trail to right. Shady spot next to lake on left. No camping here. [6.3]

0.4 Follow trail to right again at private cabin. [6.1]

0.7 Sign for official starting point of SLICK ROCK ROAD OHV ROUTE. Camping allowed after this point. After signs, trail curves to left. [5.8]
02 N38 28.122 W120 00.669

1.5 After passing two hiking trails, Silver Creek is seen on left. Gorgeous sight as water cascades over solid granite slabs. [5.0]

1.9 Narrow, steep-walled canyon marks beginning of difficult section. [4.6]

2.7 Begin steep descent down granite hill. [3.8]

2.8 Cross creek. [3.7]

3.1 Trail appears to go right. You continue straight up very difficult section of loose and embedded large boulders. [3.4]
03 N38 26.565 W120 00.716

3.2 Very difficult spot. [3.3]

3.4 Cross wooden bridge over Duck Creek. [3.1]

3.6 Difficult portion of trail ends at parking lot with portable toilets. Continue south on beautiful drive along west side of Utica Reservoir. [2.9]
04 N38 26.440 W120 00.477

4.7 Camp spot on left next to reservoir. [1.8]

5.8 Make hard right on 7N75. (Left goes to Union Reservoir.) [0.7]
05 N38 25.102 W120 00.452

6.5 Turn right on paved Spicer Road. (Left is Spicer Reservoir.) [0.0]
06 N38 24.556 W120 00.658
Right on Spicer Road takes you back to Hwy. 4 in about 8 miles. Right on 4 takes you back to Alpine Lake in 6 miles. Gas at Bear Valley.

Trail updates & GPS downloads at www.funtreks.com

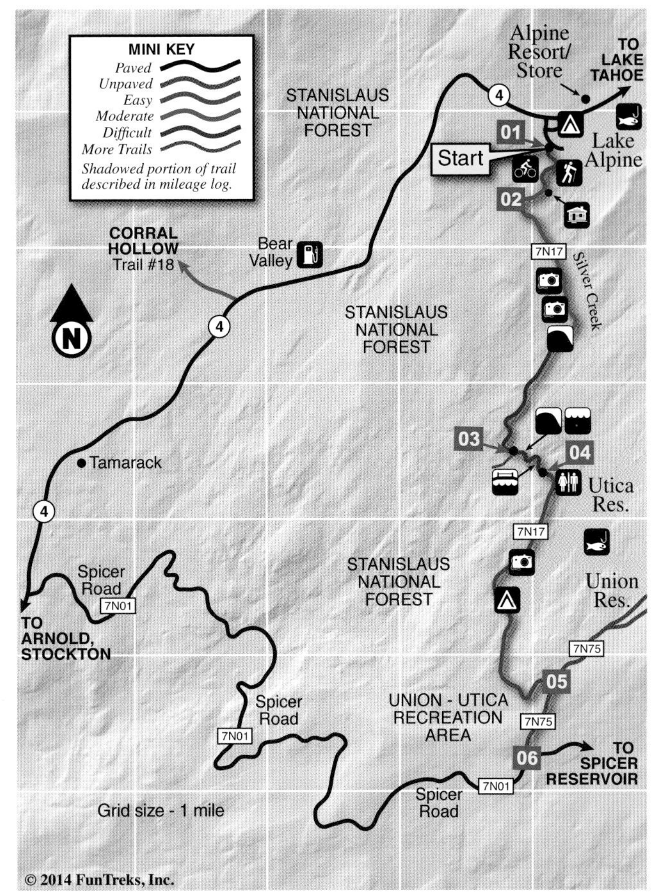

Wooden bridge over Duck Creek before Waypoint 04.

Trail runs along west shore of Utica Reservoir near the end.

18 Corral Hollow

AREA 2 map on page 50

Dispersed camp spot at Waypoint 03 has unobstructed view of Bear Valley Ski Area.

Stock SUVs descend through the mule ears.

Some maneuvering between rocks required.

Historical Highlight: *The unusual 2-story Bear Trap Cabin is believed to be an old cowboy cabin. It is owned and maintained by the U.S. Forest Service and is in remarkably good condition. Inside you'll find stairs, furniture and a functioning wood stove. There's also an outhouse in the back.*

Overview: First half of trail climbs steeply through meadows of thick mule ears to a high ridge with views of Bear Valley Ski Area and Mokelumne Wilderness. A few choice camp spots along the ridge. Second half is much easier with a stop at an historic cowboy cabin. Everything is open to green-sticker vehicles except the last mile along Cabbage Patch Road. More OHV roads available west of this trail. See MVUM.

Rating: Moderate: East side is steep, narrow, rutted and rocky in spots. West side is more downhill and easier. Suitable for stock, high-clearance 4x4 SUVs. Dusty when dry. More challenging when wet.

Stats: Length: 13.7 miles. Time: 2-3 hours. Elevation: 6,740 to 8,124 ft. Open April 15-Dec. 15. Best in July when mule ears is flowering.

Current Conditions: Stanislaus N.F., Calaveras R.D. Call (209) 795-1381.

Getting There: From Stockton, take Route 4 northeast about 93 miles. Turn left 0.1 miles after sign for Alpine County Line. If you make it to Bear Valley, you've gone ½ mile too far.

START **MILEAGE LOG:**

0.0 Zero trip odometer [Rev. Miles]
Head west then north on rough, rutted forest road. (not marked) This road is open to green-sticker vehicles. [13.7]
01 N38 27.421 W120 03.178

1.8 Steep uphill section. Cabbage-like plant along road is called "mule ears." [11.9]

2.3 Make hard left turn at top of ridge where ATV trail goes right. [11.4]
02 N38 28.768 W120 03.826

2.6 Continue straight where ATV trail goes left. [11.1]

2.8 Great views before passing through gate. [10.9]

3.0 Great camp spot on right with views of Bear Valley Ski Area. Walk out to overlook. [10.7]
03 N38 28.790 W120 04.486

4.2 More views. Salt Spring Reservoir below. [9.5]

4.8 Trail heads south away from ridge and descends more steeply. [8.9]

5.6 Stay left. [8.1]

6.1 Bear right to take side trip to Bear Trap Cabin. [7.6]
04 N38 28.298 W120 05.488

6.2 Take some time to look over the historic cabin owned by Forest Service. Leave as you find it and take only pictures. [7.5]

6.3 Return to main trail and turn right. [7.4]

7.2 Small creek crossing. Water level varies. [6.5]

8.1 Ignore lesser road on right. [5.6]

8.2 Road 7N11A joins on right. [5.5]

8.7 Ignore lesser road on right. [5.0]

8.9 Open area with view. [4.8]

12.3 Stay left on 7N11. [1.4]

12.4 Cross bridge. [1.3]

12.8 Bear left on wider Cabbage Patch Road 7N09. Licensed vehicles only from here. [0.9]
05 N38 25.403 W120 07.716

13.7 Return to Hwy. 4. [0.0]
06 N38 24.774 W120 08.196
Closest gas is left to Bear Valley, about 7 miles.

Trail updates & GPS downloads at www.funtreks.com

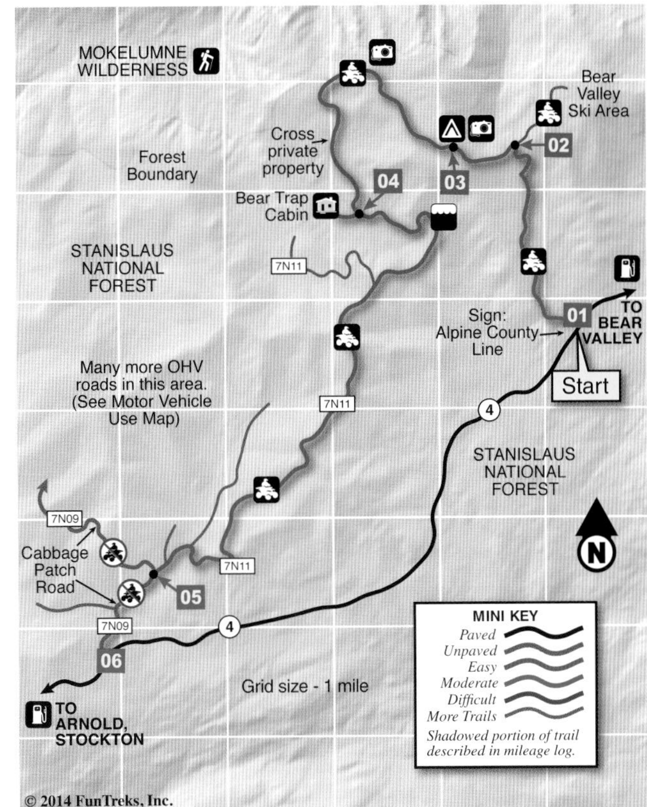

Bear Trap Cabin is two stories. Note outhouse in the back yard.

ATV riders head to cabin.

Functioning wood stove inside.

Niagara Rim

AREA 2 map on page 50

No bypass to Hard Brake Hill.

Easiest place to descend Lion's Butt.

Member of 4x4 IN MOTION tackles toughest part of optional Rock Pile. (Photo from our 2003 trip.)

Overview: Very popular hard-core trail with many marked obstacles. Harder choices on some obstacles can be extreme. Stock vehicles can access obstacles from network of interior roads starting at Niagara ORV Campground. Large area of Moab-style rock surfaces surrounds Base Camp. Green-sticker vehicles allowed except on paved roads. Trail adopted by *4x4 In Motion Club* of Modesto. See www.4x4inmotion.com.

Rating: Difficult: All obstacles can be bypassed except Hard Brake Hill. Very steep and tippy in spots. Confusing network of roads around Base Camp. Stock vehicles should use interior roads.

Stats: Length: 8.9 miles. Time: Basic trail about 3 hours. Spend a weekend camping and enjoying the area. Elevation: 6,671 to 8,150 ft. Trail open April 15 - Dec. 15. Summer is great.

Current Conditions: Stanislaus N.F., Summit R.D. Call (209) 965-3434.

Getting There: Take Hwy. 108 northeast from Sonora to Pinecrest. Stay on 108 another 14.4 miles and turn right on mostly paved Forest Road 5N01 at sign for Niagara Campgrounds. Stay on 5N01 total of 6.2 miles to trail on left marked with large brown sign saying NIAGARA RIM 4X4 TRAIL.

START **MILEAGE LOG:**

0.0 Zero trip odometer **[Rev. Miles]**
Head uphill on single-lane dirt road following RIM TRAIL markers. [8.9]
01 N38 17.768 W119 51.035

0.1 Head downhill into the trees before reaching split for No-Way-Out Hill on right. Bypass left. [8.8]

0.4 Swing right around distinctive PH Rock. [8.5]

0.5 Trail turns hard right down very steep and rocky Hard Brake Hill. [8.4]

1.0 Continue straight where roads converge across open area. Follow sign to Lion's Butt. [7.9]
02 N38 18.438 W119 51.126

1.6 Bear right at RIM sign. Straight through gate is early exit. [7.3]
03 N38 18.849 W119 51.338

1.7 Fork. Left bypasses difficult Sidewall Suicide. We went right. [7.2]

1.8 Drop down difficult Sidewall Suicide, then stay right where bypass rejoins on left. [7.1]

2.1 Turn right as you join 5N12YA. [6.8]
04 N38 19.223 W119 51.277

2.3 Left bypasses Lion's Butt. We stayed right and, just ahead, followed worn path down a big rounded ledge. After getting down, we saw harder choices we could have taken. Not sure which of the boulders was the official Lion's Butt. [6.6]

2.4 After Lion's Butt, roads split in many directions. We curved around to the left and zig-zagged in a northwest direction. [6.5]

2.9 Approach Base Camp, a large flat area in trees on left. We followed road around north side of camp to a point where 5N12Y went left. We turned right here and continued north. [6.0]
05 N38 19.497 W119 51.513

3.2 After road bent right, we continued downhill to entrance to optional Rock Pile on left. If you go up the Rock Pile, swing left at the top and return to where you started. [5.7]
06 N38 19.699 W119 51.357

3.4 After Rock Pile, continue downhill and follow RIM trail sign left. [5.5]

3.9 Make hairpin turn to right reversing direction, where 5N87 goes left. [5.0]
07 N38 19.916 W119 51.876

4.9 Arrive at viewpoint at top of ridge, then swing left and start downhill. [4.0]

5.3 Descend steep, loose rocky hill. [3.6]

5.8 Stay left at fork. Road is now easy. [3.1]
08 N38 20.243 W119 52.886

6.2 Stay left on 5N04. [2.7]

8.1 Cross bridge over Niagara Creek. [0.8]

8.9 Reconnect with paved 5N01. Follow it west to return to Highway 108 where you started. [0.0]
09 N38 19.351 W119 54.740

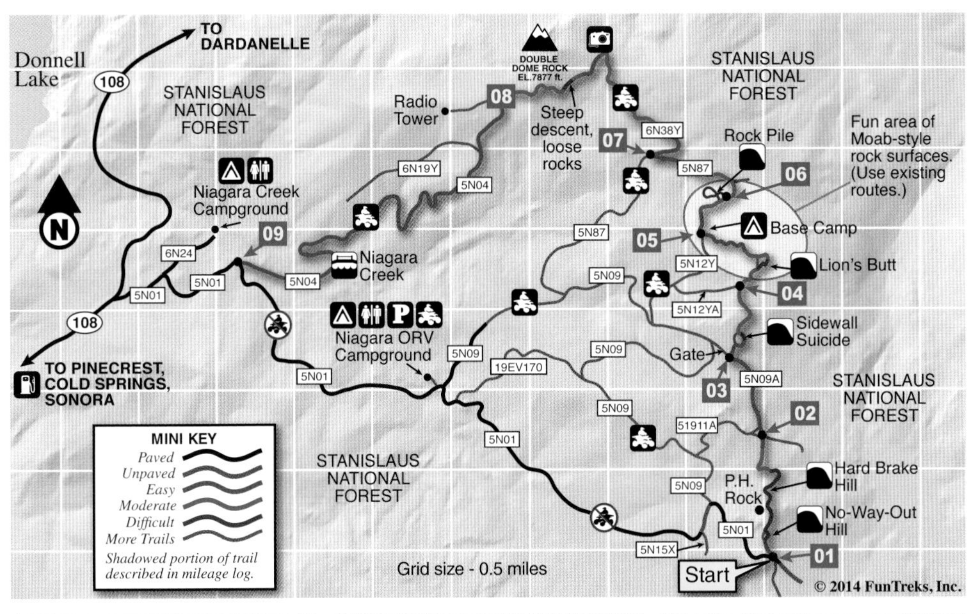

Trail is easy at the start.

Moab-style rocks at Loin's Butt.

Viewpoint at 4.9 miles.

Bodie Ghost Town

AREA 2 map on page 50

Many structures at the Chemung Mine.

View of Bridgeport from Masonic Mountain.

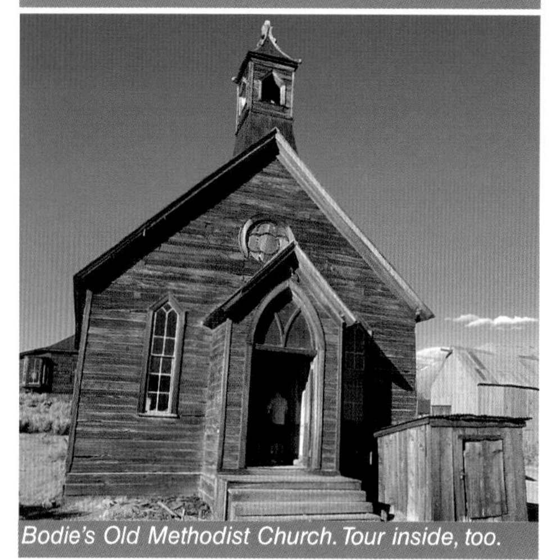

Bodie's Old Methodist Church. Tour inside, too.

Waypoint 03. Right goes to Masonic Mountain.

Historical Highlight: *In 1880, Bodie had a population of 10,000. Only 5% of the town remains but what is left is very impressive. All the remaining structures are original with only minor modifications to help preserve what is left. A small fee is charged and is used to preserve the town.*

Overview: Most tourists reach Bodie State Historic Park via paved Hwy. 270. The trip described here is a more interesting backcountry route starting north of Bridgeport. On the way you'll see great views, structures at the Chemung Mine and the historic site of Masonic. Northern end of route is in national forest with many great side roads for green-sticker vehicles to explore.

Rating: Easy: Starts as wide gravel road but soon narrows with ruts and embedded rock. Side trip to Masonic Mountain is narrow and rough, but still easy. Suitable for most stock SUVs with 4-wheel drive and moderate clearance.

Stats: Length: 26.7 miles. Time: 3 to 4 hours. Elevation: 6,528 to 9,227 ft. Best time: Mid May-Sept. Park open all year. Summer hours 9-6, winter 9-3.

Current Conditions: Humboldt-Toiyabe N.F., Bridgeport R.D. (760) 932-7070. Bodie State Park (760) 647-6445.

Getting There: From Bridgeport, head north on Hwy.182 starting at Hwy. 395. Go 3.8 miles and turn right on Masonic Road (Not marked as such. Once you start in, it's marked as 32046.)

START **MILEAGE LOG:**

0.0 Zero trip odometer **[Rev. Miles]** Head northeast on Masonic Road (wide gravel), marked 32046. Ignore numerous lesser side roads along the way. **[9.8]**
01 N38 18.560 W119 12.833

4.5 Mine on left is Success Mine (no buildings) **[5.3]**

5.1 Bear right on 32046G to visit Chemung Mine. **[4.7]**
02 N38 20.859 W119 09.120

5.2 Mine on right. Caution. Don't get too close. After looking at mine, continue ahead to main road and continue north. **[4.6]**

6.2 Camp spot in aspen grove on right. Road curves east. **[3.6]**

7.3 Turn right on 32243B to take side trip to top of Masonic Mountain. **[2.5]**
03 N38 21.359 W119 07.645

8.4 Bear left at T. **[1.4]**

8.5 At top. Return to Waypoint 03 (unless you want to try the harder roads going south and east.) **[1.3]**

9.8 At Wpt. 03 again. **[0.0]**

0.0 Zero trip odometer at Wpt. 03. Bear right and continue east on 32046. **[1.5]**

0.9 Stay left to take side trip to Masonic (site). **[0.6]**
04 N38 21.276 W119 07.083

1.2 Stop at Masonic site. Look for clues that a town was once here, then return to Wpt. 04. **[0.3]**

1.5 At Wpt. 04 again. **[0.0]**

0.0 Zero trip odometer at Wpt. 04. Bear left on 32169, Bodie Masonic Road, later marked 169. **[15.4]**

1.8 Bear left. Don't miss. **[13.6]**
05 N38 20.218 W119 07.471

6.6 Continue straight as 168 crosses. Continue south past rock painted with word "Bodie." **[8.8]**
06 N38 16.779 W119 05.961

15.4 Arrive at north side of Bodie Ghost Town. Parking just ahead. Summer hours 9-6. **[0.0]**
07 N38 12.825 W119 00.934
After visiting this incredible ghost town, head south out of park. After toll booth, continue west to leave via Bodie Road, or head south on Cottonwood Canyon Road.

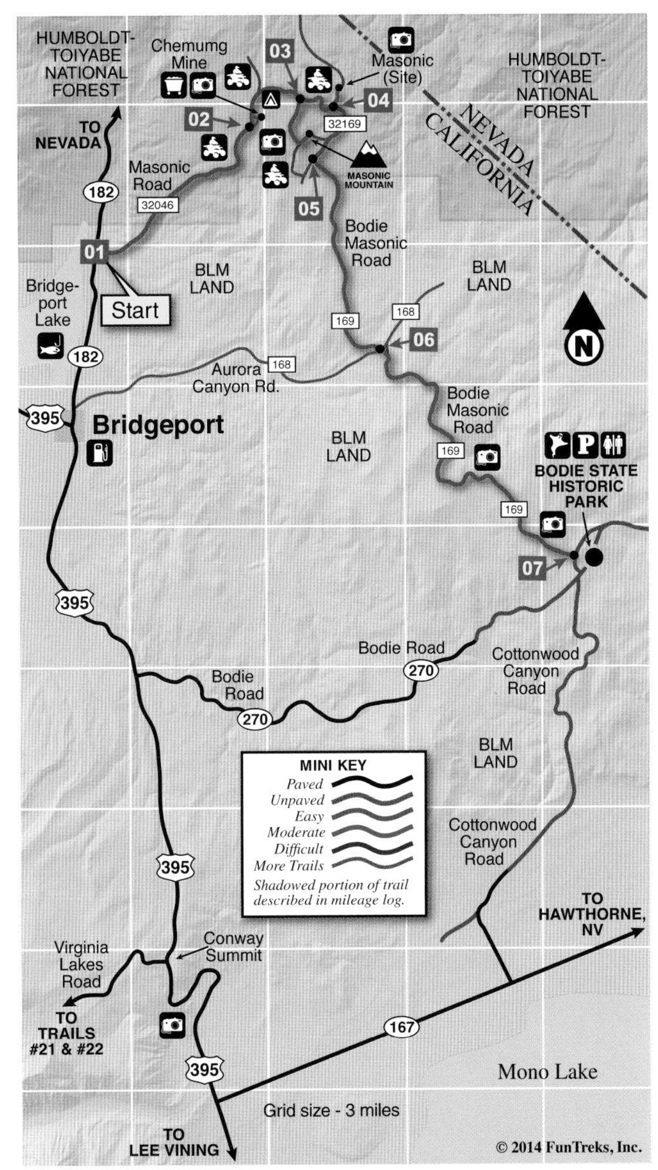

Bodie Ghost Town. Lots to see so allow plenty of time.

21 Kavanaugh Ridge

AREA 2 map on page 50

View of far-off Bridgeport Reservoir from near the top of trail between Waypoints 02 and 03.

Lake below Dunderberg Peak in July.

A few spots like this give trail moderate rating.

Historical Highlight: *Look carefully and you'll see piles of mine tailings in different directions from Waypoint 04. This was the site of Dunderberg Mill built about 1870. From Waypoint 04, a narrow rough road (not on MVUM) heads west uphill to some old log cabin ruins that mark the site of a smaller stamp mill built later. A small town existed here about 1892. We visited here in 2004 and found an old stamp press tipped on its side below the cabins.*

Overview: Trail climbs above 10,000 feet to a scenic lake below Dunderberg Peak. Beyond is Hoover Wilderness. In 2004, we ran this trail in mid July and had to push through deep snow drifts at the top. Dispersed camping along the route and at the high lake. Spring wildflowers and great fall color. Open to green-sticker vehicles. Stay on marked routes only.

Rating: Moderate: This route is mostly easy, but a few spots require a moderate rating. Rocky and narrow in places with some brush to rub against. Suitable for most stock 4x4 SUVs with moderate ground clearance.

Stats: Length: 15.2 miles. Time: About 3 hours. Elevation: 6,636 to 10,369 ft. Best time to go: Depending on winter snows, July through October.

Current Conditions: Humboldt-Toiyabe N.F., Bridgeport R.D. (760) 932-7070.

Getting There: Take Highway 395 to Conway Summit, about 8 miles north of Mono Lake, between Lee Vining and Bridgeport. Turn west on paved Virginia Lakes Road and go about 4.5 miles to Dunderberg Meadow Road on right.

START *MILEAGE LOG:*

0.0 Zero trip odometer [Rev. Miles]
Head north on wide Dunderberg Meadow Road, marked as #32020. [15.2]
01 N38 03.676 W119 14.472

0.8 Stay left where 32020E goes right. [14.4]

1.3 Dunderberg Meadow Road goes right. Make a soft left on 32178 that almost parallels Dunderberg Meadow Rd. [13.9]

1.7 Turn left on #22317. [13.5]
02 N38 04.918 W119 14.317

3.1 Enjoy lake and view of Dunderberg Peak. Great place to camp. Return to Waypoint 02. [12.1]
03 N38 04.660 W119 15.610

4.6 At Waypoint 02, bear left and continue north on 32178. [10.6]

4.7 Camp spot on right. [10.5]

5.0 Rocky, bumpy, long downhill section. [10.2]

5.6 Follow trail hard left. [9.6]

5.9 Creek crossing. [9.3]

6.1 Stay left at Y, then ignore two lesser roads. [9.1]

6.6 Continue north past Dunderberg Mines. [8.6]
04 N38 06.223 W119 15.058
(Road on left goes 1.7 mi. to a few log cabin ruins, once part of Dunderberg Ghost Town. Road was not closed off, but is not shown as legal road on MVUM. We drove this road for the first edition of this book in 2004.)

6.8 Cross Dunderberg Creek through aspen grove. Good fall color here. [8.4]

7.0 Stay right. [8.2]

7.7 Turn left. You are now back on Dunderberg Meadow Road. [7.5]
05 N38 06.818 W119 14.293

11.8 Stay right downhill on what is now Green Road. [3.4]

14.3 Continue straight as Lower Summers Meadow Road joins on left. [0.9]

15.2 Trail concludes as you return to Hwy. 395. [0.0]
06 N38 11.800 W119 13.129
Left goes to Bridgeport. Right goes back to Conway Summit.

Trail updates & GPS downloads at www.funtreks.com

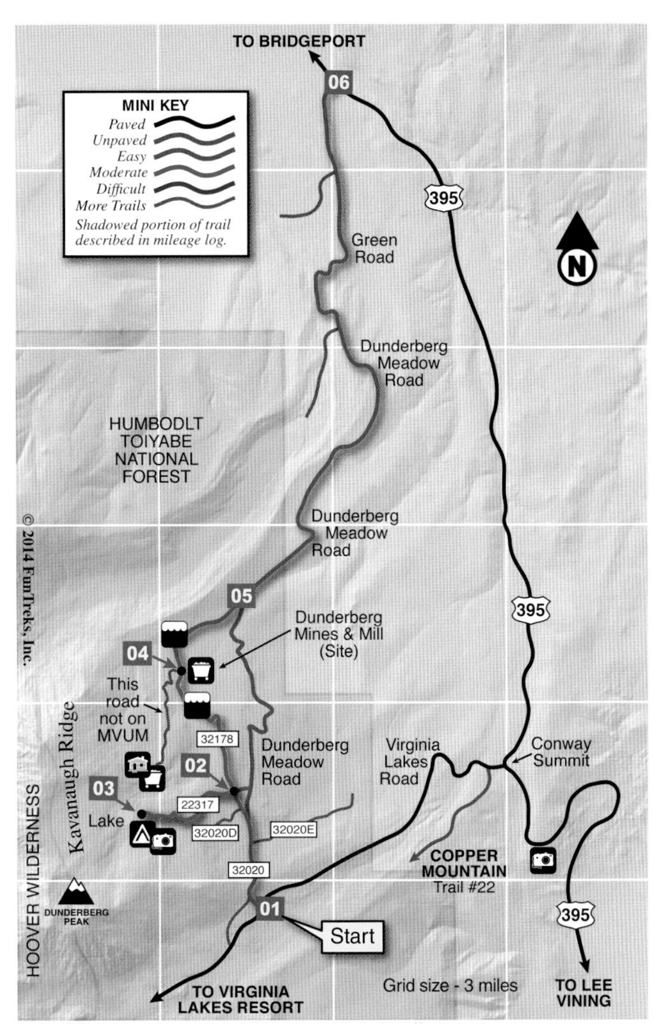

Much of route is easy.

Out of forest on way to 395.

Old stamp press from 2004 trip.

Copper Mountain

AREA 2 map on page 50

High view of Mono Lake. Don't cross this shelf road when snow is present.

Wildflowers are usually abundant in early spring.

View of Lundy Lake from Copper Mountain.

Overview: This fun SUV route traverses the eastern side of the Sierra Nevada Mountains above Mono Lake. Impressive views of the valley below. Follow a ridge with views of Lundy Lake and visit an abandoned copper mine. Popular area for green-sticker vehicles with many side roads to explore. Dispersed camping with best views between Waypoints 05 and 06.

Rating: Easy: Rocky, bumpy and narrow in places. Suitable for stock 4x4 SUVs with moderate clearance. Low-range gearing recommended because of higher altitude.

Stats: Length: 12.2 miles as described. Time: About 3 hours. Elevation: 8,274 to 9,839 ft. Best time to go: Depending on winter snows, Late June-September.

Current Conditions: Humboldt-Toiyabe N.F., Bridgeport R.D. (760) 932-7070.

Getting There: Take Highway 395 to Conway Summit, about 8 miles north of Mono Lake, between Lee Vining and Bridgeport. Turn west on paved Virginia Lakes Road and go 0.4 miles to well-marked Road 32180 on left. Wide pull-over on Virginia Lakes Road just before the turn.

START **MILEAGE LOG:**

0.0 Zero trip odometer [Rev. Miles]
Drive south on marked 32180. A small place to unload on right at 0.1 miles. [12.2]
01 N38 05.268 W119 11.383

0.5 Continue straight as another road crosses on an angle. [11.7]

1.1 Continue straight past power line road. [11.1]

1.2 Continue straight. Road joins on right. [11.0]

1.5 Continue straight. Lesser road goes left. [10.7]

2.0 Stay right on 32180. This is start of loop. [10.2]
02 N38 04.049 W119 12.490

3.2 Bear left on 32181. [9.0]
03 N38 03.422 W119 13.594

3.3 Continue straight as road crosses. Road you're on curves left and merges with just-crossed road. You'll pass through forest as you climb. [8.9]

3.9 Bear left downhill. [8.3]
04 N38 02.912 W119 13.398

4.5 Bear left. Overlook to right. [7.7]
05 N38 02.649 W119 12.923

4.9 Camp spots with views on right. [7.3]

5.6 Bear right on 32181D to take side trip to overlook of Lundy Lake, then return and continue east on 32181. [6.6]
06 N38 02.734 W119 11.943

6.8 Bear right on 32181C to take side trip to copper mine and views. Then return and continue north on 32181. [5.4]
07 N38 03.055 W119 11.787

8.3 Stay left (east) on 32181. Road on right, 32181B, is lesser alternate route back to start. It looked like a great route for ATVs and dirt bikes. [3.9]

9.3 Stay right where lesser road goes left uphill. [2.9]

10.2 Back to Waypoint 02, where loop started. Turn right to return to start. [2.0]

12.2 Return to start. [0.0]

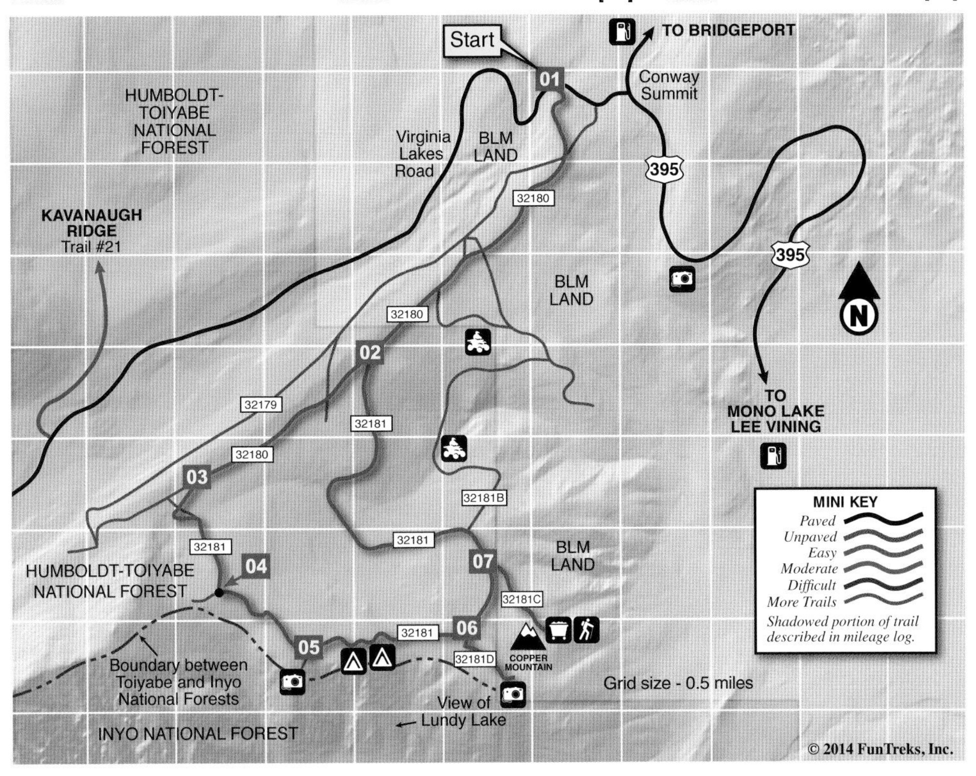

Road meanders along higher foothills of Sierra Nevada.

Shaft at the copper mine.

23 Deadman Pass

AREA 2 map on page 50

Turn right just before Minaret Entry Station.

Steeper, chewed-up section.

Suitable for stock vehicles with 4-wheel drive.

Overview: Short trail to incredible 10,000-ft. view of Mammoth Mountain Ski Area and the Minarets. Be courteous to hikers who frequent this road. When finished with this drive, consider visiting many other tourist attractions in the area, including Minaret Vista Picnic Area, Devils Postpile, Minaret Summit, Twin Lakes, Twin Falls and Lake Mary. Many Forest Service campgrounds nearby. Consult Inyo National Forest Map. Although the road is open to green-sticker vehicles, except for the view, there's not much here to ride. All side roads are closed.

Rating: Easy: Steep in a few places and one short stretch is a bit rocky. Snow sometimes lingers well into July. Compacted volcanic pumice can be dusty. Suitable for any stock 4x4 SUV.

Stats: Length: 2.5 miles one way. Time: Round trip about an hour. Elevation: 9,169 to 10,280 ft. Best time: Late July-September. Closed in winter.

Current Conditions: Inyo N.F., Mammoth R.D. Call (760) 924-5500.

Getting There: Take Highway 203 west into Mammoth Lakes from Highway 395. About 1.3 miles after the well-marked visitor center, follow 203 right uphill towards Mammoth Ski Area. Continue west about 5 more miles. Turn right on a paved road just before Minaret Vista Entry Station. Go north 200 feet to dirt road on right just after a dirt pullover area.

START **MILEAGE LOG:**

0.0 Zero trip odometer **[Rev. Miles]**
Head northeast on packed dirt road. Follow main road as it curves around to the left. Ignore all roads to right. Observe all signs. **[2.5]**
01 N37 39.268 W119 03.465

0.5 Stay right. Road on left is closed. **[2.0]**
02 N37 39.594 W119 03.649

0.8 Climb through steeper, chewed-up section. **[1.7]**

1.6 Follow road as it curves left uphill. **[0.9]**

1.8 Stay left. Road on right is closed. **[0.7]**
03 N37 40.631 W119 03.590

2.5 Road ends at Deadman Pass at wilderness boundary. Hikers only beyond this point. Return the way you came. **[0.0]**
04 N37 41.067 W119 03.919

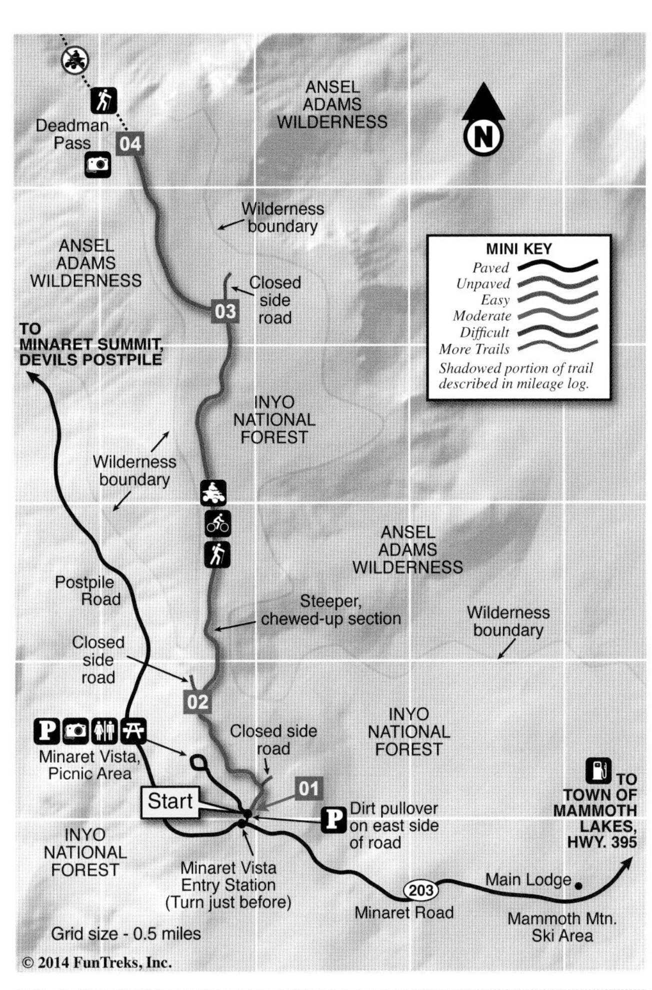

This sign near start of trail.

View of Mammoth Mountain Ski Area from near the top.

Lingering snow possible in July.

Look for the distinctive Minaret Mountains.

24 Laurel Lakes

AREA 2 map on page 50

Great camping and fishing at main lake.

No obstacles, but bone-jarring rocks in places.

Looking back down canyon from the top.

Overview: Climb to secluded, crystal-clear mountain lakes at 10,000 ft. on the edge of John Muir Wilderness. Incredible views as you climb and look down from the top. Camp and fish at the lakes and along Laurel Creek as it flows the entire length of Laurel Canyon. Open to all motor vehicles. Popular hunting area in the fall. Wildflowers and great fall color. Can get busy on holiday weekends. Snow may block top of trail into July.

Rating: Moderate: Very rocky and narrow in places, but no major obstacles. Difficult to pass in spots so watch for vehicles ahead. Perfect trail for stock, aggressive, 4x4 SUVs and new drivers looking to take on more challenge. Very steep and narrow going down to lakes.

Stats: Length: 4.9 miles to lake. Time: An hour each way unless there is heavy traffic. Elevation: 7,182 to 10,046 ft. Best time to go: Mid July-Sept.

Current Conditions: Inyo N.F., Mammoth R.D. Call (760) 924-5500.

Getting There: From Highway 395 east of Mammoth, take Sherwin Creek Road south. If you are coming from Mammoth on Highway 203, Sherwin Creek Exit is next exit east on 395. Follow Sherwin Creek Road 1.4 to sign for Laurel Lakes Road on left.

START *MILEAGE LOG:*

0.0 Zero trip odometer **[Rev. Miles]**
Head south on Forest Road 4S86. Road soon gets rocky. Side roads go to camping. **[4.9]**
01 N37 37.417 W118 54.404

2.1 Continue straight uphill. Road on right goes downhill to camping and fishing along Laurel Creek. **[2.8]**
02 N37 36.130 W118 55.026

3.3 Another road goes right downhill to creek. **[1.6]**

3.5 Large switchback goes left then right. Road is narrow. Watch for traffic coming down. **[1.4]**

4.5 Reach crest of hill with great views of Laurel Valley and Laurel Lakes below. Road continues downhill to lakes but is very narrow and steep with tight switchbacks. You may wish to turn around here where the road is a bit wider. Snow may block trail. **[0.4]**

4.9 Road ends at camp spot along edge of lake. Forks go to other camp spots. Return the way you came. **[0.0]**
03 N37 34.565 W118 54.783

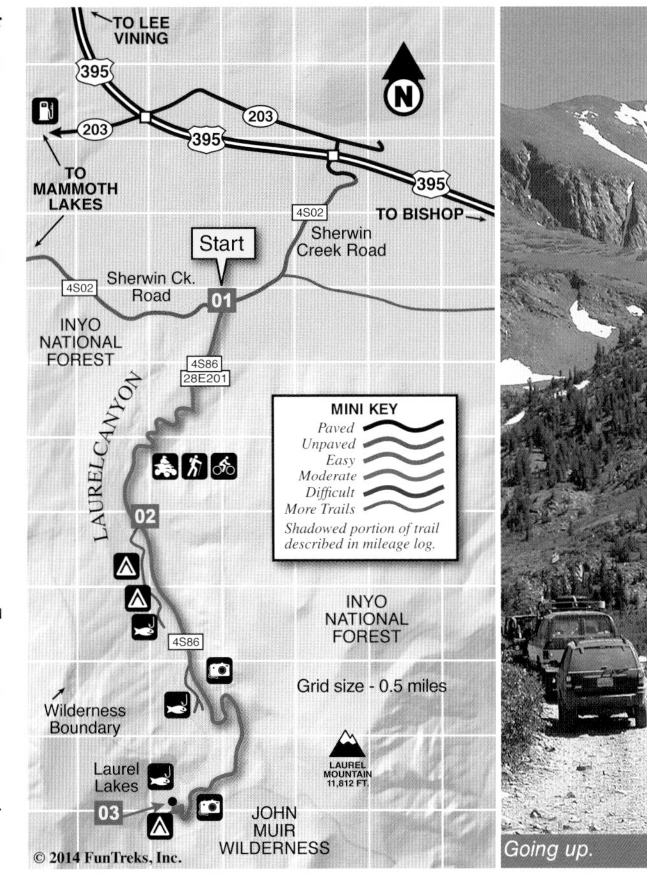

Going up.

Roads going down to main lake are steep and narrow.

Land Rover club on July 4th.

Camping in trees next to Laurel Creek in the canyon.

25 Sand Canyon

AREA 2 map on page 50

Start of trail. Forest Road 4S54 was not marked.

Rocky and steep in places.

Constant, gradual climb up Sand Canyon.

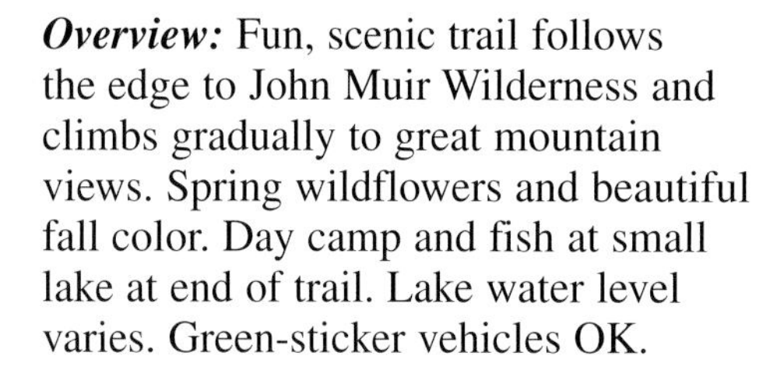

Overview: Fun, scenic trail follows the edge to John Muir Wilderness and climbs gradually to great mountain views. Spring wildflowers and beautiful fall color. Day camp and fish at small lake at end of trail. Lake water level varies. Green-sticker vehicles OK.

Rating: Moderate: Sandy in places with several steep rocky climbs and descents. Light brush in a couple of spots. Suitable for aggressive stock 4x4 SUVs with high clearance.

Stats: Length: 9.2 miles one way. Time: 3 to 4 hours for round trip. Elevation: 7,675 to 10,131 ft. Best time: Mid July-late September depending on winter snowfall.

Current Conditions: Inyo N.F., White Mountain R.D. Call (760) 873-2500.

Getting There: From Highway 395, between Mammoth Lakes and Bishop, take Lower Rock Creek Road south 4.3 miles OR Gorge Road/Old Sherwin Grade Road north 6.8 miles to Swall Meadow Road (see map). Head west on Swall Meadow Road 0.7 miles and turn right on Sky Meadows Road. Follow Sky Meadows Road north and west 0.5 miles to one-lane dirt road on right soon after pavement ends.

START *MILEAGE LOG:*

0.0 Zero trip odometer **[Rev. Miles]**
Head north on Forest Road 4S54. Stay right past gravel pit. **[9.2]**
01 N37 30.891 W118 38.295

0.8 Stay left on 30E302. Road 4S54, on right, continues north. **[8.4]**
02 N37 31.383 W118 38.633

1.3 Continue straight past lesser road on right. **[7.9]**

2.1 Stay left where road goes right. **[7.1]**

2.6 Sandy road climbs through scenic valley. Rougher with tighter brush in spots. **[6.6]**

4.5 Rockier section continues to climb. **[4.7]**

4.6 Continue straight. Road on right ends. **[4.6]**

4.7 Views open up. **[4.5]**

7.3 Stay right. Wheeler Ridge, Trail #26, goes left here. (Sign says Wheeler Ridge Mine Road.) **[1.9]**
03 N37 29.255 W118 42.577

8.0 Photo spot, especially in the fall when aspens are changing color. **[1.2]**

9.2 Camp spots next to small lake. When we drove this trail in 2004, the lake was full and beautiful. This time the lake was partially dried up. Expect more water in years with better snowfall. **[0.0]**
04 N37 27.664 W118 42.767
Return the way you came or consider driving more difficult Wheeler Ridge on the way out.

Trail updates & GPS downloads at www.funtreks.com

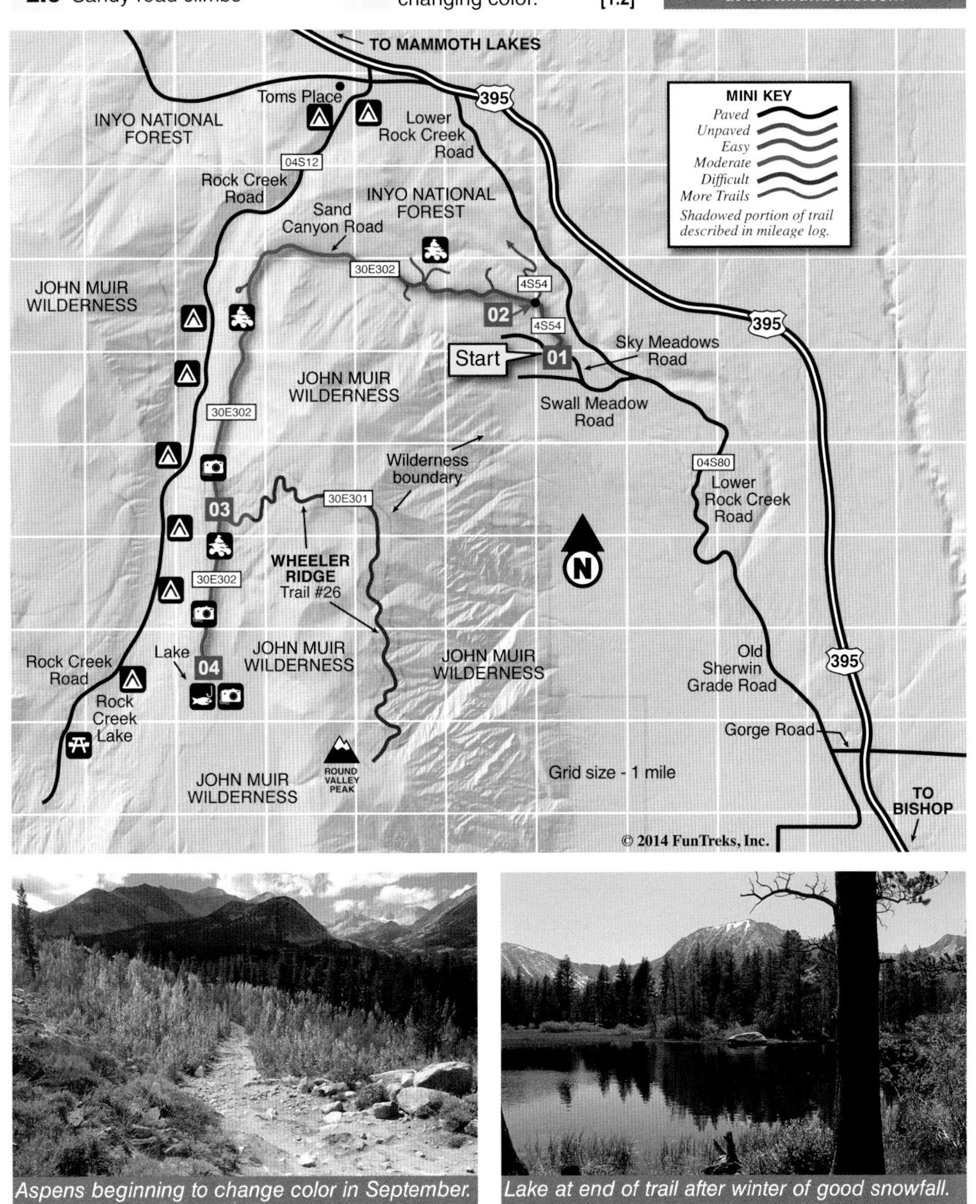

Aspens beginning to change color in September.

Lake at end of trail after winter of good snowfall.

Wheeler Ridge

AREA 2 map on page 50

Start of trail is very faint. Turn left at this sign.

Steep in spots with large boulders.

Rocky climbs, but no major obstacles.

Shelf road barely wide enough for our Rubicon.

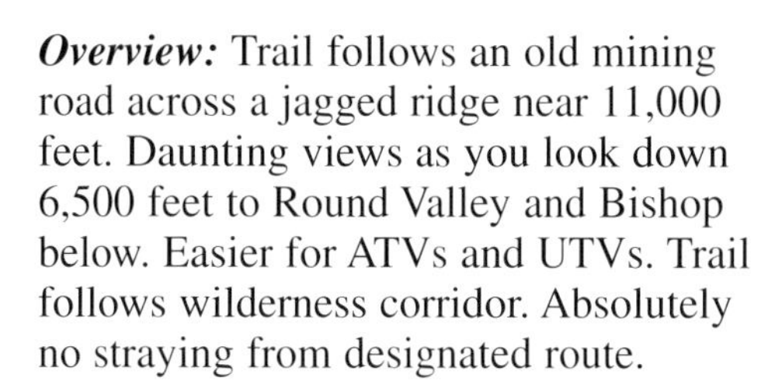

Overview: Trail follows an old mining road across a jagged ridge near 11,000 feet. Daunting views as you look down 6,500 feet to Round Valley and Bishop below. Easier for ATVs and UTVs. Trail follows wilderness corridor. Absolutely no straying from designated route.

Rating: Difficult: Steep in places with large boulders you can squeeze between, but no major obstacles. Difficulty is primarily due to a narrow, tippy shelf road after Waypoint 03. We made it in our full-size Rubicon, but just barely. The edge of the road is soft sand, which further adds to the tension. Absolutely no room to pass if you encounter an oncoming vehicle. Walk ahead to make sure no one is coming. Stay off if any snow. This can occur even in July.

Stats: Length: 6.3 miles one way, but add another 7.3 miles for the drive on Sand Canyon, Trail #25. Time: Round trip on Wheeler Ridge alone about 3 hours. Elevation: 9,802 to 10,934 ft. Best time: Late July-Sept. unless snow.

Current Conditions: Inyo N.F., White Mountain R.D. Call (760) 873-2500.

Getting There: Follow directions for Sand Canyon, Trail #25. At 7.3 miles, bear left at sign for Wheeler Ridge Mine Road.

START *MILEAGE LOG:*

0.0 Zero trip odometer **[Rev. Miles]** At sign for Wheeler Ridge Mine Trail, bear left on faint two-track road and head east. Road becomes more obvious as it heads into the forest. **[6.3]**
01 N37 29.255 W118 42.577

0.6 Short, rocky hill. **[5.7]**

1.7 Another rocky climb. **[4.6]**

1.9 Steep downhill section, then trail flattens out across a meadow alongside a lake. (Lake was full for our 2004 trip, but dry this time.) **[4.4]**
02 N37 29.404 W118 41.388

2.5 Road narrows and descends. **[3.8]**

2.9 Bear left to take short side trip to camp spot and overlook. **[3.4]**
03 N37 29.101 W118 40.539

3.2 Return to Waypoint 03. Turn left and continue south. Shelf road becomes extremely narrow with a soft, sandy edge. Wide vehicles should not continue. **[3.1]**

3.7 Shelf road ends as it drops down and crosses a little valley. Trail weaves between boulders and climbs a steep, loose hill. **[2.6]**

5.3 Rock outcrop with great views looking east. **[1.0]**

5.4 Pass through saddle and descend through an open, barren area. **[0.9]**

6.3 Trail ends at a high point where we found an American flag implanted atop a rock pile. **[0.0]**
04 N37 26.839 W118 40.543
Return the way you came.

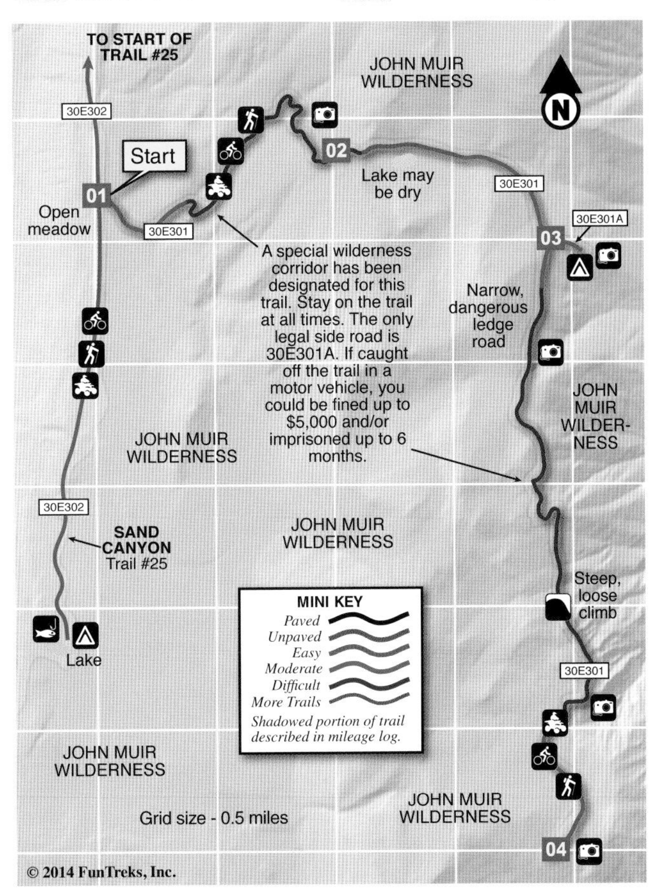

Tight squeeze at this boulder along ledge road.

Great trail for ATVs, UTVs and dirt bikes.

After ledge road, trail twists through the trees.

Trail ends here with great views.

27 Buttermilk Country

AREA 2 map on page 50

Buttermilk Road starts wide with washboard.

High clearance needed in spots.

ATVers find a wide spot to unload.

Later, road narrows and gets rougher.

Road easy enough for cars to bouldering area.

Overview: Tour scenic foothills below towering Sierra Nevada Mountains. Drive legal side roads to hiking trails into John Muir Wilderness. Watch for cars on Buttermilk Road for the first 4 miles going to a popular bouldering area near Waypoint 02. Overnight camping is allowed on numerous marked national forest side roads, but not on City of Los Angeles land. Many great roads for green-sticker vehicles to ride. We saw no signs prohibiting green-sticker vehicles from using 07S01.

Rating: Easy: Variety of dirt roads ranging from smooth gravel to narrow, rocky two-tracks. Challenging, optional side trips on network of marked forest roads (see MVUM). Main route suitable for stock, 4WD, high-clearance SUVs.

Stats: Length: 16.3 miles. Time: 3 to 4 hours. Spend weekend exploring more. Elevation: 5,500 to 9,172 ft. Best time: May-October. Hot in summer.

Current Conditions: Inyo N.F., White Mountains R.D. Call (760) 873-2500.

Getting There: From Highway 395 in Bishop, head west on Highway 168 (West Line Street). After 7.3 miles, turn right on Buttermilk Road 07S01. Green-sticker vehicles might consider running trail in reverse from Waypoint 08, as roads here are much narrower.

START **MILEAGE LOG:**

0.0 Zero trip odometer **[Rev. Miles]** Head west on Buttermilk Road 07S01. Pavement immediately changes to wide dirt road. **[9.9]**
01 N37 20.114 W118 31.022

0.6 Continue straight on 07S01. Road 07S104 goes right to network of green-sticker trails. **[9.3]**

3.7 Continue straight. Road 07S04 goes right to parking for popular bouldering area. No camping in this area, day use only. **[6.2]**
02 N37 19.698 W118 34.750

5.1 Stay right where 07S01G goes left. Ignore other side roads with letter designations at end. **[4.8]**

6.0 Continue straight (south). Right on 07S101 goes to popular Horton Lake Hiking Trailhead at wilderness boundary. **[3.9]**
03 N37 18.528 W118 36.517

7.1 Stay left even though right looks more traveled. **[2.8]**

7.6 Stay left. **[2.3]**

7.7 Cross McGee Creek. **[2.2]**

7.9 Follow main road as it makes a big curve to the right. **[2.0]**
04 N37 17.217 W118 36.300

8.3 Stay right to take side trip to camp spot and hiking trail at wilderness boundary. **[1.6]**
05 N37 17.029 W118 36.636

8.5 Stay right. Left goes back to main trail. **[1.4]**

9.8 Stay right. **[0.1]**

9.9 End. Turn around and return to Wpt. 05. **[0.0]**

0.0 Zero trip odometer at Wpt. 05 Make a hard right and continue on 07S01. **[6.4]**

0.2 Continue straight. Right goes back to side trip you just took. **[6.2]**

0.4 Continue straight downhill where road goes right. Burn area to follow. **[6.0]**

1.9 Stay left where 08S15 joins on right. **[4.5]**

2.3 Left on 07S15. (07S01 goes right here but sign says gate ahead.) **[4.1]**
06 N37 16.754 W118 34.802

4.8 Road follows pipeline for a while. **[1.6]**

5.8 Bear right uphill. **[0.6]**
07 N37 18.535 W118 31.904

6.4 Road ends at Highway 168. Left to Bishop, right to Lake Sabrina. **[0.0]**
08 N37 18.624 W118 31.453

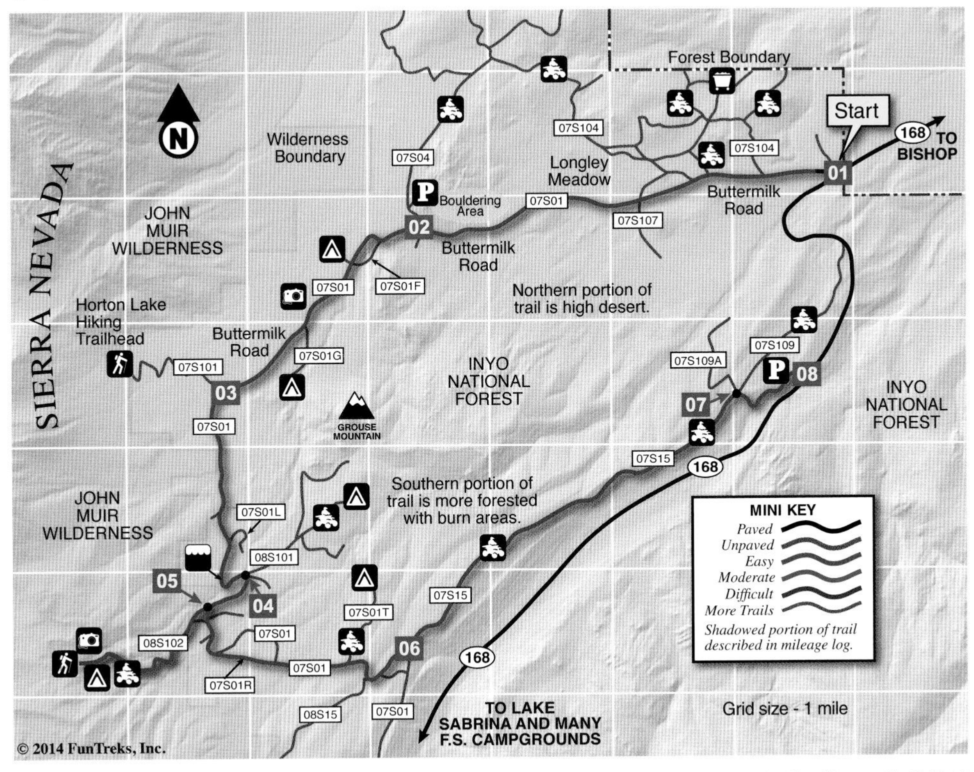

Crossing McGee Creek.

Stretches of burned forest along 07S15.

28 Coyote Flat

AREA 2 map on page 50

Panoramic mountain views. Great places to camp along the route.

Rocky and narrow in a few places.

Easy conditions much of the way.

Historical Highlight: *Most of the mining in the area was done during WWII when tungsten was in demand. A.H. Peterson built the road to Coyote Flat in 1940 to access his mining claims and mill site. The Schober Mine was discovered by Harold Schober in 1940 and was profitable for several years.*

Overview: Climb to beautiful high plateaus with panoramic views. Visit mines and fishing lakes. Explore many legal side roads and camp spots all open to green-sticker vehicles (see MVUM). Remember helmets are required. Remote camp spots with toilet at far end of trail at Waypoint 06. Hike the eastern end of King River Hiking Trail into John Muir Wilderness to Baker Lake and beyond. Wildflowers in early summer. Fishing license required.

Rating: Moderate: Much of trail is easy, but rocky sections are moderate. Most of trail is above 10,000 feet with highest point above 11,000 feet. Aggressive stock 4x4 SUVs will manage fine.

Stats: Length: Round trip returning to start about 49 miles. Time: Plan a full day. Elevation: 9,469 to 11,106 ft. Best time: July-September. Snow can block road at high points well into July.

Current Conditions: Inyo N.F., White Mountains R.D. Call (760) 873-2500.

Getting There: From Bishop, take Barlow Lane south from 395 or Schober Lane west from Main Street (also 395, see our map). Head west on Underwood 0.9 miles and turn left on Coyote Valley Road, which immediately changes to dirt. Follow Coyote Valley Road to right before substation and continue west another 3.7 miles to 2-panel forest sign.

START *MILEAGE LOG:*

0.0 Zero trip odometer **[Rev. Miles]** Bear left uphill at steel 2-panel sign. Climb to top of high ridge, then descend other side. You'll see places to camp and many side roads. **[15.6]**
01 N37 18.855 W118 29.331

6.5 Drop into valley and cross Coyote Creek. **[9.1]**

8.2 Driver's choice. We stayed right on 32E306 to go to Schober Mine. **[7.4]**
02 N37 14.632 W118 29.606

10.7 Stay right on 31E305. Left goes to Coyote Lake. **[4.9]**
03 N37 13.092 W118 31.199

11.1 Bear right on faint road. Left wanders many miles to high ridge with views. **[4.5]**

12.7 Top of ridge above 11,000 ft. Great views. Continue down other side. **[2.9]**

14.7 Pass old hunting shack, camp spots. **[0.9]**

15.3 Bear left. **[0.3]**

15.6 Stop here. Mine is uphill to left. Turn around and return to Wpt. 02. **[0.0]**
04 N37 14.404 W118 32.686

0.0 Zero trip odometer at Wpt. 02 Bear right on 32E303 to go to Baker Lake. **[9.0]**

0.8 ATV trail on left. **[8.2]**

1.4 Continue straight past 32E303A on right. **[7.6]**

2.3 Stay left. 32E304 goes right to Funnel Lake. **[6.7]**

3.0 Continue straight past other end of 32E304. **[6.0]**

4.9 Continue straight where 32E303 goes left. **[4.1]**

6.2 Cross new bridge. **[2.8]**

6.8 Make hard right uphill staying on 32E301. **[2.2]**
05 N37 10.531 W118 26.884

7.8 Make a hard right around curve where 32E301C goes left. Trail gets rockier. **[1.2]**

9.0 Stop here at camp spots with toilet. Return the way you came. **[0.0]**
06 N37 10.066 W118 28.807
Follow King River Hiking Trail west into wilderness about a half mile to Baker Lake. This trail continues many miles west to Lake Sabrina at Highway 168.

Trail updates & GPS downloads at www.funtreks.com

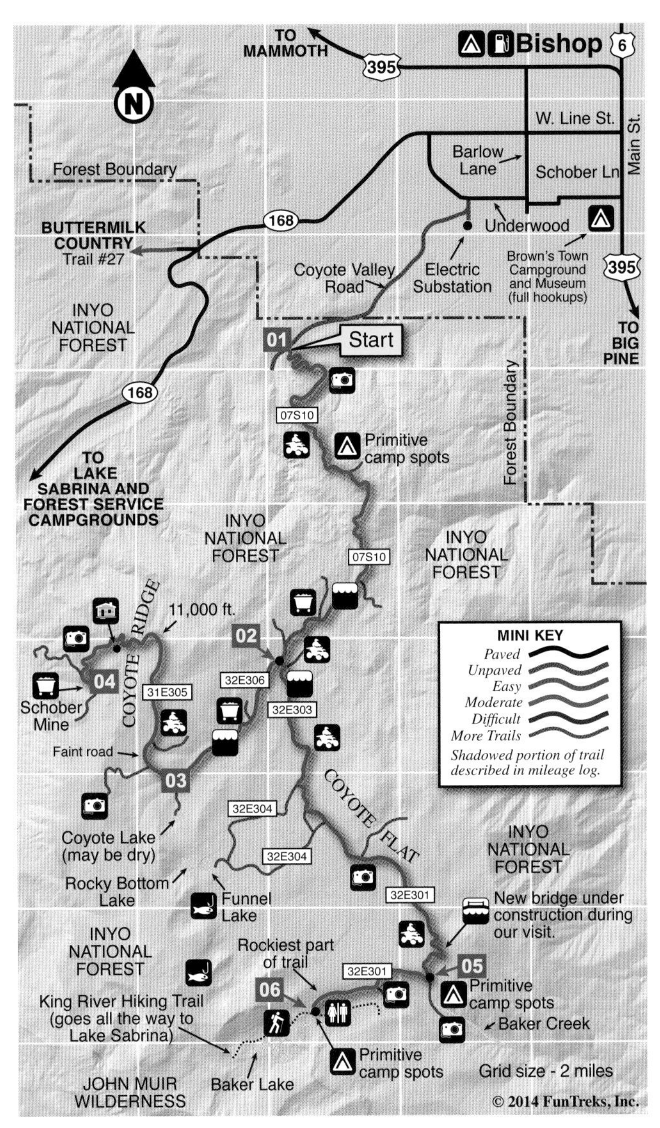

Bridge under construction.

Forest sign at start of trail.

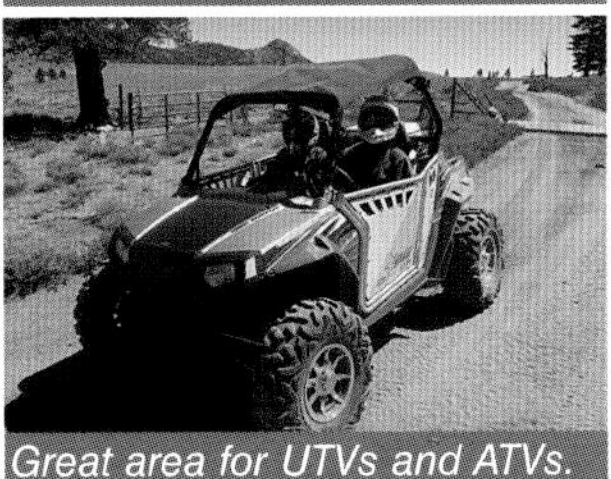
Great area for UTVs and ATVs.

29 Mazourka Canyon

AREA 2 map on page 50

Looking in direction of Big Pine from Mazourka Peak. Tinemaha Reservoir can be seen below.

Northern end of trail winds up and down hills.

Cattle loading ramp along trail.

You'll pass through this narrow rocky spot.

Overview: High views of Owens Valley and the Sierra Nevada. Scenic camp spots along the northern half of this lightly used trail. Drive to the top of 9,412-ft. Mazourka Peak. Open to green-sticker vehicles. Many side roads to explore, some to old mining locations. Parts of trail run along the edge of Inyo Mountains Wilderness. Stay on designated routes at all times.

Rating: Moderate: Southern half of route is maintained gravel road suitable for passenger cars. Northern half is hilly with several steep, narrow, rocky spots. Suitable for stock, 4x4, high-clearance SUVs. Optional side trip to Betty Jumbo Mine is very narrow and tight at the end. Rock slides possible.

Stats: Length: Almost 40 miles. Time: 4 to 6 hours. Add 3-4 hours for side trip to Betty Jumbo Mine. Elevation: 3,734 to 9,462 ft. Best time: Usually open all year, but snow can close higher roads.

Current Conditions: Inyo N.F., White Mountains R.D. Call (760) 873-2500.

Getting There: From Highway 395 on south side of Independence, take paved Mazourka Canyon Road east.

START *MILEAGE LOG:*

0.0 Zero trip odometer **[Rev. Miles]** Head east on paved Mazourka Cyn. Rd. **[21.1]**
01 N36 47.825 W118 11.742

4.5 Pavement worsens. **[16.6]**

4.9 Mine on right. **[16.2]**

6.5 Road all dirt. **[14.6]**

8.0 Enter canyon. **[13.1]**

8.3 Continue straight. Road 36E401 on right goes to Betty Jumbo Mine. (It's 8 miles one way on very twisty shelf road. Very narrow at the end.) **[12.8]**
02 N36 50.877 W118 05.052

8.9 Enter Inyo N.F. **[12.2]**

12.4 Continue straight. Left on 12S104 goes to Santa Rita Flat with network of OHV roads, camping and rock climbing. **[8.7]**
03 N36 54.018 W118 05.131

18.0 Turn left. Straight on 13S05M goes in and out of Badger Flat. **[3.1]**

18.4 Turn left again where 13S05M returns. **[2.7]**

19.2 Bear left to take side trip to Mazourka Peak on 11S01. **[1.9]**
04 N36 58.767 W118 06.282

21.1 Top of peak. Return to Waypoint 04. **[0.0]**

0.0 Zero trip odometer at Wpt. 04. Make hard left continuing north on 13S05. **[16.7]**

0.1 Stay right. **[16.6]**

0.3 Stay right. **[16.4]**

0.5 Bear left on 36E404 at Papoose Flat sign. Trail gets rougher. **[16.2]**

5.1 Stay right at triangle intersection. **[11.6]**

6.2 Where 36E404 goes right, go straight on 09S15, then stay right across Papoose Flat. **[10.5]**
05 N37 00.971 W118 07.293

7.5 Turn right. **[9.2]**

11.6 Turn hard right down steep switchbacks. **[5.1]**
06 N37 04.840 W118 06.832

12.5 Turn right at "T." **[4.2]**

13.7 Narrow, rocky spot. Stay on 09S15. **[3.0]**

16.7 Reach paved Death Valley Road. **[0.0]**
07 N37 07.369 W118 04.651

To reach Hwy. 395 at Big Pine, turn left on Death Valley Road. Go 11.3 miles and turn left on Hwy. 168. It's another 2.3 miles to Big Pine.

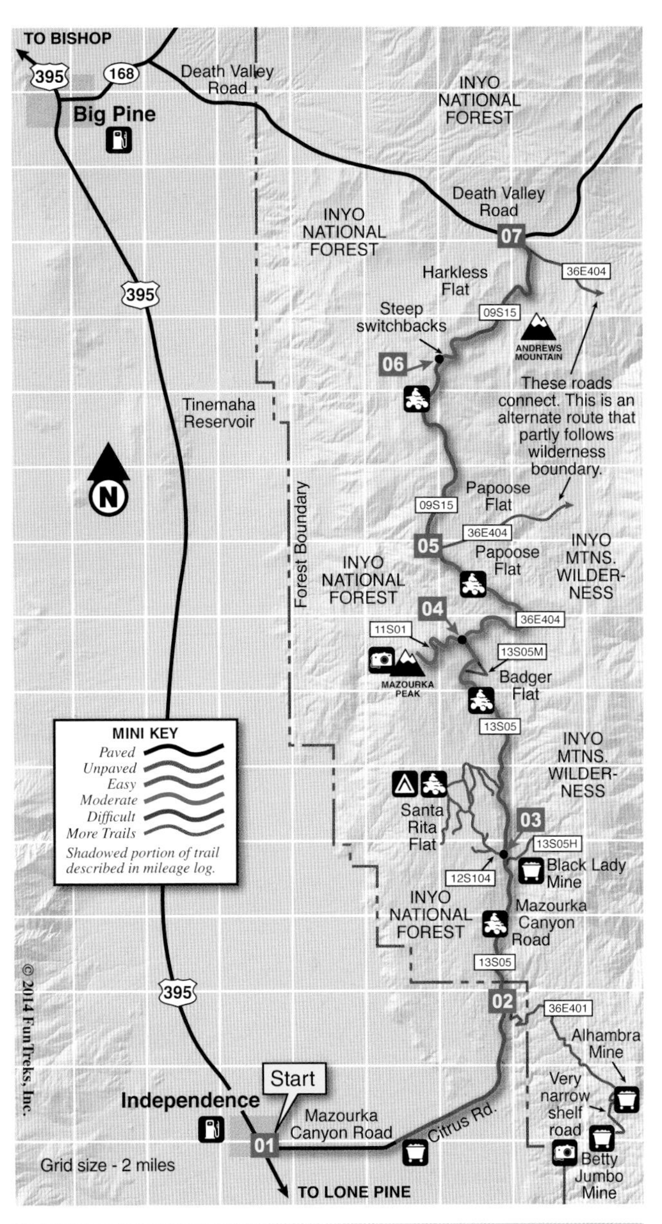

Two-track road crosses Papoose Flat.

Bald Mountain

AREA 2 map on page 50

Excellent views of Shaver Lake from Bald Mountain Lookout.

Difficult stretch after Waypoint 04.

Blue reflectors mark route across granite.

Overview: Bald Mountain Lookout is the main attraction on this trail, which features expansive views of Shaver Lake. The route consists mostly of solid granite and sand and reminds one of slickrock trails in Moab, Utah. Several obstacles will test your driving skill. The trail is well marked with cairns and reflectors, but it's still easy to get lost.

Rating: Difficult: Most of trail is easy to moderate, but difficult sections have large rocks and ledges. Aggressive stock vehicles might make it through with an experienced driver.

Stats: Length: 8.6 miles. Time: About 3 hours. Elevation: 6,816 to 7,859 ft. Typically open April 15 -Dec. 15. Opening can be delayed by heavy winter snows. Best to call ahead.

Current Conditions: Sierra N.F., High Sierra R.D. Call (559) 855-5355.

Getting There: From Highway 168 in Shaver Lake, take Dinkey Creek Road east 9.1 miles. Turn left on Rock Creek Road 9S09. Continue north 3.4 miles to wide road on left. Follow broken pavement to green gate marked Bald Mtn.

START *MILEAGE LOG:*

0.0 Zero trip odometer **[Rev. Miles]** Continue west on wide 26E219 (also marked 25E09). [4.0]
01 N37 06.079 W119 10.191

0.3 Turn right at fork. South loop to left returns here later. [3.7]
02 N37 05.916 W119 10.453

0.7 Stay right up steep rocky climb. Trail splits briefly then comes back together. [3.3]

0.8 Stay right. Shortcut to south loop on left. [3.2]
03 N37 05.758 W119 10.928

1.0 Turn right downhill at big stump, then up challenging ledges. [3.0]
04 N37 05.838 W119 11.113

1.2 Watch for cairns marking the trail. [2.8]

1.4 Stay right for easiest route over rocky obstacle. [2.6]

1.6 Driver's choice over rock obstacle. [2.4]

2.8 Trail swings south through thick forest. [1.2]

3.8 Stay right. Shortcut on left goes up steep hill to connect with south loop. [0.2]

4.0 Turn hard left at major intersection. Right goes north and reconnects with F.S. 9S09. [0.0]
05 N37 06.853 W119 12.001

0.0 Zero trip odometer Wpt. 05 Head southwest on granite slab following blue reflectors. [0.9]

0.9 Reach tower. [0.0]
06 N37 06.207 W119 12.376

0.0 Zero trip odometer Wpt. 06 Return via south loop by retracing your route a short distance until you can turn right downhill. After turn, trail zigzags and is not well marked. Look for cairns and Jeep symbols in trees. [3.4]

0.9 Bear left downhill at large rock. [2.5]

1.1 Trail swings right and heads south. [2.3]

1.7 Trail swings left and heads east. [1.7]

2.1 Stay right where trail cuts back to Wpt. 03. [1.3]
07 N37 05.582 W119 11.111

2.5 Turn left downhill. [0.9]

3.4 Reconnect with original trail. Turn right to exit via Rock Creek Road. [0.0]

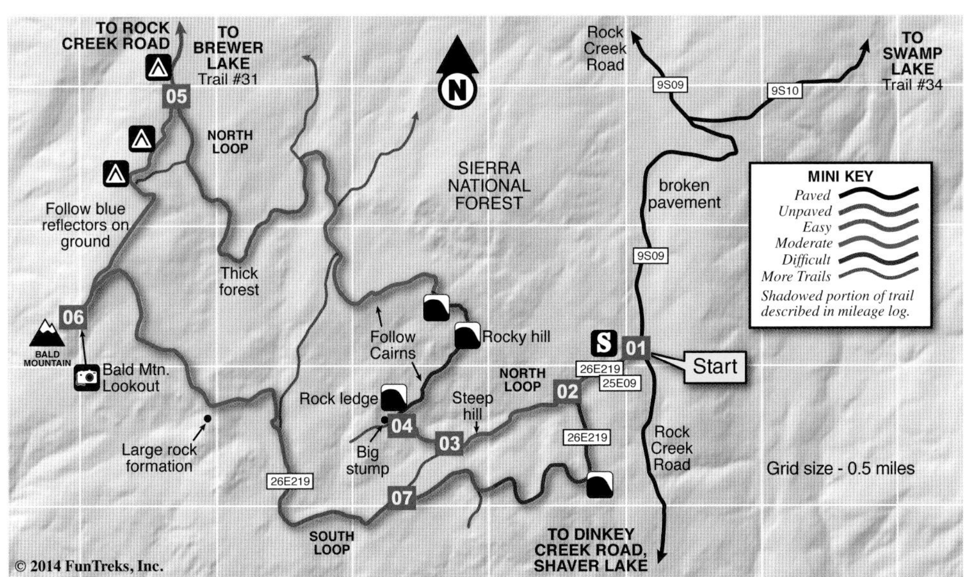

Last steep descent on south loop.

Look for cairns on the ground and Jeep symbols in trees.

31 Brewer Lake

AREA 2 map on page 50

Start of trail clearly marked.

Fun trail for ATVs, UTVs and dirt bikes.

We parked our stock 4-dr. Rubicon at Wpt. 02.

Made it to the lake with smaller Wrangler in 2004.

Overview: This trail is very short, but we think it's worth the easy drive to reach it. The lake is scenic with crystal-clear water, great camp spots and good fishing. Hard-core enthusiasts will love the last 3/4 mile.

Rating: Difficult: Most of this trail is easy to moderate, but the last ¾ mile is extremely difficult. Boulders are large, sharp and tightly spaced. Stock vehicle owners will need to hike after Wpt. 02.

Stats: Length: 3.1 miles one way. Time: About a half hour to Waypoint 02 with another 20-minute hike. You can walk the last part faster than driving it, even in the best hard-core rig. Elevation: 8,427 to 8,973 ft. Typically open June 15 -Nov. 1. Opening can be delayed by heavy winter snows. Best to call ahead.

Current Conditions: Sierra N.F., High Sierra R.D. Call (559) 855-5355.

Getting There: From town of Shaver Lake, drive north 11.4 miles on paved Highway 168. Turn right on Forest Road 9S09 at parking lot for Tamarack Snow Park. After 3.4 miles on broken pavement, turn left on wide dirt road 9S69. Go another 1.9 miles and bear right on lesser 9S10. Brewer Lake Trail is on the left in another 1.3 miles. Note: You can also reach Brewer Lake from Dinkey Creek Road via Rock Creek Rd.

START MILEAGE LOG:

0.0 Zero trip odometer **[Rev. Miles]** Head east from information board. Trail marker and MVUM shows route as 26E218, but it was also marked 9S34. **[3.1]**
01 N37 08.877 W119 09.412

0.1 Trail gets steeper and more rocky. **[3.0]**

0.4 Trail levels out along ridge with views to right. **[2.7]**

2.4 Tight squeeze between two large boulders. Trail soon becomes very difficult. Stock vehicle owners should park here and hike last part of trail, about 3/4 mile. **[0.7]**
02 N37 09.864 W119 07.764

2.9 Outhouse constructed by Fresno 4WD Club. **[0.2]**

3.0 Extremely difficult. **[0.1]**

3.1 Camp spot with stone fire ring at edge of lake. **[0.0]**
03 N37 09.997 W119 07.457
Return the way you came.

Thanks to Fresno 4WD Club.

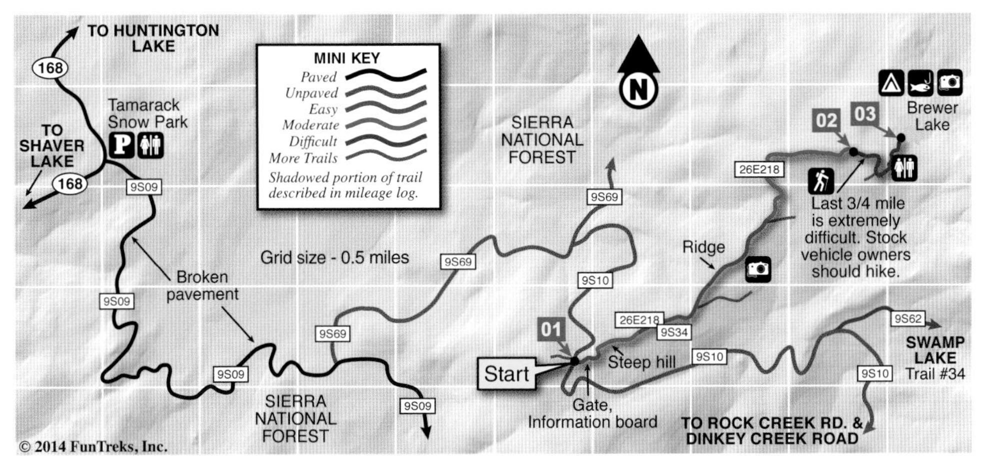

Brewer Lake: A serene, cool setting on a hot summer day.

32 Mirror Lake, Strawberry Lake

AREA 2 map on page 50

Large camping sites with fire rings near lakes.

South end of Strawberry Lake.

Difficult hill before Mirror Lake may require winch.

Overview: Remote camping and fishing at three beautiful lakes. Only hikers and hard-core vehicles can reach Mirror and Strawberry Lakes. Some stock vehicles may be able to reach West Lake. Open to green-sticker vehicles with staging at the Sand Flats. Don't camp within 100 feet of lakes or in wet areas.

Rating: Difficult: The trail to Mirror Lake has one hill that will likely require winching. The 150-yard hill is very steep with large boulders that move around. Tight trees add to the likelihood of vehicle damage. The trail to Strawberry Lake has large boulders too, but is much flatter.

Stats: Length: About 7 miles to drive to both lakes and return to start. Time: About 4-6 hours. Elevation: 8,826 to 9,033 ft. Open seasonally from mid June - November, weather permitting.

Current Conditions: Sierra National Forest, High Sierra Ranger District. Call (559) 855-5355

Getting There: From Dinkey Creek Road in Shaver Lake, head north on Highway 168. Pass Tamarack Ridge after 11 miles. Cross a bridge at 13.5 miles, then turn right on F.S. 8S10 where large grouping of signs tells which lakes are open. Drive another 1.9 miles then turn right following sign to Red Mountain OHV Area. Turn left at 3.2 miles on F.S. 8S42 by a corral. Stay right ignoring lesser side roads before reaching Sand Flats at 6.5 miles.

START *MILEAGE LOG:*

0.0 Zero trip odometer **[Rev. Miles]**
From sign posts on east side of Sand Flat, head north on F.S. 26E214. **[0.6]**
01 N37 12.034 W119 08.267

0.6 Arrive at intersection where forest sign warns of difficult hill ahead. **[0.0]**
02 N37 12.371 W119 07.878

0.0 Zero trip odometer Wpt. 02
MIRROR LAKE:
Head north on rough F.S. 26E216. **[1.3]**

0.5 Difficult hill. Walk trail before proceeding. **[0.8]**

1.1 Cross over logs through a boggy spot then turn left at fork in trail. **[0.2]**

1.3 Arrive at Mirror Lake. **[0.0]**
03 N37 12.927 W119 07.516

0.0 Zero trip odometer Wpt. 02
STRAWBERRY LAKE:
Head south on rough F.S. 26E214. **[1.7]**

0.3 Turn left following signs to Strawberry Lake. **[1.4]**
04 N37 12.168 W119 07.891

0.4 Bear left uphill. **[1.3]**

1.7 Arrive at large turnaround for Strawberry Lake. **[0.0]**
05 N37 12.321 W119 06.819

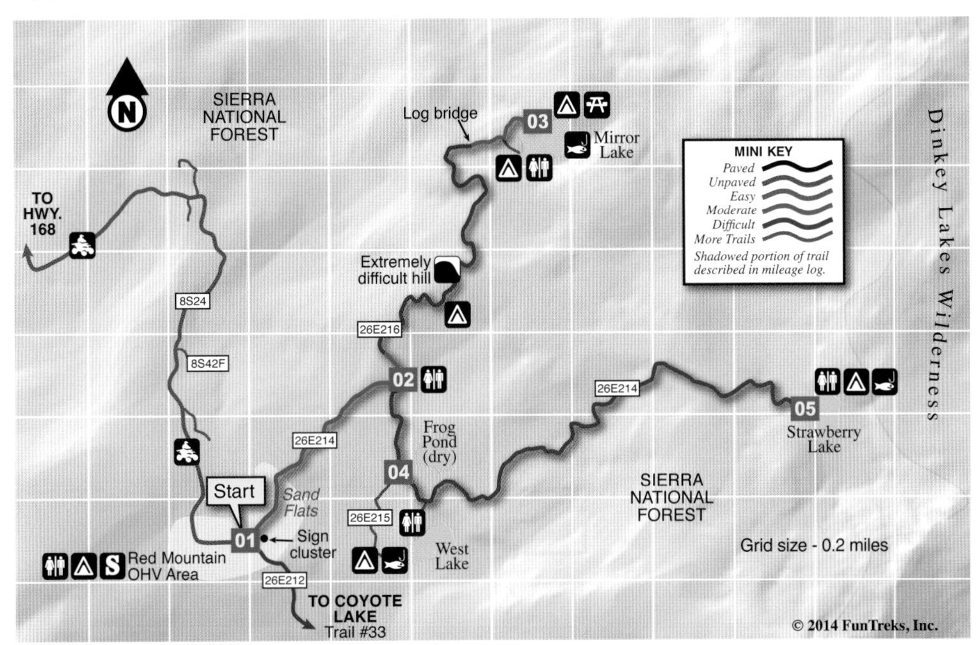

A few tight spots between trees.

All Red Mountain trails start from this point at Sand Flat.

Log bridge crosses bog before Mirror Lake.

Coyote Lake

AREA 2 map on page 50

Let's go fishing!

Camp spot at Red Lake.

This was actually the easiest line.

Overview: The longest trail in the Red Mountain area with excellent camping and fishing. Coyote Lake, because it is the largest and deepest lake, has the best fishing. A great weekend trip. Open to green-sticker vehicles. Don't camp within 100 feet of lakes or in wet areas. Pack out all trash.

Rating: Difficult. A series of challenging boulder fields, very narrow in places. One section, immediately after Red Lake, is borderline extreme with giant tree roots mixed with boulders. For modified vehicles only. Differential lockers recommended.

Stats: Length: Almost 4 miles. Time: About 2-3 hours to drive one way. Elevation: 8,620 to 9,220 ft. Open seasonally from mid June - November.

Current Conditions: Sierra National Forest, High Sierra Ranger District. Call (559) 855-5355

Getting There: From Dinkey Creek Road in Shaver Lake, head north on Highway 168. Pass Tamarack Ridge after 11 miles. Cross a bridge at 13.5 miles, then turn right on F.S. 8S10 where large grouping of signs tells which lakes are open. Drive another 1.9 miles then turn right following sign to Red Mountain OHV Area. Turn left at 3.2 miles on F.S. 8S42 by a corral. Stay right ignoring lesser side roads before reaching Sand Flats at 6.5 miles.

START **MILEAGE LOG:**

0.0 Zero trip odometer **[Rev. Miles]**
Head south on F.S. 26E212 from sign post on east side of Sand Flat. **[3.9]**
01 N37 12.034 W119 08.267

0.3 Cross creek after first challenging spot. **[3.6]**

1.1 Navigate through boulder field. **[2.8]**

2.2 Reach Red Lake with prime camping. **[1.7]**

2.4 Turn right at fork in road, then pass through gate. Trail becomes more difficult from here. **[1.5]**
02 N37 11.625 W119 06.508

3.7 Difficult obstacle. **[0.2]**

3.9 Arrive at Coyote Lake with dispersed camping along north side of lake. **[0.0]**
03 N37 11.197 W119 05.599

No bypass to this obstacle near the end of the trail.

Early creek crossing.

Coyote Lake is the deepest lake, making it a prime fishing spot.

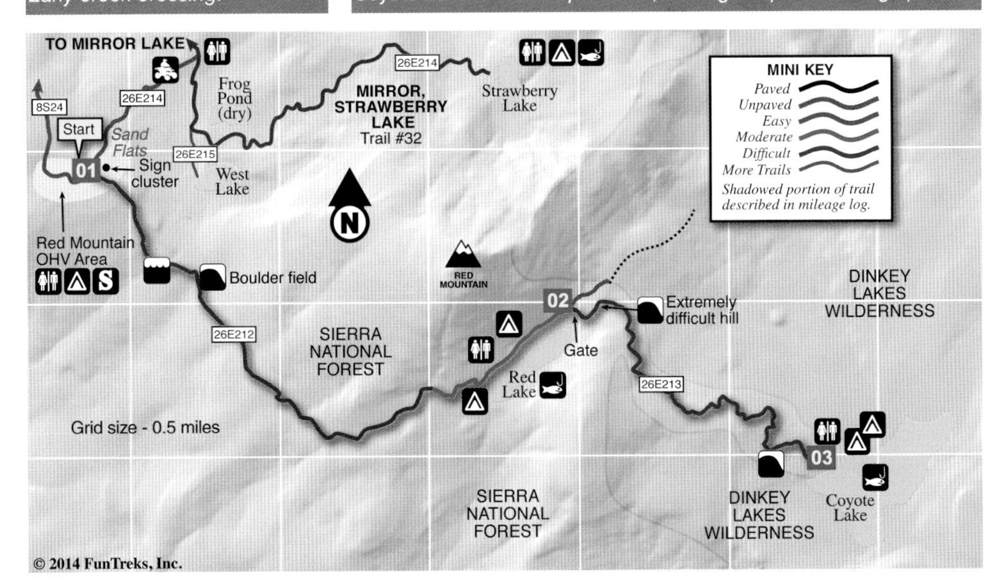

34 Swamp Lake

AREA 2 map on page 50

Swamp Lake is below the trail. Requires short, downhill hike.

Steep wall of granite.

Rocky shelf road before Waypoint 02 opens up to great views.

Overview: Contrary to what its name implies, Swamp Lake Trail is a high-elevation mountain route climbing over 9,500 feet at one point. Although much of the trail is heavily forested, the scenery is very impressive from high vistas along the route. You pass several excellent fishing lakes, although some require short hikes. The trail can be driven in a day but most people stop and camp along the way. A real challenge for green-sticker vehicles.

Rating: Difficult. Large, challenging boulders and steep climbs. Muddy in places. Snow possible in early summer. Recommend modified vehicles with high ground clearance and differential lockers. For experienced drivers only. Don't go alone.

Stats: Length: Almost 15 miles. Time: 6-7 hours one way. Elevation: 7,350 to 9,565 ft. Open seasonally mid June-November, weather permitting.

Current Conditions: Sierra N.F., High Sierra R.D. Call (559) 855-5355.

Getting There: From Highway 168 in Shaver Lake, take Dinkey Creek Road east 11.8 miles and turn right on McKinley Grove Road just before Dinkey Creek. Go 2.3 miles and turn left on Big Fir Road 10S13 at sign for Swamp Lake and Hatch Lake. Go another 3.0 miles and turn left at wide intersection on 10S66. Bear left again after another 1.2 miles on 10S31. You'll see gate for "Swamp Route" on right in another 0.8 miles.

START **MILEAGE LOG:**

0.0 Zero trip odometer [Rev. Miles]
Head east on F.S. 26E220. Trail turns to shelf road soon. [14.7]
01 N37 04.391 W119 06.110

4.1 Continue straight where lesser road on left goes to campsite with views. [10.6]
02 N37 06.006 W119 04.324

4.2 Pass through gate and follow switchbacks down the mountain. [10.5]

5.4 Cross Dinkey Creek then stay left following sign to Swamp Lake. [9.3]
03 N37 06.439 W119 04.476

5.7 Pass small lake on right then follow difficult terrain as it weaves along rocky Dinkey Creek. [9.0]

6.6 Climb extremely steep wall of granite (called Rooster Rock) followed by another hill. Then reach narrow slot at top. [8.1]

7.5 Pass Grouse Lake. [7.2]
04 N37 07.147 W119 04.368

8.1 Stay left at highest point on trail followed by views of Swamp Lake. [6.6]

8.5 Bear left where trail goes right to lake. [6.2]
05 N37 07.769 W119 04.404

10.4 Pass through large boulder field. [4.3]

11.2 Cross Dinkey Creek. [3.5]
06 N37 08.232 W119 05.936

12.0 Driver's choice followed by more creek crossings. [2.7]

12.3 Stay left after corrugated log bridge. [2.4]

12.4 Stay left. [2.3]

12.8 After passing through gate, stay left where road leads to Dinkey Lakes Trailhead. [1.9]
07 N37 08.916 W119 06.330

14.7 End at F.S. 9S10. [0.0]
08 N37 09.054 W119 07.901
Left on F.S. 9S10 connects to Rock Creek Road and heads south to Dinkey Creek Road. At Dinkey Creek Road turn right for Shaver Lake. Right on F.S. 9S10 leads to Brewer Lake Trail #31. Past Brewer Lake on F.S. 9S10, road connects to 9S09, which will then take you back to Highway 168 at Tamarack Winter Sports Area parking lot.

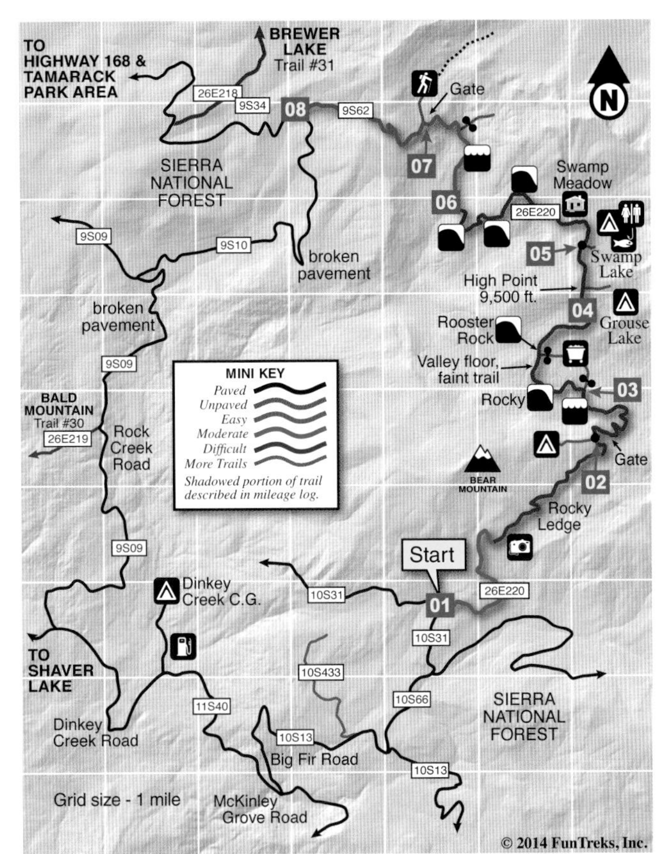

Several long boulder fields.

Narrow slot before Wpt. 04.

Cabin in Swamp Meadow.

35 Dusy/Ershim Trail

AREA 2 map on page 50

Stone bridge across Dinkey Creek at Wpt. 03.

Log road is tricky with wet tires.

Thompson Hill is tougher than it first appears.

Camp spot at Ershim Lake.

Historical Highlight: *You can't talk about this trail without talking about the Four Wheel Drive Club of Fresno. They pioneered and built this trail starting in 1956 one section at a time starting on the north end. The final section between Dusy Meadow and Thompson Lake was broken through in 1968. In all, they built 10 trails in the Shaver Lake area, most of which are in this book. A big thanks to the club for their efforts. For details go to* ***www.4wdcfresno.net****.*

Overview: Much of this long, demanding trail is enjoyable, slow-paced rock crawling. The route follows a 600-ft.-wide corridor between pristine wilderness areas. STAY ON THE TRAIL! Open to dirt bikes, ATVs and UTVs. Primitive toilets. Fire permit required.

Rating: Difficult: Variety of obstacles includes mud bogs, a slippery log road and lots of big boulders. Thompson Hill is steep with large, loose boulders. Breakage is common. Experienced drivers with modified vehicles only. Don't go alone.

Stats: Length: We measured 30.8 miles using GPS. Time: 2 or 3 days. Elevation: 8,131 to 10,114 ft. Official open dates Aug.1 to Nov. 1, but weather is bigger factor. Always check with Forest Service.

Current Conditions: Sierra N.F., High Sierra R.D. Call (559) 855-5355.

Getting There: From Fresno, take Hwy. 168 about 45 miles east to Shaver Lake. As you come into town, turn right on paved Dinkey Creek Road. Go east about 11.5 miles and turn right on paved McKinley Grove Road. After 14 more miles, turn left on paved Courtright Road. Go north 7.6 miles, and bear right to dam. Cross dam and continue another mile to gate on left marked with "DUSY" sign. It's just before hiking trail parking lot.

START MILEAGE LOG:

0.0 Zero trip odometer **[Rev. Miles]** Head north from gate on bumpy dirt road. [10.2]
01 N37 04.955 W118 57.768

1.7 Continue through Voyager C.G. (Or camp here the night before.) [8.5]

1.9 Turn left up steep Chicken Rock. Head north on granite. Trail marked with boulders each side. [8.3]
02 N37 06.339 W118 57.694

2.4 Trail turns sharp left downhill off granite and heads into trees, then heads north along edge of reservoir. [7.8]

4.2 Continue straight. Roads go left to lake. [6.0]

4.3 Cross Dinkey Creek over stone bridge built by Fresno 4WD Club. Head north after bridge. [5.9]
03 N37 07.801 W118 58.019

5.8 "Old man with beard" rock on right. [4.4]

7.2 Trail gets rougher as it begins to climb. [3.0]

8.7 Log road. Tough crossing with wet tires. [1.5]

9.5 Gets steeper as you ascend extremely difficult Thompson Hill. [0.7]

10.2 At top. Road goes right to camp spot above Thompson Lake. Good spot to camp for 3-day trip. [0.0]
04 N37 12.095 W118 57.655

0.0 Zero trip odometer at Wpt. 04. Head west. Road eases up with no major obstacles. [10.8]

2.4 Go past Summit Lake, then over Hot Springs Pass. [8.4]

5.8 Road to left goes downhill to East Lake. Halfway point. [5.0]
05 N37 10.874 W119 01.538

7.2 Trail turns north across east slope of Black Peak. [3.6]

10.8 Road on right goes to Ershim Lake. Good two-thirds-of-the-way camping area. [0.0]
06 N37 12.853 W119 03.585

0.0 Zero trip odometer at Wpt. 06. Head north to continue trail. You'll cross a log bridge. [9.8]

2.0 Sandy creek crossing at Ershim Meadow. [7.8]

3.9 Stay left. Road on right is to Mallard Lake. [5.9]
07 N37 15.182 W119 02.753

4.4 Difficult downhill to Lakecamp Lake. [5.4]

6.7 Trail swings west across scenic Kaiser Ridge, highest point of trail. [3.1]

8.5 You reach north gate of Dusy after challenging boulder fields. Just before gate is the worst. [1.3]
08 N37 17.431 W119 05.271

8.6 Gorgeous White Bark Vista on right. [1.2]

8.8 Trail swings left downhill away from ridge. [1.0]

9.8 You reach paved Kaiser Pass Road, F.R. 80. [0.0]
09 N37 17.484 W119 06.137
Campground with toilet across road. Turn left 7.4 miles to Hwy. 168, then left another 21 miles to Shaver Lake.

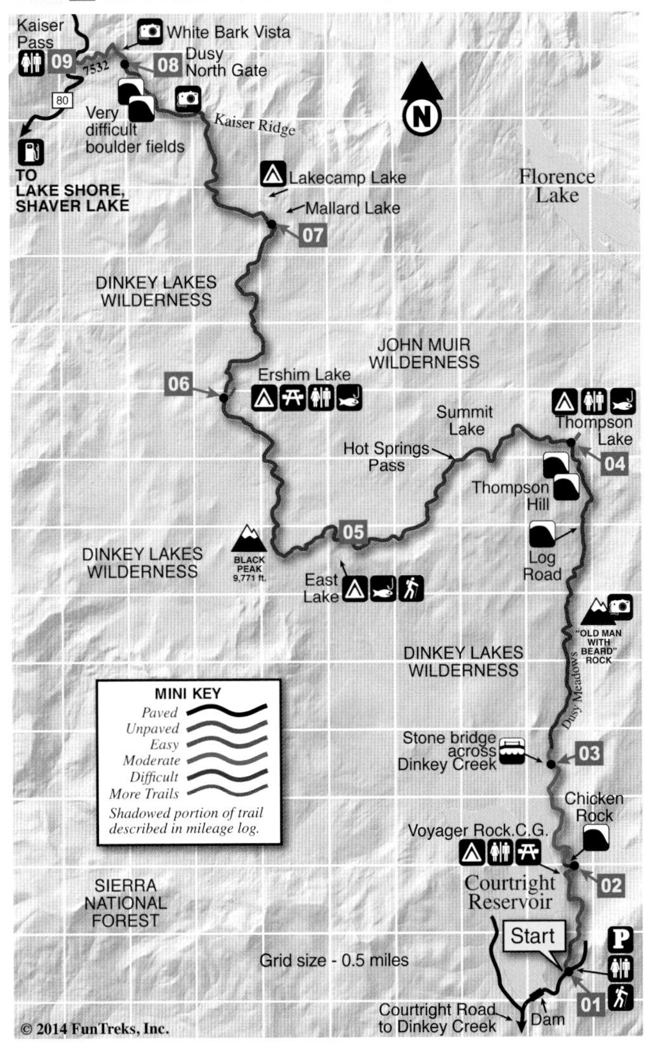

Last boulder field before north gate is surprisingly difficult.

36 Spanish Route

AREA 2 map on page 50

Start of trail leaves from paved road 11S07.

Climb to top of rock outcrop at Waypoint 02.

View from rock outcrop at Waypoint 02.

Very rocky and slow-going most of the way.

Overview: This trail doesn't see a lot of traffic because it's a long way from Shaver Lake. Fortunately, the entire drive to the trail is paved. The trail is cut through thick trees, so views are limited to the top of two large rock outcrops. There's camping at the end of the trail, which climbs above 9,000 feet, but again, trees block the views. The lakes are good size, but you must hike to them, so you're likely to find seclusion if quiet fishing is your goal. Open to green-sticker vehicles. No side trails to explore or turns to get confused.

Rating: Difficult: No major obstacles but trail is tight, steep and rocky in places. Lots of downed trees and big tree roots. Aggressive stock SUVs can do it, but damage is likely.

Stats: Length: 5.1 miles one way. Time: About 1½ hours to end of trail. Elevation: 6,642 to 9,112 ft. Typically open July 1 to Nov. 1. Opening can be delayed by heavy winter snows. Best to call ahead.

Current Conditions: Sierra N.F., High Sierra R.D. Call (559) 855-5355.

Getting There: From Highway 168 in Shaver Lake, take Dinkey Creek Road east 11.8 miles. Turn right on McKinley Grove Road (F.S.R. 40) before Dinkey Creek Inn (supplies and gas available to public). Continue southeast another 17 miles and cross Wishon Reservoir Dam. After dam, go another 2.8 miles and turn right on 11S07. Trail is on left in another 1.6 miles.

START MILEAGE LOG:

0.0 Zero trip odometer **[Rev. Miles]**
Head east on 24E224 through open seasonal gate at brown information board. **[5.1]**
01 N36 57.050 W118 58.056

0.7 Small creek crossing followed by camp spot on right. **[4.4]**

1.6 Caution. Large tree roots can grab your tires and jerk steering wheel. **[3.5]**

2.0 Maneuver through tight rocky section. **[3.1]**

2.1 Climb up and over a large rock outcrop. High point has view over trees. **[3.0]**

2.5 Large rock outcrop on right that you can drive up. More views. **[2.6]**
02 N36 56.497 W118 56.784

3.3 Another rocky spot. **[1.8]**

3.5 Climb long, steep, rocky hill. **[1.6]**
03 N36 55.950 W118 56.086

5.1 Green primitive toilet marks camping at end of trail. Fire rings and crude picnic tables. All motor vehicles must stop here at John Muir Wilderness Boundary. You must hike northeast to Spanish Lakes. Hiking trail is steep and faint in places. Compass or GPS unit recommended. It's about 0.7 and 1.2 miles to lakes. **[0.0]**
04 N36 55.362 W118 55.140
Return the way you came.

Trail updates & GPS downloads at www.funtreks.com

Trail goes up and over this rock.

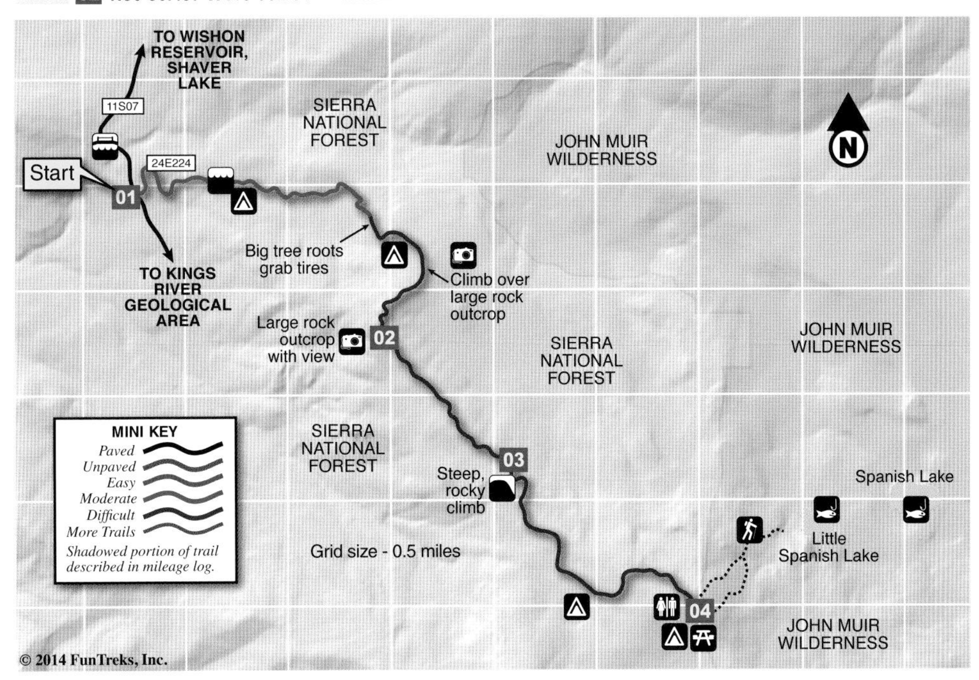

Steep, rocky climb at Waypoint 03.

One of several camp spots at end of trail.

Green = Easy, Blue = Moderate, Red = Difficult

Lone Pine, Death Valley National Park, Panamint Mountains

Death Valley National Park is one of few national parks that allows motorized travel in the backcountry. In fact, they have a free map of just backcountry roads, which describes 31 routes. We've selected eight of what we think are the best 4-wheel-drive adventures. Most are suitable for stock, high-clearance 4x4 SUVs. Our favorites include: the *Racetrack via Hunter Mountain* with Lost Burro Mine and the Moving Rocks; *Butte Valley* with the Geologist Cabin; and *Chloride City* with a great cliff view at the end. All routes require you purchase park pass available at visitor center in Furnace Creek or ranger stations. Outside the park, don't miss *Movie Road, Alabama Hills* near Lone Pine. Many famous westerns were filmed here—it's an amazing place. For more challenge, try *Swansea-Cerro Gordo Road*, featuring a large well-preserved tram station.

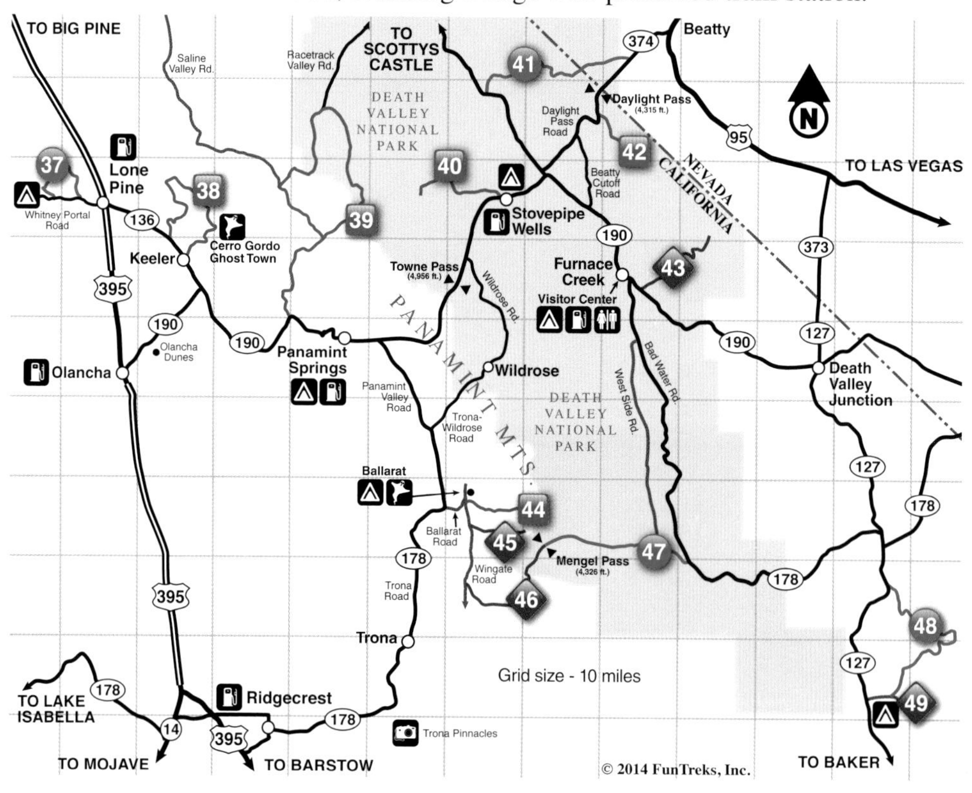

Movie Road, Alabama Hills, Trail # 37, rated easy. Just a short drive from Lone Pine.

37 Movie Road, Alabama Hills

AREA 3 map on page 94

Side roads through Movie Flat are the best part.

Picnic area at end of Whitney Portal Road.

Gene Autry Rock. One of many stops on tour.

Historical Highlight: *Some of the nearly 400 movies shot here between 1920 and present include Gunga Din, Hopalong Cassidy, The Lone Ranger, Rawhide and Star Trek V. Ironman was shot here in 2008. TV shows include Bonanza, Death Valley Days, Have Gun-Will Travel, The Lone Ranger and Wagon Train. Source: Lone Pine Film History Museum.*

Overview: This scenic loop takes you down the center of Movie Flat, then part way up Mount Whitney to a beautiful picnic area and water falls. We recommend you take a self-guided auto tour on a network of dirt side roads through Movie Flat (see detail map). See unusual rock formations and unique arches; many have been famous backdrops in western movies. "Movie Road Self-Guided Tour" booklet available at Chamber of Commerce and Film History Museum in Lone Pine. Also available as PDF online.

Rating: Easy. Main route is mix of graded dirt roads and pavement. Roads through Movie Flat are tight and narrow in spots with a few small hills. No real 4-wheel-drive challenges anywhere.

Stats: Length: 24.7 miles. Time: About 2 hours plus extra time to explore Movie Flat. Elevation: 4,462 to 8,339 ft. Best time: May-September.

Current Conditions: Eastern Sierra Interagency Visitor Center in Lone Pine. Call (760) 876-6222.

Getting There: Head west on Whitney Portal Road from Hwy. 395 at the light in the center of Lone Pine. Turn right after 2.7 miles on Movie Road.

START *MILEAGE LOG:*

0.0 Zero trip odometer [Rev. Miles]
Head north on paved Movie Road from Whitney Portal Road. [1.5]
01 N36 35.746 W118 06.550

0.6 Pavement ends. Take time to explore the many side roads of Movie Flat (See detail map.) [0.9]

1.5 Movie Road goes right after Movie Flat. [0.0]
02 N36 36.634 W118 07.540

0.0 Zero trip odometer at Wpt. 02
Bear right and continue north on Movie Rd. [23.2]

3.7 Bear left. [19.5]

4.2 Bear left on Hogback Road. [19.0]
03 N36 38.899 W118 08.562

10.0 Bear left. [13.2]

10.2 Turn right on paved Whitney Portal Road. Scenic road winds up the mountain. [13.0]
04 N36 35.826 W118 12.228

13.9 Go around loop at end of Whitney Portal Road. See waterfalls, picnic area, Mt. Whitney Hiking Trailhead. (Permit required to hike.) After enjoying the area, drive back down the mountain. [9.3]
05 N36 35.214 W118 14.397

17.9 Return to Waypoint 04 and continue east on Whitney Portal Road. [5.3]

20.9 Parking on left for optional Alabama Hills Arch. See map for details of hike. [2.3]
06 N36 35.685 W118 09.159

23.2 Return to start of Movie Road. Continue straight to Lone Pine. [0.0]

Trail updates & GPS downloads at www.funtreks.com

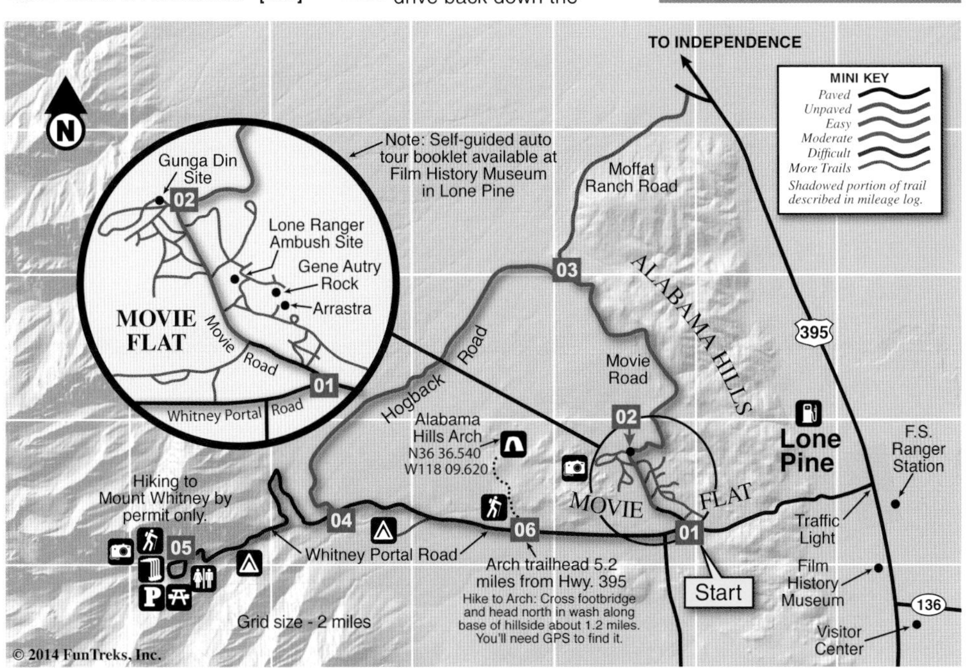

Turn right at Waypoint 04.

Kiosk explains a movie stop.

Enjoy optional hike to Alabama Hills Arch (see above map).

Swansea-Cerro Gordo Road

38

AREA 3 map on page 94

Sign at start says "Welcome to Swansea."

Lower section of trail is narrow in places.

One of the tougher spots.

Beautiful drive along ridge at top.

Be careful looking around the tram station.

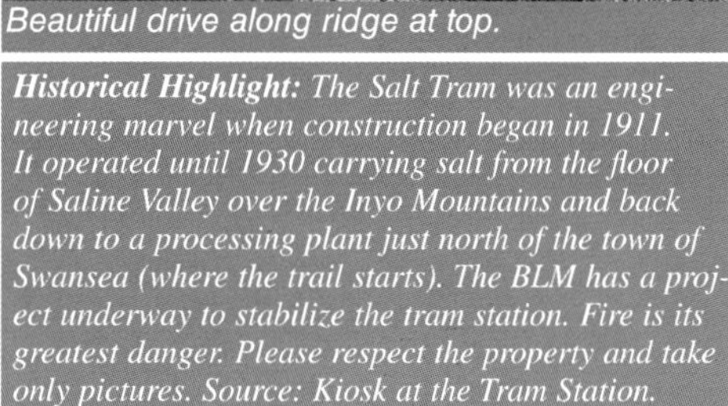

Historical Highlight: *The Salt Tram was an engineering marvel when construction began in 1911. It operated until 1930 carrying salt from the floor of Saline Valley over the Inyo Mountains and back down to a processing plant just north of the town of Swansea (where the trail starts). The BLM has a project underway to stabilize the tram station. Fire is its greatest danger. Please respect the property and take only pictures. Source: Kiosk at the Tram Station.*

Overview: Road climbs rapidly through wilderness corridor to ridge atop Inyo Mountains. Great views, wildflowers and historical mining structures including a large tramway station. Route goes past Cerro Gordo Mines and Ghost Town. This private property was once open to guided tours, but an online posting says this is no longer the case.

Rating: Moderate: Steep, narrow and rocky in places. Prone to washouts and rock slides. Suitable for aggressive stock 4x4 SUVs with high clearance and skid plates. Not for novice drivers.

Stats: Length: 31.7 miles. Time: 4 to 6 hours. Elevation: 3,607 to 9,298 ft. Best time: Open all year but summers can be hot at lower elevations and snow is possible at higher elevations.

Current Conditions: Bureau of Land Management, Bishop Field Office. Call (760) 872-5000.

Getting There: From Hwy. 395 in Lone Pine, take Hwy. 136 east 9.6 miles and turn left just before house with high fence. Small sign on mailbox says "Welcome to Swansea."

START **MILEAGE LOG:**

0.0 Zero trip odometer [Rev. Miles]
Head north along fence toward foothills on worn gravel road. [12.7]
01 N36 31.472 W117 54.298

1.2 Stay right at fork. [11.5]

2.6 Road gets steeper and rougher, but careful tire placement will get you through. [10.1]

3.2 You'll cross line of tramway towers coming down from Salt Tramway Station. Not many towers are left so you may not see anything till you get up higher. [9.5]

4.1 Another rough spot. [8.6]

5.2 Road levels out. [7.5]

7.3 Exit from wash. [5.4]

10.5 Scenic spot. [2.2]

11.2 Nice camp spot. [1.5]

12.7 Main route goes right. Left goes to Burgess Mine and a viewpoint. [0.0]
02 N36 37.525 W117 54.740

0.0 Reset trip odometer at Wpt. 02
Continue east on trail. [19.0]

2.3 Steep descent with tight brush. [16.7]

4.2 Historic Salt Tramway Station on left. [14.8]
03 N36 36.474 W117 51.230

8.6 Tree line. [10.4]

10.4 Narrow, rocky ledge road. You'll see Cerro Gordo Mines and Ghost Town as you descend. This private land is no longer open to public. [8.6]

11.2 Bear right and head down the mountain on easier Cerro Gordo Road. [7.8]
04 N36 32.365 W117 47.668

19.0 Return to Highway 136. Right goes back to start and on to Lone Pine. Left goes to Trail #39. [0.0]
05 N36 29.186 W117 51.998

Trail updates & GPS downloads at www.funtreks.com

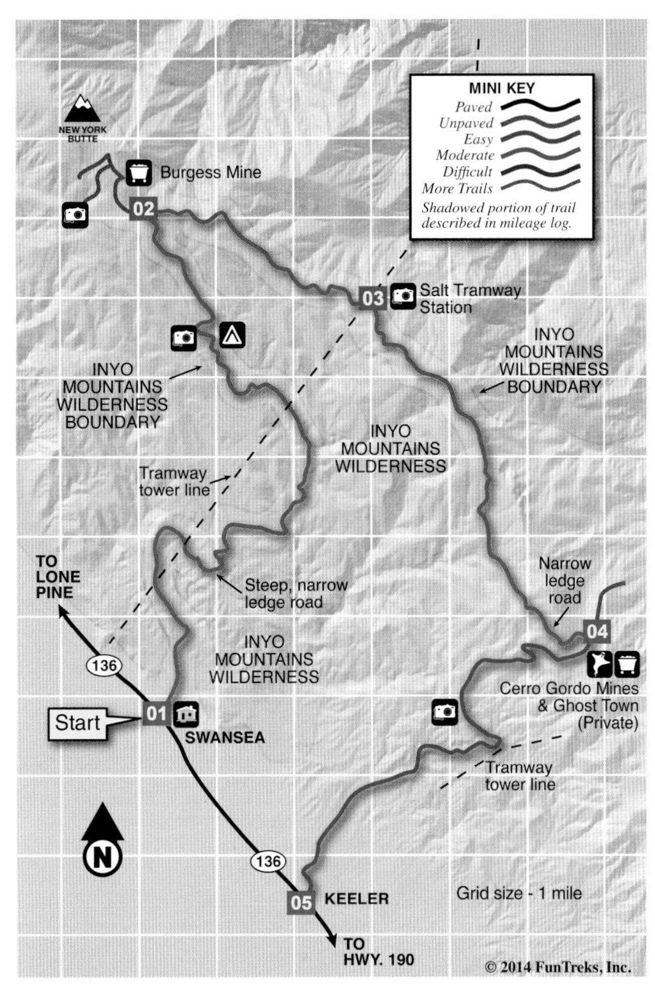

View of tram station as you continue east on trail.

Cerro Gordo Ghost Town.

Cerro Gordo Road is well maintained. Owens Valley in distance.

39 Racetrack via Hunter Mountain

AREA 3 map on page 94

One of many great views as you descend Hunter Mountain Road.

Cabin at Lost Burro Mine.

Inside cabin at Lost Burro Mine.

Teakettle Junction.

Historical Highlight: *The Lost Burro Mine operated off and on between 1907 and 1938 under different ownership. It was one of the richest gold mines in the area. Mystery of the moving rocks: Some scientists think the moving rocks at the Racetrack are simply pushed by the wind when the playa is wet. Others think the surface must also be icy.*

Overview: Large loop winds through mountains and across desert inside Death Valley National Park. Great scenery with stops at old mining camp and Racetrack Playa, known for its mysterious moving rocks. If you're on north side of park, you can start loop from Waypoint 04 by heading south on Racetrack Valley Road from Grapevine Station south of Scottys Castle. Street-legal vehicles only. Pay park fee.

Rating: Moderate: Conditions vary depending on recency of maintenance. Lippincott Grade is not maintained. Steep and narrow in places with possible washouts and large ruts. Usually okay for stock 4x4 SUVs with higher ground clearance. Call ahead to be sure.

Stats: Length: 85.3 miles. Time: 7 to 8 hours plus significant time to reach start of trail. Elevation: 1,934 to 7,154 ft. Best time: Oct.-April. Spring best for wildflowers. Don't go in summer.

Current Conditions: Death Valley National Park. Call (760) 786-3200. Ask for official copy of Death Valley Backroads Map.

Getting There: From Panamint Springs, go west 13.8 miles on Hwy. 190 to well-marked Saline Valley Road on right. From Lone Pine, take Hwy. 190 east about 35 miles. To start loop at Wpt. 04, head south on Racetrack Valley Road (lots of washboard) about 26 miles from Grapevine Station.

START MILEAGE LOG:

0.0 Zero trip odometer **[Rev. Miles]**
Head north on wide. Saline Valley Road. Mix of broken pavement and dirt. **[42.7]**
01 N36 21.849 W117 37.551
4.8 Old Saline Valley Road joins on left. **[37.9]**
6.0 Continue straight. Road to Lee Mines on right. **[36.7]**
7.5 Enter D.V.N.P. **[35.2]**
8.3 Bear right. Left goes to Lee Flat. **[34.4]**
9.0 Road all dirt now. **[33.7]**
15.7 Bear right on Hunter Mountain Road. This is start of loop. **[27.0]**
02 N36 31.600 W117 32.818
21.1 Two-track road on right goes to log cabin. **[21.6]**
22.8 Stay right. Left goes to overlook of Racetrack in about 3.4 miles. **[19.9]**
23.2 Begin winding descent into Hidden Valley. **[19.5]**
26.1 Stay left. Right goes to Goldbelt Spring site. **[16.6]**
26.5 Stay left. **[16.2]**
27.4 Stay left. **[15.3]**
30.6 Continue straight. **[12.1]**
33.7 Soft sand possible. **[9.0]**
37.2 Turn left on one-lane road to take great side trip to Lost Burro Mine. **[5.5]**
03 N36 43.776 W117 30.311
38.4 Turn around at mine. **[4.3]**
39.5 Return to Waypoint 03 and turn left. **[3.2]**
40.7 Pass through narrower Lost Burro Gap. **[2.0]**
42.7 Turn left at Teakettle Junction. Right goes to Grapevine Station and Scottys Castle. (Alternate route to Racetrack.) **[0.0]**
04 N36 45.599 W117 32.544
0.0 Zero trip odometer at Wpt. 04.
Head southwest. **[42.6]**
2.1 Stay left. **[40.5]**
5.8 Parking for Grandstand, Information board. **[36.8]**
7.9 Parking for Moving Rocks, information board. **[34.7]**
9.5 Turn right to go down Lippincott Grade. **[33.1]**
05 N36 38.488 W117 34.476
16.5 Left on Saline Valley. **[26.1]**
06 N36 37.193 W117 38.932
22.2 Enter narrow, twisty Grapevine Canyon. Washouts possible. **[20.4]**
26.9 Return to Wpt. 02. Right returns to start. **[15.7]**
42.6 Return to start of trail. **[0.0]**

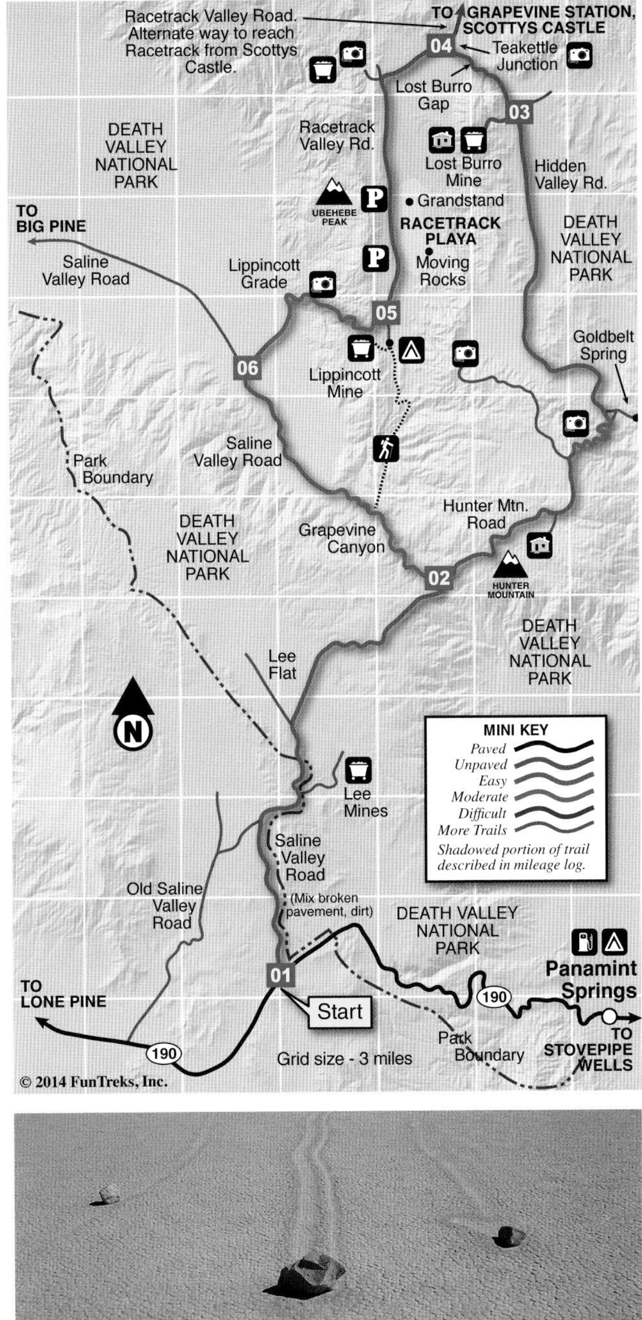

Hike west from southern parking area to see moving rocks.

Sign marks roughest drive.

Washout in Grapevine Canyon.

40 Marble & Cottonwood Canyons

AREA 3 map on page 94

General store at Stovepipe Wells.

Road is well defined at first.

Later, watch for cairns to stay on course.

First part of hike into Marble Canyon is flat.

Historical Highlight: *For many years, this has been a popular backpacker's destination. The two canyons connect in a loop. The route is challenging and dangerous if you get lost. No permit other than park pass is required. Check at the ranger station in Stovepipe Wells for latest conditions and recommendations.*

Overview: Route crosses a wide alluvial plain then turns into the mountains following twisting wash bottoms. Route is inside Death Valley National Park and offers great photo opportunities, especially at sunrise and sunset. Once you pay the general fee to be in the park, there are no additional fees. To get the most out of this trip, we suggest you hike a mile or so into Marble Canyon. Street-legal vehicles only.

Rating: Moderate: Conditions can change quickly after heavy rainstorms. Stock vehicles with 4-wheel drive and moderate ground clearance are usually sufficient to handle conditions. Route-finding can be challenging in Cottonwood Canyon, especially south of Waypoint 05. Flash floods are rare but possible.

Stats: Length: Round trip is 34.3 miles as described. Add 9 miles if you go to end of Cottonwood Canyon. Time: 4-5 hours. Elevation: -14 ft. to 1,884 ft. Open all year. Avoid summer.

Current Conditions: Stovepipe Wells Ranger Station, call (760) 786-2342.

Getting There: Take Highway 190 to Stovepipe Wells in Death Valley National Park. Head north on paved road that enters large campground southwest of gas station.

START **MILEAGE LOG:**

0.0 Zero trip odometer **[Rev. Miles]**
Head north on thinly paved road following sign to air strip. Swing left past RV campground. **[15.6]**
01 N36 36.362 W117 08.862

0.5 Turn right at air strip following graded road across alluvial plain. Mix of sand and gravel. **[15.1]**

6.4 Pace slows as road begins to climb and gets rockier. **[9.2]**

8.4 After short climb, road curves left and drops down into a wide, rocky wash. Follow best-traveled road. Watch for cairns and rocks marking edge of road. **[7.2]**
02 N36 38.562 W117 16.235

10.0 Curve left (south) following cairns. Route is not always easy to see. **[5.6]**

10.7 Bear right at fork and start into Marble Canyon. Look for faded crossroads sign. **[4.9]**
03 N36 37.924 W117 17.727

13.1 Sign marks end of motorized portion. **[2.5]**
04 N36 37.131 W117 19.839
Park here and hike another mile or so into canyon.

15.6 Return to Wpt. 03. **[0.0]**

0.0 Zero trip odometer at Wpt. 03
Bear right and head south into Cottonwood Canyon. Trail winds back and forth across wash bottom and may not always be obvious. **[4.0]**

1.6 Avoid lesser wash that splits off to the left. Stay slightly right heading south-southwest. Watch for cairns. **[2.4]**

4.0 Large cave on left. This is good place to turn around. Return the way you came. **[0.0]**
05 N36 34.803 W117 18.702
We drove another 4.5 miles to end of canyon where vehicles must stop. Trail was rougher and not well traveled.

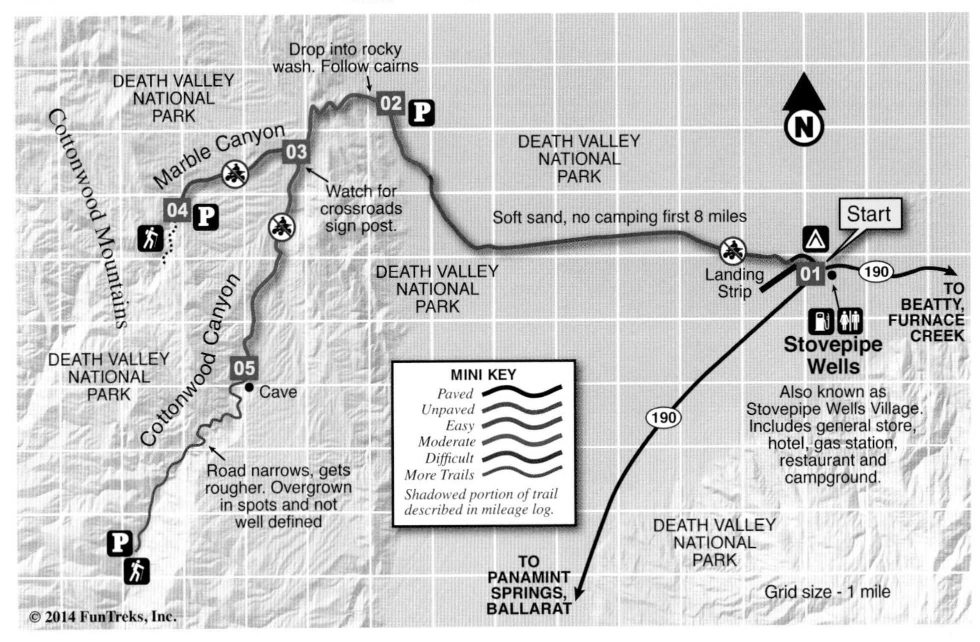

Faded sign at Waypoint 03.

Cave at Waypoint 05 is good spot to turn around.

41 Titus Canyon

AREA 3 map on page 94

Great views as you climb to nearly a mile high at Red Pass.

A few buildings still stand at Leadfield ghost town.

Sign marks the entrance to Titus Canyon.

Historical Highlight: *The town of Leadfield never delivered on its promise of rich lead claims and lasted less than a year despite getting a post office in 1926. The canyon is named after mining engineer Morris Titus, who died prospecting the canyon.*

Overview: One of the most popular backroads in Death Valley National Park. Very scenic after the first 10 miles. Visit historic Leadfield where mines and a few buildings remain. Interesting geologic rock formations and a few petroglyphs. Street-legal vehicles only. Trail is one way east to west. Park pass required.

Rating: Easy: A well-maintained gravel road, but steep and narrow in a few places. Four-wheel drive seldom necessary under dry conditions. Road is closed when rain is expected due to extreme flash flood danger through the narrow canyon.

Stats: Length: 26.6 miles. Time: Drive by itself only takes an hour, but allow extra time for stops. Elevation: 179 ft. to 5,265 ft. Open all year unless closed by flash-flood warnings. Dangerously hot in summer.

Current Conditions: Stovepipe Wells Ranger Station. Call (760) 786-2342.

Getting There: Head northeast from Stovepipe Wells or north from Furnace Creek on Highway 190 and connect to Highway 374 heading northeast towards Beatty, NV. Turn left on well-marked road 6.5 miles east of state line. Start is 6.2 miles southwest of Beatty, NV.

START **MILEAGE LOG:**

0.0 Zero trip odometer
From Highway 374, head west on wide, well-maintained gravel road.
01 N36 51.552 W116 50.767

1.9 Enter Death Valley National Park.

9.6 Road descends into Titanothere Canyon. Great views.

11.1 Climb to Red Pass.

12.3 Arrive at Red Pass, nearly a mile high. More great views.
02 N36 49.730 W117 01.974

15.4 Arrive at historic Leadfield. Take some time here to look around. Follow hiking trail.
03 N36 50.906 W117 03.554

16.0 Interesting exposed folded layers of different colored rock.

16.2 Sign marks entry into Titus Canyon.

18.0 Look high up on walls for petroglyphs.

23.5 Narrowest part of canyon. Just one lane wide.

23.9 Exit Titus Canyon. Parking lot, vault toilet and hiking trail on left. Two-way traffic from here.
04 N36 49.333 W117 10.405

26.6 Paved Highway 267.
05 N36 47.269 W117 11.489
Right on 267 goes to Scottys Castle. Left goes to Stovepipe Wells, Furnace Creek or back to Beatty, NV.

Trail updates & GPS downloads at www.funtreks.com

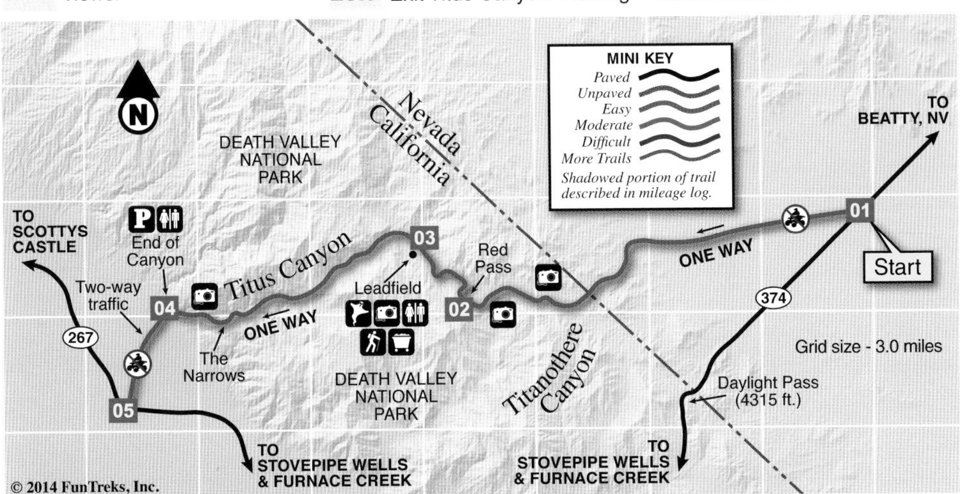

Colorful and interesting geology as you enter Titus Canyon.

Canyon is well maintained but rock slides are always possible.

The narrows.

42 Chloride City

AREA 3 map on page 94

Even on a rainy day we had great views looking southwest from Chloride Cliff.

Trail is steep and rocky in a few places.

Trail climbs over 1,700 feet in the Funeral Mtns.

Historical Highlight: *Chloride City was first established in the early 1870s when silver was discovered at Chloride Cliff. Poor profits led to the town's abandonment by 1880. New investors reopened the mine in 1908. Enough ore was discovered to warrant construction of a cyanide mill in 1916, but by 1918 the town, once again, shut down.*

Overview: Fun, scenic trail climbs gradually over 1,350 feet to site of historic Chloride City, then climbs another 400 feet to Chloride Cliff high above the Keane Wonder Mine. (Accessed from Beatty Cut-Off Road, but now closed to the public. Explained on kiosk at Chloride City.) Not much remains at Chloride City except an old mining shack and a grave marker. Street-legal vehicles only. Park pass required.

Rating: Moderate: Mostly easy but a few sections are steep and rough. Narrow shelf roads at Chloride Cliff subject to deterioration. Use prudent judgment when to stop as no barricades mark ends of roads. Suitable for most stock high-clearance 4x4 SUVs with low-range gearing.

Stats: Length: 7.7 miles one way. Time: Allow 3-4 hours round trip. Elevation: 3,408 to 5,176 ft. Open all year. Very hot in summer, but not quite as bad as on valley floor.

Current Conditions: Visit Furnace Creek Visitor Center, or call general number at (760) 786-3200. To bypass recorded answer, call Stovepipe Wells Ranger Station at (760) 786-2342.

Getting There: Head northeast from Stovepipe Wells or north from Furnace Creek on Highway 190 and connect to Highway 374 heading northeast towards Beatty, NV. Look for dirt road on right 3.3 miles after Hells Gate Rest Area. Sign says "4x4 High Clearance, No Camping Next 2 Miles."

START **MILEAGE LOG:**

0.0 Zero trip odometer **[Rev. Miles]**
Head east on easy gravel road which gradually circles south. **[7.7]**
01 N36 45.035 W116 56.192

2.2 Bear left at T intersection. **[5.5]**
02 N35 44.461 W116 13.280

2.5 After going past water tank, road starts to climb and gets rougher. **[5.2]**

4.5 Join wash that comes in on right. Stay left. **[3.2]**

4.7 Continue straight where road goes right. **[3.0]**

5.2 At T intersection, bear hard right as you join Chloride Cliff Road. **[2.5]**
03 N36 43.060 W116 53.106

6.2 Stay left where lesser road goes right. **[1.5]**

6.3 Continue straight. Ignore faint road on left. **[1.4]**

6.5 At 5-way intersection. Pick your way uphill on maze of roads. You are now passing through site of Chloride City. **[1.2]**

6.6 Stay right to see mine shack and grave, then continue southeast. **[1.1]**
04 N36 42.225 W116 52.914

7.0 Make a hard left uphill at T intersection. Road continues to climb ridge and circles around. Straight takes you to the same place. **[0.7]**

7.3 Continue straight. Other road from last intersection joins on right. **[0.4]**

7.4 Continue straight. Ignore road on left. **[0.3]**

7.5 Driver's choice. We stayed right to reach viewpoint along Chloride Cliff. Left goes to different viewpoint. Proceed with caution either way. Road conditions subject to deterioration and may be dangerous. **[0.2]**
05 N36 41.807 W116 52.736

7.7 We stopped here. Road continued downhill but soon ended. **[0.0]**
Return to Highway 374 via the reverse route.

Trail updates & GPS downloads at www.funtreks.com

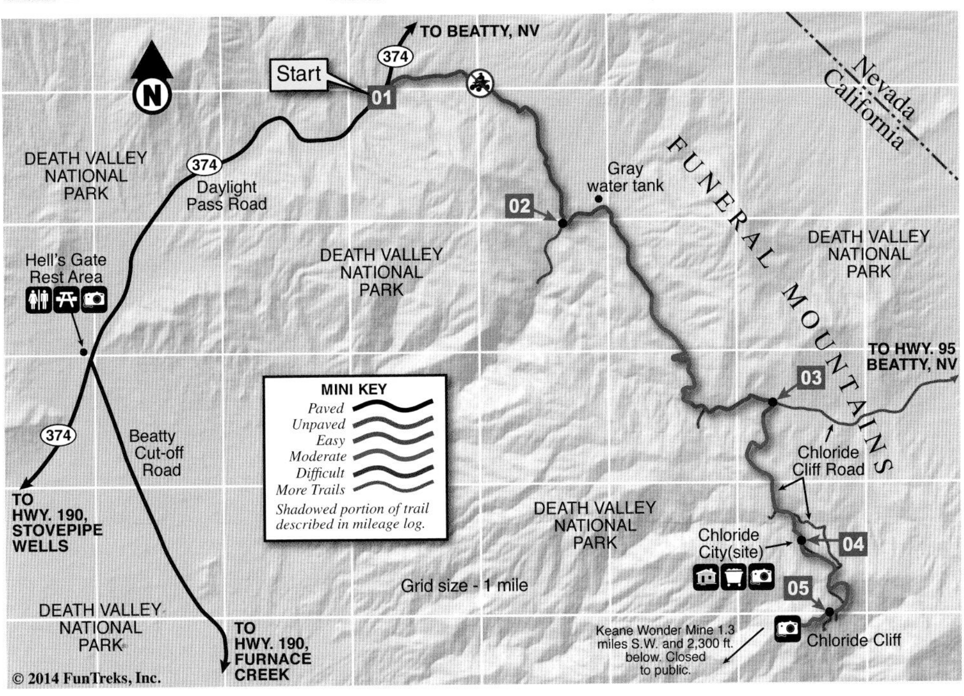

Grave marker for James McKay.

Mining shack covers entry to mine.

Inyo Mine, Echo Pass

AREA 3 map on page 94

Trail starts here on north side of Highway 190.

Backside view of Eye of the Needle.

Skeletal remains of mill at mine site.

Inside view of one of the remaining buildings.

Historical Highlight: *Inyo Mine is a favorite spot for visitors because it has structures still standing. Gold was discovered here in 1905. Water had to be hauled in from Furnace Creek, so production costs were high. Despite good ore, the mine shut down in 1912. Another attempt was made between 1932 and 1938 when a 25-ton crushing mill was built. In 1907, the town included a boarding house, blacksmith shop and company store. Lack of water doomed the mine.*

Overview: First part of trip takes you past Eye of the Needle to Inyo Mine, where you'll find several well-preserved structures and old mining equipment. Please take only photographs. The second part of trip has a challenging obstacle and ends at a relatively high pass with good views. Street-legal vehicles only. Park pass required.

Rating: Difficult: Easy to Inyo Mine. A little rocky in spots but stock 4x4 SUVs will have no problem to this point. The second part is easy to moderate with a few more rocks and steep places; however, there's one tight passage with steep rock ledges. An experienced driver in a stock vehicle with lockers and high clearance should be able to get through.

Stats: Length: 9.5 miles to Inyo Mine. Another 5.2 to Echo Pass. Time: Round trip allow 3 hours to mine or 5 hours to pass. Elevation: 412 ft. to 4,857 ft. Best time: Oct.-April. Spring best for wildflowers. Don't go in summer.

Current Conditions: Death Valley National Park. Call (760) 786-3200. At visitor center, ask for copy of the park's official backroads map.

Getting There: From the intersection of Highway 190 and Badwater Road south of Furnace Creek, continue 2.1 miles southeast on Highway 190. Watch for a gravel road on left. Everything is gravel so the road blends in. After you turn, look for sign with Jeep symbol.

START **MILEAGE LOG:**

0.0 Zero trip odometer **[Rev. Miles]** Head northeast on well-defined road. Sign says Echo Canyon and has Jeep symbol. No camping is allowed the first two miles. **[9.5]**
01 N36 26.258 W116 49.442

3.4 Start into the mouth of the canyon. **[6.1]**

4.7 Stop here for best view of Eye of the Needle. **[4.8]**

9.0 Bear right to take side trip to Inyo Mine. **[0.5]**
02 N36 29.779 W116 42.639

9.5 Arrive at mine. Lots of structures to see here. Be careful around mine. **[0.0]**
03 N36 29.606 W116 42.231

Return to Wpt. 02.

0.0 Zero trip odometer at Wpt. 02 Make a hard right at sign that says "Short Wheel-base Vehicles Only. **[5.2]**

0.2 Stay left. Road on right is shortcut. **[5.0]**

0.3 Follow trail as it curves around to right. You'll pass a small parking area for hiking trail to Schwab Townsite on left. **[4.9]**

2.5 Continue straight where lesser road goes right. **[2.7]**

2.9 Foundations of cabin remain on right. **[2.3]**

3.0 Climb difficult rock ledges through narrow opening in rock wall. We used our rear locker. Aggressive, high-clearance SUVs should be able to get through this section with skilled driver. After this section, trail gets easier again. **[2.2]**

3.5 Make sharp left turn uphill out of wash. **[1.7]**
04 N36 30.845 W116 40.731

3.6 Continue straight over top of hill and start down other side. **[1.6]**

4.5 Bear right and follow road as it climbs to pass. **[0.7]**

5.2 Top of pass at about 4,900 ft. Great views. Road continues many miles to Hwy. 95, but we recommend returning the way you came. **[0.0]**
05 N36 31.799 W116 40.341

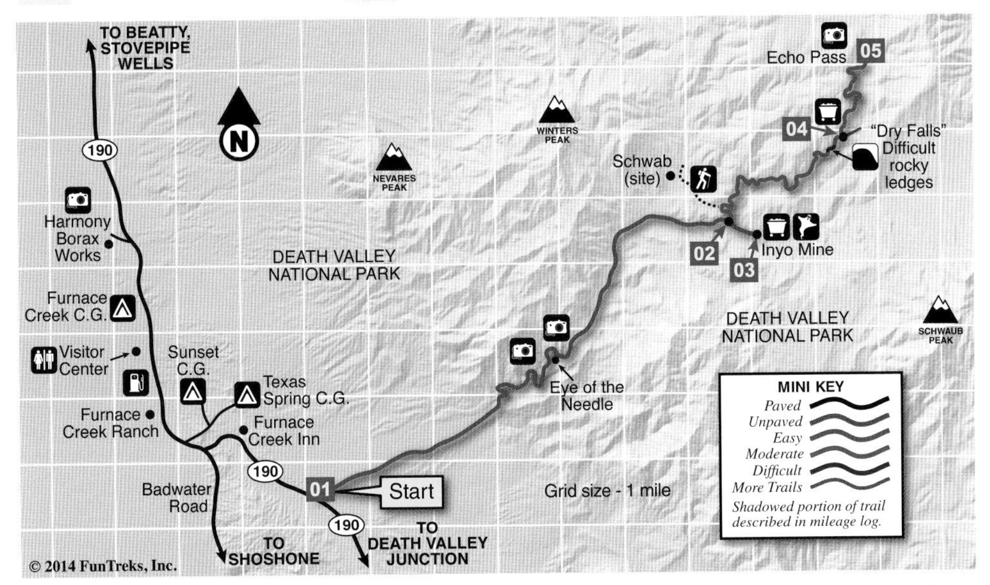

Lockers recommended for "Dry Falls."

Echo Pass. Our GPS elevation read 4,857 ft.

Lonely wildflower in October. Spring better time.

Pleasant Canyon

AREA 3 map on page 94

Clair Camp. Standing structures provide a great photo opportunity.

Ballarat Ghost Town.

Shelf road descends into Pleasant Canyon.

Historical Highlight: *In 1897, over 200 men worked the Ratcliff Mine and lived at Clair Camp (later named). The mine shut down in 1905 after producing a half million dollars in gold. In 1930, W.D. Clair bought the mine and was able to extract another $60,000. Source: Secret Places in the Mojave Desert, Vol. II, by Jim Mattern.*

Overview: You'll head east into the Panamint Mountains just past Ballarat Ghost Town and drop into Pleasant Canyon. First stop is Clair Camp, which features standing structures and historic mining ruins. Green-sticker vehicles must stop at boundary to Death Valley N.P., but street-legal vehicles can proceed to Rita's Cabin and explore other mining roads around Rogers Pass. Return the way you came. An unsafe bridge now prohibits returning via South Park Canyon. Dispersed camping at Ballarat.

Rating: Moderate: High shelf road has several steep, narrow sections. Okay for stock vehicles, but high clearance, 4WD and low-range gears are necessary. Optional route has extremely tight and scratchy brush.

Stats: Length: 10 miles one way. Time: About 3 hours including return trip from Rita's Cabin. Elevation: 1,090 to 6,394 ft. Best time: October-April.

Current Conditions: BLM, Ridgecrest Field Office (760) 384-5400. Death Valley National Park (760) 786-3200.

Getting There: **From Trona:** Take Hwy. 178 north about 22 miles and turn right on Ballarat Road. Head east 3.6 miles to the ghost town of Ballarat. **From intersection of Highway 190 and Panamint Valley Road:** Drive 14 miles south on Panamint Valley Road. Turn right on Trona Wildhorse Road and drive another 9.5 miles. Turn left on Ballarat Road and head east 3.6 miles to the ghost town of Ballarat.

START **MILEAGE LOG:**

0.0 Zero trip odometer **[Rev. Miles]** Head east on Ballarat Road where it intersects with Wingate Road. **[10.0]**
01 **N36 02.873 W117 13.447**

0.5 Immediately after turn for Jackpot Canyon on left, continue straight (slightly left) on better-traveled road. Right is lesser-used optional route. **[9.5]**
02 **N36 03.029 W117 12.983**

2.2 Bear right. Lesser road on left dead ends. **[7.8]**

3.1 Follow more traveled road as you cross over ridge and drop into canyon. **[6.9]**

3.4 Bear left up canyon as optional road joins on right. **[6.6]**
03 **N36 01.972 W117 10.539**

6.0 Be careful exploring ruins at Clair Camp. **[4.0]**
04 **N36 02.003 W117 07.987**

7.0 Continue straight. **[3.0]**

8.2 Pass natural spring. **[1.8]**

8.4 Stay right following more-traveled road. Lesser roads on left go to Porter and Copper mines. **[1.6]**

10.0 Arrive at boarded-up Rita's Cabin. There's a little shade here and a few picnic tables. Return the way you came. **[0.0]**
05 **N36 01.500 W117 04.283**
On our first drive of this trail years ago, we were able to loop back down South Park Canyon. Today, a small bridge above Briggs Camp is closed to full-size vehicles.

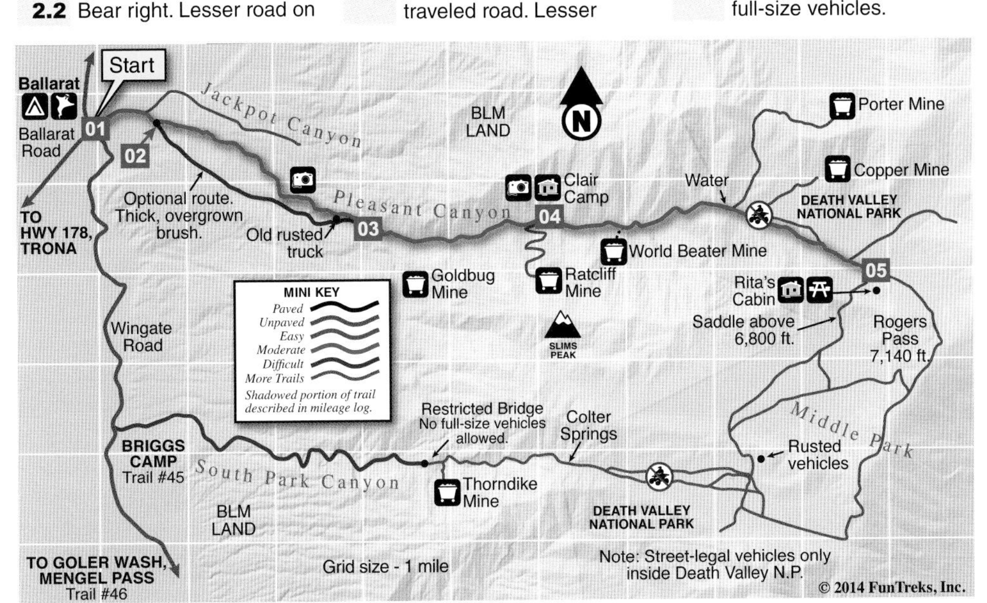

Shade and a few picnic tables at Rita's Cabin.

Optional route is overgrown with tight brush.

Remains of old mill at Clair Camp.

45 Briggs Camp

AREA 3 map on page 94

View as you arrive at Briggs Camp. Cabins are available to public on a first-come, first-served basis.

Conditions vary considerably. Call ahead.

BLM has plans for new bridge in the future.

Historical Highlight: *All we know about Harry Briggs is that he lived here in the 1930s and was in charge of surrounding mining operations. A picture of him hangs in Briggs Cabin. Purportedly, the cabins are in better shape today then when he lived there. The cabins are maintained by volunteers of "Friends of Briggs Camp." Please follow posted rules. Maximum stay 4 days. Read and follow hantavirus advisories posted at cabins.*

Overview: This challenging hard-core route takes you to an old mining camp with two amazingly well-kept Adopt-A-Cabins, which are open to the public on a first-come, first-served basis. Signs say full-size vehicles should not proceed above the camp, where there's a small bridge for ATVs and motorcycles only. (Bridge may be rebuilt in the future.) Green-sticker vehicles can explore Thorndike Mine above the bridge, but must turn around at the boundary to Death Valley National Park.

Rating: Difficult: Condition of trail varies greatly depending on recent storms. At times it may be impassable until volunteers repair it. Prepare for a narrow, rocky trail, very tippy in spots. We don't recommend this trail for stock SUVs.

Stats: Length: Almost 5 miles. Time: About 2 hours to Briggs Camp. Elevation: 1,026 to 4,081 ft. Best time: October-April.

Current Conditions: BLM, Ridgecrest Field Office, (760) 384-5400.

Getting There: **From Trona:** Head north on Highway 178 about 22 miles to Ballarat Road. Turn right heading east and go another 3.6 miles to the ghost town of Ballarat. Turn right on Wingate Road and head south 4 miles to start of trail on left.

START **MILEAGE LOG:**

0.0 Zero trip odometer **[Rev. Miles]**
From Wingate Road, head east on lesser road. **[4.7]**
01 N36 00.012 W117 13.217

1.7 Pass flat camping area on right. **[3.0]**

1.9 Stay left as difficult short-cut goes right uphill. **[2.8]**
02 N35 59.849 W117 11.787

2.6 Follow more traveled road left into canyon. **[2.1]**

4.0 Continue following wash in canyon as lesser road goes up to mine. **[0.7]**

4.7 Arrive at Briggs Camp. Lots to see here. **[0.0]**
03 N35 59.728 W117 09.860
Full-size vehicles return the way you came. Green-sticker vehicles must stop at boundary to D.V.N.P.

Trail climbs over 2,000 feet in the first 2 miles.

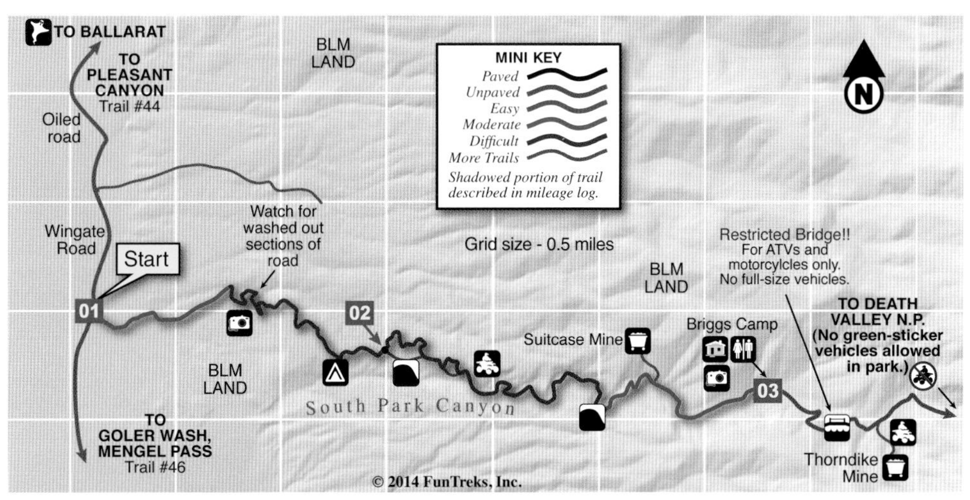

Sign above Briggs Camp.

Kitchen in Briggs Cabin.

Briggs Mine Cabin is in excellent condition thanks to volunteers.

Goler Wash, Mengel Pass

AREA 3 map on page 94

Passing through canyon after road was graded.

We barely got across this ungraded section.

Rocky descent down north side of Mengel Pass.

Historical Highlight: *Charles Manson is perhaps the most notorious mass murderer of all time. He and his "Manson Family" accomplices were caught hiding out at the Barker Ranch in 1969. It was a major news event. A fire in 2009 destroyed the wooden part of the structure, but the stone portion of the house still remains. Don't miss this interesting side trip.*

Overview: This trail is a real backcountry adventure; you never know what to expect (see rating below). Features along the route include Newman Cabin, Lotus Mine, Manson Hideout and Mengel's grave. End of trail reaches Butte Valley, where you can explore a network of roads that lead to three amazing cabins, shown in Trail #47. Street-legal vehicles only in Death Valley N. Park. Park pass required.

Rating: Difficult: There's one rocky section descending the north side of Mengel Pass that will always be difficult for stock vehicles. The balance of the trail ranges between easy to impassable, depending upon recency of maintenance. We drove through while the trail was being graded. The graded portion was very easy, but the ungraded portion was extremely difficult due to major washouts (see photo above).

Stats: Length: 11.8 miles one way. Add 26 miles if you drive out via Trail #47. Time: Allow 2-3 hours for described portion, but you'll need a whole day before you're done with everything. Elevation: 1,120 to 4,292 ft. Best time: Oct.-April. Spring best for wildflowers. Don't go in summer.

Current Conditions: BLM, Ridgecrest Field Office (760) 384-5400. Death Valley National Park (760) 786-3200.

Getting There: Take Highway 178 north from Trona about 22 miles. Turn right on Ballarat Road to Wingate Road. Head south on Wingate Road 15.1 miles to BLM Road P52 on left.

START **MILEAGE LOG:**

0.0 Zero trip odometer **[Rev. Miles]** Head east on wide dirt road marked P52. Some maps show this as Coyote Canyon Road. **[11.8]**
01 N35 51.538 W117 10.787

1.4 Road narrows to single lane and enters canyon. Road had just been graded so it was easy, but we've seen this road extremely difficult after a rainstorm. For that reason, we show trail as difficult through this entire section. **[10.4]**

3.8 Bear right to take short side trip to Newman Cabin. **[8.0]**
02 N35 51.706 W117 07.675

3.9 After visiting cabin, return to Waypoint 02 and continue east. **[7.9]**

4.3 Road grading ended and half the road was washed away, but we were able to get through. We assumed road grading was not complete. **[7.5]**

4.7 Continue straight. Road on right goes to Lotus Mine. Lots to see. **[7.1]**

5.1 Stay left. Road on right hadn't been driven in a long time. **[6.7]**

5.8 Bear left even though right looked better. Because road grader hadn't reached this point yet, we had to get across an extreme washout. **[6.0]**

5.9 Stay left at sign that marks entry into DVNP. Street-legal vehicles only beyond this point. **[5.9]**

6.0 Make hard right to take side trip to Manson's famous hideout at Barker Ranch. **[5.8]**
03 N35 51.642 W117 05.801

6.6 Turn around at hideout. It burned in 2009, but stone portions remain. **[5.2]**

7.2 Return to Waypoint 03 and bear right to continue on main trail. **[4.6]**

7.4 Stay left. Lesser wash to right. **[4.4]**

7.8 Trail turns left uphill. **[4.0]**

7.9 Bear right up steep limestone hill. **[3.9]**

10.4 After alternating easy washes and more difficult rocky spots, you arrive at Mengel Pass. Look for grave marker on left. **[1.4]**
04 N35 53.999 W117 04.934

10.5 Descend steeply down difficult boulder field. Trail then alternates between easy and moderate. **[1.3]**

11.8 Fork marks entry into Butte Valley. Visit 3 amazing cabins shown in detail map and explore other great side roads. **[0.0]**
05 N35 54.863 W117 04.960
Continue straight to exit via Butte Valley Trail #47, or return the way you came.

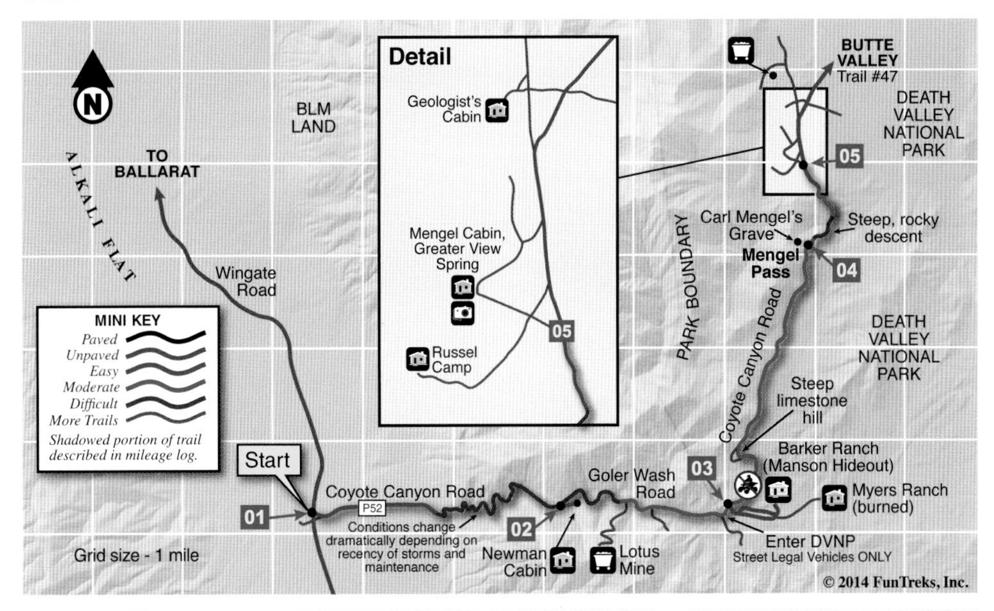

Manson Hideout at Barker Ranch. Only stone portion remains.

Russel Camp in Butte Valley.

Butte Valley

AREA 3 map on page 94

Looking east past Striped Butte towards Warm Springs Canyon. Wild burros in foreground.

Geologist's Cabin is best condition of the three.

Cozy interior of Geologist's Cabin.

Narrow, mildly rocky through Warm Springs Cyn.

Historical Highlight: *Carl Mengel, 1868-1944, devoted his life to mining in the area. There's a grave marker at the top of Mengel Pass south of his cabin. The Geologist's Cabin, Russel Camp and his cabin are open to the public on a first-come, first-served basis. The stone Geologist's Cabin is usually taken first. Please read hantavirus warnings posted at the cabins. Only you can decide if it is safe.*

Overview: You'll follow a wide road across open desert inside Death Valley National Park, then go through Warm Springs Canyon passing several talc mines. Explore an abandoned summer resort with decayed buildings and eerie swimming pool. End of trip opens into scenic Butte Valley featuring distinctive Striped Butte. Here you'll explore three historic, well-preserved cabins. Several interesting side roads to explore in Butte Valley. Watch for wild burros. Street-legal vehicles only. Park pass required.

Rating: Easy: Long gradual climb. Narrow, rough and mildly rocky in a few spots. Okay for stock 2-wheel-drive SUVs with moderate ground clearance.

Stats: Length: 25.5 miles one way plus a few extra miles to reach cabins. Time: Allow 5-7 hours for round trip. Elevation: -248 ft. to 4,245 ft. Best time: Oct.-April. Spring best for wildflowers. Don't go in summer.

Current Conditions: Death Valley National Park. Call (760) 786-3200. Ask for official copy of Death Valley Backroads Map.

Getting There: From Furnace Creek, head south about 42 miles on Badwater Road and turn right on West Side Road.

START *MILEAGE LOG:*

0.0 Zero trip odometer **[Rev. Miles]** Head west on West Side Road. Pass through gate with information board explaining history of road. Wide road continues west then heads north. **[25.5]**
01 N35 56.262 W116 42.277

2.9 Turn left on wide road towards Warm Spring Canyon (see photo). **[22.6]**
02 N35 57.247 W116 44.796

10.2 Stay to the right. **[15.3]**

12.6 Pass through area of talc mines. **[12.9]**

13.7 Bear left off main road to take side trip to Warm Springs Camp. **[11.8]**
03 N35 58.155 W116 55.622

14.0 Arrive at Warm Springs Camp. Explore area, then head north. **[11.5]**

14.1 Turn left on main road and continue west past interesting display of mining equipment. **[11.4]**

18.5 Continue straight where road goes right. **[7.0]**

23.1 Road straightens out as you go past Striped Butte on right. **[2.4]**

25.5 Driver's choice: Right goes to Geologist's Cabin. Straight to Mengel's Cabin and Russel Camp. Explore area using Detail Map A. Main road continues south and connects to difficult Goler Wash, Trail #46. Rough climb to Mengel Pass. See Trail #46 for details. **[0.0]**
04 N35 55.413 W117 04.957

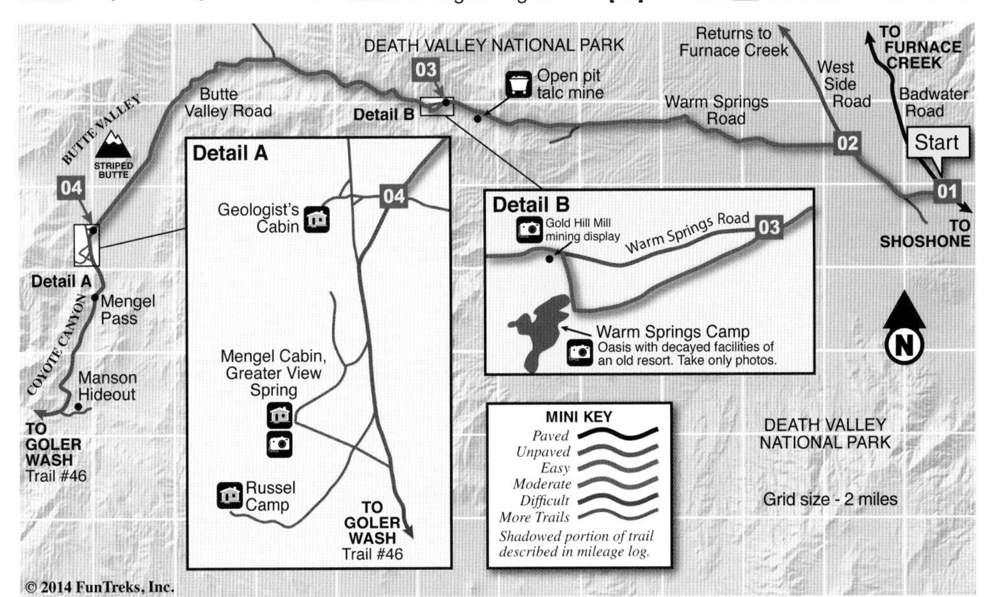

Talc soil, not snow. Looking west from Wpt. 02.

Gold Hill Mill mining equipment next to road.

Empty pool at Warm Springs Camp.

Mengel's Cabin at Greater View Spring.

48 Sperry Wash

AREA 3 map on page 94

Soft soil results in deep erosion and unusual looking buttes like this.

Amargosa River is usually shallow or dry.

Mine structure on right before Waypoint 05.

Historical Highlight: *As you pass through Amargosa Canyon, look for remains of the old Tonopah & Tidewater Railroad that was built in 1905. It continued up Amargosa Canyon and serviced many important mining operations in Death Valley. The town of Sperry serviced the railroad during that time.*

Overview: Many people drive or ride this trail as a diversion from the sand-only routes at Dumont Dunes. Snowbirds come to Tecopa to enjoy a variety of campgrounds and resorts with mineral hot springs. Rockhounds search for petrified wood, amethyst and opals. Green-sticker vehicles are allowed to Wpt. 04. Stay on marked route only.

Rating: Easy: Trail follows mostly sandy wash bottoms where flash floods are possible. You'll cross the Amargosa River many times, but it is usually dry or very shallow. Route markers are often washed away, and route-finding can be challenging in spots.

Stats: Length: Dirt portion is 8.7 miles with another 12.3 miles of deteriorated pavement. Entire route is 28.8 miles. Time: 3 to 5 hours. Elevation: 655 to 2,312 ft. Best time: Late October to early May. Very hot in summer.

Current Conditions: Bureau of Land Management, Barstow Field Office. Call (760) 252-6000.

Getting There: Take Highway 127 north from Baker about 34 miles and turn right on Dumont Dunes Road. Drive east 2.8 miles and turn left before entering Dumont Dunes. Look for ranch-style entry portal.

START MILEAGE LOG:

0.0 Zero trip odometer **[Rev. Miles]**
Pass through ranch-style entry with overhead sign for Sperry Wash. Head east following wide wash of Amargosa River. **[28.8]**
01 N35 41.928 W116 15.146

0.3 First of several crossings of Amargosa River (may be dry). **[28.5]**

0.7 Stay right and cross river again. This part of trail may be very hard to see. Many of the unique cairns that once marked trail have been washed away. **[28.1]**

2.8 Trail is better defined and is marked with brown carsonite posts. **[26.0]**

3.1 Sign marks entry into non-wilderness corridor. Stay on trail. **[25.7]**

3.9 Sign marks entry into Amargosa Canyon ACEC. This is Sperry Townsite, but there's not much to see but foundations. **[24.9]**
02 N35 42.287 W116 14.502

4.3 Trail turns east into Sperry Wash and leaves Amargosa Canyon. Large sign with separate mileage for motorized and hikers. Canyon walls close in with more interesting terrain. **[24.5]**
03 N35 44.779 W116 13.262

8.7 Trail changes to broken pavement. **[20.1]**

10.7 Stay right at fork, then in less than tenth of a mile, make a sharp left and follow trail north. **[18.1]**

11.5 Pass through north entry gate and stay left on Western Talc Road. Pass through area of talc mines, popular with rockhounds. Unlicensed vehicles must turn around here. **[17.3]**
04 N35 47.058 W116 08.339

15.1 Water tank, collapsed mine building on right. **[13.7]**

15.3 Bear left on Furnace Creek Road. **[13.5]**
05 N35 48.066 W116 05.902

21.0 Continue straight. Left goes to China Ranch Date Farm, a popular tourist attraction for snowbirds in winter. **[7.8]**

22.8 Bear left on Old Spanish Trail. **[6.0]**

24.3 Bear right on Tecopa Hot Springs Road. **[4.5]**
06 N35 50.900 W116 13.533

26.1 Public mineral hot springs on right. Separate facilities for men and women. Popular with locals and snowbirds. Small fee. **[2.7]**

28.8 Highway 127. **[0.0]**
07 N35 53.971 W116 15.514
Right goes to Shoshone and Death Valley. Left returns to Dumont Dunes.

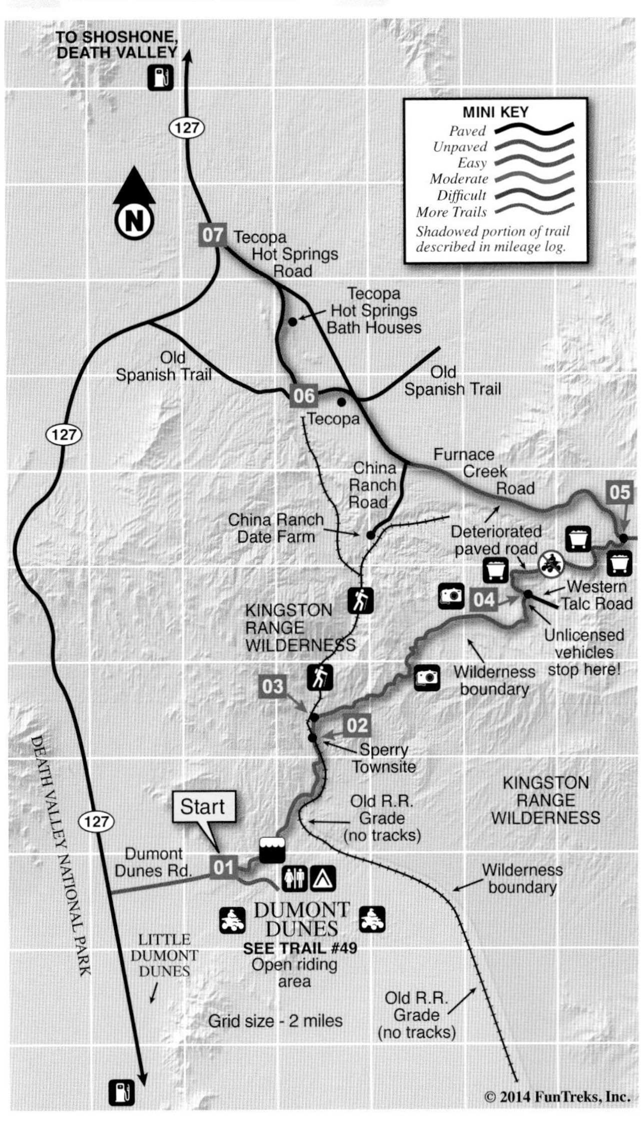

Look for paw print on cairns.

Large cairns mark trail.

Dumont Dunes

AREA 3 map on page 94

Almost 13 square miles to cruise and enjoy. Air down tires before attempting smaller dunes.

North Pole—landmark and meeting place.

ATV and UTV riders enjoy the slopes.

Overview: Area is obviously best suited for dune buggies and vehicles with paddle tires; however, owners of regular 4x4s can have a great time, too. Just use common sense. Stay on smaller dunes and away from the drift side of dunes where sand is super soft. Drive or ride anywhere within park boundary. A great place to camp and enjoy the sun. A pass is needed for each vehicle you drive into park. Overnight camping allowed. All vehicles must be licensed or have OHV sticker. Flags required.

Rating: Difficult: Steep slopes, soft sand and off-camber hills are available. Be extremely careful when turning across side hills. Air-down tires. Vault toilets only. NO water, shade, picnic tables or trash removal.

Stats: Almost 13 square miles of open riding. Elevation: 700 to 1,200 ft. Best time: October-April. Avoid summer.

Current Conditions: Bureau of Land Management, Barstow Field Office. Call (760) 252-6000.

Getting There: From Baker, drive north 34 miles on Hwy. 127. Turn right on Dumont Dunes Road. Stay right at 2.8 miles heading towards fee station. Climb up to plateau and park anywhere.

START *MILEAGE LOG:*

No mileage log is needed since you can ride or drive anywhere within the park boundary.

It's a good idea to purchase park passes before you go since solar-powered, "credit card only" dispensers do not always work.

For information on the area and a **list of vendors who sell park passes go to:** http://www.blm.gov/ca/st/en/fo/barstow/dumont.html

FunTreks Scout Team arrives at the dunes ready for fun.

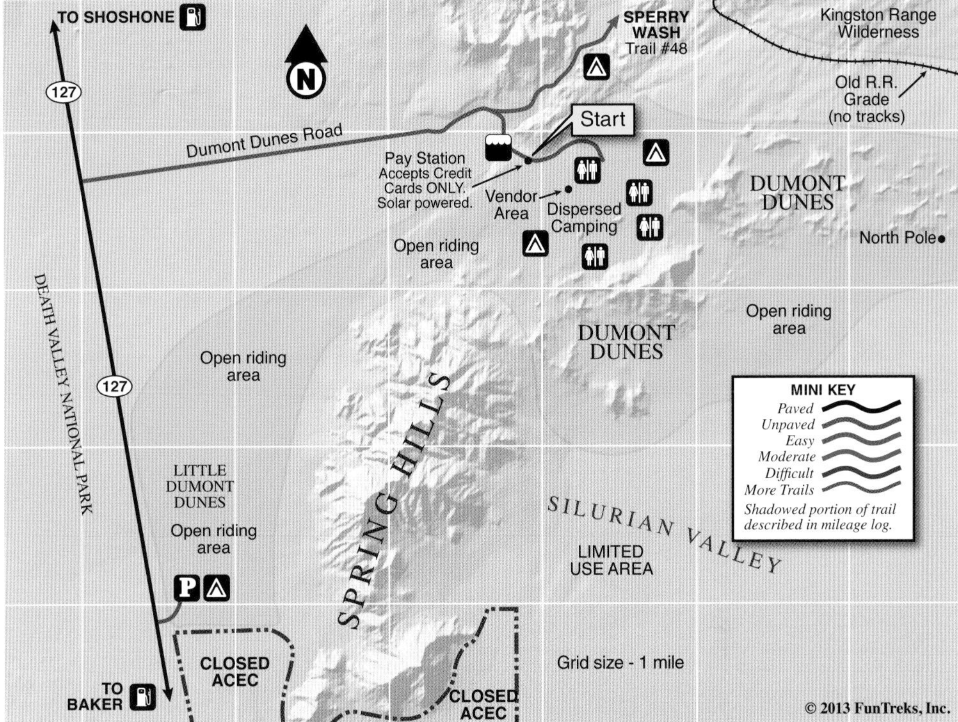

Wishing we had one of these for just a day.

Hike to top of dunes for amazing photos.

Lake Isabella, Ridgecrest, Barstow

As you travel from east to west across Area 4, the trails change from low rugged desert to high scenic forest. Nowhere is this more obvious than Trail 53, which starts at 2,500 feet at Jawbone Station and climbs to 8,200 feet looking down on Lake Isabella. The terrain north of Barstow (trails 58, 59 & 60) is about as rugged and barren as it gets. As you move west to Red Rock Canyon State Park and surrounding BLM land (trails 55, 56 & 57), it's flatter and more desert like. Farther west, above Lake Isabella (trails 50, 51 & 52), it's all forested, with *Sherman Pass 4x4 Trail* topping out near 10,000 feet. Our favorite trail in Area 4 is easy *Bonanza Gulch*, which features well-preserved miners' cabins and amazing *Bickel Camp*. For hard-core enthusiasts, we recommend difficult *Odessa-Doran Loop,* so unusual, you'll only understand after driving it.

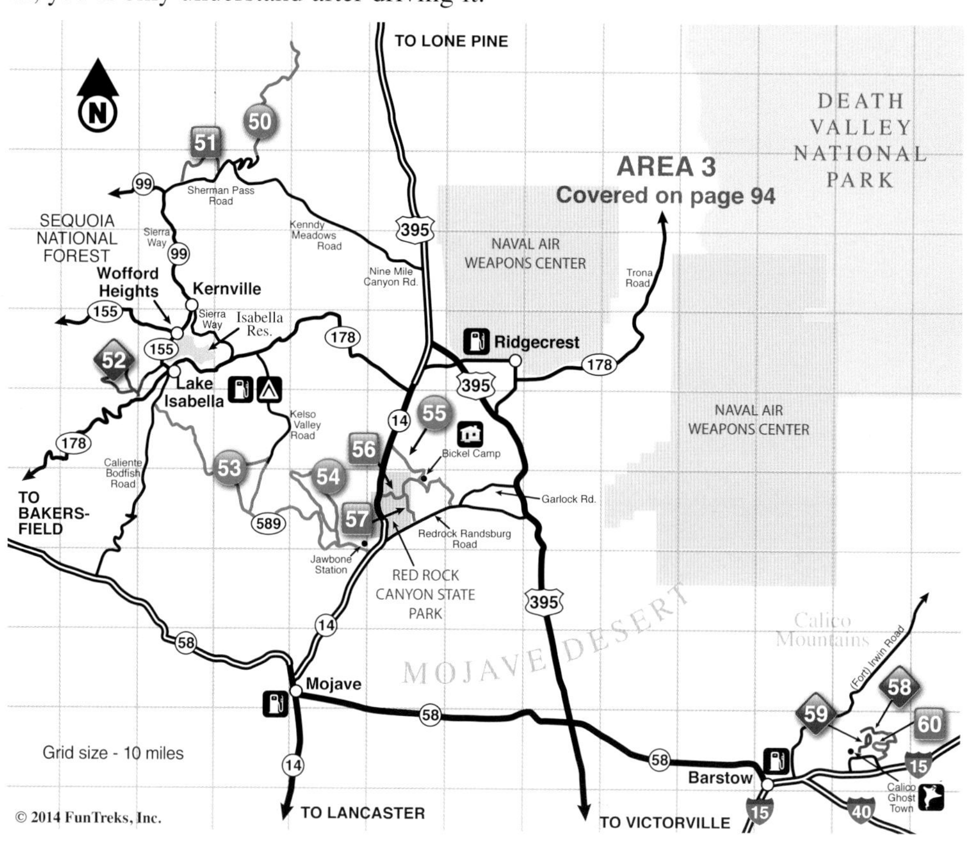

Odessa-Doran Loop, Trail #59, rated difficult. Hard to believe this was once a paved road.

50 Monache Meadows

AREA 4 map on page 122

Start of trail is well marked.

Highest point of trail is before first half mile.

Monache Meadow is surrounded by wilderness.

Deeper river crossing at end of trail is optional.

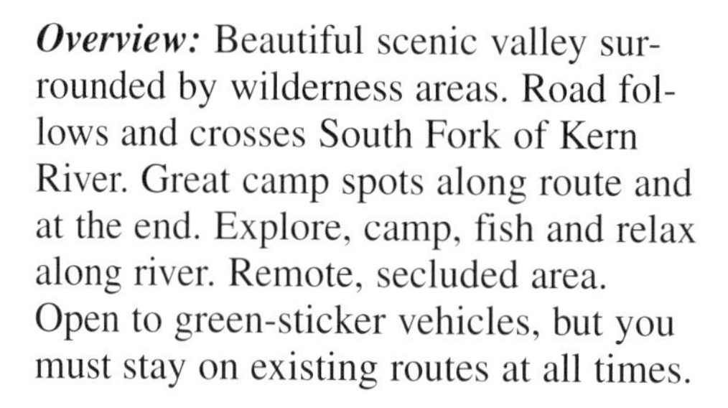

Overview: Beautiful scenic valley surrounded by wilderness areas. Road follows and crosses South Fork of Kern River. Great camp spots along route and at the end. Explore, camp, fish and relax along river. Remote, secluded area. Open to green-sticker vehicles, but you must stay on existing routes at all times.

Rating: Easy: A few small hills and mildly rocky in places. Sandy whoop-ti-dos crossing Monache Meadows. River crossings usually shallow, but may be deeper in the spring. Suitable for high-clearance stock SUVs. Four-wheel drive is recommended but is not always necessary if you stay on main route.

Stats: Length: 9.1 miles one way. Time: 3-4 hours round trip. Elevation: 7,831 to 8,576 ft. Best time: May-September.

Current Conditions: Most of the trail is in Inyo N.F., Mount Whitney Ranger District. Call (760) 876-6200.

Getting There: From Kernville, take Sierra Way north about 20 miles and turn right on Sherman Pass Road. Go another 32 miles following signs to Black Rock Work Station. Continue north 3.5 miles on 21S03 and turn right on 21S36. Go another 3.6 miles and turn left on dirt road 34E38. Trailhead is on left in another mile.

START *MILEAGE LOG:*

0.0 Zero trip odometer **[Rev. Miles]**
Continue north on Forest Road 34E38. **[9.1]**
01 N36 09.740 W118 13.958

0.5 Pass Blackrock single-track trail 34E26. **[8.6]**

1.6 Trail curves right past camp spots. **[7.5]**

1.7 Driver's choice. Toughest part of trail. **[7.4]**

1.8 Granite Knob single-track trail on right. **[7.3]**

2.3 Enter Inyo N.F., cross Snake Creek bridge and swing right. **[6.8]**

2.5 Enter open area. This is Monache Meadows. **[6.6]**

3.3 Sandy trail has a few whoop-ti-dos. **[5.8]**

5.1 Stay left. Two-track trail on right goes down closer to river. **[4.0]**

5.7 Sign says Overflow Camping to left. **[3.4]**

5.9 Sign marks area as National Wild and Scenic Rivers System. **[3.2]**

6.0 Road swings right then left past camp spot at closed road. **[3.1]**

6.1 Continue north. Road that joins on right crosses river to other side of meadow. **[3.0]**
02 N36 12.522 W118 10.578

7.0 Continue straight then curve left. Road to right crosses river to other side of meadow. **[2.1]**
03 N36 13.274 W118 10.690

7.7 Turn right and continue north. West crosses large, flat sandy area. **[1.4]**

8.8 Enter area of dispersed campsites. **[0.3]**

8.9 Fun river crossing through wooded section. **[0.2]**

9.1 Trail ends at campsites with primitive toilet. **[0.0]**
04 N36 14.350 W118 11.258
Return the way you came. Explore other roads you passed earlier. All end at wilderness boundary.

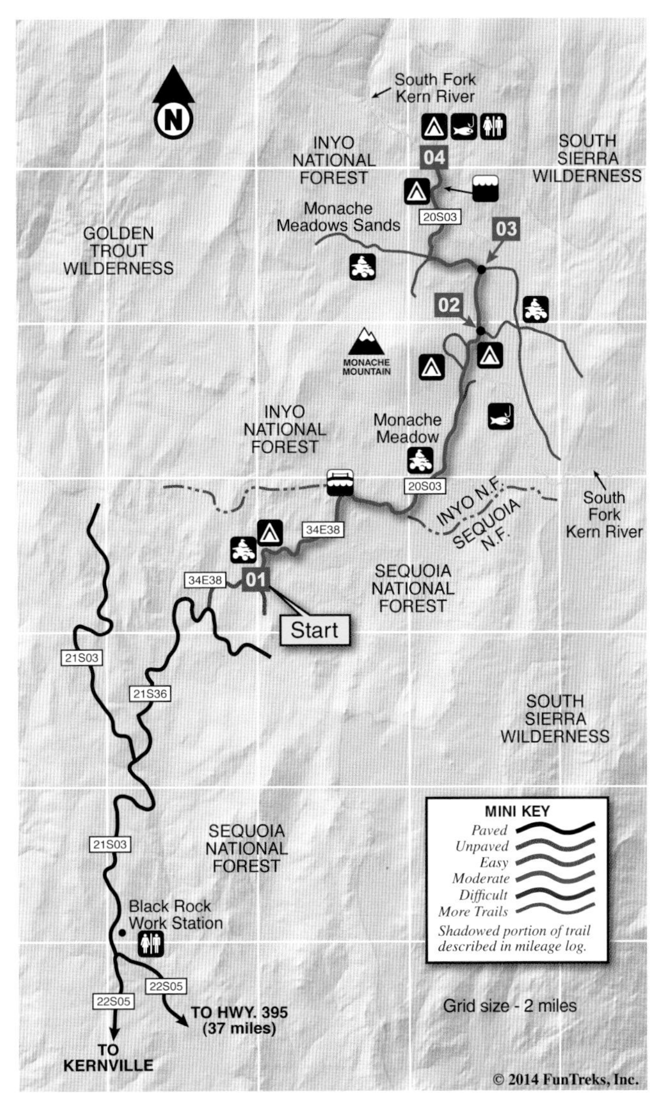

Special river designation.

One of many great camp spots along the route.

51 Sherman Pass 4x4 Trail

AREA 4 map on page 122

Summit of Sherman Peak is just short of 10,000 feet. Walk around for great views.

Fire-damaged west side looks like this today.

Trail is steep and rocky in a few spots.

Historical Highlight: *The western half of this trail was destroyed by the huge McNally Fire in the summer of 2002. For the first edition of this book, we drove the route with the Bakersfield Trailblazers the following year along with a ranger from the Sequoia National Forest. They assessed damage and repaired what they could. The Trailblazers and Ridgecrest Gear Grinders have continued to maintain the trail since then. As a result of improvements, we have upgraded the trail's rating from difficult to moderate.*

Overview: Trail climbs to the top of Sherman Peak just below 10,000 ft. Many legal side roads for green-sticker ATVs on the west end. More single-track trails for dirt bikes on the east end. Helmets required. Great camp spots along the route including several at popular Bonita Meadows. Wildflowers in abundance after spring runoff.

Rating: Moderate: Steep and narrow in spots with possible muddy sections. Burned trees may fall across the road blocking the trail. No major obstacles. Suitable for aggressive, high-clearance stock SUVs with experienced driver.

Stats: Length: 16.2 miles as described. Time: 3-5 hours. Elevation: 6,606 to 9,843 ft. Best time: June-mid October.

Current Conditions: Sequoia N.F. Kern River R.D. Call (760) 376-3781.

Getting There: From Kernville, head north about 20 miles on scenic Sierra Way, Highway 99. Turn right on paved Sherman Pass Road. Go east another 8.2 miles to well-marked Sherman Pass 4x4 Trail on left.

START MILEAGE LOG:

0.0 Zero trip odometer **[Rev. Miles]**
Head north uphill through burn area on steep, narrow road marked 33E48. Small area to park. **[16.2]**
01 N35 59.248 W118 24.853

2.4 Creek crossing. **[13.8]**

3.2 Turn right to take side trip to Sherman Peak. **[13.0]**
02 N36 01.160 W118 24.174

4.0 Bear left uphill. **[12.2]**

4.9 Turn around at top, marked by cell tower and shed. Views. **[11.3]**
03 N36 00.610 W118 23.427

6.6 Return to Waypoint 02 and turn right. You leave burn area behind. **[9.6]**

6.7 Driver's choice. We went right down steep rocky hill. **[9.5]**

6.9 Bear right downhill at "T." Alternate route rejoins on left. **[9.3]**

7.8 Boggy section. **[8.4]**

9.8 Turn left past corral. **[6.4]**
04 N36 01.767 W118 22.090

9.9 Go past dirt bike trail 33E28, camp spot. **[6.3]**

10.0 Stay left on 33E48. **[6.2]**

12.1 Stay left. **[4.1]**

12.8 At "T," bear right on better road. **[3.4]**
05 N36 03.047 W118 20.796

13.9 Follow road around curve to right, where dirt bike trail 21S57 goes left. **[2.3]**

14.8 Popular area to camp at Bonita Meadows. Signs say no green-sticker vehicles south of this point. **[1.4]**

16.2 Return to paved Sherman Pass Road. **[0.0]**
06 N36 01.376 W118 19.170
Right returns to start. Left goes to Black Rock Station and Monache Meadows, Trail #50.

Trail updates & GPS downloads at www.funtreks.com

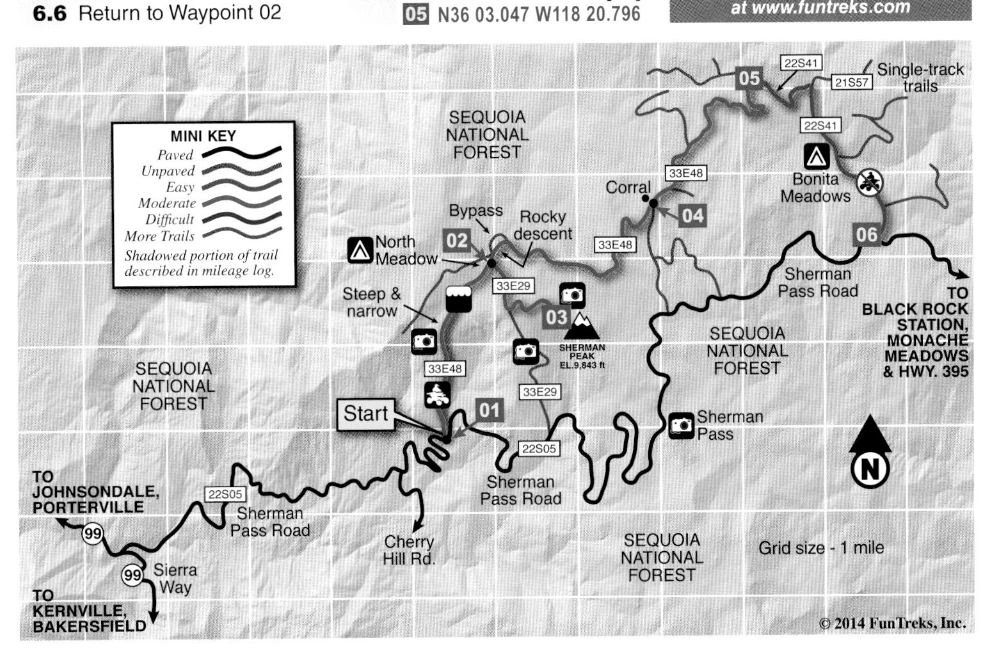

Bakersfield 4x4 club clears giant sequoia that blocked trail in 2003.

Typical damage in 2003.

52 Freeway Ridge, Black Gulch Trail

AREA 4 map on page 122

Coming up Freeway Ridge.

Driver's choice on 32E58. This is the easier side.

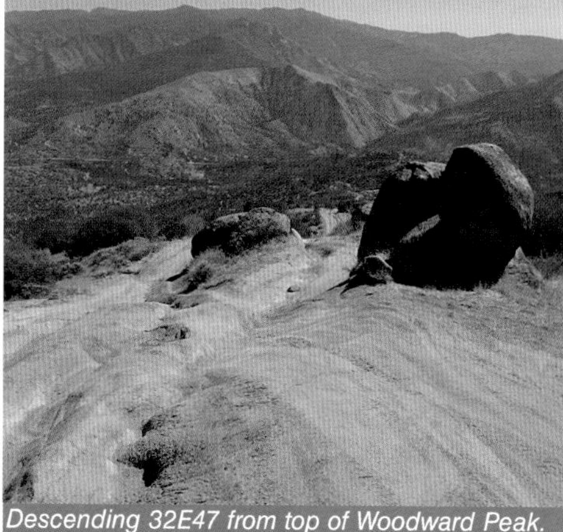

Descending 32E47 from top of Woodward Peak.

Steep and tippy in places coming down 32E47.

Historical Highlight: *Keyesville is named after Richard Keyes, who discovered gold here in 1853 and set off a major gold rush along the Kern River. The town had about 60 permanent residents. Structures included 8 houses, a saloon, a small hotel and an earthen fort for protection against Indian attacks.*

Overview: Trail circles around and climbs 4,000 feet to the top of 6,500-ft. Woodward Peak. This once active mining area features high views of Isabella Lake as you descend from top. Recommend you obtain MVUM to see all the roads in the area. For maximum challenge, we approach trail from the south side via Freeway Ridge. Lots of camping and side roads to explore for green-sticker vehicles north of Keyesville Road on BLM land.

Rating: Difficult: Steep, rutted climb up Freeway Ridge at the start. Long, steep descent down 32E47. Deep ruts are very tippy in spots. High clearance and at least one locker recommended. Experienced drivers only.

Stats: Length: 23.5 miles. Time: About 5 hours. Elevation: 2,486 to 6,490 ft. Upper roads open April 15 to Dec. 31. Hot in summer at lower elevations.

Current Conditions: Sequoia N.F., Kern River R.D. (760) 379-5646. BLM Bakersfield F.O. (661) 391-6000.

Getting There: From Hwys. 155 and 178 south of Isabella Lake, drive south 6 miles on Hwy. 178. Turn right at trailhead just before mile marker 37. If coming north on 178 from Bakersfield, you can't legally turn left at trailhead. Go to next exit and circle back.

START **MILEAGE LOG:**

0.0 Zero trip odometer **[Rev. Miles]**
Close gate and head uphill on steep, rutted Forest Road 31E77. **[9.9]**
01 N35 34.917 W118 33.275

1.8 Bear left on Black Gulch Trail 32E58. You'll return to this point later. **[8.1]**
02 N35 35.572 W118 32.931

2.7 Stay left where 32E47 goes right. **[7.2]**
03 N35 36.004 W118 33.566

4.1 Driver's choice. **[5.8]**

4.7 Continue straight. (Road soon crosses private land. Can be bypassed on right via 32E48, 32E65 and 27S13. See map.) **[5.2]**

5.3 Stay right on 26S06. **[4.6]**

5.6 Go past Jack's Cabin. Private, keep out. **[4.3]**

6.6 Stay left. **[3.3]**

6.7 Continue straight where 27S13 joins on right. **[3.2]**

6.9 Turn right on wide, easy Rancheria Road **[3.0]**
04 N35 36.999 W118 36.999

9.9 Turn right at sign for Evans Flat C.G. **[0.0]**
05 N35 38.628 W118 35.534

0.0 Zero trip odometer at Wpt. 05.
Follow road 26S27 thru campground. **[5.5]**

0.3 Continue straight where 32E30 goes left. **[5.2]**

0.7 Bear left on 32E47 where 32E53 goes right. **[4.8]**
06 N35 38.474 W118 34.985

0.8 Stay right. **[4.7]**

1.2 Stay right where 32E42 goes left. This begins long difficult descent. **[4.3]**

1.5 Driver's choice at difficult steep, rutted spot. **[4.0]**

2.2 Stay left past unmarked road on right. **[3.3]**

2.6 Continue straight past 32E48 on right. **[2.9]**

4.6 Return to Waypoint 03. Turn left on 32E58. **[0.9]**

5.5 Return to Wpt. 02. **[0.0]**

0.0 Zero trip odometer at Wpt. 02.
Make hard left staying on 32E58. **[8.1]**

1.8 Continue straight as road gets easier. This is the official start of Black Gulch Trail that you've just completed. **[6.3]**

3.8 Stay left. Right is Black Gulch North Trail. **[4.3]**
07 N35 36.985 W118 31.472

4.8 Stay on best-traveled road. **[3.3]**

6.2 Road swings right past historical marker for Keyesville Townsite. **[1.9]**
08 N35 37.575 W118 30.642

6.3 Stay left and follow paved Keyesville Rd. Camping and OHV trails on both sides of road. **[1.8]**

7.2 Pearl Harbor Road on right. From this point on, no motorized vehicles are allowed on south side of Keyesville Road. **[0.9]**

7.4 Parking, toilets on right for mountain bike park. **[0.7]**

8.1 Highway 155 just south of Isabella Lake. **[0.0]**
09 N35 38.464 W118 29.035
See map for nearby places to visit, including visitor center.

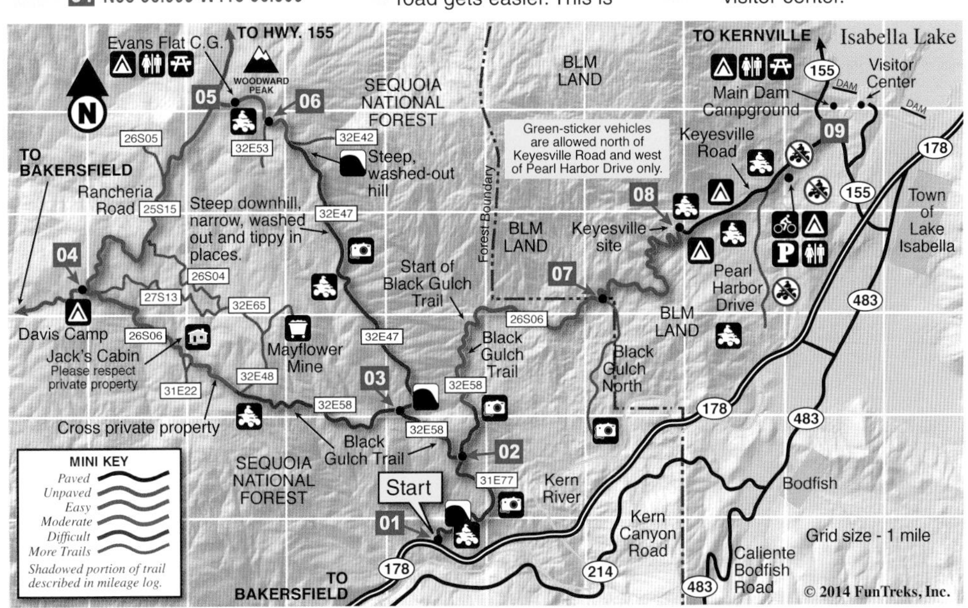

You'll pass through Evans Flat Campground on 26S27.

Keyesville historical marker.

53 Jawbone to Lake Isabella

AREA 4 map on page 122

Eastern half of trail crosses high desert. Make sure you have plenty of gas and drinking water.

Jawbone Station and Visitor Center.

Road is steep and narrow as it climbs into forest.

Keep your eyes peeled for this old chip burner.

Historical Highlight: *The rusty teepee-like structure you encounter on this trip was used to burn mill waste for a saw mill located nearby. At one time you could find these odd structures all over California. The Clear Air Act 1970 did away with their use and by 1980 all were shut down. Please respect the structure and take only pictures.*

Overview: Long scenic route crosses sprawling high desert from Jawbone OHV Area, climbs above 8,000 feet across the Piute Mountain Range inside Sequoia National Forest, then descends quickly to Lake Isabella. Vast areas of dispersed camping with open riding around Jawbone Station. No green-sticker vehicles allowed on Jawbone Canyon Road. Although Forest Road 27S02 is open to green-sticker vehicles, we don't recommend riding here.

Rating: Easy: We found the road well graded the entire way, but be prepared for ruts and washed-out sections on steep grades. Winter snows may close the road for brief periods at higher elevations. Mud possible in spring.

Stats: Length: Almost 49 miles. Time: 4 to 5 hours. Elevation: 2,593 to 8,213 ft. Open all year except when closed by snow. Jawbone OHV hot in summer.

Current Conditions: Jawbone Station Visitor Center, (760) 373-1146. Sequoia N.F., Kern River R.D. (760) 379-5646

Getting There: From town of Mojave, take Hwy. 14 northeast about 19 miles and turn left on Jawbone Canyon Rd. Continue west 4.9 miles to SC176 on right just before distinctive Blue Point.

START *MILEAGE LOG:*

0.0 Zero trip odometer [Rev. Miles]
Head west on paved Jawbone Cyn. Rd. [13.6]
01 N35 19.015 W118 04.551

1.5 Follow Jawbone Canyon Road to right as it changes to dirt. [12.1]

2.9 Road turns uphill to right and heads north along ridge. [10.7]

6.5 Cross wash and bear left staying on wide Jawbone Canyon Road. (On right is SC251, Trail #54 described pg. 132.) [7.1]

7.0 Bear left. Head west away from OHV Area. [6.6]
02 N35 22.359 W118 07.005

10.2 Descend from high ridge south of Butterbredt Peak. Views to west. [3.4]

13.2 Continue straight. Right cuts over to Kelso Valley Road. [0.4]

13.6 Arrive at Kelso Valley Road (marked Kelso Way). [0.0]
03 N35 22.666 W118 13.006

0.0 Zero trip odometer at Wpt. 03.
Continue west on Jawbone Canyon Road, County Road 589. [13.0]

6.4 Road enters Sequoia N.F. as it climbs series of steep switchbacks. [6.6]

7.8 Bear right. [5.2]

9.9 Stay right on 589. Left is forest road 29S02. [3.1]

10.9 Rusty teepee-like structure on left is chip burner from old sawmill. [2.1]

13.0 Intersect Piute Mountain Road, C.R. 501. [0.0]
04 N35 26.632 W118 19.566

0.0 Zero trip odometer at Wpt. 04.
Bear left on 501. [21.9]

0.6 Bear left where Ferrell Lane goes right. [21.3]

1.9 Stay on wide Piute Mtn. Road (second left). Right on 28S27 goes to French Meadow. [20.0]

5.6 High point, views. [16.3]

5.7 Bear right uphill on Saddle Spring Road 27S02. [16.2]
05 N35 26.884 W118 22.701

7.1 Stay right uphill. [14.8]

10.6 Stay right. [11.3]

11.7 Stay right as you go past Saddle Sprg. C.G. [10.2]
06 N35 31.254 W118 24.735

11.8 Stay left on 27S02. [10.1]

16.7 Descend switchbacks through burn area. [5.2]

21.9 At bottom, intersect paved Caliente Bodfish Road, County Road 483. [0.0]
07 N35 34.106 W118 30.409
Bear right on 483 to Bodfish and Lake Isabella, where you can connect to Hwy. 178 to Bakersfield.

Trail updates & GPS downloads at www.funtreks.com

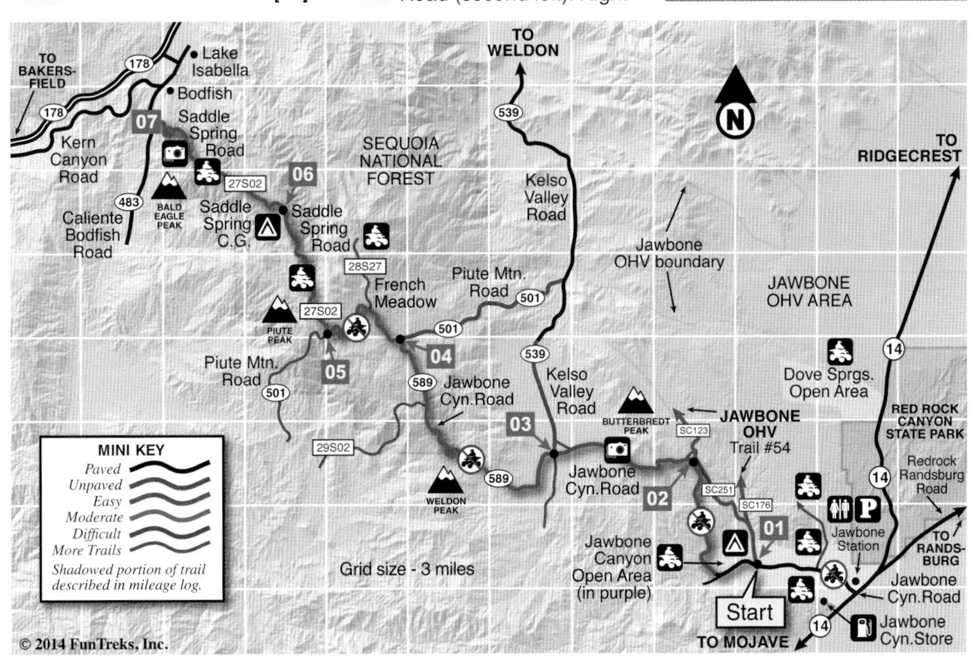

Great road for stock SUVs.

Switchbacks as you descend to Lake Isabella.

54 Jawbone OHV Area

AREA 4 map on page 122

You'll climb to an elevation over 5,600 feet as you cross the south slope of Gold Peak.

Easy, winding road is fun to drive.

Joshua trees are plentiful in Butterbredt Canyon.

To learn more about this incredible area and how you can help keep it open, contact "Friends of Jawbone" at (760) 373-1146 or go to www.jawbone.org.

Overview: The start of this route offers open riding with free camping and vault toilets. You'll head north staying on numbered roads inside Jawbone OHV area. The route climbs over 3,000 feet and traverses the southern slope of 5,950-ft. Gold Peak. You'll see abundant Joshua trees and enjoy high desert views. Stop at Jawbone Station for a detailed map of the area.

Rating: Easy: Soft sand and one steep hill climb. Any stock SUV with 4-wheel drive and moderate clearance can handle this trail. Take plenty of water.

Stats: Length: Loop measures 27.6 miles. Time: About 3 hours. Elevation: 2,582 to 5,674 ft. Open all year. Hot in summer.

Current Conditions: Jawbone Station Visitor Center, (760) 373-1146.

Getting There: From town of Mojave, take Highway 14 northeast about 19 miles and turn left on paved Jawbone Canyon Road following sign to Jawbone Station. Continue west 4.9 miles to SC176 on right just before distinctive Blue Point.

START *MILEAGE LOG:*

0.0 Zero trip odometer **[Rev. Miles]** Head north on wide SC176. Sandy road crosses wide wash. **[27.6]**
01 N35 19.015 W118 04.551

0.1 Continue straight. Left goes to flat R.V. camping area. **[27.5]**

0.3 Continue north. Vault toilet and flat camping area on left. Note white arrows on brown posts point to camp spots. **[27.3]**

1.0 Bear left on lesser SC251. This starts loop. You'll return here later. **[26.6]**
02 N35 19.882 W118 04.638

1.4 Scenic camp spots in rock formations. **[26.2]**

4.7 Stay right on SC251 which runs parallel to wider Jawbone Canyon Road, Trail #53. **[22.9]**

5.3 Stay right on SC123 away from Jawbone Canyon Road. **[22.3]**
03 N35 22.359 W118 07.005

6.2 Follow road left as it passes Butterbredt Springs & Wildlife Sanctuary. After this point, you'll see more Joshua trees. **[21.4]**

12.3 Bear right on SC124, where SC123 goes straight. **[15.3]**
04 N35 26.689 W118 11.132

14.0 Crest of hill, views. **[13.6]**

15.0 Road descends along scenic ridge. **[12.6]**

16.2 Bear right at fenced intersection on SC176. **[11.4]**
05 N35 27.050 W118 08.047

20.1 Road twists through spot with large rocks. **[7.5]**

20.8 Road curves left up steep hill. You'll need 4-wheel drive here. **[6.8]**

21.1 Stay left. (Right on SC176 bypasses San Antonio Mine.) **[6.5]**

21.2 Bear right at clearing. Mine straight ahead. Everything is fenced off for safety. **[6.4]**
06 N35 24.058 W118 05.147

21.3 Continue straight (south) as you rejoin SC176. **[6.3]**

26.6 Continue straight as you return to Wpt. 02. **[1.0]**

27.6 Return to start. **[0.0]** Left returns to Hwy. 14. For gas, head south 0.4 miles on Highway 14 to Jawbone Canyon Store.

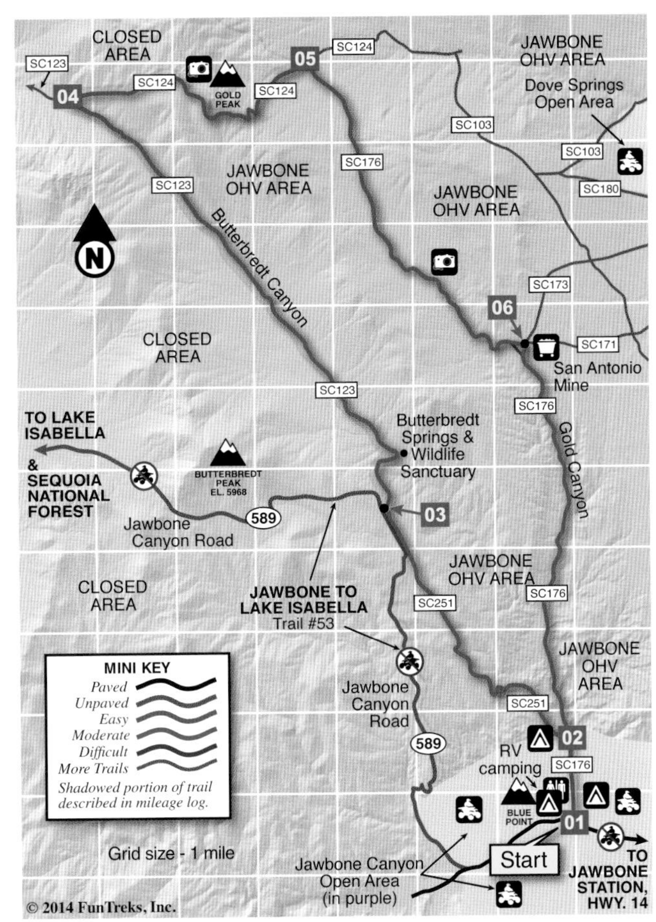

Final descent heading south through Gold Canyon.

Vault toilets near camping.

Great area for UTVs.

Bonanza Gulch

AREA 4 map on page 122

Holly Ash Cleanser Mine. Side trip before Wpt. 03.

Head north from Waypoint 03 on marked EP15A.

Miner's cabin on south end of Bonanza Gulch.

Route passes directly in front of post office.

Flag marks entrance to Bickel Camp.

Historical Highlight: *Everyone is welcome at Bickel Camp, where you can spend hours looking at a large collection of mining artifacts and memorabilia, accumulated over a lifetime by the late prospector, inventor and humanitarian Walter Bickel. The camp is staffed by volunteers who watch over the camp 24-7. Learn more at www.bickelcamp.org.*

Overview: Amazing desert trip includes stops at giant white caverns at the Holly Ash Cleanser Mine, historic Bonanza Gulch Post Office, several well-preserved miners' cabins, sprawling Bickel Camp, and Burro Schmidt Tunnel. Many more roads to explore. Green-sticker vehicles allowed, but stay on designated routes only. This is a BLM limited-use area. Take only pictures.

Rating: Easy: Much of route is easy wide sandy road. Steep, narrow and rough as you descend through Bonanza Gulch. Soft sand in washes. Suitable for stock, high-clearance SUVs. Follow directions carefully. Easy to get lost.

Stats: Length: 17.9 miles. Time: 4-5 hours. Elevation: 2,095 to 4,120 ft. Open all year. Avoid hot summer.

Current Conditions: BLM, Ridgecrest Field Office. Call (760) 384-5400.

Getting There: From Highway 14, at a point about 35 miles north of Mojave and 0.3 miles north of mile post 50, turn east on well-marked EP15. Look for large sign for Burro Schmidt Tunnel.

START *MILEAGE LOG:*

0.0 Zero trip odometer **[Rev. Miles]** Head southeast on EP15. Stay on this wide road ignoring side roads. **[4.8]**
01 N35 30.044 W117 56.932

0.9 Large flat area on right for staging, camping. **[3.9]**

1.7 Continue straight where Redrock-Inyokern Road crosses. **[3.1]**

3.6 Continue straight on EP15. Right goes to historic Cudahy Dutch Cleanser Mine. **[1.2]**
02 N35 27.501 W117 54.698

4.6 Main route continues straight on EP15. (Right on EP474 goes to interesting Holy Ash Cleanser Mine. Lots of confusing roads. You can cut over to Wpt. 03 after visiting the mine.) **[0.2]**

4.8 Stay left as you approach a large clearing. From here, head northeast on EP15(A) following sign for Bonanza Trail. Do not go south on EP15. **[0.0]**
03 N35 26.941 W117 53.694

0.0 Zero trip odometer at Wpt. 03

0.9 Descend steep, rocky hill. Note that trail is now marked EP15. **[2.2]**

1.0 Stay left on EP15. **[2.1]**

1.1 After stopping to see Bonanza Post Office, continue downhill on EP15 as it circles south along wash. This is Bonanza Gulch. **[2.0]**

1.4 Continue south. Left goes to Sears Cabin. **[1.7]**

1.6 Road in wash. **[1.5]**

1.8 Bear right out of wash to well-tended green cabin. Open for use if not occupied. EP15 continues south along wash. **[1.3]**

2.1 Another miner's cabin on right. **[1.0]**

2.5 Confusing spot where two large washes intersect. You're looking for EP30 which goes NE (left) to Bickel Camp. **[0.6]**

2.8 Arrive at Bickel Camp, then return to EP15. **[0.3]**

3.1 Look for sign for Schmidt Tunnel on south side of wash. **[0.0]**
04 N35 25.993 W117 53.443

0.0 Zero trip odometer at Wpt. 04
Head southeast on EP15 following sign to Schmidt Tunnel. **[10.0]**

0.1 Stay left on EP15. **[9.9]**

1.5 Stay right at metal drum on EP103. **[8.5]**
05 N35 25.201 W117 52.343

2.2 Turn right and go past ransacked Burro Schmidt cabins. **[7.8]**

2.4 Stop at parking area before tunnel. Then return to Waypoint 05. **[7.6]**

3.3 Bear right at Wpt. 05 and stay on well-marked EP15, ignoring many side roads. **[6.7]**

5.0 Continue straight where EP30 joins on left. **[5.0]**

5.7 EP15 goes both ways. Stay right. **[4.3]**

5.8 Intersect with EP100, Mesquite Canyon Road, and bear right. Follow this road south. **[4.2]**
06 N35 26.122 W117 50.408

6.4 Continue south where EP204 joins on right. **[3.6]**

8.6 Stay right downhill. Left uphill is alternate exit that goes to Garlock Ghost Town. **[1.4]**

10.0 Intersect paved Redrock Randsburg Road. **[0.0]**
07 N35 23.314 W117 49.020
Left goes to Randsburg. Right to Hwy. 14.

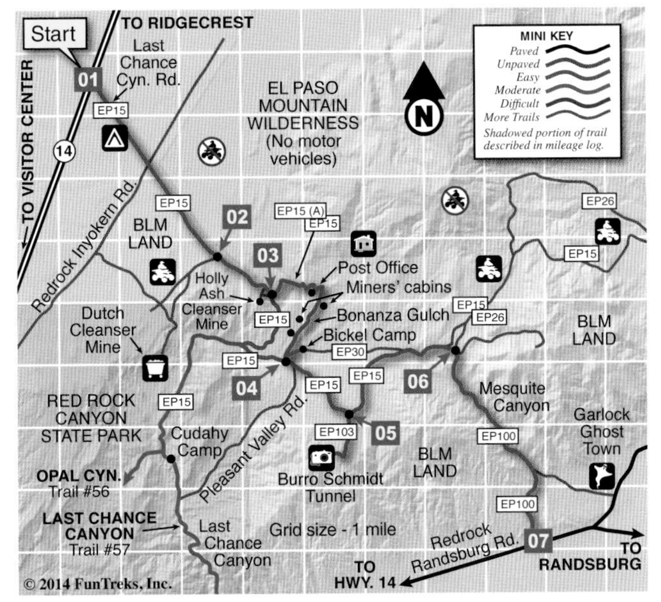

Just a small part of the artifacts on display at Bickel Camp.

Inside Walt Bickel's cabin.

Burro Schmidt Tunnel entrance.

56 Opal Canyon

AREA 4 map on page 122

Interesting terrain after Waypoint 06 as you near the bottom of Last Chance Canyon.

Steep, rough road descends after Waypoint 05.

Historical Highlights: *Cudahy Camp housed about 12 miners who worked the Dutch Cleanser Mine from about 1923 to 1947. Pumicite was extracted from the mine and used to make Old Dutch Cleanser, a kitchen and bathroom scouring powder still manufactured today (but from a different mine location). The Dutch Cleanser Mine is located about 2 miles north of the camp. Ore was brought down the mountain by tram and trucked down Last Chance Canyon to the Pacific Railroad at Saltdale.*

In the late 1990s, Barnett Opal Mine was open to the public for a fee. When owner Barnett died, the mine became part of the park in 2005. In 2012, the park removed the road to the mine due to illegal activities. Today the mine is permanently closed to all.

Overview: Fun desert route meanders through Red Rock Canyon State Park, then drops over 600 feet to historic Cudahy Camp in bottom of Last Chance Canyon. Great views of multicolored bluffs as you descend. Green-sticker vehicles are allowed in the park, but riders must have a driver's license. Limited-use area. Stay on designated roads only. No camping along route.

Rating: Moderate: First half is easy, but soft sand in the washes may require airing down. Moderate rating applies after Wpt. 05 where road is steep and rough. Aggressive stock SUVs with high ground clearance should manage fine.

Stats: Length: 5.7 miles one way. Time: 1½ to 2 hours. Elevation: 2,664 to 3,288 ft. Open all year but summers are very hot.

Current Conditions: Red Rock Canyon State Park. Call (661) 946-6092. Park itself has no direct number. This is general number for Mojave Sector Office.

Getting There: Take Highway 14 to mile marker 44 across from entrance to Dove Springs OHV Area. This is about 29 miles north of Mojave and 3.5 miles north of entrance to Red Rock Canyon State Park Ricardo Campground and Visitors Center.

START MILEAGE LOG:

0.0 Zero trip odometer **[Rev. Miles]**
From Hwy. 14, head east across cattle guard and follow dirt road north parallel to Hwy. 14. **[5.7]**
01 N35 24.831 W117 58.825

0.7 Turn right at "OPAL" sign. Also follow signs to Randsburg. **[5.0]**
02 N35 25.378 W117 58.604

1.3 Road enters wash where sand is soft. May need to air down. **[4.4]**

2.2 Follow road as it swings left around curve. Sign says "Opal Trail." **[3.5]**
03 N35 24.203 W117 57.978

2.9 Road climbs out of wash on right-hand side. **[2.8]**

3.2 Follow road as it curves around to right. Ignore several roads that go left here. **[2.5]**
04 N35 24.679 W117 57.338

3.5 Continue straight over crest of hill. Continue to follow Randsburg signs. **[2.2]**

3.8 No longer road on left that went to Barnett Opal Mine. **[1.9]**

3.9 Follow best-traveled road as other roads branch off and join. Correct road is marked with Randsburg signs. It curves left and climbs up to ridge. **[1.8]**
05 N35 24.445 W117 56.932

4.0 Come over crest of hill and start down rougher road on other side. Great view of multicolored bluffs below. **[1.7]**

4.6 Turn left at 3-way fork following Randsburg sign. Straight goes to Cudahy Camp, too, but is difficult and dangerous. (See map.) **[1.1]**
06 N35 24.229 W117 56.432

5.6 Stay left. Ignore roads on right that shortcut over to Cudahy Camp. **[0.1]**

5.7 Connect to wash in bottom of Last Chance Canyon. Cudahy Camp is right about 0.1 miles. Left follows EP15 to Burro Schmidt Tunnel and much more. (See Trail 57.) **[0.0]**
07 N35 24.727 W117 55.641

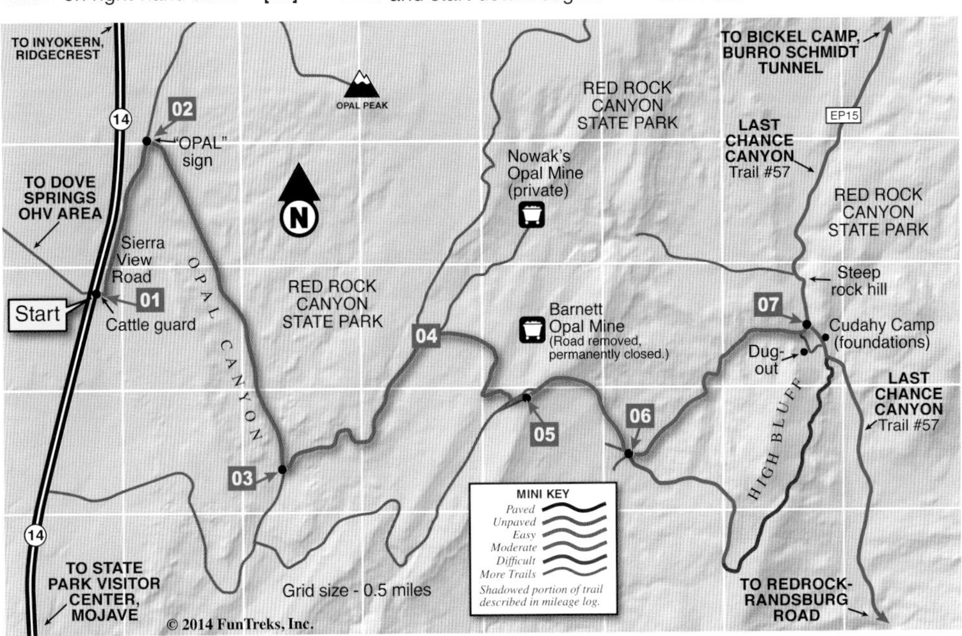

Dugout west of Cudahy Camp.

View of Cudahy Camp coming down difficult road to the south.

57 Last Chance Canyon

AREA 4 map on page 122

What we saw when we visited in 2002.

What we saw this time.

The V-slot. Wide vehicles can use bypass.

Rocky section south of Waypoint 02.

Steep spot just north of Waypoint 03.

Historical Highlight: *Dubbed the "human mole" by Time Magazine in the 1940s, William "Burro" Schmidt spent 38 years digging his half-mile-long tunnel. He operated it as a tourist attraction until his death in 1954. During our first visit in 2002, we met a 90-year-old woman, Tonie Seger, who was still living in the main cabin. Artifacts were everywhere. Today, nothing remains but bare cabins (see photos).*

Overview: This alternate way to Bickel Camp and Burro Schmidt Tunnel offers a bit more challenge than Bonanza Gulch, Trail #55. Towering red buttes surround the canyon as you pass through Cudahy Camp and continue north. Don't miss the interesting dugout west of the camp. Area is open to green-sticker vehicles but you must stay on designated routes at all times. No camping in Red Rock Canyon State Park.

Rating: Moderate: One spot, we call the V-slot, is very narrow and will challenge wider vehicles. A bypass is only slightly easier. Stock, high-clearance, 4x4 SUVs can manage this trail with an experienced driver. Be aware of the possibility of flash floods.

Stats: Length: 19.3 miles. Time: About 4 hours. Elevation: 1,988 to 4,120 ft. Open all year. Avoid hot summer.

Current Conditions: California State Parks, (661) 946-6092. BLM, Ridgecrest F. Office, (760) 384-5400.

Getting There: From Highway 14 about 21 miles north of Mojave, turn right (northeast) on Redrock-Randsburg Road and go 6 miles to wide dirt road on left. Look for signs after you turn. This point is 14.4 miles west of Randsburg.

START MILEAGE LOG:

0.0 Zero trip odometer **[Rev. Miles]** Head north on wide dirt road into Red Rock Canyon State Park. **[9.3]**
01 N35 21.701 W117 53.917

0.8 Continue straight down into wash where EP107 goes right. **[8.5]**

1.9 Canyon narrows and gets rocky. **[7.4]**

2.6 Pass through narrow V-Slot or take bypass on right. **[6.7]**

2.8 Trail gets easier, but will narrow again. **[6.5]**

3.2 Wash widens. Stay to right. **[6.1]**

3.7 Turn right out of wash, then make immediate left heading north along east side of wash. Pleasant Valley Road heads east from this point. **[5.6]**
02 N35 23.984 W117 55.402

4.4 Cross wash, then re-enter soon after. **[4.9]**

4.5 Turn right out of wash at red post and go through Cudahy Camp. Note dugout on west side of canyon (see photo on pg. 137 and below). **[4.8]**

4.7 Stay right in bottom of canyon. Opal Canyon, Trail #56, comes downhill on left. **[4.6]**
03 N35 24.727 W117 55.641

4.8 Trail blocked. Turn hard left and climb steep rock hill. **[4.5]**

4.9 Go over hill and drop down into wash on other side, then stay as far right as possible continuing north in wash. **[4.4]**

6.1 Look uphill to left. This is location of Cudahy Dutch Cleanser Mine, accessed from Trail #55. **[3.2]**

7.8 EP15 goes both ways. Stay right. Left is alternate route to Trail #55. **[1.5]**
04 N35 26.220 W117 54.227

8.2 Stay right on EP15. Ignore roads to left. **[1.1]**

8.7 Important intersection. Stay slight left on EP30 to see Bickel Camp. **[0.6]**
05 N35 25.991 W117 53.445

9.0 Visit Bickel Camp, then return to Wpt. 05. **[0.3]**

9.3 Back at Waypoint 05. **[0.0]**

0.0 Zero trip odometer at Wpt. 05. Make a hard left and continue southeast on EP15 following signs to Schmidt Tunnel. **[10.0]**

0.1 Stay left on EP15. Pleasant Valley Road goes right here. **[9.9]**

1.5 Stay right of metal drum on EP103 to reach Schmidt Tunnel. **[8.5]**
06 N35 25.195 W117 52.344

2.2 Turn right and go past ransacked Burro Schmidt cabins. **[7.8]**

2.4 Stop at parking area before tunnel. Then return to Waypoint 06. **[7.6]**

3.3 Bear right at Wpt. 06 and stay on well marked EP15, ignoring many side roads. **[6.7]**

5.0 Continue straight where EP30 joins on left. **[5.0]**

5.7 EP15 goes both ways. Stay right. **[4.3]**

5.9 Intersect with EP100, Mesquite Canyon Road, and bear right. Follow this road south. **[4.1]**
07 N35 26.115 W117 50.394

6.4 Continue south where EP204 joins on right. **[3.6]**

8.6 Stay right downhill. Left uphill is alternate exit that goes to Garlock Ghost Town. **[1.4]**

10.0 Intersect paved Redrock Randsburg Road. **[0.0]**
08 N35 23.314 W117 49.020
Left goes to Randsburg. Right to Hwy. 14.

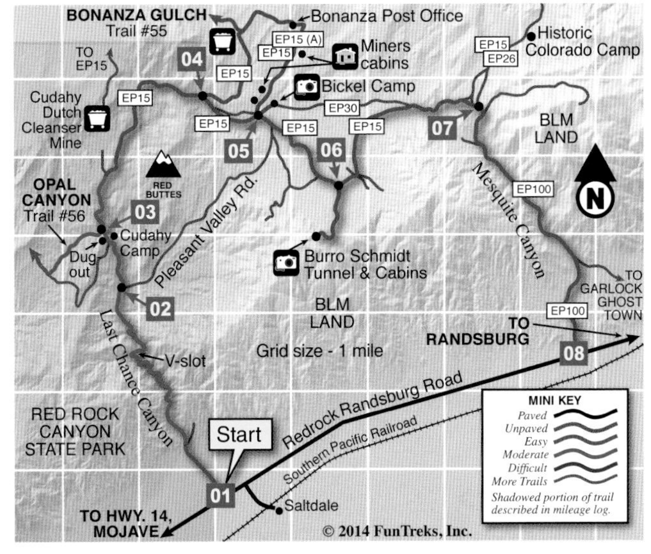

Parking area at entrance to Burro Schmidt Tunnel.

Dugout west of Cudahy Camp.

Lots to see at Bickel Camp.

58 Wall Street Canyon Overlook

AREA 4 map on page 122

This part of Mule Canyon is slippery when wet.

Exposed catacombs of Bismarck Mine.

UTVs head out to find the trails.

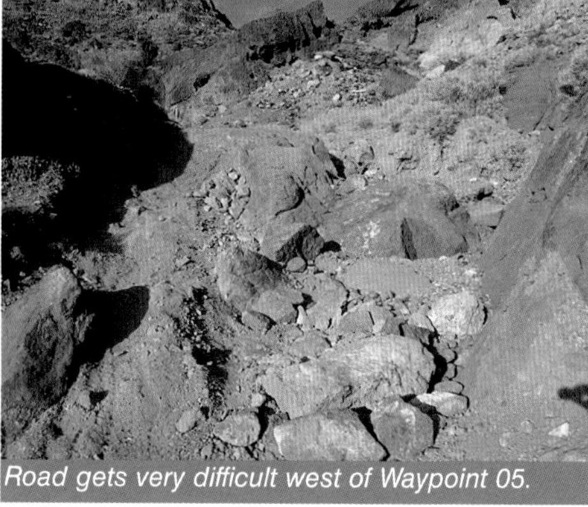

Road gets very difficult west of Waypoint 05.

Looking east from top of saddle.

Historical Highlight: *This area was one of the richest mining districts in California with over 500 mines. Bismarck Mine was one of the largest. The exposed catacombs at the mine are the result of modern-day strip mining over top of the original mine. To go to work, miners hiked up Wall Street Canyon from Calico and climbed 100-ft. ladders at the overlook.*

Overview: A rugged, fun drive through the heart of the Calico Mountains. Visit massive Bismarck Mine, then continue into narrow Wall Street Canyon. Trip ends at 100-ft.-high ledge above the lower end of the canyon. Great area for green-sticker vehicles with many miles of legal side roads to explore. Lots of dispersed camping along with nearby fee campgrounds.

Rating: Difficult: Most of this route is easy to moderate, but the last half mile is extremely difficult with large boulders and narrow passages. Most people will have to walk the last portion. Mule Canyon Road, in places, is extremely slippery when wet. Flash floods possible in narrow canyons.

Stats: Length: 9.6 miles one way. Time: Allow 3-4 hours for round trip. Elevation: 2,000 to 3,235 ft. Open all year. Extremely hot in summer.

Current Conditions: BLM, Barstow Field Office. Call (760) 252-6000.

Getting There: Exit I-15 at Calico Road near Yermo and head north about a mile to well-marked Mule Canyon Road on right. Drive in short distance to kiosk.

START **MILEAGE LOG:**

0.0 Zero trip odometer **[Rev. Miles]**
Head northeast on Mule Canyon Road, soon marked CM7630. **[8.4]**
01 N34 55.266 W116 50.928

0.6 Where 7600 joins on left, continue straight on 7630 in main wash as you enter Mule Canyon. **[7.8]**

1.5 Popular camp spot on right. **[6.9]**

1.6 Stay right past entrance to Phillips Loop, Trail #60, on left. **[6.8]**

2.0 Stay right on 7630. Phillips Loop exits left. **[6.4]**

2.5 Stay right uphill. **[5.9]**

3.1 Stay left downhill. **[5.3]**

3.3 Stay left. **[5.1]**

3.5 Continue straight where 7632A goes left. **[4.9]**

4.3 Hard left at big rock with arrow, "NEW CBH." **[4.1]**
02 N34 57.346 W116 48.537

4.4 Rusty cans of Tin Can Alley. **[4.0]**

4.5 Stay left on 7632. **[3.9]**

4.7 Stay left on 7632 where 7634 goes right. **[3.7]**

5.7 Continue straight where 7632A joins on left. **[2.7]**

6.6 Climb to top of saddle with small parking area. Hike to views. **[1.8]**

6.7 Driver's choice. Main route left. **[1.7]**

6.9 Stay right. **[1.5]**

7.1 Hard left on 7635. Right goes to Calico Peak, but may be gated. **[1.3]**

7.3 Turn right on 7631. Straight enters Odessa Canyon, Trail #59. **[1.1]**
03 N34 58.148 W116 50.881

7.5 Sweetwater Spring on right. Continue uphill on 7631. Avoid two roads that go right. **[0.9]**

8.0 At high point with views, bear right downhill towards mine below. **[0.4]**

8.1 Road gets steeper as you descend. **[0.3]**

8.3 Right goes to Wall Street Canyon Overlook, but continue south another 200 ft., then turn right to visit Bismarck Mine. **[0.1]**
04 N34 58.001 W116 51.530

8.4 Turn around at mine and return to Wpt. 04. (Unsafe to enter mine.) **[0.0]**

0.0 Zero trip odometer at Wpt. 04
At Waypoint 04 the second time, bear left (west) downhill and descend into canyon just north of mine. **[1.1]**

0.4 Stay left. Right connects to large network of confusing roads. **[0.7]**

0.7 Stay left. Trail becomes extremely difficult. Hardcore vehicles only, or park here and hike. **[0.4]**
05 N34 57.973 W116 52.026

0.9 Stay left downhill through narrow canyon. **[0.2]**

1.1 Small flat area to turn around. Dangerous cliff ahead with view into Wall Street Canyon. **[0.0]**
06 N34 57.745 W116 52.258
We recommend you return the way you came to avoid getting lost. However, left at previous intersection eventually connects to Fort Irwin Road. Much to see if you have someone who knows the way.

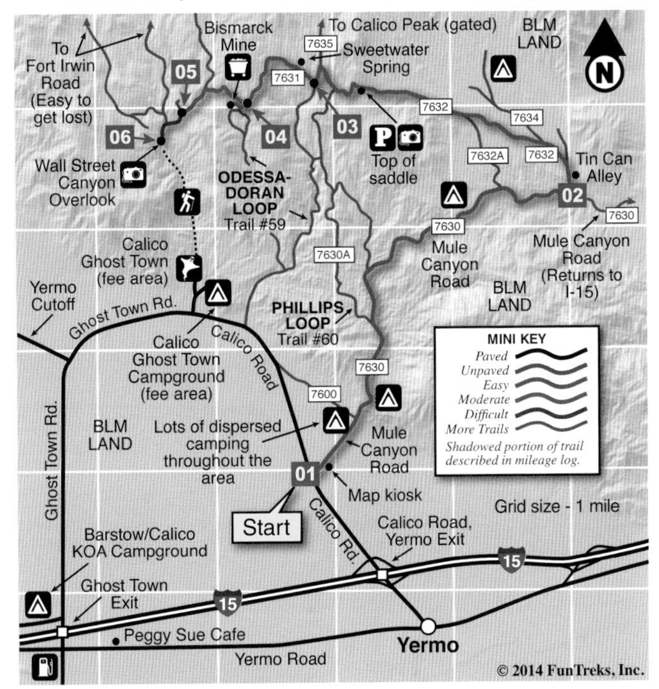

Calico Peak in distance.

View at end of trail.

59 Odessa-Doran Loop

AREA 4 map on page 122

Entrance to trail is wide with multiple roads.

Fun side trip on Mule Canyon Cut-Across Road.

Odessa Canyon is extremely narrow in spots.

Big ledge coming down Doran Canyon.

Historical Highlight: *The eroded paved portions of this trail are remnants of old Doran Scenic Drive, constructed in the 1930s and popular for about a decade. A few old signs remain and many maps, including Google Earth, still refer to this loop as Doran Scenic Drive.*

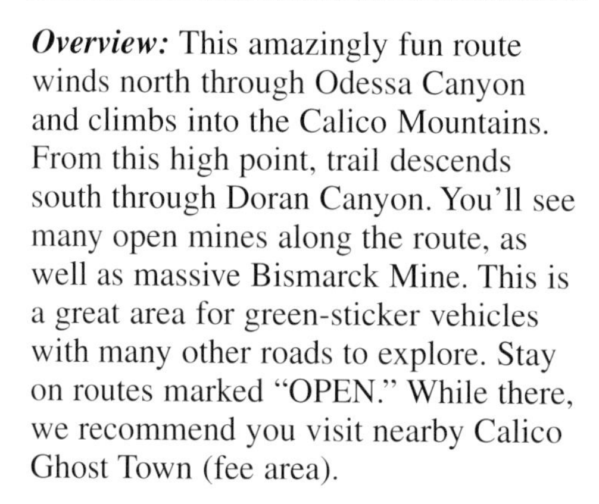

Overview: This amazingly fun route winds north through Odessa Canyon and climbs into the Calico Mountains. From this high point, trail descends south through Doran Canyon. You'll see many open mines along the route, as well as massive Bismarck Mine. This is a great area for green-sticker vehicles with many other roads to explore. Stay on routes marked "OPEN." While there, we recommend you visit nearby Calico Ghost Town (fee area).

Rating: Difficult: Large rocks with big ledges and steep drop-offs. Extremely narrow in places. Numerous side roads make route-finding challenging. To see extreme obstacle, go left at Wpt. 02.

Stats: Length: About 6 miles. Time: 3 to 4 hours. Elevation: 2,160 to 3,255 ft. Open all year. Summer extremely hot.

Current Conditions: BLM, Barstow Field Office. Call (760) 252-6000.

Getting There: Get off I-15 at Ghost Town Road and head north. After 3.5 miles, you'll go past entrance to Calico Ghost Town. Continue another half mile to start of trail on left, marked Doran Scenic Drive (later marked CM 7635).

START *MILEAGE LOG:*

0.0 Zero trip odometer **[Rev. Miles]** Head north in wide sandy wash CM7635. We stayed to the right. Lots of room to stage and camp. [2.7]
01 N34 56.392 W116 51.519

0.2 Road to left is exit route. Continue north. [2.5]

0.4 Continue straight. Note fun road on right that cuts across to Trail #60. [2.3]

0.6 Stay in canyon to right. Left goes to extreme obstacle. [2.1]
02 N34 56.778 W116 51.206

0.7 Canyon narrows with steep rock walls. [2.0]

0.8 Larger rocks and ledges with very tight spots to squeeze through. [1.9]

1.4 Difficult ledge. Very narrow. Trail continues to get tougher. [1.3]

1.9 Stay right. Lesser road on left goes uphill to mine adits. [0.8]

2.2 Continue north in bottom of canyon. Road joins on left, another goes uphill to right. Gets easier. [0.5]
03 N34 57.741 W116 51.050

2.3 Driver's choice. Left uphill is easier. [0.4]

2.6 Continue straight in canyon bottom. Road comes downhill on right. Canyon flattens out. [0.1]

2.7 Bear left on 7631. [0.0]
04 N34 58.149 W116 50.882

0.0 Reset odometer at Wpt. 04. [3.4]

0.2 Continue straight. Hiking trail on right goes to Sweetwater Spring. [3.2]

0.4 Bear left at fork. [3.0]

0.5 Stay left uphill. Lesser road to right. [2.9]

0.7 High saddle with view of Bismarck Mine below. Bear right and drop steeply downhill. [2.7]

1.0 Continue south on east side of Bismarck Mine. Right is Trail #58. [2.4]
05 N34 58.020 W116 51.514

1.1 Wide area. Stay slightly right downhill. Lots of confusing roads. [2.3]

1.2 Road curves south downhill. Stay left as roads branch to right. [2.2]

1.5 Drop south into Doran Canyon marked by series of big ledges. [1.9]

2.0 Alternate road down mountain joins on right, followed by major drop-off ledge (see photo). [1.4]

2.4 Stay right downhill in main canyon. Left exits. [1.0]

2.6 After a large pile of rocks in the middle of the trail, bear right uphill out of the canyon to avoid a major obstacle ahead. [0.8]

06 N34 56.978 W116 51.213

3.4 After following a ridge east of Calico Ghost Town Campground, you'll drop downhill back to the main canyon. Right returns to start. [0.0]

Note: Mileages may vary due to inconsistent GPS signals in the deep, narrow canyons.

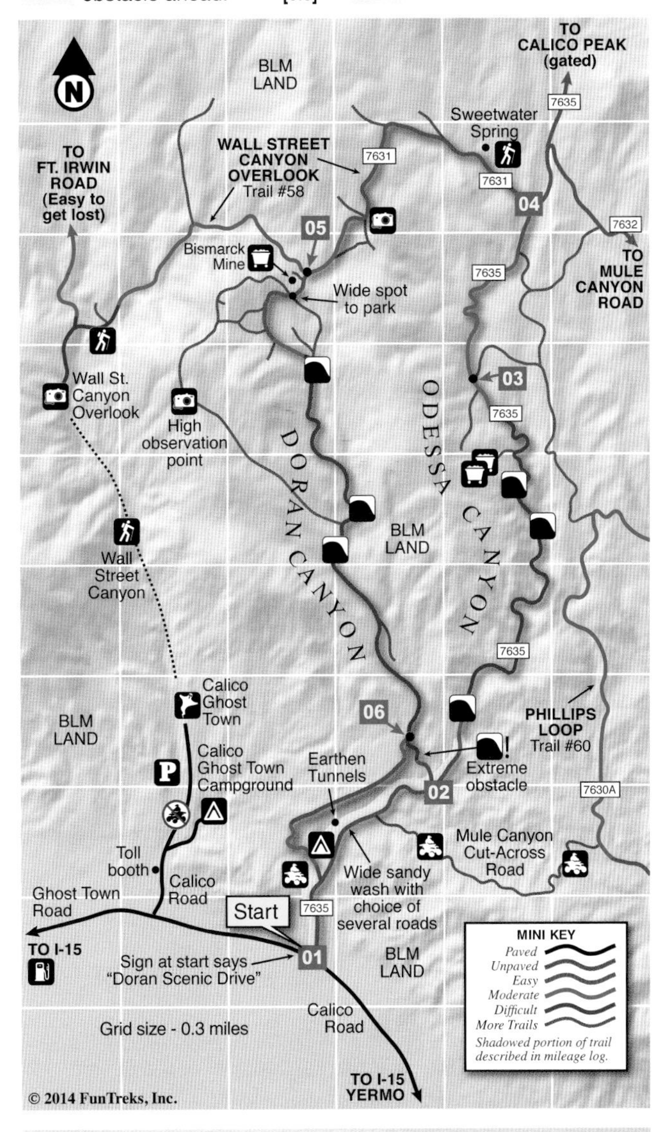

Looking down on Bismarck Mine from high saddle above Wpt. 05.

60 Phillips Loop

AREA 4 map on page 122

Leftover pavement from the 1930s.

Starting up the rocky shelf road.

This rock ledge is the toughest spot.

Short side trip to Kramer Arch at Waypoint 04.

Historical Highlight: *Like Doran Scenic Drive, Phillips Loop was also paved back in the 1930s and was a popular tourist destination for about 10 years. Today, what little pavement remains only serves as an obstacle to make the drive more challenging.*

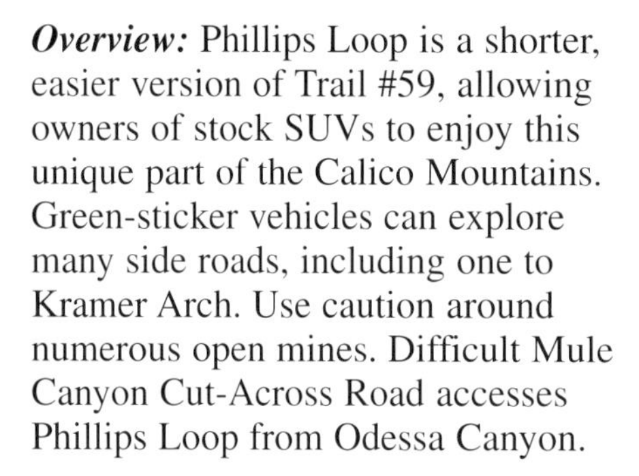

Overview: Phillips Loop is a shorter, easier version of Trail #59, allowing owners of stock SUVs to enjoy this unique part of the Calico Mountains. Green-sticker vehicles can explore many side roads, including one to Kramer Arch. Use caution around numerous open mines. Difficult Mule Canyon Cut-Across Road accesses Phillips Loop from Odessa Canyon.

Rating: Moderate: Much of the road is fairly easy. A section of narrow, rocky shelf road after the turn for Kramer Arch is more challenging. High-clearance stock SUVs can get through with experienced driver. Side roads are more difficult.

Stats: Length: 6.2 miles as described. Loop itself is just 2.6 miles. Cut-Across Road measures 1.7 miles. Time: About an hour. Elevation: 1,989 to 2,830 ft. Open all year. Very hot in summer.

Current Conditions: BLM, Barstow Field Office. Call (760) 252-6000.

Getting There: Exit I-15 at Calico Road near Yermo and head north about a mile to well-marked Mule Canyon Road on right. Drive in short distance to kiosk.

START MILEAGE LOG:

0.0 Zero trip odometer [Rev. Miles]
Head northeast on Mule Canyon Road 7630. [6.2]
01 N34 55.266 W116 50.927

0.6 Continue straight where Rd. 7600 joins on left. We saw motorhomes camped along 7600. [5.6]

1.6 After passing through Mule Canyon, another popular camping area, bear left in side wash to start Phillips Loop. [4.6]
02 N34 56.413 W116 50.372

2.0 Stay right and continue north on 7630A. On left is steep and hilly Mule Canyon Cut-Across Road that connects to Odessa Canyon, Trail #59. [4.2]
03 N34 56.628 W116 50.673

2.5 Bear left staying on 7630A. Right is shortcut to east side of Phillips Loop and goes past Kramer Arch. [3.7]
04 N34 57.001 W116 50.678

2.6 Climb rocky, narrow shelf road, the hardest part of trail. [3.6]

3.0 Stay right. Left goes steeply uphill to network of ATV roads. [3.2]

3.1 Stay right through area of many open mine shafts. Left connects to Odessa Canyon, Trail #59. [3.1]
05 N34 57.432 W116 50.690

3.4 Bear right downhill. [2.8]

3.7 Stay right at tire as you come down section of broken pavement. [2.5]

3.8 Continue straight. Road that joins on right is shortcut that comes from Kramer Arch. [2.4]
06 N34 57.030 W116 50.384

4.2 Rejoin Mule Canyon Road and continue south. (Hard left goes to Trail #58. [2.0]

4.6 **07** N34 56.738 W116 50.444
Back to Waypoint 02. Continue south to return to start. [1.6]

6.2 Return to start at Calico Road. [0.0]
Right at Calico Road goes to Calico Ghost Town. Left in about a mile goes to I-15 at Yermo.

Trail updates & GPS downloads at www.funtreks.com

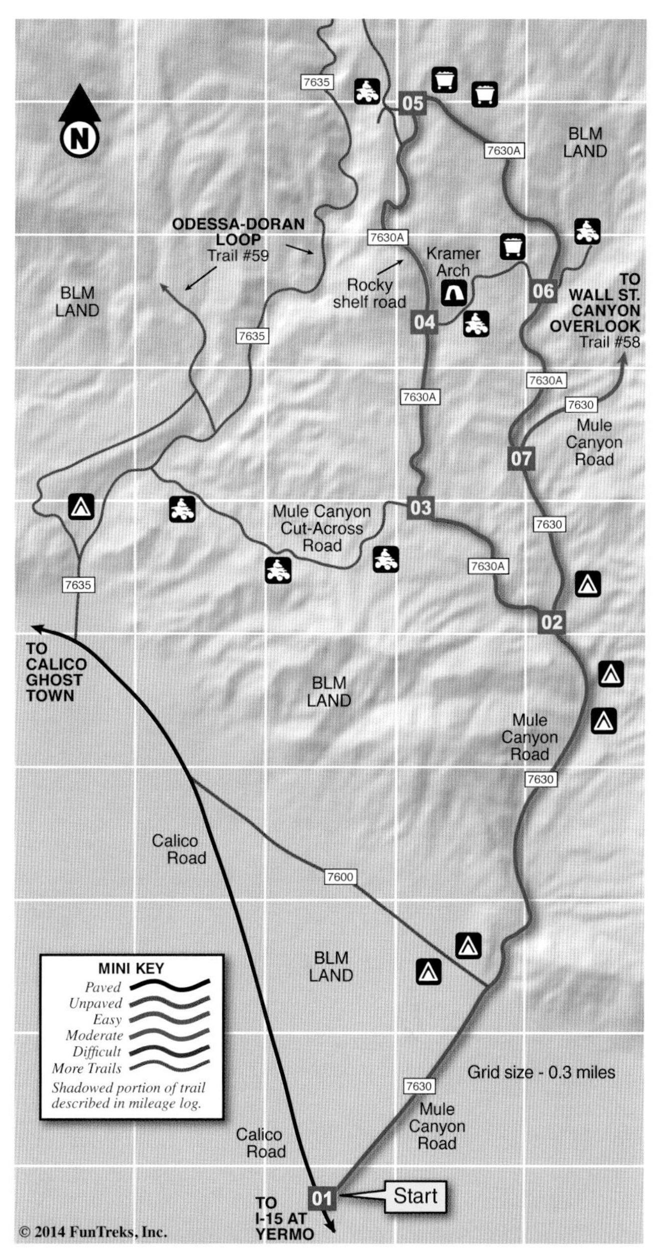

Cut-Across Road is very steep.

Much of trail is rough but easy.

Frazier Park, Santa Clarita, Big Bear, Lake Arrowhead

You don't have to drive far from the Los Angeles metropolitan area to find great 4-wheeling. Surrounding Big Bear and Arrowhead Lakes, just north of San Bernardino, is a network of trails adopted by local 4-wheel-drive clubs. They work in cooperation with the San Bernardino National Forest to maintain and keep trails open. These trails see heavy use so it's important to be a responsible 4-wheeler at all times. Difficult trails 69, 70 and 71 can be strung together and run in a single day, so they are a big draw for hard-core enthusiasts.

You can also head north on I-5 past Santa Clarita to two popular OHV areas, *Hungry Valley SVRA* and *Rowher OHV Area*. In each of these areas, we've picked out one trail that gives you a flavor for the terrain.

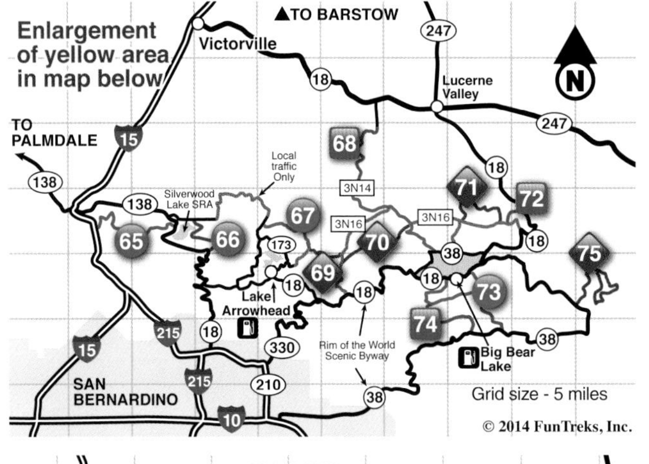

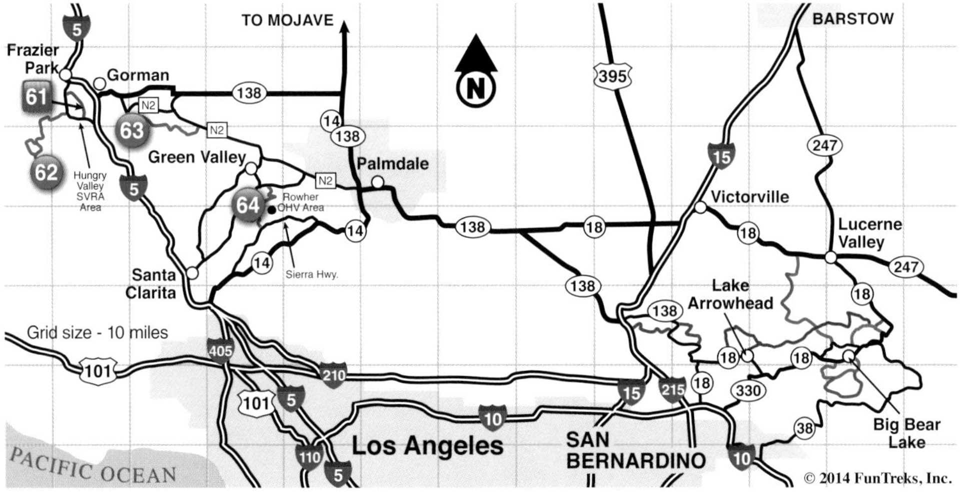

Hungry Valley, Trail #61, rated moderate (easy spot shown here). SVRA has over 130 miles of trails.

61

Hungry Valley SVRA

AREA 5 map on page 146

Start of Pronghorn Trail at Waypoint 02.

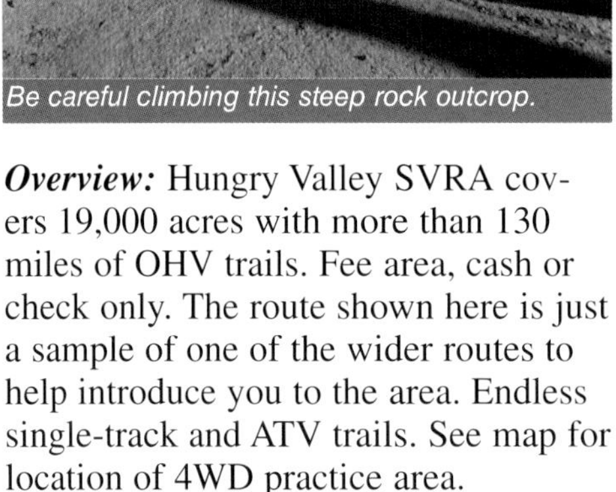

Be careful climbing this steep rock outcrop.

Entrance is well marked.

You'll begin Powerline Road here at Wpt. 03.

Overview: Hungry Valley SVRA covers 19,000 acres with more than 130 miles of OHV trails. Fee area, cash or check only. The route shown here is just a sample of one of the wider routes to help introduce you to the area. Endless single-track and ATV trails. See map for location of 4WD practice area.

Rating: Moderate: Powerline Road is easy. Pronghorn Trail is sandy, narrow and undulating in places with one steep, tippy climb over large rock outcrop. Short wheel-based vehicles best. We managed in our stock 4-door Rubicon.

Stats: Length: 12.5 miles this trail only. Time: 2-3 hours. Elevation: 3,051 to 4,506 ft. Best spring and fall. Park open all year, 24 hours a day, 7 days a week to green-sticker vehicles. Closed to red-sticker vehicles May 1 - Sept. 30.

Current Conditions: Hungry Valley District Office (661) 248-7007. Online: http://ohv.parks.ca.gov/hungryvalley.

Getting There: Get off Interstate 5 at Smokey Bear Exit and head west. Follow signs to Hungry Valley Road and continue west 2.8 miles to sign for Freeman Canyon on right. Starting point is one-half mile east of Lane Ranch Campground.

START MILEAGE LOG:

0.0 Zero trip odometer [Rev. Miles]
Head north on Lower Freeman Trail. [12.5]
01 N34 43.113 W118 50.277

0.4 Turn right on wide, straight Pipeline Rd. [12.1]

1.1 Pipeline Road bends right and heads S.E. [11.4]

1.4 Bear left on marked Pronghorn Trail. [11.1]
02 N34 43.099 W118 49.367

2.1 Continue straight past closed road on right. [10.4]

2.9 Road narrows and climbs steeply over large rock outcrop. Be very careful. Misplaced tire could result in tip-over. [9.6]

4.3 Continue north across paved road to Quail Canyon Special Events Area. Motocross track is also located here. [8.2]

4.7 Continue straight. Quail Pass Trail on left. [7.8]

5.9 Bear left uphill on sandy Powerline Road. [6.6]
03 N34 45.725 W118 48.705

6.0 Continue straight where Cow Trail goes right. [6.5]

6.2 Stay left. Right goes to overlook. [6.3]

6.9 After twisty climb, bear left at fork and follow along top of scenic ridge. All side roads end at overlooks. [5.6]

7.5 Follow Powerline Road as it curves left where Cow Trail crosses. [5.0]

8.0 Stay left where Wheatfield Trail joins on right. [4.5]

8.6 Follow main road as it curves right uphill past a road on left. Follow powerline downhill ignoring roads that head away from powerline. [3.9]

9.3 Powerline Road heads north away from powerline then returns. Many twists and turns along high ridge. [3.2]

11.2 Hard right turn reversing direction. Straight narrows to single-track. [1.3]

11.8 Stay right where Edison Trail goes left to massive single-track area. [0.7]

12.5 Intersect paved Gold Hill Road. [0.0]
04 N34 46.740 W118 52.876
Right goes to north gate. Left returns to start.

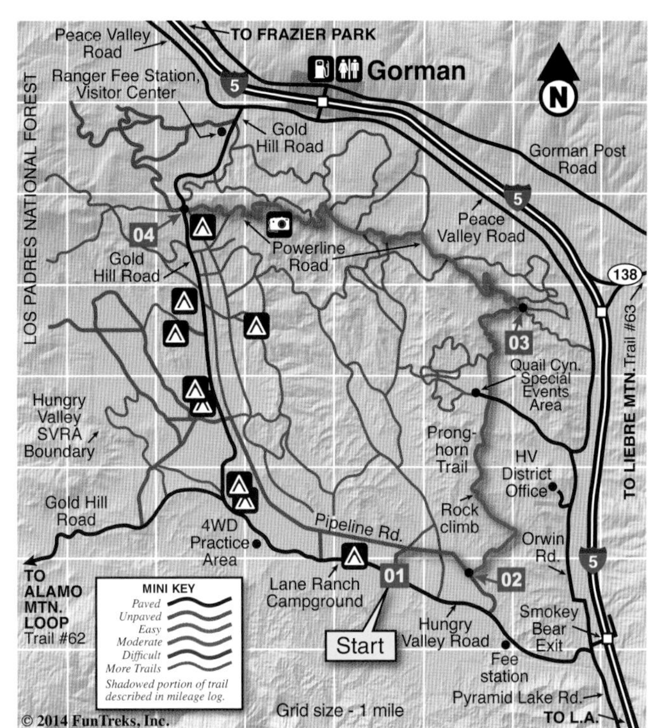

Many campgrounds adjacent to massive riding areas.

Much of Powerline Road follows along a high, scenic ridge.

62 Alamo Mountain Loop

AREA 5 map on page 146

Easy road climbs high into Los Padres National Forest. Much of area was burned in 2006.

Little Mutau Hiking Trailhead has vault toilet.

Great camp spot on side road. See map.

Historical Highlight: *Fire damage on this trail is the result of the Day Fire in 2006. The ninth largest fire in California history burned 162,700 acres. It started on Labor Day, September 4, and wasn't contained until October 13. The fire cost over $70 million and involved 4,600 fire fighters.*

Overview: A relaxing forest drive adjacent to Hungry Valley State Recreation Area. Escape the noise and dust for a little quiet time away from the crowds. Climb above 7,000 feet to cooler temperatures in the summer. Secluded camping. Two fun hiking trails into Sespe Wilderness. See how forest has recovered from devastating Day Fire in 2006. Green-sticker vehicles allowed after pavement ends 8 miles from start.

Rating: Easy: Two-wheel drive adequate for loop portion of route when dry. More steep and narrow approaching Sewart Mountain on Forest Road 6N10.

Stats: Length: Round trip returning to start 41.2 miles. Time: About 4 hours. Elevation: 3,543 to 7,028 ft. Trail open May 1 to November 1. Hot in summer.

Current Conditions: Los Padres N.F., Mt. Pinos R.D. Call (661) 245-3731.

Getting There: Get off Interstate 5 at Smokey Bear Exit and head west. Follow signs to Hungry Valley Road and continue west about 5 miles to Gold Hill Road. No fee is required if you are just passing through SVRA, but you must tell ranger. You can also reach start from Gorman Exit via Gold Hill Road.

START MILEAGE LOG:

0.0 Zero trip odometer [Rev. Miles]
Head west on paved Gold Hill Road. [23.0]
01 N34 43.876 W118 52.397

1.4 Enter Los Padres National Forest. [21.6]

5.2 Continue straight. Paved road on left goes to Kings Campground. [17.8]

5.9 Staging area on right accesses popular motorcycle trail 20W07. [17.1]

6.0 Paved water crossing over Piru Creek. [17.0]

6.2 Enter burn area. [16.8]

8.0 Pavement ends. [15.0]

10.8 High views. [12.2]

12.2 Continue straight. Left 0.2 miles goes to scenic camp spot and natural spring. [10.8]

12.3 Bear left to start loop around Alamo Mtn. [10.7]
02 N34 40.180 W118 56.929

13.9 Motorcycle trail 19W04 on left circles back to Kings Campground. [9.1]

15.5 Bear left to take side trip to Sewart Mtn. [7.5]
03 N34 39.044 W118 57.394

16.2 Little Mutau Hiking Trailhead on right. Road narrows along Sespe Wilderness. [6.8]

19.2 Trail ends at Buck Creek Hiking Trailhead. Turn around. [3.8]
04 N34 38.298 W118 55.197

23.0 Return to Wpt. 03 [0.0]

0.0 Zero trip odometer Wpt. 03
Continue straight around loop. [5.9]

2.8 Campground on left. [3.1]

3.3 Continue straight. Dutchman C.G. on left with toilet. (Left here connects to Lockwood/Miller Jeep Trail 20W06.) [2.6]

5.5 Continue straight. (Right goes to views and camping in 0.4 miles. Street-legal vehicles only.) [0.4]

5.9 Return to start of loop at Waypoint 02. Bear left and return the way you came. [0.0]

Trail updates & GPS downloads at www.funtreks.com

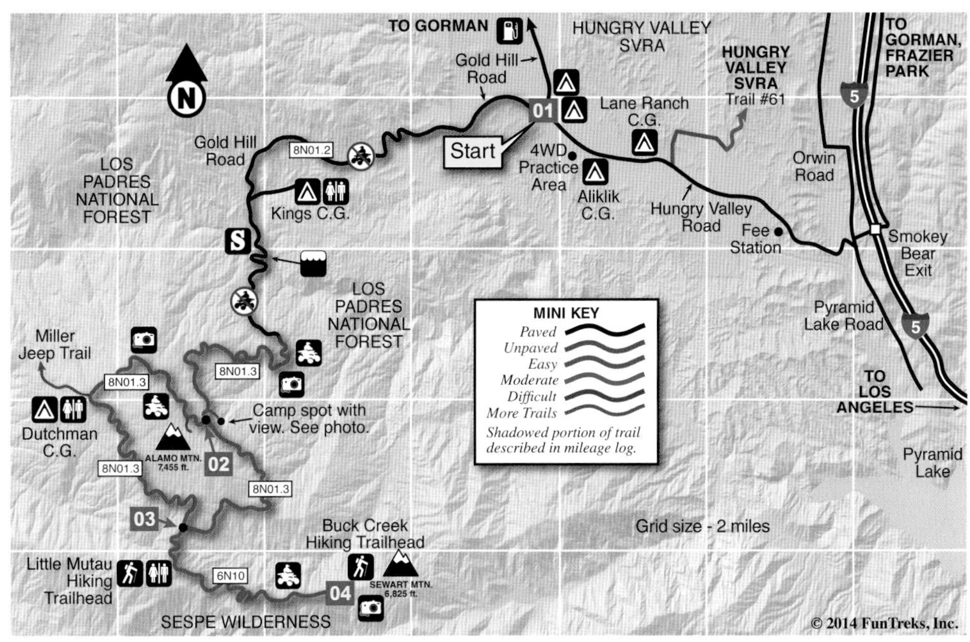

Forest Road 6N10 is steep and narrow as it climbs towards Sewart Mountain.

63 Liebre Mountain

AREA 5 map on page 146

First part of route is open as it climbs to the top of the ridge on a wide, easy road.

Bear Campground has picnic tables. Good place for lunch.

Great views as you climb.

Overview: A stressless drive with views along both sides of a high ridge. Lots of camp spots and a fun place to spend a relaxing weekend. Great hiking along the Pacific Crest Hiking Trail that winds back and forth along 7N23. The main route and larger side roads are open to green-sticker vehicles. Check Motor Vehicle Use Map for legal access. Expand trip by continuing south on 7N08 to Lake Hughes Road.

Rating: Easy: The road narrows to one lane in places with a few mildly steep descents and climbs. Suitable for any stock SUV; however, 4-wheel-drive may be needed when road is wet. Snow possible at higher elevations in winter.

Stats: Length: 18 miles as described. Time: 2 to 4 hours. Elevation: 3,973 to 5,785 ft. Best time: Open all year. Spring through fall best.

Current Conditions: Angeles N.F., Santa Clara/Mojave Rivers Ranger District. Call (661) 269-2808.

Getting There: From Interstate 5 just south of Gorman and east of the Hungry Valley SVRA, head east on Highway 138 about 4.2 miles past Quail Lake. Turn right and head south on Old Ridge Route. After 2.2 miles, continue straight on deteriorating paved road. Just after sign for Angeles N.F. boundary in another 3 miles, turn left on 7N23.

START *MILEAGE LOG:*

0.0 Zero trip odometer [Rev. Miles]
Head east on 7N23. Climb series of tight, scenic switchbacks. [18.0]
01 N34 42.931 W118 42.657

0.6 Continue straight. (Right is 7N22.) [17.4]

2.3 Continue straight on the main road. You'll see many lesser side roads as you continue. Some are illegal. Others go to camp spots. [15.7]

4.2 Road levels out along ridge. [13.8]

4.7 Forest gate. [13.3]

6.7 Continue straight. Lesser road on left goes to water collection station. [11.3]

7.6 Stay right. [10.4]

8.2 One of several places where Pacific Crest Hiking Trail crosses. [9.8]

8.5 Continue straight. Bear C.G. on right. [9.5]
02 N34 42.780 W118 37.888

9.6 Stay right. Left rejoins up ahead. [8.4]

10.6 Stay right. Great overlook 0.1 miles to left. [7.4]

11.6 Continue straight. Right goes to Atmore Meadows C.G in 2.5 miles. [6.4]
03 N34 42.618 W118 35.670

12.1 Parking for Pacific Crest Hiking Trail. [5.9]

13.5 Continue straight. Left goes to Sawmill C.G. [4.5]

14.9 Large circular intersection. Turn hard left to stay on 7N23. Right to Burnt Peak is hiking only. Straight on 7N08 continues many miles to Lake Hughes Road. [3.1]
04 N34 41.499 W118 33.280

16.0 Stay left on 7N23. Road on right goes to Upper Shake C.G. [2.0]

18.0 Eastern end of 7N23 at Pine Canyon Road, F.R. N2. More parking. [0.0]
05 N34 42.184 W118 31.668
Left on Pine Canyon Road connects to Three Points Road, which returns to Hwy. 138.

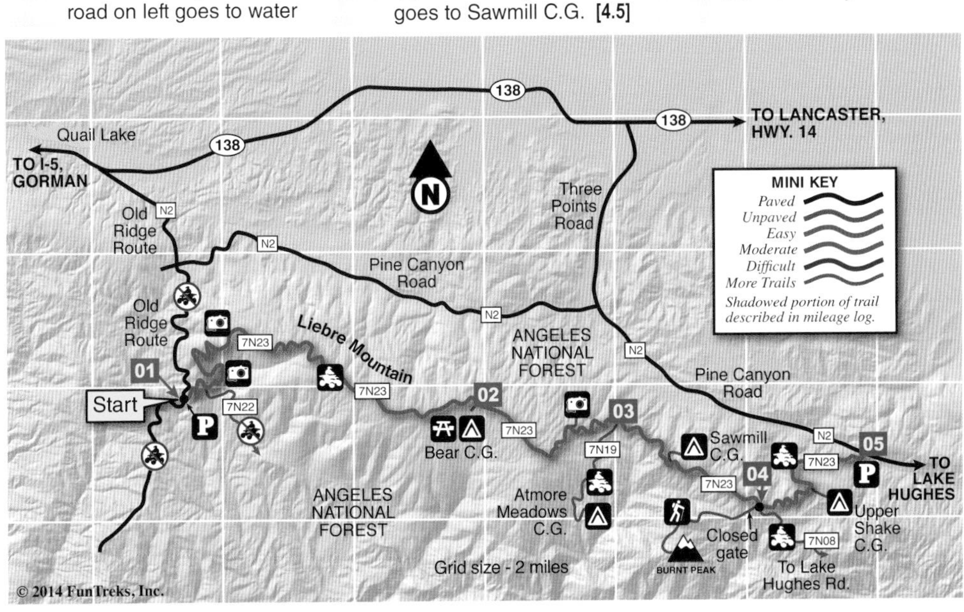

Narrows to one lane in a few places, but still easy when dry.

Pacific Crest Hiking Trail.

Sierra Pelona Ridge/Rowher OHV

AREA 5 map on page 146

Follow posted rules at Rowher Flats OHV Area.

Unloading dock at Staging Area #1.

Starting down Fall Canyon Road from Waypoint 03 as sun begins to set.

Overview: This rugged backcountry drive climbs high to the ridgeline of the Sierra Pelona. After traversing the ridge for several scenic miles, it switchbacks down the northern side of the mountain, offering outstanding views of Bouquet Reservoir. Most of the route is inside Rowher Flat OHV Area, open to green-sticker vehicles. If you're looking for a difficult route, follow Rowher Trail shown on the map. Sierra Pelona Road crosses Rowher Trail several times on the north side.

Rating: Easy: Single-lane shelf road much of the way with adequate room to pass most of the time. Mildly steep in places with vertical dropoffs at the top. Suitable for stock 4x4 SUVs with decent ground clearance. Skid plates helpful.

Stats: Length: 15 miles. Time: 2-3 hours. Elevation: 2,100 to 4,800 ft. Best time: Open all year. Hot in summer. Good alternative to Hungry Valley SVRA when it is snow covered.

Current Conditions: Angeles N.F., Santa Clara/Mojave Rivers Ranger District. Call (661) 269-2808.

Getting There: Take I-5 to Highway 14. Get off 14 at Sand Canyon and head north to Sierra Highway. Go northeast about 4.5 miles to Rush Canyon Road on left. Follow Rush Canyon Road north 2.9 miles to Staging Area #1.

START *MILEAGE LOG:*

0.0 Zero trip odometer **[Rev. Miles]** After Staging Area #1, turn left on Texas Canyon Road 5N14. Follow this wide gravel road southwest. **[15.0]**
01 N34 31.630 W118 22.940

2.0 Turn hard right on Fall Canyon Road and begin steep scenic climb. **[13.0]**
02 N34 30.876 W118 24.507

5.5 Continue straight as you join Sierra Pelona Road that heads east across a high ridge. Follow most-traveled road marked 6N07. **[9.5]**
03 N34 32.869 W118 24.098

6.6 Continue straight as downhill road crosses. **[8.4]**

8.9 Continue straight across Rowher Trail. **[6.1]**

9.6 Cross Rowher Trail again. Lots of confusing spurs. Follow 6N07. **[5.4]**

9.8 Cross Rowher again as it comes uphill from the OHV area. **[5.2]**

10.0 Turn left downhill on Artesian Springs Road 6N08. **[5.0]**
04 N34 33.737 W118 20.748

10.6 Turn right staying on 6N08. **[4.4]**

11.6 Turn left. **[3.4]**

11.8 Continue straight across Rowher Trail. **[3.2]**

12.6 Continue straight across Rowher Trail. **[2.4]**

14.5 Continue straight as lesser road joins on right. **[0.5]**

15.0 Trail ends at paved Bouquet Canyon Road. **[0.0]**
05 N34 34.799 W118 22.122
Left here goes to Santa Clarita, right to Palmdale.

Trail updates & GPS downloads at www.funtreks.com

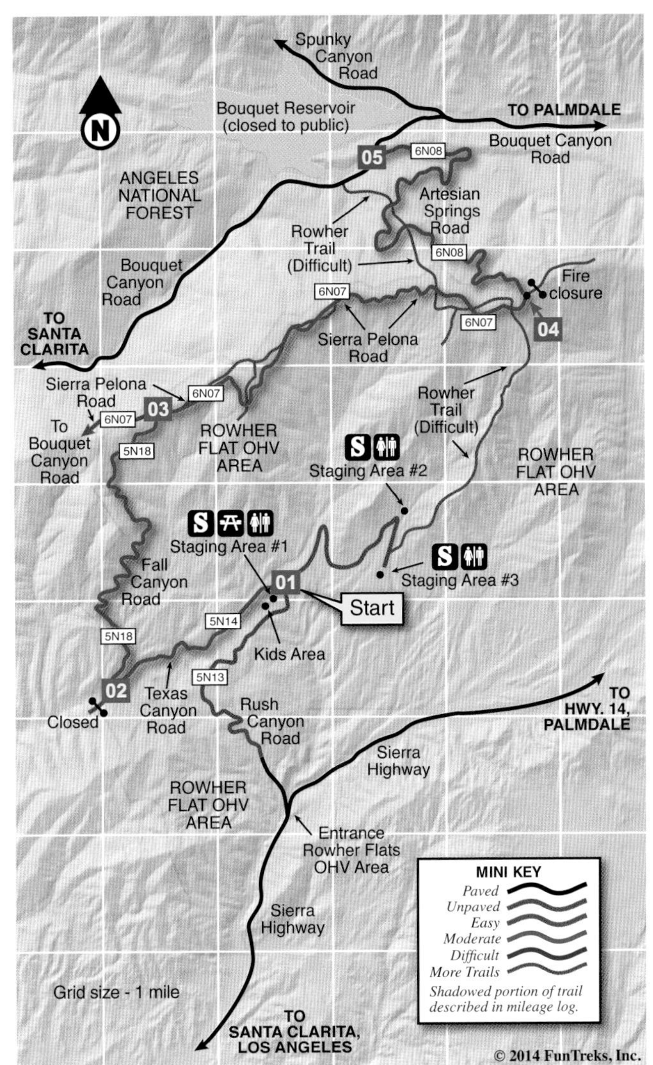

Fire closure east of Wpt. 04.

View of Bouquet Reservoir from Artesian Springs Road.

Cleghorn Ridge

AREA 5 map on page146

Start of trail is immediately east of I-15. Limited parking here.

Winding shelf road at first.

View of Silverwood Lake from east end of trail. Popular boating and camping recreation area.

Overview: A fun drive along a scenic ridge with views of Silverwood Lake on east end. A difficult trail is intertwined with an easy road starting at Waypoint 03. A great route for less experienced drivers to try something harder. If you find it too hard you can immediately get back to the easy road. A popular area for green-sticker vehicles. Parking limited at start and finish, but adequate room at wide places along the road. Dispersed camping allowed but no campfires or BBQ grills. Propane stoves OK.

Rating: Easy: Road 2N47 is fairly smooth most of the way except for a steeper, rougher section going over Cleghorn Mountain. The tougher alternate route varies from moderate to very difficult.

Stats: Length: Easy 2N47 measures 15 miles. Time: 2 to 3 hours. Add time for harder route. Elevation: 3,020 to 5,282 ft. Best time: Open all year. Winter snow possible. Hot in summer.

Current Conditions: San Bernardino National Forest, Lytle Creek Ranger District. Call (909) 382-2851.

Getting There: About 15 miles north of San Bernardino. Trail starts on the east side of I-15 at the Cleghorn Exit.

START MILEAGE LOG:

0.0 Zero trip odometer [Rev. Miles] Continue east uphill on wide dirt road after pavement ends. Note: You can park here on the side of the road away from "NO PARKING" signs. Don't block road. [15.0]
01 N34 17.977 W117 27.394

0.7 Stay right. Lesser road on left is closed. [14.3]

0.8 Equal size road goes left. Continue straight on 2N47. [14.2]

2.4 Follow main road as it curves right past powerline tower. [12.6]

4.0 Continue straight. Left is 3N22, which goes north to Hwy. 138. Right here is now closed. [11.0]
02 N34 18.735 W117 26.294

4.8 Take the outside lane to the left, then continue to stay left on 2N47. [10.2]

5.4 Easy route continues straight. The steep rutted climb on left begins a difficult alternate route that weaves back and forth across 2N47. This is a legal route according to the ranger we spoke with, as long as you stay roughly parallel with 2N47. [9.6]
03 N34 18.323 W117 25.887

6.6 Main route 2N47 gets steeper and rougher. Difficult alternate route continues to join and leave 2N47. [8.4]

7.7 Cross over Cleghorn Mountain. [7.3]
04 N34 17.676 W117 24.729

9.0 First glimpse of Silverwood Lake. [6.0]

10.9 Pacific Crest Hiking Trail crosses 2N47. [4.1]
05 N34 17.692 W117 22.681

14.1 Photo opportunity. Great view of lake below. [0.9]

15.0 Trail ends at paved Highway 138. [0.0]
06 N34 18.025 W117 20.226
Left takes you back to I-15, Cajon Junction, in about 10 miles. Right goes to camping and boating at Silverwood Lake State Recreation Area. Right also goes to Pilot Rock Rd., Trail #66.

Trail updates & GPS downloads at www.funtreks.com

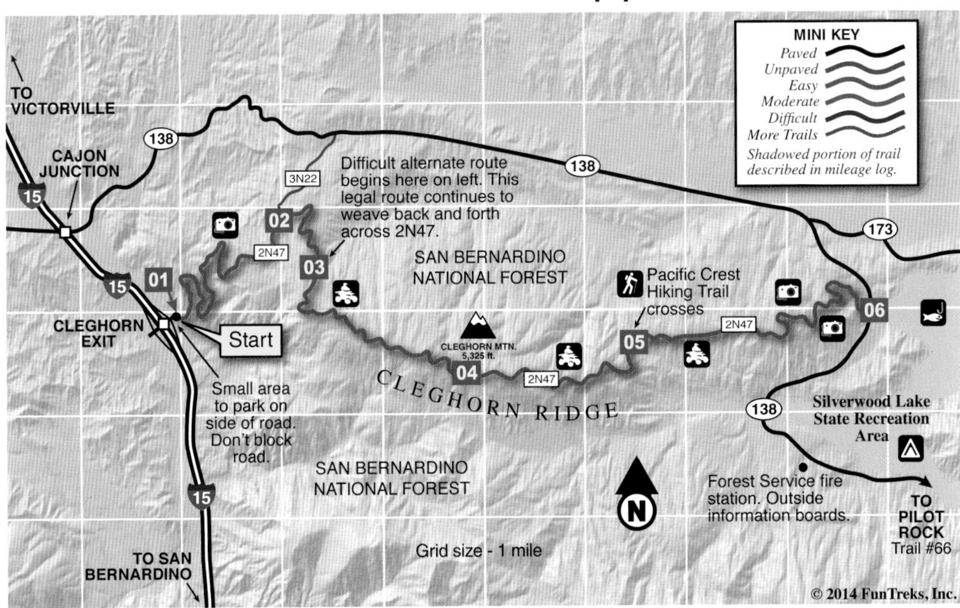

Difficult alternate route branches off here at Waypoint 03.

Steeper at Cleghorn Mountain.

66 Pilot Rock Road

AREA 5 map on page 146

North side of Silverwood Lake as seen from high point of trail.

Main route is easy cruise in good weather.

More difficult ridge route goes left here at Wpt.03.

Historical Highlight: *The dam at Silverwood Lake, aka Cedar Springs Dam, was built in 1971. In the early part of the 1900s, about 100 farming families lived in the small town of Cedar Springs, which would now be located at the bottom of the lake, had it not been razed before the lake was filled.*

Overview: This scenic backcountry route meanders through forest along a high ridge east of Silverwood Lake. Great views of the lake after Wpt. 04. Starting at Wpt. 03, you can choose a more difficult route that runs along the top of the ridge. From Wpt. 06, you can take a difficult OHV route that circles all the way back to Wpt. 03. Open to green-sticker vehicles. Combine with Cleghorn Ridge, Trail #65.

Rating: Easy: The main route described here is steep and narrow in a few places but suitable for any high clearance 4x4 vehicle. Ridge route is much steeper with large ruts. Road 2N17X is a hard-core OHV route.

Stats: Length: 8.7 miles. Time: 2 hours. Elevation: 3,407 to 4,658 ft. Best time: Open all year with exception of rare winter snowfall. Hot in summer.

Current Conditions: San Bernardino National Forest, Lytle Creek Ranger District. Call (909) 382-2851.

Getting There: Take Highway 138 east about 16 miles from Interstate 15 at Cajon Junction. Turn left on a small paved road at a sign for Silverwood Lake State Recreation Area/Miller Canyon. Go north about 400 feet to Forest Road 2N37 on right. If you've driven Cleghorn Ridge, Trail #65, first, turn right on 138 and go 5.8 miles.

START *MILEAGE LOG:*

0.0 Zero trip odometer **[Rev. Miles]**
Head east on 2N37. **[8.7]**
01 N34 16.257 W117 17.419

0.3 Pavement ends after going past camp spots on the left. **[8.4]**

0.8 Turn left on 2N36, cross paved water crossing and begin climbing. **[7.9]**
02 N34 16.243 W117 16.749

2.6 Continue west at top of ridge as you join 2N33, which comes in on right. In another 200 feet, stay right to follow easy Pilot Rock Road. Two steep roads on left follow more difficult ridge route. This is a legal route. **[6.1]**
03 N34 16.885 W117 17.371

3.0 Stay right. Ridge route merges here on left. **[5.7]**

3.8 Stay right. Once again you can see more difficult ridge route on left. **[4.9]**

4.6 Stay right. Left connects to ridge route. **[4.1]**

4.9 Continue straight. Ridge route ends on left. **[3.8]**

5.0 Pilot Rock Road curves around to right, reversing direction. Good views of lake at this point. **[3.7]**
04 N34 17.017 W117 19.247

6.1 Stay right on main road past overlook on left. **[2.6]**

6.2 Stay right past wide area on left with roads that go downhill to lake. **[2.5]**
05 N34 17.483 W117 18.693

8.2 Continue straight on main road. Uphill to right is difficult OHV route 2N17X. It circles all the way back to 2N33. This is a fun trip for hard-core rigs. **[0.5]**
06 N34 18.160 W117 18.198

8.7 Bear right on paved road and follow it downhill to Highway 173. Left on 173 connects to 138 back to I-15 at Cajon Jct. **[0.0]**
07 N34 18.315 W117 18.586
Left at Waypoint 07 goes to overlook of dam.

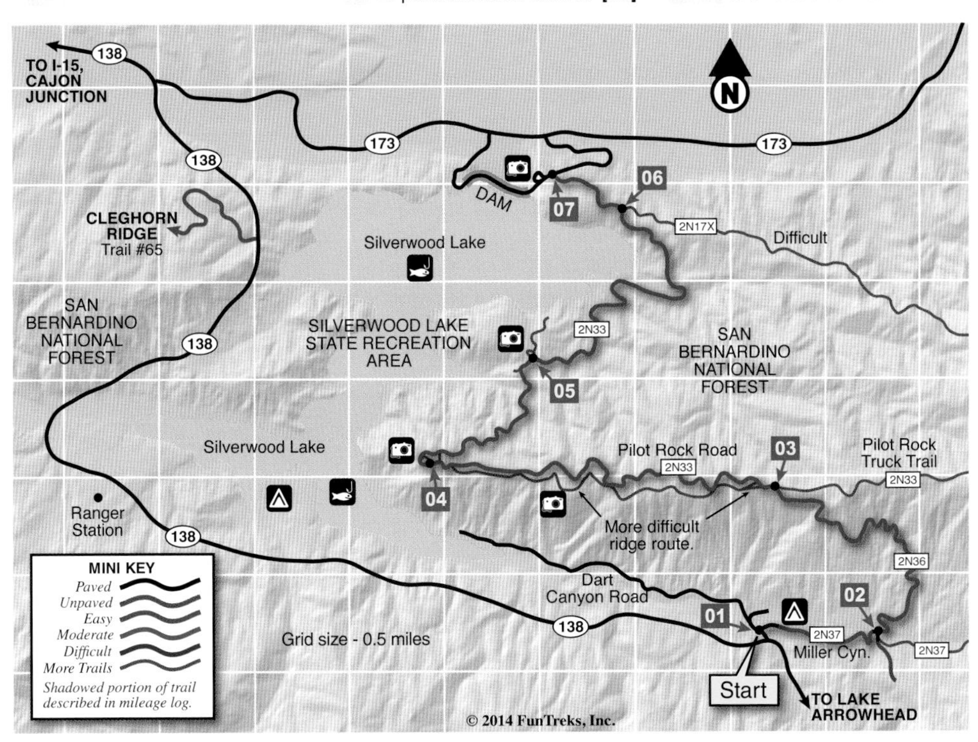

Start of difficult OHV route 2N17X at Waypoint 06.

Turn left at Waypoint 07 to overlook of dam.

Willow Creek Road

AREA 5 map on page 146

Most of the Willow Creek Road is wide, easy and well marked.

Green-sticker vehicles will want to start at the Pinnacles Staging Area, where we ended our drive.

Overview: A fun, easy route for just about any 4x4 SUV. Road is open to green-sticker vehicles with many legal side roads to explore. Green-sticker vehicles usually start at Pinnacles Staging Area where we end our description. Stay on paved Highway 173 to go to staging area.

Rating: Easy: Most of this route, when dry, does not require 4-wheel drive; however, you'll want 4-wheel drive and a little ground clearance for one rocky climb after Waypoint 03. Willow Creek has the potential to be deep after a heavy rainstorm.

Stats: Length: 6.5 miles. Time: About 1 hour. Elevation: 4,387 to 4,917 ft. Open all year weather permitting. Winter snow possible. Hot in summer.

Current Conditions: San Bernardino National Forest, Big Bear Discovery Center. Call (909) 382-2790.

Getting There: From Highway 18 near mile marker 24.5, go north on Highway 173 to Lake Arrowhead. Hwy. 173 turns right after 1.5 miles. After 3.2 miles, turn right on Hook(s) Creek Road at small gas station. After another 3.2 miles downhill, turn left at fork just after pavement ends. This fork has a large white sign with a forest map showing routes in the area.

START MILEAGE LOG:

0.0 Zero trip odometer **[Rev. Miles]**
At white sign, stay left on easy F.S. 3N34. **[6.5]**
01 **N34 16.184 W117 08.267**

0.1 Bear left where Splinter Trailhead goes right. **[6.4]**

0.6 Bear right where difficult 2N27Y goes left. **[5.9]**

1.0 Bear right. **[5.5]**

2.3 Turn left following F.S. 3N34. Right goes to Devil's Hole. **[4.2]**
02 **N34 17.584 W117 08.723**

2.4 Turn left. F.S. 3N38 goes right then rejoins. **[4.1]**

2.7 Stay right. **[3.8]**

3.1 Bear left, lesser road joins on right. **[3.4]**

3.2 Hard right on F.S. 3N34. The next mile is the roughest part of the trail. **[3.3]**
03 **N34 17.591 W117 09.465**

4.7 Stay right where difficult F.S. 3W13 goes left. **[1.8]**

5.0 Cross Willow Creek. **[1.5]**

5.1 Stay right where Willow Creek Road splits. Left is longer and easier. **[1.4]**
04 **N34 18.042 W117 11.022**

6.1 Turn right at Pinnacles Staging Area. **[0.4]**

6.5 End trail at Hwy. 173. **[0.0]**
05 **N34 18.014 W117 12.302**
To exit, turn left on Highway 173 and follow it back to Highway 18 through Lake Arrowhead.

Toughest part of trail.

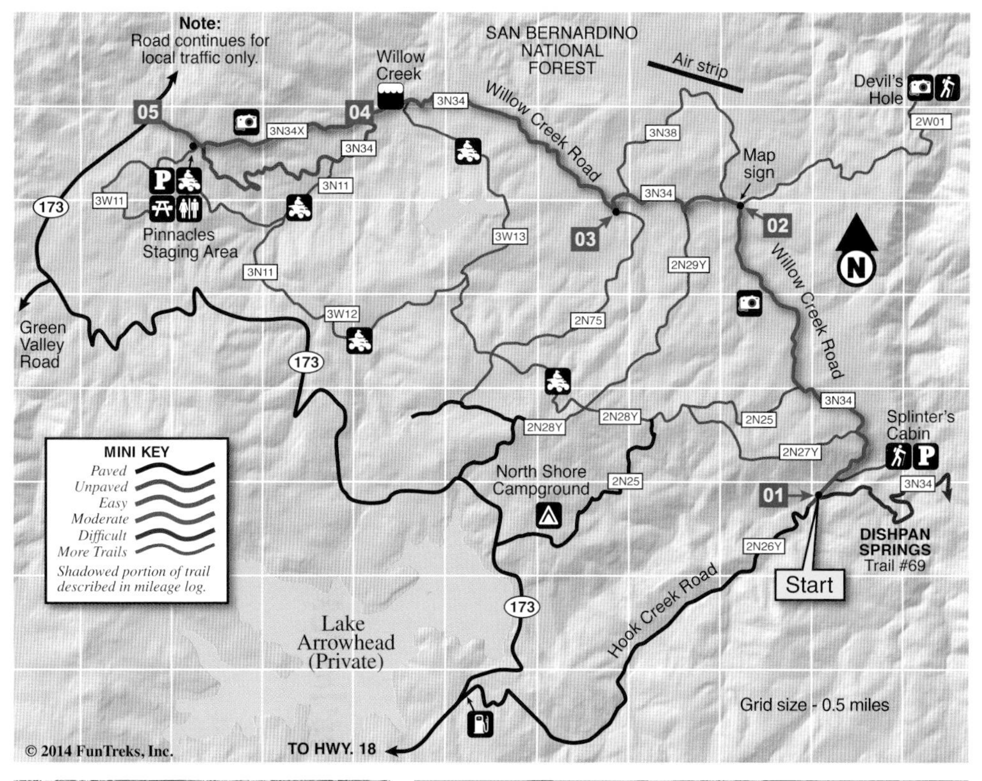

Most of route does not require 4WD.

Stay left here on Forest Road 3N34 to begin route.

68 Grapevine Canyon

AREA 5 map on page 146

Look for fawn statues in town of Fawnskin.

Trail moderate after boulder outcrop at Wpt. 05

Grapevine Canyon Road has many forks.

Be very careful where trail is washed out.

Overview: You'll pass through the heart of a popular area of San Bernardino National Forest northwest of Big Bear Lake. After passing several large F.S. campgrounds, you'll exit the forest and descend steeply down a wild and scenic BLM road into Lucerne Valley. Large boulders provide great photo opportunities. Green-sticker vehicles allowed after Waypoint 04. Fun riding down Grapevine Canyon.

Rating: Moderate: Very easy mix of gravel and paved roads to Waypoint 04. After boulder outcrop, sandy road becomes moderate as it descends steeply. Washouts of road are possible after rainstorms. Use extreme caution.

Stats: Length: 23.3 miles. Time: 3 to 4 hours. Elevation: 7,192 to 2,968 ft. Best time: May-November. Hot in summer at lower elevations. Snow possible at higher elevations in winter.

Current Conditions: San Bernardino National Forest, Big Bear Ranger Station & Discovery Center. Call: (909) 382-2790. BLM Barstow Field Office. (760) 252-6000.

Getting There: Take Highways 18 and 38 to the little town of Fawnskin on the north side of Big Bear Lake. Look for three fawn statues in the center of town that mark start of paved Rim-of-the-World Drive.

START MILEAGE LOG:

0.0 Zero trip odometer **[Rev. Miles]**
Head northwest from Fawnskin on paved Rim-of-the-World Drive. **[23.3]**
01 N34 16.175 W116 56.826

0.5 Pavement ends. **[22.8]**

1.3 Follow Forest Road 3N14 right past the road to Butler Peak on left. **[22.0]**

1.8 Continue straight. (Road 3N12 goes right.) **[21.5]**

2.0 Stay right on 3N14 past YMCA camp. **[21.3]**

2.4 Continue straight on paved part of road past Hanna Flat C.G. **[20.9]**

4.3 Continue straight. After crossing Holcomb Creek, Road 3N93 goes left, then 3N08 goes right. **[19.0]**
02 N34 18.024 W116 58.938

6.8 Continue straight through paved 4-way intersection past Big Pine Flat C.G. Still on 3N14. **[16.5]**
03 N34 19.192 W117 00.611

12.2 Bear right on 4N16 following large sign to Lucerne Valley. Green-sticker vehicles OK now. **[11.1]**
04 N34 20.594 W117 03.845

13.2 Continue straight past road on left that goes to Horse Springs C.G. **[10.1]**

14.1 Leave San Bernardino National Forest. Now on BLM JF3223. **[9.2]**

15.6 Stay left past large boulder outcrop. **[7.7]**
05 N34 22.949 W117 03.291

15.7 Stay right. **[7.6]**

15.9 Follow road as it curves left, ignoring roads to right. **[7.4]**

17.2 Stay right after passing through fence. **[6.1]**

18.4 At valley bottom, circle to left and head north. Ignore roads right. **[4.9]**

19.6 Wait until you reach R.R. tracks and turn right. **[3.7]**

20.3 Turn left at paved High Road and cross R.R. tracks. **[3.0]**
06 N34 24.432 W117 01.999

23.3 You reach Hwy. 18 **[0.0]**
07 N34 27.025 W117 01.998
At Highway 18, right goes into Lucerne Valley and back to Big Bear Lake. Left goes to Apple Valley.

Trail updates & GPS downloads at www.funtreks.com

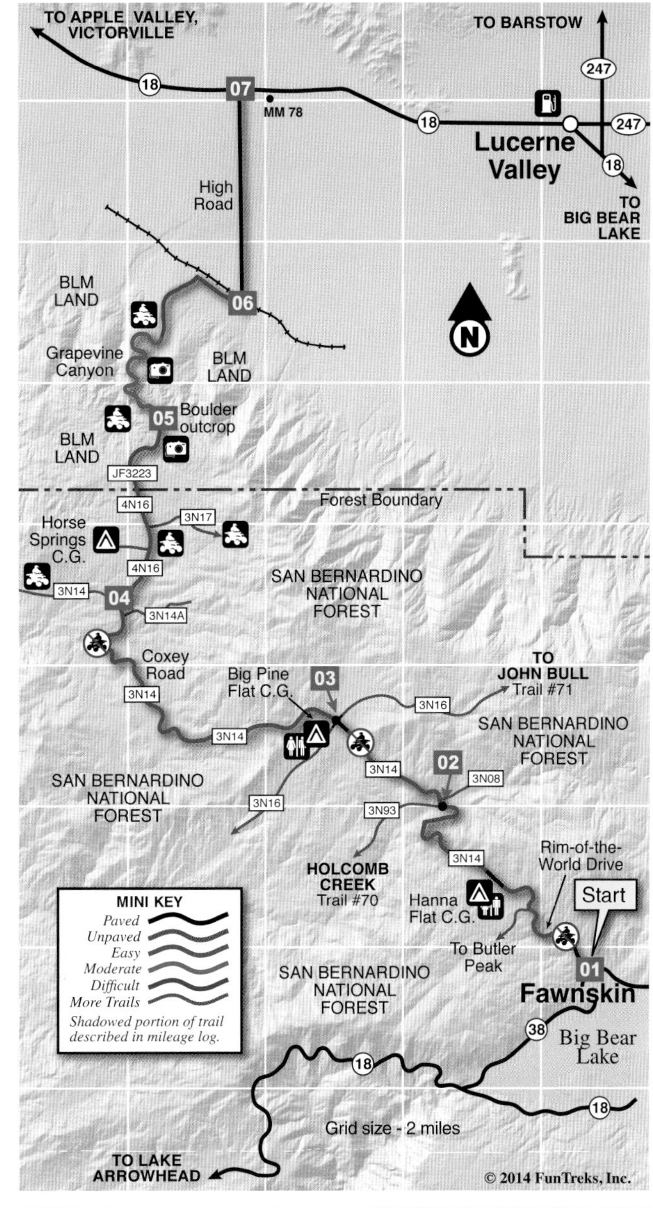

You'll see damage from the Willow Fire, which happened in 1999.

Dishpan Springs

AREA 5 map on page 146

Bottom of hill starting at Waypoint 02.

Kids will like the sandy beach below bridge.

New bridge that crosses Deep Creek.

Historical Highlight: *We've heard two stories as to why some call this trail Dishpan Springs. One is that it is simply named after a natural spring along the trail. Two is that, before the bridge was built over Deep Creek, the crossing was so deep that gear, including dishpans, floated out of open vehicles. We'll let you decide if either is true.*

Overview: This trail is also called Deep Creek after the creek it crosses at the beginning. It's the first of three short but satisfying hard-core trails that can be run in sequence in one day. The mileage log on the opposite page includes directions from the end of this trail to the next trail, Holcomb Creek. Trail is open to green-sticker vehicles, but it takes a very good rider to get up it.

Rating: Difficult: Steep rocky climbs with large boulders. Rocks are often covered with fine sand making for poor traction. Hard-core modified vehicles only. Somewhat easier if driven downhill in reverse direction.

Stats: Length: Almost 5 miles. Time: About 2 hours. Elevation: 4,689 to 5,968 ft. Best time: May-November. Snow possible in winter.

Current Conditions: San Bernardino National Forest, Big Bear Discovery Center. Call (909) 382-2790.

Getting There: From Highway 18 near mile marker 24.5, go north on Highway 173 to Lake Arrowhead. Hwy. 173 turns right after 1.5 miles. After 3.2 miles, turn right on Hook(s) Creek Road at small gas station. After another 3.2 miles, when pavement ends, stay right uphill at fork with white forest sign.

START *MILEAGE LOG:*

0.0 Zero trip odometer [Rev. Miles]
Head uphill on F.S. 3N34, moderate to start. [4.7]
01 N34 16.184 W117 08.267

0.4 Continue straight. Large parking area and picnic tables on left. [4.3]

0.7 Cross bridge over Deep Creek. [4.0]

1.3 Driver's choice. [3.4]

2.3 Difficult hill. [2.4]
02 N34 15.907 W117 07.060

3.5 Bear left on more-traveled road. Right goes to Tent Peg Campground. [1.2]
03 N34 15.729 W117 06.021

3.9 Continue straight. [0.8]

4.2 Bear right. [0.5]

4.5 Continue straight past Crab Flats Campground on left. [0.2]

4.7 Trail ends at intersection with F.S. 3N16. [0.0]
04 N34 15.646 W117 05.070
To get to Holcomb Creek, Trail #70, turn left on F.S. 3N16 and head north 2.7 miles. To reach Hwy. 18, turn right on F.S. 3N16, which later becomes Green Valley Lake Road.

First rocky hill just after Deep Creek Bridge.

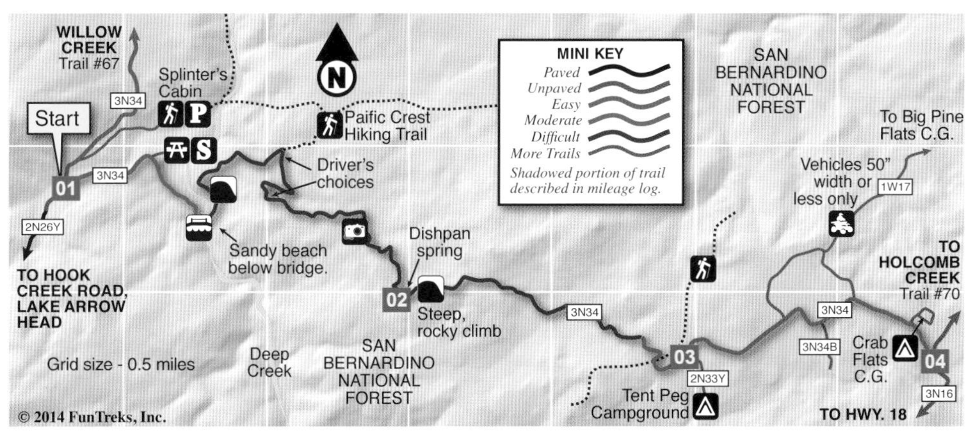

Toughest part of hill after Waypoint 02 is at the top.

70 Holcomb Creek

AREA 5 map on page 146

We had to use our winch a couple of times while crossing the rock garden at the start.

Stock SUV attempts trail in reverse direction.

Burn area still visible on parts of the trail.

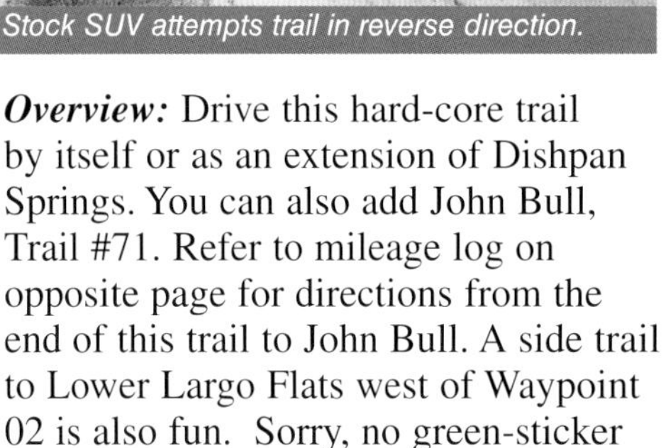

Overview: Drive this hard-core trail by itself or as an extension of Dishpan Springs. You can also add John Bull, Trail #71. Refer to mileage log on opposite page for directions from the end of this trail to John Bull. A side trail to Lower Largo Flats west of Waypoint 02 is also fun. Sorry, no green-sticker vehicles on this route.

Rating: Difficult: No single large obstacle, just two tough boulder fields. Wet tires add to the difficulty as you cross Holcomb Creek several times. Stock vehicles not recommended, but some try it going downhill. Winch, lockers and skids plates highly recommended. Best to go with a second vehicle.

Stats: Length: Almost 6 miles. Time: About 1 hour. Elevation: 5,492 to 6,642 ft. Best time: May-November. Snow possible in winter.

Current Conditions: San Bernardino National Forest, Big Bear Discovery Center. Call (909) 382-2790.

Getting There: Go north on Green Valley Road from Hwy. 18 near mile marker 34.5. After 2.7 miles, turn left on F.S. 3N16 following signs to Crab Flats Campground. Ignore lesser side roads continuing on F.S. 3N16. At 6.5 miles stay right on F.S. 3N16 as you pass Crab Flats Campground. Reach F.S. 3N93 on right at 9.2 miles.

START *MILEAGE LOG:*

0.0 Zero trip odometer **[Rev. Miles]**
Head east on F.S. 3N93 over rock garden. **[5.8]**
01 N34 16.519 W117 03.063

1.3 Cross small creek. **[4.5]**

2.6 Enter burn area. **[3.2]**

2.9 Short steep hill with water crossing at bottom. **[2.9]**

3.3 Challenging stretch of wet boulders. **[2.5]**

3.8 Continue straight. F.S. 2N06X goes left to Lower Largo Flats. **[2.0]**
02 N34 16.947 W117 00.203

5.1 Driver's choice. **[0.7]**

5.8 Trail ends at F.S. 3N14. **[0.0]**
03 N34 18.022 W116 58.944
To reach Big Bear Lake turn right on F.S. 3N14 and follow to Fawnskin. To reach John Bull, Trail #71, turn left on F.S. 3N14 and go a short distance to F.S. 3N08 on right. Follow this well-marked road 4.4 miles east to F.S. 3N16. Reset odometer and turn right, heading east, on F.S. 3N16. After 1.3 miles turn right, then turn left at 1.4 miles continuing on F.S. 3N16. At 5.4 miles, F.S. 3N02 will be on the left and is the start of John Bull Trail.

Friendly driver helps another at boulder field, near Waypoint 02.

As forest grows back, a bit of fall color returns.

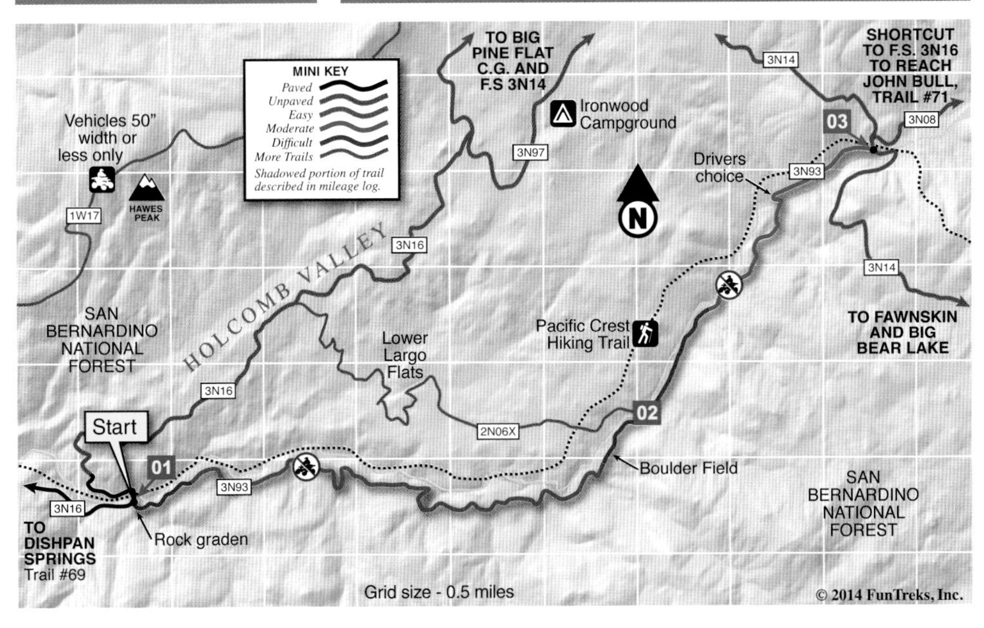

John Bull Trail

AREA 5 map on page 146

"Gate Keeper" obstacle may take a while.

Traffic back-ups are common on weekends.

Walk to edge of ridge for views of Lucerne Valley.

Top end of "Gate Keeper" may require winching.

Overview: This popular hard-core trail is considered by many the toughest in the Big Bear area. Often driven in the opposite direction. Can also be run in sequence with trails #69 and #70. Can get busy on weekends and holidays causing traffic back-ups. Not open to green-sticker vehicles. Trail climbs above 8,100 feet with views of Lucerne Valley along a high ridge.

Rating: Difficult: Trail officially begins at Waypoint 03, not far from the *Gate Keeper*. A good spotter here will speed up the process. Winch points are hard to find. Many more boulders follow.

Stats: Length: Almost 7 miles. Time: 2-3 hours depending on traffic. Elev: 7,305 to 8,176 ft. Best time: Late June - early October. Can snow late October.

Current Conditions: San Bernardino National Forest, Big Bear Discovery Center. Call (909) 382-2790.

Getting There: From Highway 18 east of Big Bear Lake, follow signs to Big Bear Landfill, heading northwest from mile post 58. Turn left before the substation and follow Holcomb Valley Road, F.S. 3N16, uphill 2.2 miles to F.S. 3N02 on the right.

START **MILEAGE LOG:**

0.0 Zero trip odometer **[Rev. Miles]**
Head north on easy Forest Road 3N02. **[6.7]**
01 **N34 18.296 W116 50.820**

1.1 Turn left on F.S. 3N10, at sign for John Bull Trail. **[5.6]**
02 **N34 19.145 W116 51.270**

2.7 Turn right continuing on 3N10. Left is 3N32. **[4.0]**
03 **N34 19.036 W116 52.439**

2.9 Gate Keeper obstacle begins hard-core. **[3.8]**

4.6 Walk to right for views of Lucerne Valley. **[2.1]**

5.7 Bear right downhill heading southwest. (Left on 3N43 will also take you to 3N16.) **[1.0]**
04 **N34 19.107 W116 54.289**

6.2 Follow F.S. 3N10 south through intersection. **[0.5]**
05 **N34 18.802 W116 54.546**

6.7 Trail ends at Forest Road 3N16. **[0.0]**
06 **N34 18.390 W116 54.718**
To reach Big Bear, turn left and go 0.2 miles on 3N16. Then stay right (south) on 2N09. At some point 2N09 becomes Polique Cyn. Road, which connects to Hwy. 18.

Official start at Waypoint 03.

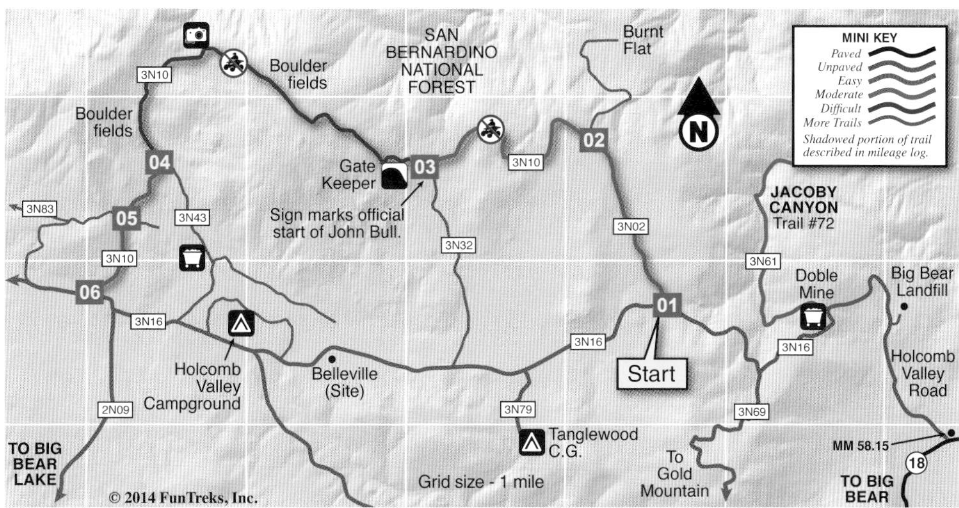

Some say John Bull Trail gives them a taste of the Rubicon. We agree—but just a little taste!

Jacoby Canyon

AREA 5 map on page 146

Turn left here on 3N16 before landfill.

Start of trail is well marked.

First half of route in canyon bottom is an easy shady drive.

Overview: This short trail drops down into Jacoby Canyon, then winds its way north in the bottom of the canyon through a mostly shaded area. You'll find two dispersed camp spots next to boulder outcrops along the last part of the trail. Street-legal vehicles only.

Rating: Moderate: The first half is fairly easy, but large embedded boulders and several steep spots, starting at Waypoint 03, offer some challenge for stock 4x4 SUVs. Narrow in places. Skid plates recommended.

Stats: Length: 2.9 miles. Time: Less than an hour. Elevation: Starts at 7,256 ft. and drops to 6,002 ft. Best time: Late spring through early fall.

Current Conditions: San Bernardino N.F., Big Bear Ranger Station and Discovery Center. Call (909) 382-2790.

Getting There: From the northeast side of Big Bear, after the crossover point of Highways 38 and 18, follow Highway 18 east along the north side of Baldwin Lake (mostly dry). Continue 3.7 miles and turn left on paved Holcomb Valley Road near mile marker 58. Go north about a mile and turn left on Forest Road 3N16 just before entrance to Big Bear Landfill Substation. Follow 3N16 north, then west about 0.8 miles to start of 3N61 on right.

START MILEAGE LOG:

0.0 Zero trip odometer **[Rev. Miles]**
Head west downhill on F.S. Road 3N61. Start of trail is well marked. **[2.9]**
01 N34 18.285 W116 49.794

0.4 Trail turns north at switchback and follows bottom of Jacoby Canyon. **[2.5]**
02 N34 18.191 W116 50.173

1.7 Large imbedded boulders require more careful tire placement. Tight squeeze for wide vehicles. **[1.2]**
03 N34 19.092 W116 49.917

1.9 Short, steep hill. **[1.0]**

2.0 Large boulders on left mark primitive camp spot. Views to the north. **[0.9]**

2.4 Another primitive camp spot on left. **[0.5]**

2.7 Tougher rocky section. **[0.2]**

2.9 Trail ends at paved Highway 18. **[0.0]**
04 N34 19.034 W116 48.904

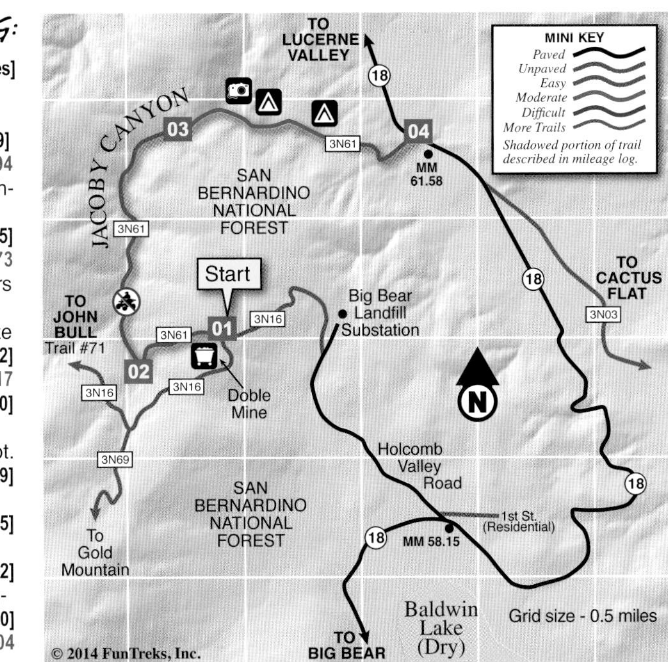

Large embedded boulders at Waypoint 03.

Tight maneuvering in places.

Scenic camp spot at boulder outcrop.

Prickly pear cactus is about ready to bloom.

Skyline Drive

AREA 5 map on page 146

Road passes just below Grandview Point at Waypoint 03. Hike a short distance to the top.

Views through occasional breaks in the trees.

The road couldn't be any easier.

Overview: Follow a high, scenic ridge above the town of Big Bear Lake. The route passes between two tree-hidden ski areas. The road is heavily used by hikers and mountain bikers, so avoid the temptation to drive fast on the smooth dirt road. Many side roads to explore. Street-legal vehicles only. Best views require short walks from your vehicle. You can extend trip and add difficulty if you go down and back up the south side of the mountain via Clarks Summit, Trail #74.

Rating: Easy: Suitable for 2-wheel-drive passenger cars when road is dry. You'll want 4-wheel drive for optional Grandview Loop.

Stats: Length: 12.4 miles. Time: 2-3 hours. Elevation: 6,871 to 8,024 ft. Best time: Late spring through fall or until first snowfall. Parked vehicles may require Adventure Pass.

Current Conditions: San Bernardino National Forest, Big Bear Discovery Center. Call (909) 382-2790.

Getting There: From Highway 18 on the southeastern end of Big Bear Lake, head southeast on Moonridge Drive. Bear right after one mile on Club View Drive. After another 1.2 miles, bear right on Balsam Drive. It circles counterclockwise past Aspen Drive to start of Forest Road 2N10. No parking here.

START **MILEAGE LOG:**

0.0 Zero trip odometer **[Rev. Miles]**
Head west on Forest Road 2N10. No parking at start of trail. **[12.4]**
01 **N34 13.634 W116 52.042**

0.7 Stay right on 2N10. Road 2N10F goes left here towards Bear Mountain Ski Area. **[11.7]**

1.3 Continue straight on 2N10. The east side of Clarks Summit, 2N06, Trail #74, is on left. **[11.1]**
02 **N34 13.046 W116 52.789**

2.3 Views on left. **[10.1]**

2.6 Continue straight. Road 2N51Y goes right here. This is the east side of Grandview Loop, a shorter and slightly more challenging way to drive to the top. **[9.8]**

4.6 Continue straight on 2N10. Road 2N08 goes downhill on the right. This is the west side of Grandview Loop. Hike uphill to the left to see great views at Grandview Point. **[7.8]**
03 **N34 12.906 W116 55.354**

5.6 View of Big Bear Lk. **[6.8]**

6.4 Continue straight on 2N10. The west side of Clarks Summit, 1N54, Trail #74, is on left. **[6.0]**
04 **N34 12.572 W116 56.680**

8.0 Stay right on 2N10. Road 2N11 goes left here to Lookout Point. **[4.4]**

8.8 Stay right. Road 2N86 goes left here to Bluff Mesa Campground. **[3.6]**
05 **N34 13.376 W116 57.716**

10.3 Continue straight passing spur roads 2N10B and 2N10C. **[2.1]**

10.9 Continue straight where 2N17 goes right. **[1.5]**

11.4 Start of paved Mill Creek Road. Continue downhill. **[1.0]**
06 **N34 13.550 W116 56.020**

12.4 We end our description here. Left on Tulip Lane takes you to Highway 18 heading west. Right on Mill Creek Road takes you to Highway 18 heading east. **[0.0]**
07 **N34 14.128 W116 55.729**
Right also goes to Aspen Glen Picnic Area, where you'll find restrooms and the start of the 3-mile hiking trail to Grandview Point. If you want to drive back up the mountain via the Grandview Loop, bear right to reach Knickerbocker Road.

Trail updates & GPS downloads at www.funtreks.com

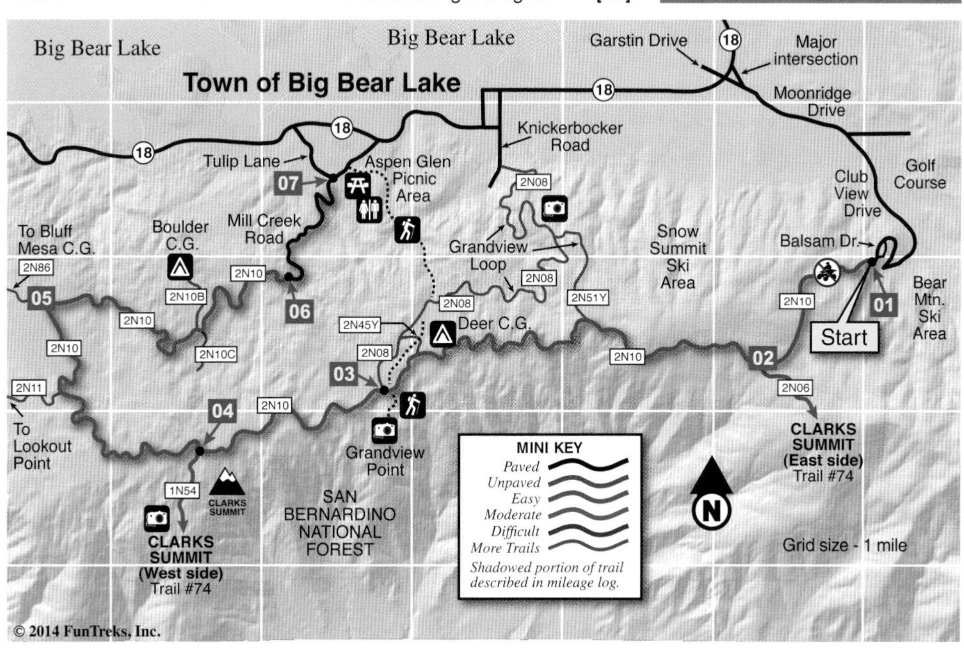

Look for this sign at start.

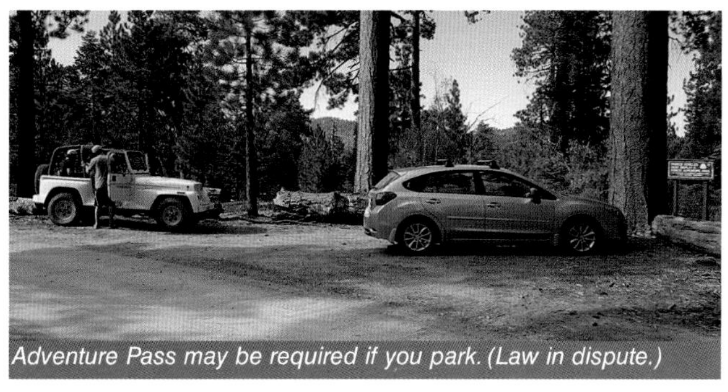
Adventure Pass may be required if you park. (Law in dispute.)

74 Clarks Summit

AREA 5 map on page 146

Passing can be challenging at several places along the trail. Tight brush for wide vehicles.

Great views as you descend switchbacks.

Much of trail is forested and shady.

Overview: Explore lesser-traveled roads on back side of Snow Summit Ski Area. Upper portion of Clarks Summit shares the same road as the easier Skyline Drive, Trail #73. Enjoy outstanding views to the south at higher elevations. Street-legal vehicles only.

Rating: Moderate: Steep and narrow in sections, especially on the descent from Clarks Summit. A couple of spots are so narrow there is barely enough room to get out of your vehicle. Tight brush in places for wide vehicles. OK for most stock 4x4 SUVs with skid plates.

Stats: Length: 29.7 miles. Time: 4 to 5 hours. Elevation: 4,830 to 8,095 ft. Best time: Late spring through fall or until first snowfall. Call ahead to be sure gates are open.

Current Conditions: San Bernardino National Forest, Big Bear Ranger Station and Discovery Center. Call (909) 382-2790.

Getting There: Take Highway 38 east from San Bernardino or south from Big Bear Lake to Forest Road 1N04 at mile marker 30.97.

START **MILEAGE LOG:**

0.0 Zero trip odometer **[Rev. Miles]** Head northwest uphill on Forest Road 1N04. **[17.0]**
01 N34 10.245 W116 49.569

1.1 Lesser road on left goes to camp spot. **[15.9]**

2.4 Bear right on Seven Oaks Road, F.R. 1N45. **[14.6]**

2.7 Bear right staying on 1N04. (Seven Oaks Road goes left.) **[14.3]**
02 N34 11.067 W116 51.881

6.1 Continue straight (slightly left) across large road. **[10.9]**

6.3 Turn hard right on 2N06. Road climbs and narrows as views unfold. **[10.7]**
03 N34 11.679 W116 54.705

10.7 Forest gate. **[6.3]**

11.2 Stay left where 2N21 joins on right. **[5.8]**

11.9 Bear left on 2N10. This is Skyline Drive. See Trail description #73. **[5.1]**
04 N34 13.036 W116 52.780

17.0 Bear left on 1N54. **[0.0]**
05 N34 12.574 W116 56.678

0.0 Zero odometer at Wpt. 05. **[12.7]**

0.1 Stay left where 1N54A goes right. **[12.6]**

2.2 Series of steeper switchbacks. **[10.5]**

5.7 Continue straight on 1N54 where 1N64 goes right. **[7.0]**
06 N34 11.001 W116 58.257

7.0 Continue straight where 1N04 goes left. **[5.7]**

7.4 Continue straight where 1N09 joins on right. **[5.3]**

7.6 Go through gate and bear left on paved Seven Oaks Road. **[5.1]**
07 N34 10.373 W116 57.004

10.4 Turn right on Glass Road and head downhill. **[2.3]**

12.7 Return to Hwy 38. **[0.0]**
08 N34 10.136 W116 53.600

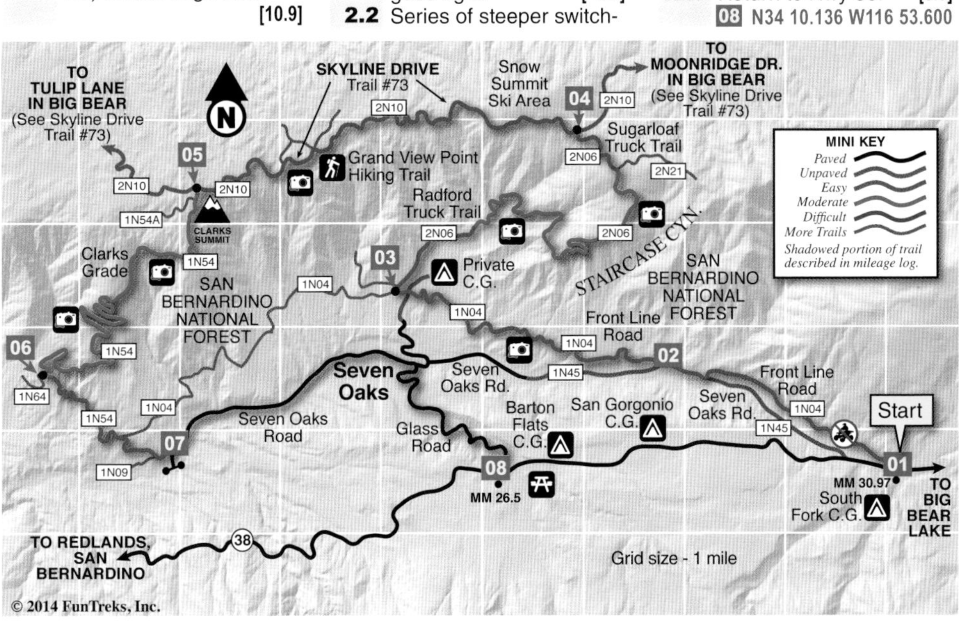

One of the wider sections of road descending from Clarks Summit on Forest Road 1N54.

75 Burns Canyon

AREA 5 map on page 146

Start of route at Highway 38 is well marked.

Looking west from high point along 2N01.

Challenging descent between Wpts. 03 and 04.

Take short side trip to this stone arrastra.

Historical Highlight: *The arrastra you pass on this trip is an indication that mining took place here a very long time ago. Arrastras were primitive devices used to pulverize gold or silver ore. A long arm connected to a center post was turned in a circle powered by horse, mule, human, water power, steam power and even electricity in later years. Flat stones were attached to the arm and dragged over the ore inside the circle.*

Overview: Take an easy forest road to a challenging loop through scenic Burns Canyon. Visit a stone arrastra from bygone mining days. Green-sticker vehicles are allowed after Waypoint 02. Get a copy of the San Bernardino N.F. Motor Vehicle Use Map so you can differentiate numerous legal and illegal side roads. We were disappointed to learn that Heartbreak Ridge 4x4 Trail, which we drove for the first edition of this book in 2003, does not show on the latest MVUM.

Rating: Difficult: Much of this trail is easy to moderate; however, two steep hills have large boulders to maneuver around. Modified vehicles are best, but some aggressive, high-clearance stock vehicles will be able to get through.

Stats: Length: 19.1 miles if you return to start. Time: 3 to 5 hours. Elevation: 8,080 to 6,198 ft. Open all year weather permitting. Expect snow in winter. Best spring through fall.

Current Conditions: San Bernardino National Forest, Big Bear Discovery Center. Call (909) 382-2790.

Getting There: Head southeast from Big Bear Lake, or northeast from Redlands on winding Highway 38. Turn east on well-marked Forest Road 2N01 near mile marker 41.

START *MILEAGE LOG:*

0.0 Zero trip odometer **[Rev. Miles]**
After a brief stretch of pavement, continue on wide dirt road. **[8.3]**
01 **N34 12.444 W116 44.274**

0.5 Road turns north after point where Pacific Crest Hiking Trail crosses. **[7.8]**

2.3 Continue northeast across Broom Flat after roads go right and left. Right goes to Juniper Springs Group C.G. **[6.0]**

4.3 High point with good views to the west. **[4.0]**

5.8 Stay right on 2N89Y to begin loop. Trail gets rougher. **[2.5]**
02 **N34 14.616 W116 42.414**

6.1 Bear right to take side trip to arrastra. **[2.2]**

6.3 Remains of arrastra on left. Camp spots ahead if you continue. We turned around here. **[2.0]**

6.6 Bear right and continue south on 2N61Y. **[1.7]**

8.3 Bear left staying on 2N61Y. Unmarked road on right goes to Heartbreak Ridge (see disclaimer). **[0.0]**
03 **N34 13.429 W116 41.713**

0.0 Zero odometer at Wpt. 03 **[10.8]**

0.5 Most difficult part of trail as rocky road descends steeply. **[10.3]**

1.3 Stay left on 2N61Y. **[9.5]**

1.6 Cross wash. **[9.2]**

1.7 Turn hard left on easier 2N02, Burns Canyon Road. Right goes to interesting Pioneertown. **[9.1]**
04 **N34 13.641 W116 40.291**

2.1 Driver's choice. We went left on more difficult 2N70Y. **[8.7]**

2.4 Another driver's choice. Right more difficult. **[8.4]**

3.1 Series of difficult spots as you climb. **[7.7]**

3.5 Rejoin easier 2N02 and continue north staying on most-traveled road. **[7.3]**

4.6 Continue straight. Right uphill is Rose Mine and unusual dune-like terrain. **[6.2]**

4.7 Turn left on 2N01. **[6.1]**
05 **N34 14.778 W116 42.175**

5.0 Return to start of loop at Waypoint 02. Bear right and go out the way you came in. **[5.8]**

10.8 Return to start at paved Highway 38. **[0.0]**
Right returns to Big Bear Lake. Left circles west back to Redlands.

Trail updates & GPS downloads at www.funtreks.com

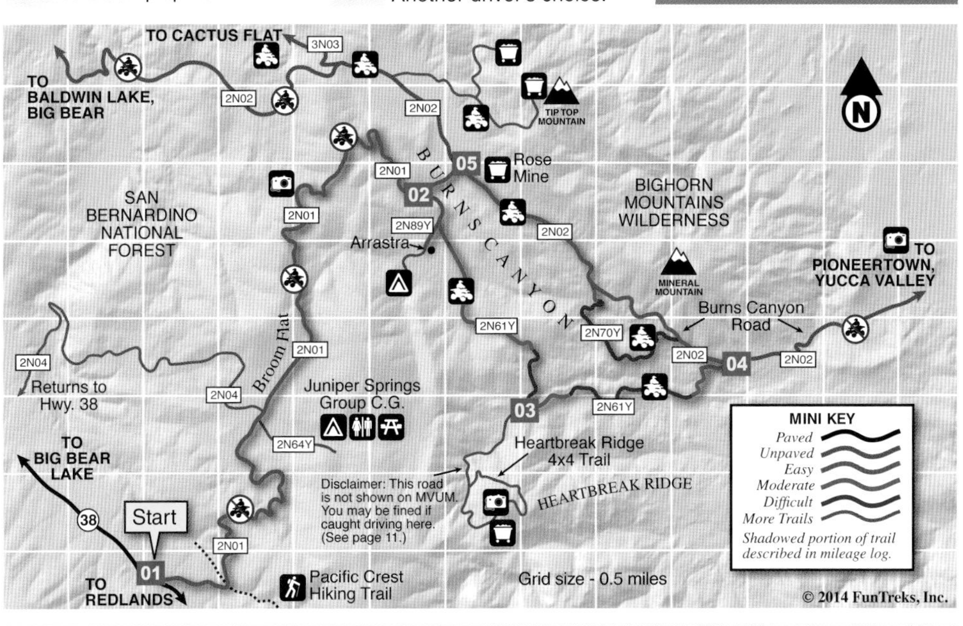

You'll see large Joshua trees along portions of the route.

Ocotillo, Anza-Borrego Desert, Superstition Mountain, Imperial Sand Dunes

You can't discuss Area 6 without talking about "sand." Thirteen of the 18 trails in this southernmost area deal with soft-sand conditions. We recommend you review our tips on driving in sand on page 15. *Superstition Mountain, Trail #92,* and *Glamis, Oldsmobile Hill, Trail #93,* feature large shifting dunes, which is the most challenging of all sand conditions. It goes without saying that it's easy to get stuck, but first-timers don't realize how easy it is to roll a vehicle going over the back side (or drift side) of a dune. We recommend you avoid this situation entirely. Fortunately, many of the routes we've chosen are mostly packed sand, like trails in Ocotillo Wells SVRA. You are usually on solid ground if you stay on the best-traveled route.

Trails 80 through 87 are inside fabulous Anza-Borrego Desert State Park. Sport utility vehicle owners will love the park, as five of the seven trails are suitable for stock 4x4 SUVs. Sorry, green-sticker vehicles are not allowed in the park.

Several trails are very close to the Mexico border, where you may come in contact with illegal immigrants. This happened to us on *Mortero Wash, Trail #87.* Ours was a friendly encounter, but this is not always the case. Be careful.

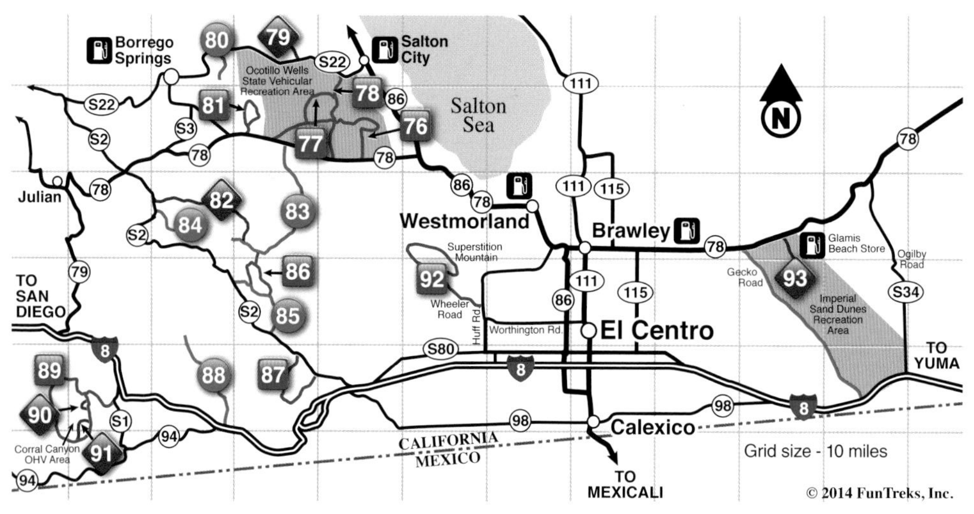

Glamis, Oldsmobile Hill, Sand Canyon Highway, Trail #93, difficult. Easy to get stuck if you're not careful.

76 Ocotillo Wells SVRA

AREA 6 map on page 178

Scouts at Ranger Station. Land Rover 3rd in line.

Crossing Tarantula Wash. Markers often missing.

Cahuilla Trail washed out west of Artesian Well.

Shell Reef Expressway.

Historical Highlight: *The "Wells" in "Ocotillo Wells" is said to be derived from exploratory oil wells that existed here from 1919 to 1984. During WWII, portions of the area were used for military training. After the war, surplus Willys Jeeps were bought by civilians and used here for recreation. In April of 1976, Ocotillo Wells was officially designated as an SVRA (State Vehicular Recreation Area).*

Overview: This trail passes west to east through the heart of Ocotillo Wells SVRA and provides an introduction to the area. You'll get a feel for the obscure terrain and have access to many side roads of greater difficulty. The area is free and open 24 hours a day, 7 days a week. Lots of camping with vault toilets. Pay showers at Holmes Camp and along Ranger Station Road. Get an official map at ranger station.

Rating: Moderate: Most of this route is easy, but a few rutted washes offer challenges for stock 4x4 SUVs. Route-finding can be challenging when wind blows down signs and covers tire tracks.

Stats: Length: Our route covers 21.7 miles. Time: 3 to 4 hours. Elevation: 26 to 355 ft. Best time: Late October through mid May. Very hot in summer.

Current Conditions: Call Discovery Center at the park at (760) 767-5391.

Getting There: Take State Route 78 to Ranger Station Road about halfway between Borrego Springs and Highway 86. If coming from Highway 86, Ranger Station Road is west 18.5 miles. Head north on Ranger Station Road about 0.2 miles to Quarry Road on right. Before you turn, you'll see the Discovery Center and Ranger Station just ahead.

START *MILEAGE LOG:*

0.0 Zero trip odometer [Rev. Miles]
Head east on Quarry Road from Ranger Station Road. [21.7]
01 N33 09.231 W116 10.037

1.1 Stay left on Quarry Road where Main street goes right. [20.6]

1.6 Bear right on Shell Reef Expressway. [20.1]
02 N33 09.834 W116 08.831

3.6 Continue east past Devil's Slide (on left). [18.1]

5.5 Continue east crossing wide Bank Wash. [16.2]

5.7 Continue east. (A left turn here goes north up East Bank Wash to Pumpkin Patch Trail #77.) [16.0]
03 N33 11.156 W116 04.971

6.2 Continue east past fenced-off Shell Reef (on left) [15.5]

7.8 Continue straight on Shell Reef Expressway. Left is Cross Over Trail #78. After this point, Shell Reef Expressway curves to the south. [13.9]
04 N33 11.308 W116 02.902

8.8 Bear left on Cahuilla Trail and head northeast. [12.9]
05 N33 10.975 W116 02.096

11.4 Bear left on Gas Dome Road. [10.3]
06 N33 10.742 W115 59.700

12.6 At toilet, cross Pole Line Road and continue NE on Gas Dome Road. You must stay on existing roads and trails from this point on. [9.1]

14.3 Pass through area of fenced-off gas domes. [7.4]
07 N33 10.789 W115 57.390

15.2 Trail swings right and winds south through a narrow, fun wash. [6.5]

16.0 Arrive at Artesian Well. Turn right here and follow Cahuilla Trail west again. Parts of this route were very hard to see due to wind-blown sand covering the trail. [5.7]
08 N33 09.993 W115 56.642

16.6 Trail gets very washed out with deep ruts. Careful tire placement needed. [5.1]

18.5 Bear left on Pole Line Road and head straight south. [3.2]
09 N33 10.559 W115 58.699

18.8 Main road splits left and continues south parallel to lesser road under power lines. [2.9]

21.7 Return to paved Highway 78. Turn right to return to ranger station. Left goes to Highway 86 . [0.0]
10 N33 07.547 W115 58.630

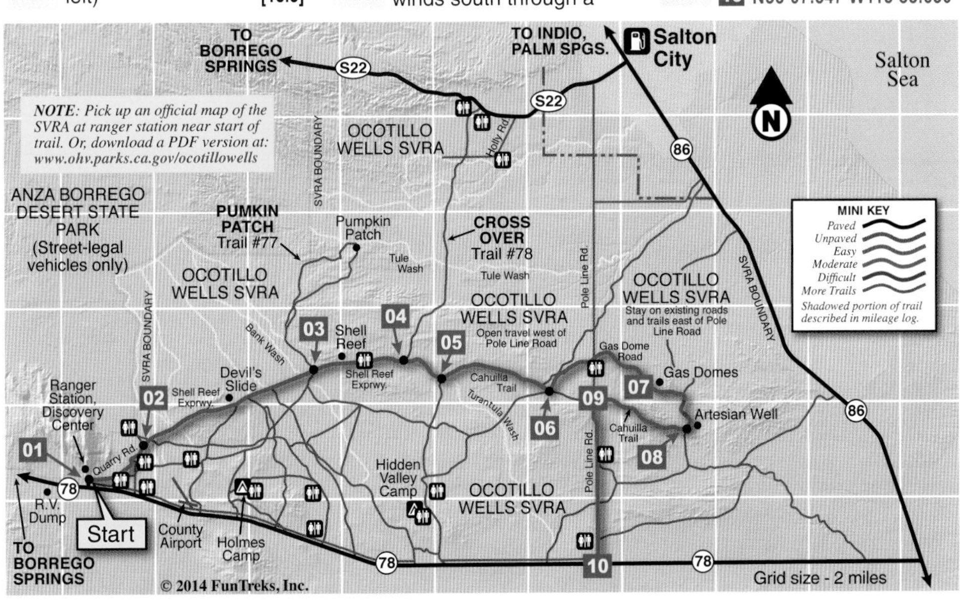

Artesian Well provides enough water for a natural palm tree to grow, rare in the desert.

77

Pumpkin Patch

AREA 6 map on page 178

Finding the Pumpkin Patch was not easy, but it was worth the effort.

Not many sign posts mark the route.

Heading north after Waypoint 02.

Historical Highlight: *The round rocks at the Pumpkin Patch are called "concretions." They were formed deep under the sand by water carrying cementing precipitates that began building around an organic nucleus such as a leaf, piece of shell or a fossil. Wind eroded away the sand, bringing the rocks to the surface, where further wind erosion rounded them to their present shape. Do not remove any of the rocks. Take only pictures.*

Overview: The end of this trail features unique geologic rock formations. We've chosen the most direct route from the ranger station. This trail is often obscured by sand and is very hard to find at times. Look for rock cairns and a few sign posts. Lots of open terrain to explore along the way. Great area for ATVs and UTVs. Get detailed map of SVRA from ranger station at start of Trail #76. Visit the Discovery Center to learn more about the rock formations.

Rating: Moderate: Most of the route follows wash bottoms, where conditions vary tremendously depending on recent rains. Be prepared for anything. We recommend using a GPS unit.

Stats: Length: 4.1 miles one way. Time: About an hour if you don't get lost. Elevation: 153 to 305 ft. Best time: Late October through mid May. Very hot in summer.

Current Conditions: Call Discovery Center at the park at (760) 767-5391.

Getting There: Follow directions for previous Trail #76. After 5.7 miles, turn left and head north in East Bank Wash. If you reach the information boards at Shell Reef, you've gone past the turn by 0.4 miles.

START MILEAGE LOG:

0.0 Zero trip odometer **[Rev. Miles]**
From Shell Reef Expressway, head north in massive Bank/East Bank Wash. Stay to the east side as far as possible. [4.1]
01 N33 11.156 W116 04.971

0.4 Continue north in main wash past a small wash on the right. [3.7]

1.0 Swing right into lesser wash on right as you leave East Bank Wash. We found a Pumpkin Patch Trail marker here, but it's easy to miss. [3.1]
02 N33 11.750 W116 05.598

1.2 Driver's choice. Stay left following easier shortcut. Look for cairns that mark trail. Right follows difficult wash, then circles back to rejoin trail at next waypoint. [2.9]
03 N33 11.941 W116 05.608

1.7 Stay left. Alternate route through difficult wash rejoins on right. [2.4]
04 N33 12.267 W116 05.353

2.0 Look for cairns. Route is very hard to find. [2.1]

2.2 Bear left. [1.9]
05 N33 12.653 W116 05.210

2.4 Trail changes to small hills and whoop-ti-dos. [1.7]

3.1 Trail becomes more obvious as you pass through hilly area. [1.0]
06 N33 13.201 W116 04.932

4.0 Come out of hills and follow trail east. [0.1]

4.1 After going past vault toilet, bear right to Pumpkin Patch. Look for large signs. [0.0]
07 N33 13.369 W116 04.103
Return the way you came, or follow Tule Wash east to Cross Over Trail #78.

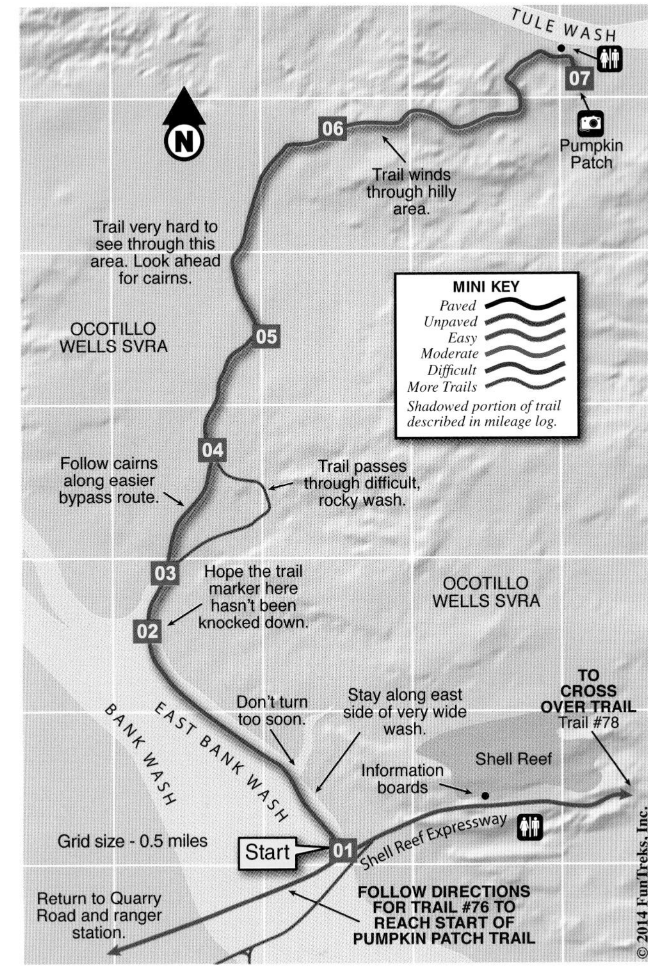

Trail was better defined after Waypoint 06.

Stay to the east side of East Bank Wash or you'll miss the turn at Waypoint 02.

78 Cross Over Trail

AREA 6 map on page 178

Marker at start of trail.

Single lane most of the way.

Moon-like landscape offers many fun side roads to explore.

Overview: This is the main route to reach the northern part of Ocotillo Wells SVRA. It provides access to many fun side trails and ends at camping and picnic facilities along Hwy. S22. The north end has many ATV and dirt bike trails and a training track for kids. It's also the main access point from Salton City.

Rating: Moderate: Most of this route is single lane with lots of twists and whoop-ti-dos. It's fairly slow-going in places. We found the route well-marked, but it is still easy to make a wrong turn if you're not paying attention. Avoid this trail when it is wet.

Stats: Length: 6.4 miles. Time: 2-3 hours. Elevation: 59 to 202 ft. Best time: Late October through mid May. Very hot in summer.

Current Conditions: Call Discovery Center at the park at (760) 767-5391.

Getting There: Follow directions for Trail #76 starting at the ranger station. After 7.8 miles, turn left at sign for Cross Over Trail. Follow reverse mileage if starting on the north end.

START **MILEAGE LOG:**

0.0 Zero trip odometer [Rev. Miles]
Head north from Shell Reef Expressway at sign for Cross Over Trail. [6.4]
01 N33 11.310 W116 02.907

0.2 Cross Tarantula Wash and continue north. [6.2]

0.5 Stay left on better-traveled road. [5.9]
02 N33 11.694 W116 02.747

1.5 Follow signs and stay in wash. [4.9]

2.2 Continue north and cross Tule Wash (secondary branch). [4.2]

2.6 Continue north and cross wide Tule Wash. [3.8]
03 N33 13.040 W116 01.942

3.5 Continue north where unmarked road goes right. [2.9]

4.0 Continue north across Arroyo Salado. [2.4]
04 N33 14.232 W116 01.873

4.3 Tierra Del Sol joins on right. [2.1]

4.5 Continue north. Tierra Del Sol goes left. [1.9]

5.1 Cross north fork of Arroyo Salado. [1.3]

5.2 Continue north across Holly Road. If you are in a hurry, you can take faster Holly Road east, then north to Hwy. S22. [1.2]
05 N33 15.069 W116 01.514

5.6 Cross another wash, then drop into a wash heading north. Trails crisscross everywhere. [0.8]

6.1 Bear right out of wash and head east past camping area with covered tables. This is a popular ATV area. [0.3]
06 N33 15.875 W116 01.419

6.4 Arrive at Highway S22. Right goes into Salton City in 2.5 miles. Convenient point to gas up. Left goes to Fonts Point, Trail #80, and Calcite Mine, Trail #79. [0.0]
07 N33 15.966 W116 01.125

Holly Road, quick way out.

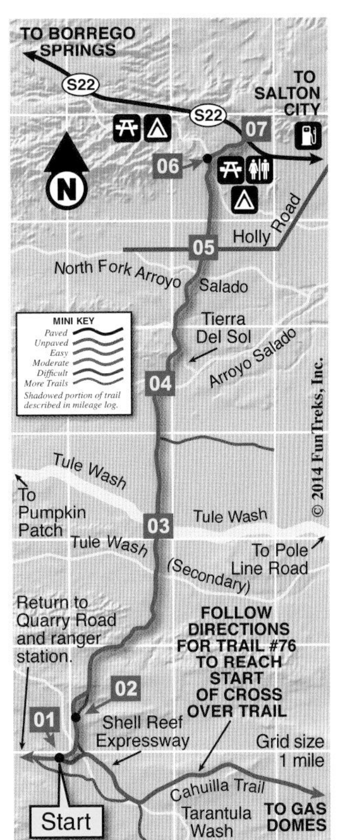

Point where Tierra Del Sol joins on right.

Shaded picnic tables.

Entrance at north end along Highway S22. Obey all posted regulations.

79 Calcite Mine

AREA 6 map on page 178

We stopped here at edge of overlook at the mine. Look around but be careful of deep trenches.

Initial descent to South Fork of Palm Wash.

Steep in spots with large ruts.

Historical Highlight: *Calcite Mine contained a high-quality colorless calcite that was used to make Norden bombsights during WWII. It was mined by digging trenches following calcite seams. You can see bits of the calcite when it reflects the sun. It is illegal to remove any plant, animal or mineral from the park.*

Overview: A short but challenging climb to an old WWII calcite mine and a high overlook with views of Anza-Borrego State Park and the Salton Sea. See map for side trips to hiking trails into two amazing slot canyons. Street-legal vehicles only in state park.

Rating: Difficult: Steep, narrow and tippy with large ruts and washouts. Impassable when wet. Stay out if rain is expected. Modified vehicles are best, but aggressive stock vehicles can do it with experienced driver. Extreme flash flood danger hiking in the slot canyons.

Stats: Length: 1.9 miles one way. Time: Allow 1 hour to reach mine with capable vehicle. Elevation: 516 to 1,131 ft. Open all year. Avoid summer.

Current Conditions: Anza-Borrego Desert State Park Visitor Center. Call 760-767-4205.

Getting There: Located on the north side of Highway S22 between Borrego Springs and Salton City. From Highway 86 in Salton City, drive 8.3 miles west on S22. Trail entrance is 0.65 miles west of large microwave tower on S22.

START **MILEAGE LOG:**

0.0 Zero trip odometer [Rev. Miles]
Follow road downhill. It first bends left then continues north. [1.9]
01 N33 16.868 W116 05.795

0.1 When you reach wash, bear slightly left and head across wash to yellow ROUGH ROAD sign. [1.8]
(Note: You can drive west and east in this wash. West leads to a popular slot-canyon hike. East goes to Salton City.)

0.2 On north side of wash, head uphill on well-marked trail. [1.7]

0.7 Continue straight. Road on right drops downhill to Palm Wash. [1.2]
02 N33 17.253 W116 06.234

0.9 Steep section with big ruts. [1.0]

1.2 Caution. Spot prone to washouts could be dangerous. [0.7]

1.4 Steep, rocky climb after crossing wash. [0.5]
03 N33 17.666 W116 06.660
(Hiking north in wash leads to another amazing slot canyon.)

1.7 Tippy spot. Big hole on outer edge of trail. [0.2]

1.8 Bear right across flat area at mine location. [0.1]

1.9 We continued east a short distance before stopping at edge of overlook. Nearby deep crevices are left from the mining operations. Watch your step. [0.0]
04 N33 17.933 W116 06.582

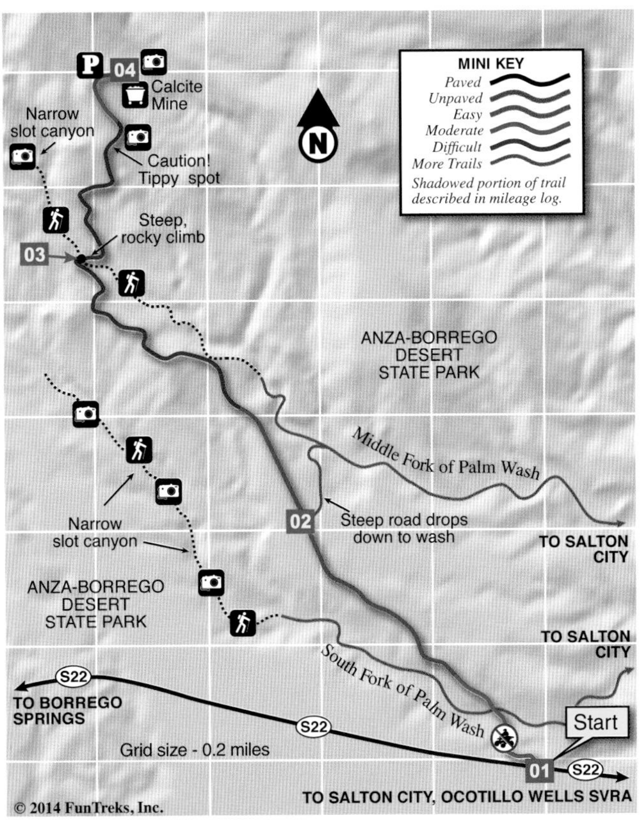

Open trench at the mine.

Steep, rocky climb after Wpt. 03. Hike left in wash to slot canyon.

80 Fonts Point

AREA 6 map on page 178

Looking down on Borrego Badlands from Fonts Point at midday.

Fonts Wash is very wide with soft sand.

Historical Highlight: *Fonts Point is one of the most popular viewpoints in Anza-Borrego Desert State Park. Try to time your visit to be there before sunset when views of the ancient Badlands are the most spectacular. You'll gain a better appreciation of the geology if you stop at the visitor center beforehand.*

Overview: Not much to see along the route until you get to the end. Stay in the main wash and obey all signs. Views at the end are definitely worth this short drive. All vehicles in Anza-Borrego Desert State Park must be street legal.

Rating: Easy: The route climbs gradually the entire way, but the climb is almost imperceptible until the end. Soft sand is the only real challenge. You should definitely have 4-wheel drive. Stock tires will do better if aired down a bit. Be aware that flash floods are possible in Fonts Wash.

Stats: Length: Just 4 miles one way. Time: Half hour each way. Elevation: 717 to 1,250 ft. Best time: Late October through mid May. Very hot in summer.

Current Conditions: Anza-Borrego Desert State Park Visitor Center. Call (760) 767-4205. Open 9-5 Oct. 1 - May 31, weekends only the rest of the year. The visitor center is located at 200 Palm Canyon Drive in Borrego Springs.

Getting There: Take Highway S22 east from Borrego Springs about 11 miles from center of town. Look for a sign on the right near mile marker 29. From Salton City, take S22 west about 17 miles.

START **MILEAGE LOG:**

0.0 Zero trip odometer **[Rev. Miles]**
Head south in very wide Fonts Wash. Consider airing down your tires to avoid getting stuck in soft sand. **[4.0]**
01 N33 18.205 W116 14.346

1.7 Move over to right side of wash. Avoid lesser wash to left. **[2.3]**

1.9 Stay in wash on right. Everything left is for foot traffic only. **[2.1]**
02 N33 16.905 W116 13.308

2.2 Wash narrows. **[1.8]**

2.4 Less sandy, more of a road. **[1.6]**

3.7 Stay left at start of one-way loop. Single lane traffic. **[0.3]**
03 N33 15.696 W116 14.038

3.9 Climb uphill out of wash. **[0.1]**

4.0 Arrive at small parking area. Stop here and hike less than one-tenth mile to see views of Borrego Badlands. **[0.0]**
04 N33 15.468 W116 14.007
Return the way you came.

Trail updates & GPS downloads at www.funtreks.com

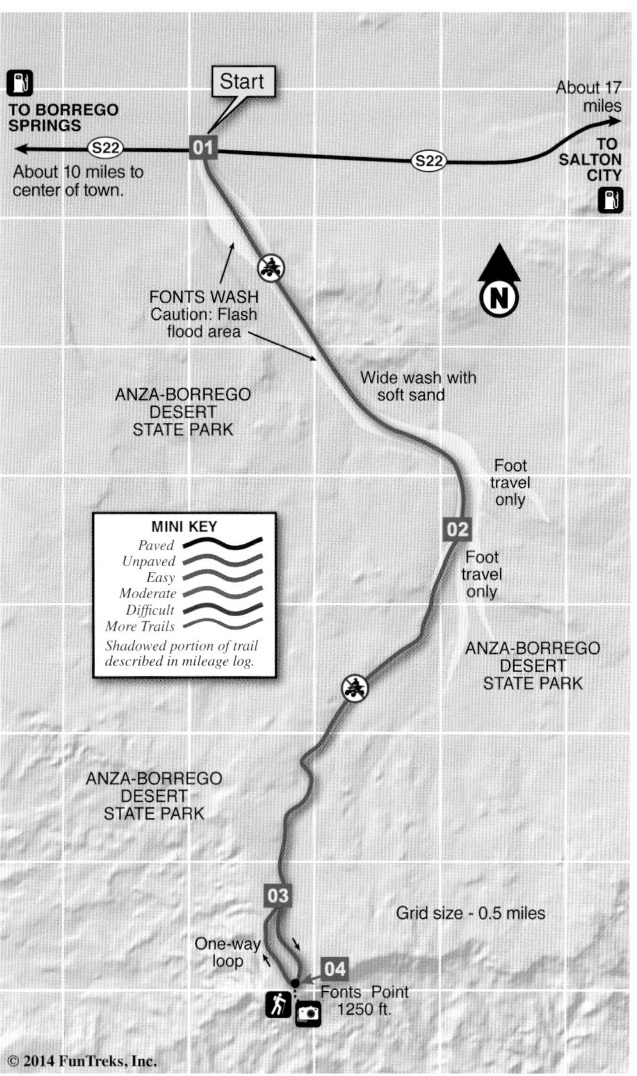

Start of trail is well marked.

The wash narrows as you get closer to Fonts Point. FunTreks scout passes native ocotillo plant.

81 The Slot

AREA 6 map on page 178

The hike into slot is great fun. Stay out if rain is expected.

Most of the route is very easy.

Before Waypoint 03, walk this hill before starting down.

Hill was not too bad on this day.

Overview: There are several beautiful slot canyons like this in Anza-Borrego State Park (see Trail #79). Hiking the canyon is great fun, but be very careful; walls can collapse and rainstorms can flood the canyon in minutes. Kids should be accompanied by their parents. No green-sticker vehicles allowed.

Rating: Moderate: Much of this route is in wide washes with soft sand. However, one hill drops steeply into the canyon before Waypoint 03. This moderate spot has the potential to be difficult if the hill gets washed out. Drive loop other way to avoid the hill. Hill is closed to uphill traffic. Route is usually OK for stock, high-clearance 4x4 SUVs. Air down tires if necessary.

Stats: Length: 11.6 miles. Time: Trail can be driven in 1 hour, allow extra time for hike. Elevation: 292 to 826 ft. Best time: Open all year. Avoid summer.

Current Conditions: Anza-Borrego Desert State Park. Call (760) 767-5311.

Getting There: Follow signs for Buttes Pass located on Hwy. 78 about 3 miles west of the ranger station at Ocotillo Wells SVRA. From points west, turn left 1.5 miles east of Borrego Springs Road near mile post 87.

START *MILEAGE LOG:*

0.0 Zero trip odometer [Rev. Miles]
Head north on a wide single-lane dirt road. [3.5]
01 N33 09.542 W116 13.123

1.0 Bear left following marker to Borrego Mtn. [2.5]
02 N33 10.277 W116 12.793

1.8 Turn left and follow ridge of canyon. (If you do not want to drive the steep section of this trail, you may stop here and hike down to The Slot.) [1.7]

2.8 Bear right down steep hill. Walk it first if you have any concerns. [0.7]

3.0 At bottom of hill, turn right and follow the wash. [0.5]
03 N33 11.198 W116 13.268

3.5 Stop and park here. Hike to The Slot then return to Waypoint 03 when done exploring. [0.0]

0.0 Zero trip odometer at Wpt. 03
At bottom of steep hill, continue north in Borrego Mountain Wash. [7.6]

1.0 Turn left after a peculiar-looking rock. [6.6]

2.3 Bear right in the San Felipe Wash. This is a wide wash and the trail meanders from the right to the left side of the wash. We tried to stay on the right as much as possible. [5.3]
04 N33 12.758 W116 12.762

4.1 Turn right on Buttes Canyon, a wide wash. [3.5]
05 N33 11.916 W116 11.327

5.9 Continue straight. Hawk Canyon goes right. [1.7]

6.2 Stay right. [1.4]

6.7 Reconnect with Waypoint 02. Turn left to return to starting point. [0.9]

7.6 Highway 78. [0.0]

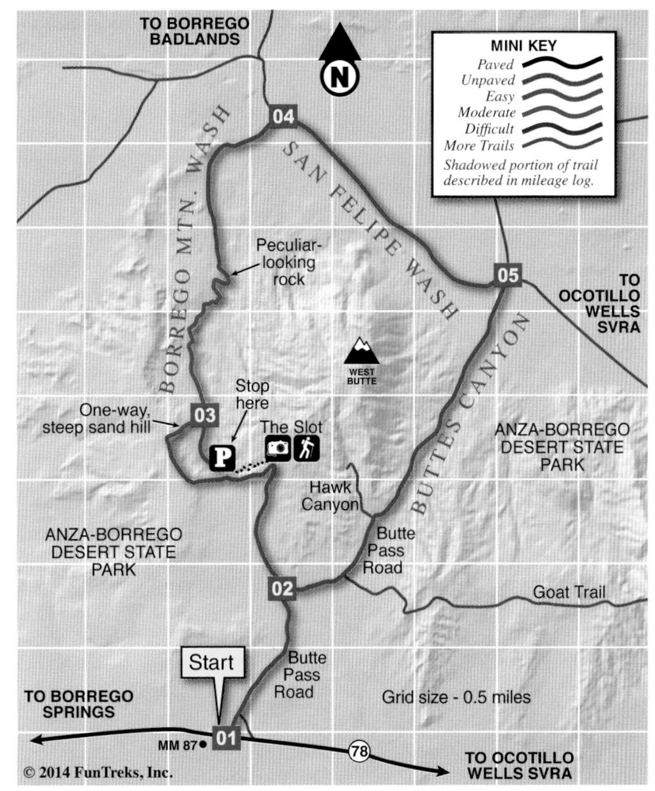

Main washes are very wide, but flash floods are still possible.

Route is well marked.

The Slot doesn't look like much from above.

82 Pinyon Mountain Valley

AREA 6 map on page 178

Trail starts here. Head east on single-lane road.

Be very careful descending "Pinyon Dropoff."

"The Squeeze" has no bypass.

Steep climb out of wash after Waypoint 04.

Overview: Very scenic, long desert crossing with special challenges. (See rating below.) Entire trail is in beautiful Anza-Borrego Desert State Park. All vehicles must be street legal. Travel recommended west to east. Unique side trip into Sandstone Canyon (Trail #83, described separately). Take 1-mile hike to curious Wind Caves. At Wpt. 06, access difficult Broken Shaft Gulch to bottom of Diablo Dropoff.

Rating: Difficult: Much of this trail follows sandy washes, which are mostly easy with occasional moderate rocky sections. Two major obstacles, however, are for hard-core vehicles only. Wide vehicles can expect side damage getting through *The Squeeze*. *Pinyon Dropoff* is extremely steep. Avoid trail if rain is expected due to flash flood danger.

Stats: Length: 30.1 miles. Time: About 5 hours. Add for side trips. Elevation: 226 ft. to 3,977 ft. Best time: Open all year. Avoid summer.

Current Conditions: Anza-Borrego Desert State Park. Call (760) 767-5311.

Getting There: From Scissors Crossing on Highway 78 between Julian and Ocotillo Wells, take Highway S2 south 4.4 miles. Turn left on sandy road in bushes immediately after large sign that says: Welcome to Anza-Borrego Desert State Park. Sign for trail says *Pinyon Mountain Area* (hidden in bushes).

START MILEAGE LOG:

0.0 Zero trip odometer [Rev. Miles]
Head east on one-lane, rutted, sandy road. [17.9]
01 N33 03.416 W116 25.266

0.1 After wide circular area, stay right on road marked "Pinyon Mtn. Valley." [17.8]

3.5 Stay right. Road on left is closed. [14.4]

3.7 Rock challenge. [14.2]

3.8 Stay right. Left closed. Gets easy again. [14.1]

4.2 Jog slightly right, then continue east across sandy wash. [13.7]
02 N33 03.206 W116 21.378

4.5 Enter wide sandy wash and continue east along base of ridge on left. [13.4]

5.7 Continue east passing hiking trail to Whale Peak. [12.2]

5.8 Ignore road on left. [12.1]

6.3 Ignore road on right. [11.6]

7.0 "The Squeeze" [10.9]

7.6 Important right turn uphill out of wash. Trail gets narrow and difficult. [10.3]
03 N33 03.062 W116 18.216

7.9 Steep descent down Pinyon Dropoff. [10.0]

8.8 Turn right at "T" following marker to Fish Canyon. Left closed. [9.1]
04 N33 03.263 W116 17.254

9.4 Bear right up steep rocky hill out of wash. [8.5]

10.2 Easy sandy road winds across Hapaha Flat. Now in Fish Creek Wash. [7.7]

12.5 Bear right at sign to Mc-Cain Spring (dry). [5.4]

14.5 Maneuver through boulders in wash. [3.4]

16.7 Stay left joining larger wash. [1.2]

17.2 Continue south in main wash where lesser wash joins on right. [0.7]

17.9 Sandstone Canyon, Trail #83 on right. [0.0]
05 N32 58.766 W116 12.877

0.0 Zero trip odometer at Wpt. 05
Continue south in wide Fish Creek Wash. [12.2]

2.8 Follow main wash as it curves left. (Narrow wash on right is Broken Shaft Gulch that goes to bottom of Diablo Dropoff. (Sometimes closed due to washouts.) [9.4]
06 N32 57.635 W116 10.715

3.7 Stay right in main wash. Left is alternate loop that rejoins later. [8.5]

5.4 Follow main wash to right. Alternate loop rejoins on left. [6.8]

8.0 Continue north in main wash. North Fork joins on left. Wind Caves Hiking Trail on right. [4.2]
07 N32 59.554 W116 07.098

12.2 After passing through dramatic high walls of Split Mountain, bear left on what soon becomes paved road. [0.0]
08 N33 02.338 W116 05.811
Follow paved Split Mountain Road north 8.1 miles to Highway 78 at Ocotillo Wells.

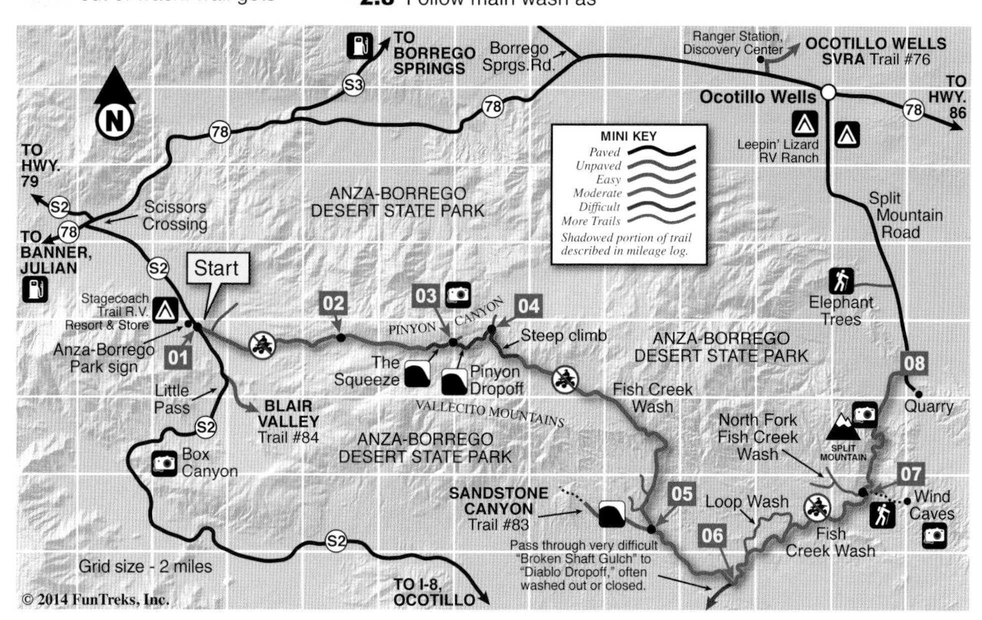

Challenging spot in wash.

No place to be in flash flood.

Much of route is easy.

83 Sandstone Canyon

AREA 6 map on page 178

Towering walls going through Split Mountain.

Sandstone Canyon is very narrow at the end.

Fallen rocks block canyon at 1.7 miles.

Historical Highlight: *A fault occurred through Split Mountain about 20 million years ago. As flood waters passed through the fault it gradually widened, exposing fascinating rock layers. Over 40,000 acres of watershed is funneled through the canyon and continues eastward about 20 miles to the Salton Sea.*

Overview: You'll pass through Split Mountain with its towering walls and interesting exposed rock layers, then wander back and forth in super-wide Fish Creek Wash before entering narrow Sandstone Canyon. Giant rocks block this canyon at 1.7 miles, but some hard-core vehicles are getting through. The last 0.7 miles can be driven or hiked. Hike to Wind Caves is worth the extra time. Anza-Borrego Park is restricted to street-legal vehicles only.

Rating: Easy: Conditions in the canyon sometimes worsen after heavy rains, but this route is usually suitable for stock 4x4 SUVs. Dangerous flash floods are possible. Avoid if rain is forecast.

Stats: Length: 13.9 miles one way. Time: Allow 3 to 4 hours plus time to explore side canyons. Elevation: 226 to 1,553 ft. Best time: Open all year. Avoid extremely hot summer months.

Current Conditions: Anza-Borrego Desert State Park. Call (760) 767-5311.

Getting There: From Ocotillo Wells on Highway 78 on the south side of Ocotillo Wells SVRA, take Split Mountain Road south 8.1 miles. Turn right at sign for Fish Creek Wash after break in pavement.

START **MILEAGE LOG:**

0.0 Zero trip odometer [Rev. Miles]
Head west on dirt portion of Split Mountain Road following wide wash. [13.9]
01 N33 02.338 W116 05.811

1.6 Gradually sides of road begin to rise as you start into canyon. [12.3]

2.6 Canyon narrows through towering walls. Observe folded rock layers in exposed walls. [11.3]

4.2 Stay left in main part of Fish Canyon Wash. Right is North Fork. On left is 1-mile hiking trail to photogenic Wind Caves. [9.7]
02 N32 59.554 W116 07.098

6.7 Stay left in main wash. alternate Loop Wash goes right here. [7.2]
03 N32 58.874 W116 08.989

8.4 Continue straight. Alternate Loop Wash rejoins on right. Consider going this way on return trip. [5.5]

9.4 Continue straight in main wash. Left is difficult Broken Shaft Gulch that leads to base of Diablo Dropoff. [4.5]
04 N32 57.635 W116 10.715

12.2 Turn left into Sandstone Canyon. Canyon narrows quickly, but sandy bottom is flat and easy. [1.7]
05 N32 58.766 W116 12.877

13.9 We found trail blocked by SUV-size rocks. Most people stop here and hike. If you can get over rock, trail remains easy (but very narrow) for another 0.7 miles, with a great hike beyond. [0.0]
06 N32 59.382 W116 14.052
Return the way you came or take alternate Loop Wash. You may also wish to explore the North Fork of Fish Creek Wash.

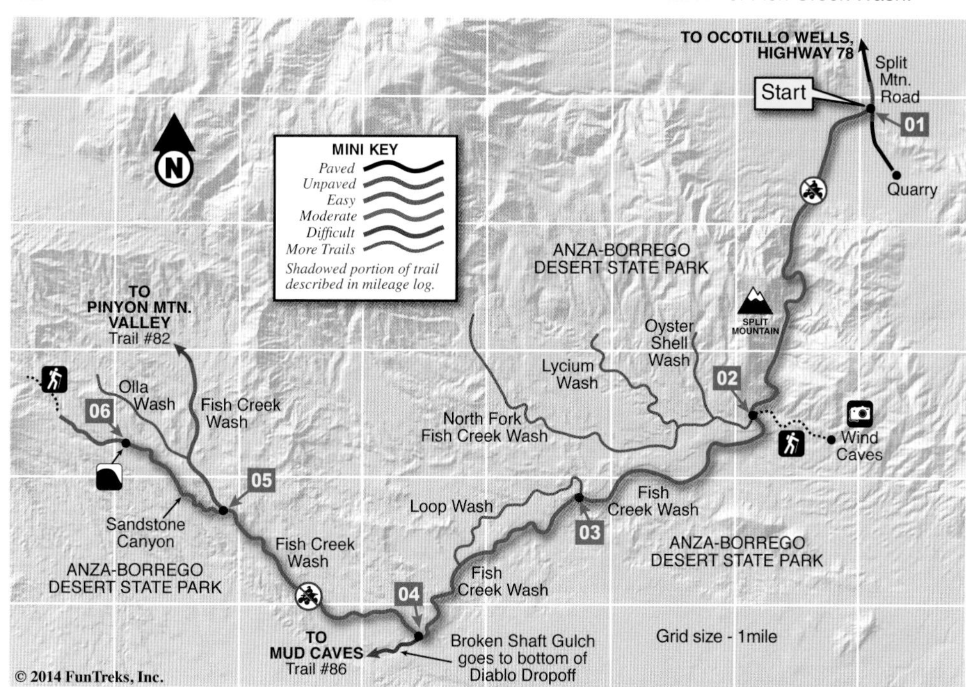

Fish Creek Wash.

Hike one mile to see Wind Caves.

84 Blair Valley

AREA 6 map on page 178

Ruins of the Marshal South home on Ghost Mountain. The Souths called their home "Yaquitepec."

Great views from Ghost Mountain.

We started loop on the north end.

Historical Highlight: *All three of the hikes are fun, but don't miss the one to the Marshal South home. Although this is the longest and steepest hike (we GPS'd it 0.8 mile, not a mile), it's the most unique of the three. Marshal and Tanya South came here in the early 1930s, built an adobe home and managed to survive for 16 years, raising 3 children in the process. To learn more about this fascinating story, go to: www.californiahistorian.com/articles/marshall-south.html.*

Overview: This scenic desert loop passes through a sensitive archaeological area featuring pictographs, Indian morteros and ruins of a 1930s desert home at the top of Ghost Mountain. Hikes are required to see each feature. Historical kiosks at three parking areas. Stay on existing roads at all times. Street-legal vehicles only. Loop can be driven in either direction. Many dispersed camp spots along route.

Rating: Easy: Soft sand possible in wash bottoms, but most of route is hard-packed sand. Suitable for stock high-clearance 4x4 SUVs.

Stats: Length: 11.2 miles. Time: We did everything in 4 hours including the hikes. Elevation: 120 to 3,081 ft. Open all year, but avoid summer.

Current Conditions: Anza-Borrego Desert State Park. Call (760) 767-5311.

Getting There: From Scissors Crossing on Hwy. 78 between Julian and Ocotillo Wells, take Highway S2 south 5.3 miles. Watch for sandy road on the left with small sign that says "Little Blair."

START **MILEAGE LOG:**

0.0 Zero trip odometer [Rev. Miles] Head south on sandy road that parallels Highway S2. [11.2]
01 N33 02.754 W116 24.794

0.9 Follow road as it curves left. Right is Foot & Walker Hiking Trail, once part of Butterfield Stage Route. [10.3]

1.2 Road curves left then right and continues east along foothills. [10.0]

1.7 Follow road as it curves right out of wash. [9.5]

1.8 Bear right at fork following sign to pictographs. [9.4]
02 N33 02.201 W116 23.400

2.3 We made a right off main road to see camp spot nestled in boulders. View of Blair Valley beyond boulders. At camp spot we swung left and reconnected to main road continuing south. [8.9]

2.6 Stay left on main road. Camp spot right. [8.6]

4.1 Make hard left to visit pictographs. [7.1]
03 N33 00.574 W116 22.684

5.5 Stop at parking area. Hike about 0.8 mile to pictographs, then return to Waypoint 03. [5.7]
04 N33 01.182 W116 21.593

6.9 Continue southwest through Wpt. 03 and immediately bear left into parking area to see morteros at Indian site. Park and follow hiking trail 0.3 mile. When finished continue southwest on main road. [4.3]

7.5 Bear left. [3.7]
05 N33 00.345 W116 23.237

7.7 Parking area. Hike 0.8 mile to ruins of Marshal South Home on Ghost Mountain (Yaquitepec), then return to Waypoint 05. [3.5]

8.0 Bear left at Waypoint 05 and follow main road north along base of mountain ridge. [3.2]

8.2 Stay right. Shortcut joins on left. [3.0]

9.8 Stay left across Blair Valley. Many roads go right to camping. [1.4]

11.1 Continue west through large intersection. Kiosk and vault toilet to left. Road on left goes to camping and eventually connects to S2. [0.1]

11.2 Highway S2. Right returns to start. [0.0]
06 N33 02.239 W116 24.631

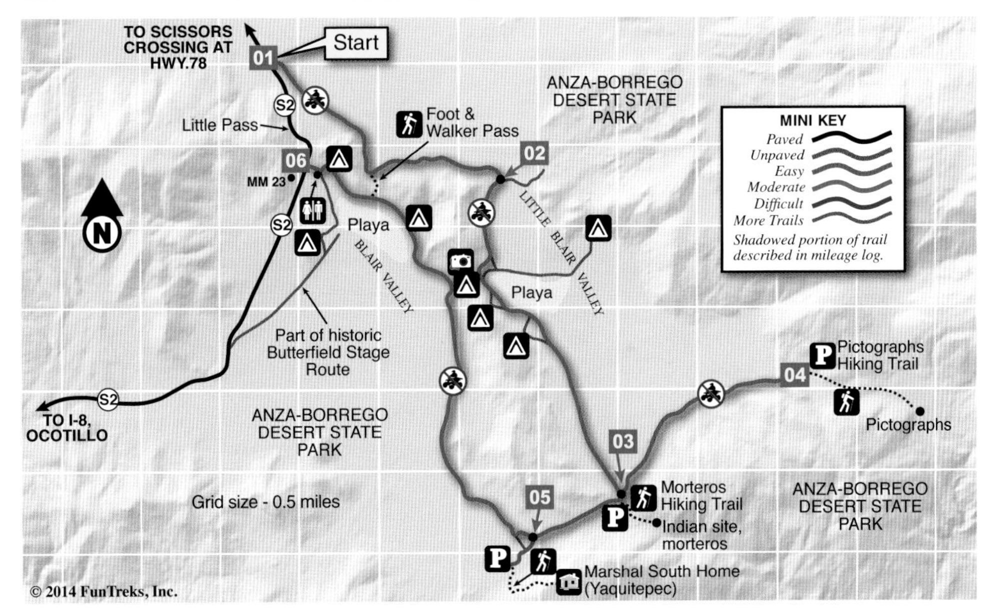

Easy hike to pictographs.

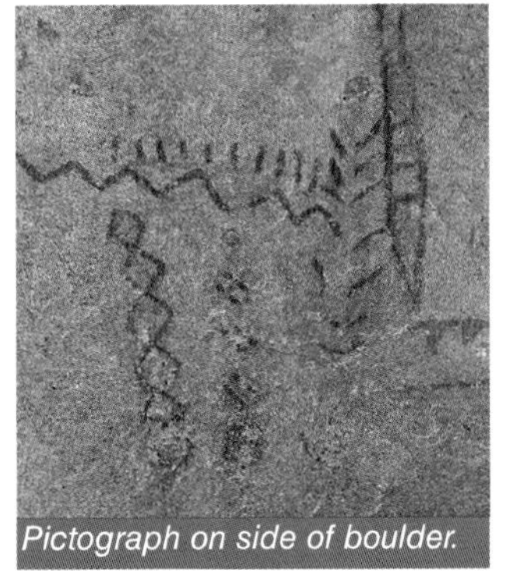
Pictograph on side of boulder.

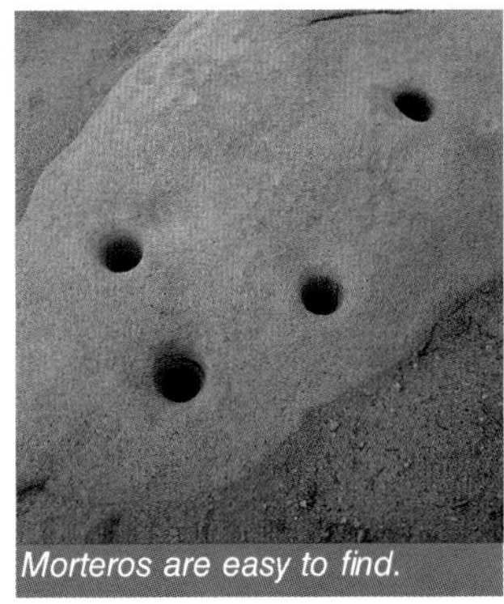
Morteros are easy to find.

85 Canyon Sin Nombre

AREA 6 map on page 178

Start of trail is well marked at Highway S2.

Short, rocky stretch in Canyon Sin Nombre.

Camp spot in slot canyon. Flash floods possible.

Historical Highlight: *We found two explanations for the curious "Hollywood & Vine" street sign at Waypoint 05. One explanation claims a jokester painted over a county mileage sign of a bygone era. Another attributes the act to Army tank crews who trained here during World War II. Purportedly, Anza Borrego Park rangers maintain the sign. To learn more, we recommend the book "The Anza-Borrego Desert Region" by Lowell & Dianna Lindsay.*

Overview: This route twists northeast through narrow, geologically interesting Canyon Sin Nombre, then follows the historic Butterfield Stage Route northwest through a series of wide sandy washes. Approximately 1.6 miles from the end, the route passes just south of a mesquite-shaded watering hole called "Palm Spring," once used as a relay station on the Butterfield Stage Route. The area is now a popular camping spot. Street-legal vehicles only on this trail.

Rating: Easy: You'll want 4-wheel drive for the soft sand and skid plates to get through Canyon Sin Nombre. The wide, obscure washes make route-finding very challenging. GPS is recommended.

Stats: Length: 11.5 miles. Time: About 2 hours. Elevation: 526 ft. to 1,210 ft. Best time: Late October through mid May. Very hot in summer.

Current Conditions: Anza-Borrego Desert State Park Visitor Center. Call (760) 767-4205. Open 9-5 Oct. 1 - May 31, weekends only the rest of the year.

Getting There: From Interstate 8, take Imperial Hwy., Exit 89, north through town of Ocotillo. The highway turns west, then heads northwest, marked as S2. The trail is well marked with a large brown sign on the right after a total of 13.2 miles, just after Carrizo Badlands Overlook and before Sweeney Pass.

START **MILEAGE LOG:**

0.0 Zero trip odometer **[Rev. Miles]** Head northeast on defined sandy road toward badland foothills. [11.5]
01 N32 49.799 W116 10.211

0.3 Trail swings right in sandy wash along foothills. Sand is softer here. [11.2]

1.0 Enter Canyon Sin Nombre. Rocky trail zigzags through canyon. Use caution going over rocks. [10.5]

1.9 Check canyon walls for interesting rock folds in sedimentary rock. [9.6]

2.3 Camp spot on left in narrow slot canyon. Don't camp here if rain is expected due to possibility of flash flood. [9.2]

2.8 Exit Canyon Sin Nombre and begin following poorly defined, smoke-tree wash. [8.7]

3.9 Stay along left half of wash, don't go right. [7.6]

4.3 Bear left and follow wide sandy wash northwest. Right goes to remains of Carrizo Stage Station in about 3 miles. [7.2]
02 N32 52.394 W116 08.604

5.5 Continue straight. Right goes to the Diablo Dropoff via Arroyo Seco del Diablo. [6.0]
03 N32 52.970 W116 09.582

6.6 Continue straight. Don't enter wash on right. [4.9]

7.0 Stay left. Arroyo Tapiado goes right to Mud Caves, Trail #86. [4.5]
04 N32 53.718 W116 10.758

8.9 Note historic "Hollywood & Vine" sign atop small knoll on right. [2.6]
05 N32 54.424 W116 12.279

9.2 Stay left following tracks in wider wash. Smaller Arroyo Hueso goes right here. [2.3]

9.9 Trail continues northwest in wide Vallecito Wash. About 1/4 mile north of this point is "Palm Spring," a natural oasis of mesquite with a water hole. This was a Butterfield Stage Stop in 1858. [1.6]

11.2 Follow road left. [0.3]

11.5 Return to paved County Road S2. [0.0]
06 N32 54.928 W116 14.429

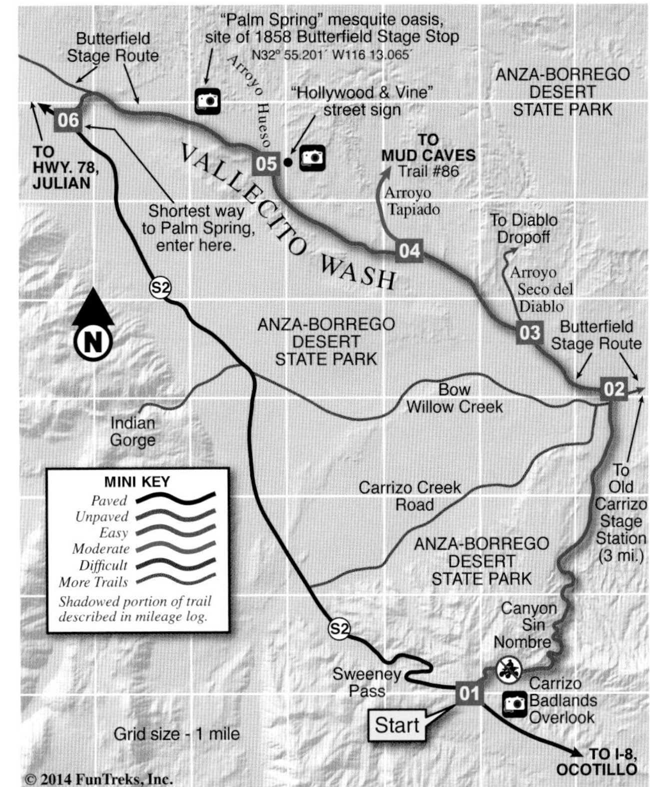

This sign marks exit of trail.

Barrel cactus along route.

"Holllywood & Vine" street sign atop knoll at Waypoint 05.

86 Mud Caves

AREA 6 map on page 178

Great trail for stock, high-clearance SUVs.

Caves can be dangerous. Enter at your own risk.

High clearance is needed through this section.

Historical Highlight: *Maps of the mud cave network are available online. In 2012, a hiker fell into a giant crevice and died. So, for liability reasons, the state park no longer sells the maps or encourages people to go in the caves. However, they do not prohibit people from entering and the caves are still very popular. FunTreks also advises that if you go into the caves, you do so at your own risk. Please be careful.*

Overview: At least 22 mud caves have been counted in Anza-Borrego State Park, some up to 1,000 feet long and 80 feet high. Thousands of people come here to explore the caves and accidents are rare. However, they do happen from time to time. Never enter the caves if it is raining, has rained recently or if rain is expected. This trail connects to Sandstone Canyon, Trail #83, via a hard-core route if Diablo Dropoff is open. Sorry, no green-sticker vehicles are allowed in park.

Rating: Moderate: Mostly sandy washes with hard-packed dirt. High clearance needed for last 3 miles where loose rock is mixed with soft sand.

Stats: Length: 18.1 miles including trip to Diablo Dropoff. Time: About 2 hours, allow more if exploring Mud Caves. Elevation: 604 to 1,249 ft. Best time: Open all year. Avoid summer.

Current Conditions: Anza-Borrego Visitor Center, (760) 767-4205.

Getting There: Follow directions to Canyon Sin Nombre, Trail #85. After 7 miles, turn right into the Arroyo Tapiado Wash.

START **MILEAGE LOG:**

0.0 Zero trip odometer **[Rev. Miles]**
Head north in Arroyo Tapiado Wash. **[10.5]**
01 N32 53.701 W116 10.765

2.4 Popular parking area for hiking. **[8.1]**

3.0 Parking on right for mud caves. **[7.5]**
02 N32 55.542 W116 11.473

4.9 Stay right following main wash. **[5.6]**

6.3 Turn right into smaller wash. Small rocks prevent continuing straight. **[4.2]**
03 N32 56.899 W116 12.933

6.7 Turn right climbing out of wash. Follow sign to Arroyo Diablo Turnoff. **[3.8]**
04 N32 57.181 W116 12.937

8.9 Bear right joining larger wash. **[1.6]**

9.1 Turn left out of wash. Follow signs to Diablo Dropoff. **[1.4]**
05 N32 56.336 W116 11.408

10.5 Reach Diablo Dropoff overlook. **[0.0]**
06 N32 57.301 W116 11.286
After enjoying view from overlook, return to Waypoint 05. (When Diablo Dropoff is open, hard-core vehicles can go down dropoff and pass through difficult "Broken Shaft" Gulch to Trail #83.)

0.0 Zero trip odometer at Wpt. 05
Turn left and continue south in wash. Canyon narrows in spots. **[6.2]**

6.2 End trail at larger wash. Use Canyon Sin Nombre, Trail #85 to exit. **[0.0]**
07 N32 52.957 W116 09.561

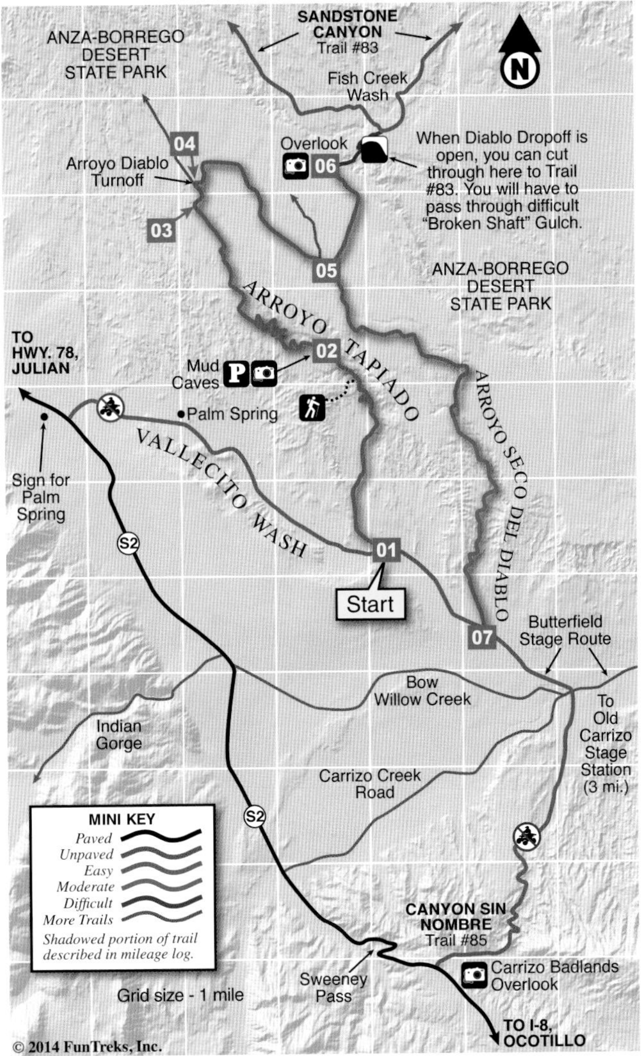

Canyon is narrow in places

When we drove the trail, Diablo Dropoff was temporarily closed after a heavy rain storm.

87 Mortero Wash

AREA 6 map on page 178

Start of trail is well marked.

Dos Cabezas Water Tower.

First trestle just west of Waypoint 02.

One of 21 tunnels. Hike required to see.

Historical Highlight: *It took 12 years to build the 11 miles of railroad through hellish Carrizo Gorge. Twenty-one tunnels and 14 trestles were needed including curved Goat Canyon Trestle. It's a difficult hike to this trestle but worth the effort. The railroad operated over 50 years starting in 1919. Learn more at the Anza-Borrego State Park Visitor Center.*

Overview: Remote desert route visits remains of historic railroad station and water tower. Road accesses hiking trail to Indian Hill Archeological Site featuring burnt caves and pictographs. Allow additional time for hike to Carrizo Gorge to see Goat Canyon Trestle. Lots of dispersed camping except where restricted. Street-legal vehicles only in state park. Watch for illegal immigrants along tracks.

Rating: Moderate: Mostly easy with a few moderate challenges. Air down for soft sand when necessary. One steep bumpy hill to climb. Rocky spot has bypass. Suitable for stock 4-wheel-drive SUVs. Flash floods possible in washes.

Stats: Length: 17.7 miles as described. Time: 3-4 hours plus hikes. Elevation: 820 to 1,928 ft. Best time: Open all year. Avoid hot summer months.

Current Conditions: Anza-Borrego Desert State Park. Call (760) 767-5311.

Getting There: Exit Interstate 8 at Ocotillo and head north through town. Follow Hwy. S2 west 9.2 miles from I-8. Watch for sign for Mortero Wash on left after mile marker 56.

START *MILEAGE LOG:*

0.0 Zero trip odometer [Rev. Miles] Head south on well-marked road to Mortero Wash. [8.5]
01 N32 47.569 W116 06.457

1.7 Road follows sandy wash. Soft sand possible. [6.8]

2.8 Go left out of wash. [5.7]

4.0 Stay left. Right goes to Cabezas Mine. [4.5]

4.1 Bear right along tracks to take side trip to Indian Hill Pictographs. [4.4]
02 N32 44.784 W116 08.379

4.3 Small trestle on left. [4.2]

4.5 Steep, bumpy climb. [4.0]

4.6 Stay left along tracks. [3.9]

6.3 Parking for hiking trail to Indian Hill Pictographs. Turn around here and return to Wpt.02. [2.2]
03 N32 45.940 W116 10.003

8.5 At Waypoint 02. [0.0]

0.0 Reset odometer at Wpt. 02 Cross tracks near water tower. Road goes slightly right, then continues south. [9.2]

1.2 Stay left. Closed road on right is hiking only to Piedras Grandes Archeological Site. [8.0]

1.5 Continue south where road joins on left. [7.7]

1.6 Drive through rocky section or go around. [7.6]

1.7 Continue straight where road joins on left. [7.5]

1.9 Continue straight. Right goes to camp spot behind rock outcrop. [7.3]

2.1 Stay left. Right goes to hiking trail to Goat Canyon Trestle. [7.1]
04 N32 43.125 W116 08.441

2.2 Bear left. [7.0]

3.1 Continue straight. Right goes to camp spot. [6.1]

3.3 Road curves right past more camping. [5.9]

3.8 Stay left and follow wide wash northeast. [5.4]

4.7 Stay left in wash where road goes right. [4.5]

5.0 Bear left and pass by four culverts. [4.2]
05 N32 43.206 W116 06.184

5.2 Cross tracks and bear right on uphill road. [4.0]

5.6 Stay left along west side of tracks. [3.6]

6.1 Continue straight on BLM Road 109. [3.1]

6.3 Cross over major dirt road and continue north along left side of tracks. [2.9]

7.1 Follow road as it curves right past 158, which joins on left. [2.1]

7.5 Turn left on 109 away from tracks. [1.7]
06 N32 44.576 W116 05.161

8.7 Desert viewpoint. [0.5]

8.9 Continue straight where road crosses. [0.3]

9.2 Return to Hwy. S2. [0.0]
07 N32 45.486 W116 03.751
Right goes to Ocotillo and Interstate 8.

Trail updates & GPS downloads at www.funtreks.com

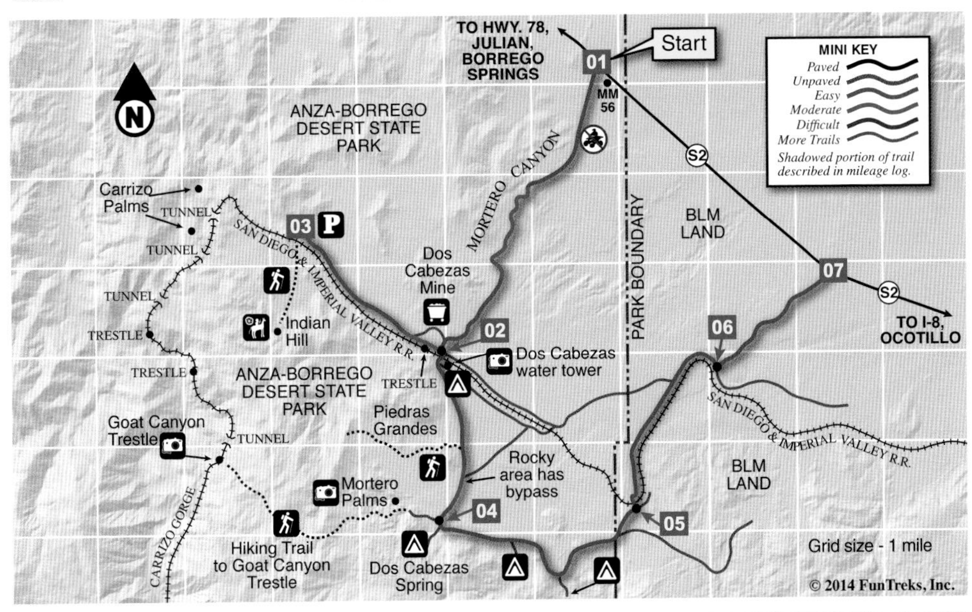

Stock SUV maneuvers through rockier part of trail.

Steep spot will test articulation.

88 McCain Valley Road

AREA 6 map on page 178

View from Sacatone Overlook. Take binoculars to see railroad trestles (barely visible top, center).

Lark Canyon OHV Area has 40 miles of trails.

Hiking trail at Carrizo Overlook.

Overview: Scenic high desert drive with two overlooks of Carrizo Canyon. Corrizo Overlook, with picnic tables, makes great lunch spot. Take binoculars. Fun hiking trails. Overnight camping at Lark Canyon Recreation Site, fee area. Street-legal vehicles only on McCain Valley Road. Lark Canyon OHV Area is for vehicles less than 40 inches wide.

Rating: Easy: Passenger cars can reach the overlooks. High clearance best after Carrizo Overlook.

Stats: Length: 16.7 miles one way counting overlooks. Time: 3 to 4 hours for round trip. Elevation: 3,581 to 4,502 ft. Best time: Open all year. Winter snows possible. Not too hot in summer.

Current Conditions: BLM, El Centro Field Office. Call (760) 337-4400. PDF map of OHV area available on website.

Getting There: Get off Interstate 8 at Highway 94, exit 65. Drive south 0.5 miles and turn left on Old Highway 80. Go east 1.8 miles and turn left on McCain Valley Road. Go north 2.4 miles to fork where pavement ends.

START **MILEAGE LOG:**

0.0 Zero trip odometer [Rev. Miles] Stay right when road forks at end of pavement. Pass sign for McCain Valley Conservation Area. [16.7]
01 N32 41.761 W116 15.565

0.4 Turn right to visit to Sacatone Overlook. [16.3]
02 N32 42.080 W116 15.518

0.8 Continue straight. [15.9]

1.9 Stay left slightly. [14.8]

2.0 Continue straight. Small cave on left next to narrow uphill road. [14.7]

2.2 Stay left. [14.5]

2.4 Sacatone Overlook. With binoculars you can easily see several wooden trestles of the Carrizo Canyon Railroad. Return to Wpt. 02. [14.3]

4.4 Bear right at Wpt. 02 and continue north on McCain Valley Road. [12.3]

5.9 Follow main road as it curves to left past gated road on right. [10.8]

6.5 Stay right past entrance to Lark Canyon OHV Staging Area on left. Sign at this entrance has map of OHV area. [10.2]
03 N32 43.425 W116 16.172

6.9 Continue straight on McCain Road. Left goes to camping at Lark Canyon Recreation Site. [9.8]

9.7 Continue straight where road crosses. [7.0]

10.4 Bear right to take short side trip to Corrizo Canyon Overlook. [6.3]
04 N32 46.275 W116 17.024

10.6 Overlook. Good spot for lunch. Return to McCain Valley Road. [6.1]

10.9 At Wpt. 04, bear right and continue on McCain Valley Road. [5.8]

13.9 Continue straight. Road narrows and gets a bit rougher. [2.8]

15.0 Continue straight. Left goes to Cottonwood Campground, a popular equestrian area. [1.7]

16.7 Road ends. Turn around and return the way you came. [0.0]
05 N32 49.410 W116 20.719

Trail updates & GPS downloads at www.funtreks.com

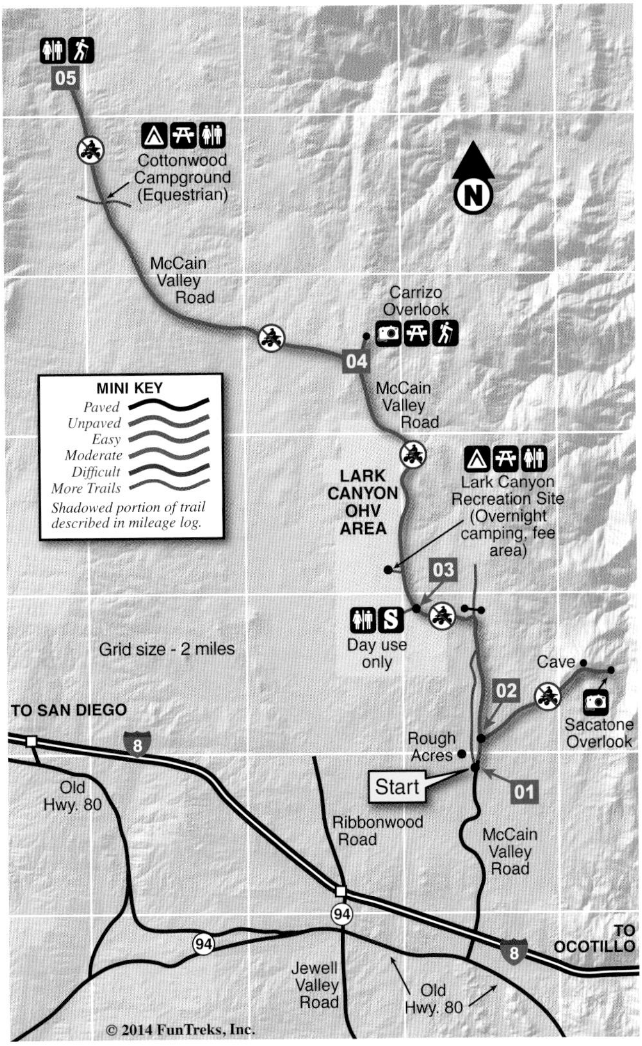

Plenty of room to turn around at Carrizo Overlook.

McCain Valley Road gets rougher towards the end.

89 Los Pinos Mountain Loop

AREA 6 map on page 178

Great views from Los Pinos Mountain lookout tower. From here fires can be seen 20 miles away.

Steep downhill spot...toughest spot on the trail.

Spots like this can be slippery when wet.

Historical Highlight: *"Los Pinos" is Spanish for "The Pines," which you'll see in abundance from the Forest Service fire tower at the top of the mountain. The tower, originally built in the 1920s and replaced in the 1960s, is one of few remaining in California manned full time.*

Overview: The first part of this loop to the fire lookout tower has been paved since our last visit in 2002. ATVs are not allowed on this portion. The remainder of the loop is all dirt as it circles south around the outside of Corral Canyon OHV Area, which is open all year to green-sticker vehicles. Great views along the route including from the top of Los Pinos Mountain. Fee and dispersed camping available.

Rating: Moderate: Mostly easy except for the section between Waypoints 02 and 04. This portion is narrow, steep, brushy and rutted in spots, but suitable for high clearance stock 4x4 SUVs.

Stats: Length: 19.4 miles. Time: 3 to 4 hours. Elevation: 2,675 to 4,800 ft. Best time: Spring and fall.

Current Conditions: Cleveland N.F., Descanso R.D. Call (619) 445-6235.

Getting There: Take Interstate 8 to the Buckman Springs exit. This exit has a rest stop. Head south on Buckman Springs Road 3.3 miles to Corral Canyon Rd. Turn right and go 5.8 miles west to a parking area near a paved 4-way intersection called Four Corners.

START **MILEAGE LOG:**

0.0 Zero trip odometer **[Rev. Miles]** From Four Corners, bear right on paved Los Pinos Road 16S17. **[19.4]**
01 N32 43.504 W116 33.557

2.1 View point. **[17.3]**

2.3 If gate is open, turn right and climb to lookout. Get permission from ranger to climb tower. Return to Waypoint 02. **[17.1]**
02 N32 44.168 W116 34.753

2.8 From Wpt. 02, continue north on 16S17. Dirt road is much rougher. **[16.6]**

3.4 Bear left. **[16.0]**

3.5 Bear left again. **[15.9]**

4.6 Make a hard left off 16S17 onto 4E03. **[14.8]**
03 N32 44.855 W116 34.530

5.5 Steep downhill. **[13.9]**

6.5 Squeeze between large boulders. **[12.9]**

6.9 Stay right. **[12.5]**

7.5 Stay left where road goes right. Trail widens and gets easier. **[11.9]**
04 N32 45.250 W116 37.179

7.8 Clearing with shade is good lunch spot. **[11.6]**

9.9 Follow road as it curves left. Right closed. **[9.5]**

11.6 Hard left turn. Right gated closed. **[7.8]**

13.4 Stay right uphill on Skye Valley Road. Left downhill on Corral Canyon Road is shortest way back to start. **[6.0]**
05 N32 42.219 W116 35.824

15.4 Continue straight. Left is exit point of Bronco Peak Trail #91. **[4.0]**

16.2 On left is first of several ATV trails that go into OHV Area. **[3.2]**

16.8 Viewpoint. **[2.6]**

17.6 Continue straight. Start of Bronco Peak on left. **[1.8]**

18.4 Bobcat Meadow Campground on right. Exit of Sidewider, Trail #90, on left. Road becomes paved. **[1.0]**
06 N32 42.767 W116 33.500

18.8 Start of Sidewinder on left. **[0.6]**

19.4 Return to start at Four Corners Staging Area. Right here returns the way you came in. **[0.0]**

Trail updates & GPS downloads at www.funtreks.com

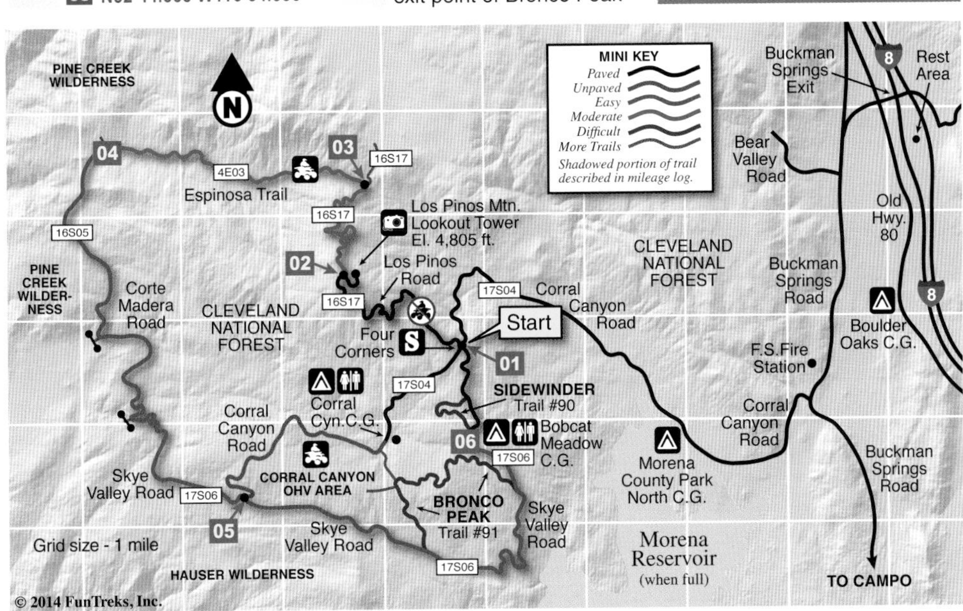

After Waypoint 04, trail gets easier.

Morena Reservoir in distance.

90 Sidewinder

AREA 6 map on page 178

Last obstacle is a real challenge. We found the left side easier.

Much of trail is exposed rock slabs like this.

Be prepared for brush marks.

Historical Highlight: *In 2006, most of Corral Canyon was destroyed by the Horse Fire. Today the area is fully open thanks to the efforts of volunteers working with fire rehabilitation funds.*

Overview: This trail is short but packed with difficult obstacles. It's located in popular Corral Canyon OHV Area, which is relatively close to San Diego. Weekends can get busy, so arrive early if you expect to get a camp spot in either of two developed Forest Service Campgrounds. Besides 4WD trails, you'll find designated routes for ATVs and dirt bikes. Adventure pass may be required. Call number at right.

Rating: Difficult: Steep rock slabs and large boulders. Two obstacles can cause extreme tipping. Lockers, high ground clearance and excellent articulation are needed. Tight, scratchy brush. Not for stock vehicles. Watch for snakes and poison oak. Very hot in summer.

Stats: Length: Just over 1 mile long. Time: 1 hour or less. Elevation: 3,658 to 3,846 ft. Best time: Spring and fall.

Current Conditions: Cleveland N.F., Descanso R.D. Call (619) 445-6235.

Getting There: Follow directions to Corral Canyon OHV Area as described in Los Pinos Mountain Loop, Trail #89. When you reach the Four Corners parking area, bear left heading south on a narrow, paved road. Trail is 0.6 mile from the staging area on the right.

START MILEAGE LOG:

0.0 Zero trip odometer **[Rev. Miles]**
Head west on marked Route #8. Several single-track trails cross this route. **[1.0]**
01 N32 43.048 W116 33.501

0.1 Continue straight. ATV Route #1 crosses. **[0.9]**

0.4 Bear left where single-track trail goes right. **[0.6]**
02 N32 42.924 W116 33.809

0.5 Turn left uphill. **[0.5]**

0.6 Cross a large, steep, tippy rock slab. **[0.4]**

0.7 Steep obstacle. **[0.3]**

0.9 Last obstacle. We found the left side easier. **[0.1]**

1.0 Trail ends at Los Pinos Road marked by forest information kiosk. **[0.0]**
03 N32 42.761 W116 33.505
Turn right to reach Bronco Peak, Trail #91.

Trail updates & GPS downloads at www.funtreks.com

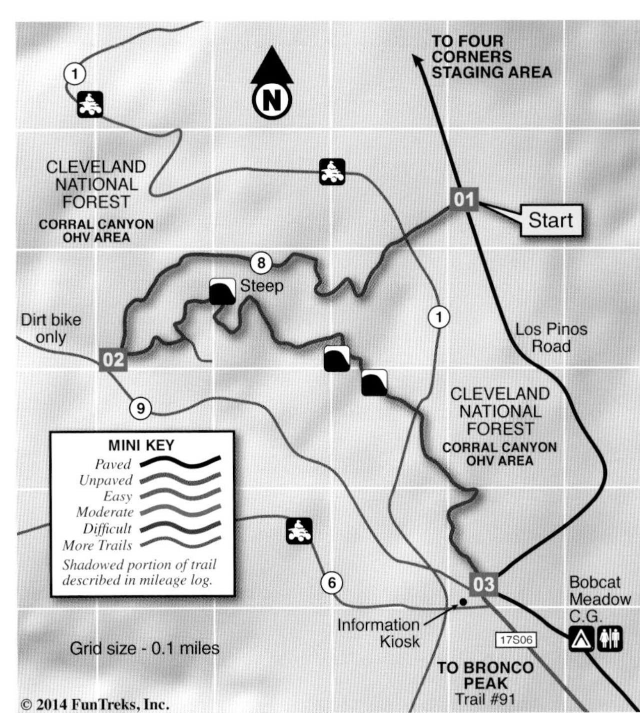

Very steep climbs and descents. Make sure everything inside your vehicle is tied down.

Bronco Peak

AREA 6 map on page 178

Use extreme caution. Body damage and rollovers are not uncommon.

Tight squeeze here. Don't count on bypasses.

Trail starts here. Look for brown post with #3.

Overview: This is the main 4-wheel-drive trail in Corral Canyon OHV Area. It's often run in combination with Sidewinder, Trail #90. Most other trails in the OHV area are designated for ATVs and dirt bikes. The trail climbs to top of Bronco Peak, then drops steeply over 800 ft. to Los Pinos Mountain Loop, Trail #89. If you camp overnight, try to get a spot in Bobcat Meadow Campground (fee area).

Rating: Difficult: This trail will test your articulation to the max. It's extremely tight with large boulders and few bypasses. Body damage and rollovers are not uncommon. We recommend front and rear lockers.

Stats: Length: 2.6 miles. Time: One to two hours depending on vehicle setup and driver skill. Add more time for weekend traffic. Elevation: 3,307 to 4,178 ft. Best time: Spring and Fall.

Current Conditions: Cleveland N.F., Descanso R.D. Call (616) 445-6235.

Getting There: Follow directions to Corral Canyon OHV Area as described in Los Pinos Mountain Loop, Trail #89. When you reach the Four Corners parking area, bear left heading south on a narrow, paved road. Once you reach Bobcat Meadow Campground, continue another 0.8 mile, after the road turns to dirt. Trail is on the right marked #3.

START *MILEAGE LOG:*

0.0 Zero trip odometer [Rev. Miles]
Head west uphill on steep, twisty road. [2.6]
01 N32 42.290 W116 33.025

0.5 Optional obstacle. [2.1]

0.7 Continue straight, ATV Route #1 crosses. [1.9]

1.1 Cross over the top of Bronco Peak and begin steep, treacherous half-mile descent. [1.5]
02 N32 42.326 W116 33.761

1.7 Turn left heading south. Right is Bronco Peak, connector Route #3A, rated extreme, limited to 72″ wide vehicles. [0.9]
03 N32 42.324 W116 34.163

2.0 Continue straight downhill towards Bronco Flats marked Route #5. (Right is moderate Gun Slinger, Route #11, an alternate way to exit.) [0.6]
04 N32 42.172 W116 34.184

2.6 Reach main road. [0.0]
05 N32 41.764 W116 34.000
To return to Four Corners Staging Area, turn left on Skye Valley Road, which is the last part of Los Pinos Mountain Loop, Trail #89.

Trail updates & GPS downloads at www.funtreks.com

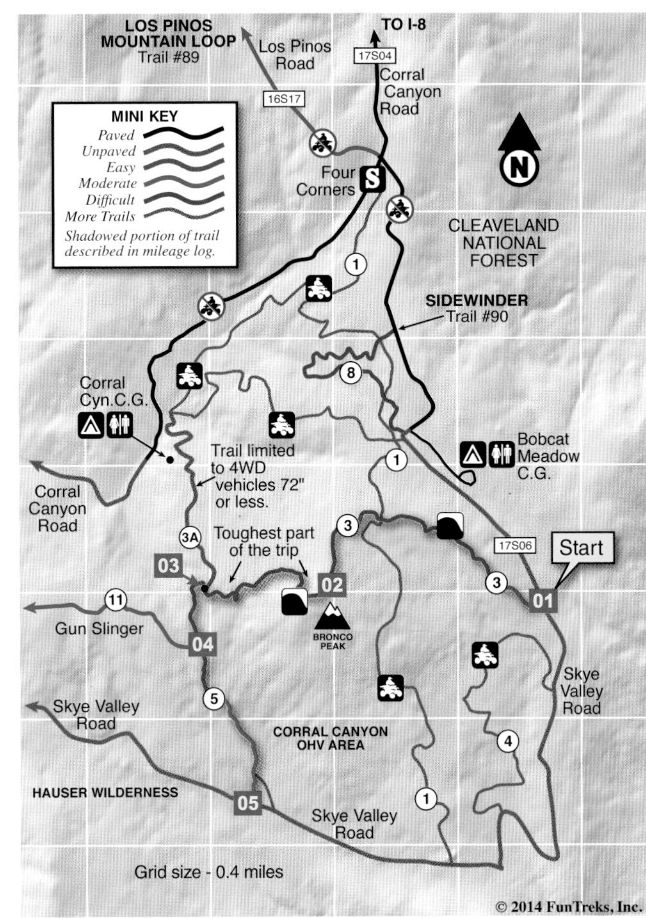

View from top of Bronco Peak is impressive. Toughest part of trip begins after this point.

92 Superstition Mountain

AREA 6 map on page 178

Trail starts at this information board at the end of Wheeler Road. This is also the camping area.

Massive play area for all green-sticker vehicles.

Interior trails can be extremely difficult.

Overview: You must first understand this route before you can find all the other routes. It is an extremely confusing area, especially during the off season when there are no tire tracks to follow. We recommend first-timers participate in the San Diego 4-Wheelers Annual Superstition Mountain Run in January (www.sd4wheel.com). Great area for green-sticker vehicles. Camp on desert floor near Waypoint 01 where the ground is firm and well-suited for large campers and motorhomes.

Rating: Moderate: Rating applies to this route only and even that could change with drifting sand. Interior routes shown on map range from moderate to extremely difficult. Route-finding can be nearly impossible at times. Use the three towers and paved roads as directional landmarks. Avoid drift side of dunes where rollovers are possible.

Stats: Length: Almost 19 miles. Time: About 1 hour to complete loop. Elevation: 85 to 358 ft. Best time: Open all year, avoid summers.

Current Conditions: BLM El Centro Field Office. Call (760) 337-4400.

Getting There: Get off Interstate 8 at Dunaway Road or Drew Road west of El Centro. Take S80 east to Huff Road. Follow Huff Road north about 6.3 miles. Reset odometer, turn left on Wheeler Road and stay on this wide dirt road as it heads west then northwest. After 4.8 miles, bear right heading almost north. You should see the information board near a fork at 7 miles.

START *MILEAGE LOG:*

0.0 Zero trip odometer [Rev. Miles]
Bear right at information board and follow more-traveled road northeast. [18.8]
01 N32 55.593 W115 48.648

2.2 Turn left. [16.6]

2.5 Turn sharp left and follow telephone poles northwest. [16.3]
02 N32 55.739 W115 46.417

4.4 Continue straight as you cross paved road. [14.4]

6.7 Continue straight where difficult "Wrangler Canyon" goes left. [12.1]
03 N32 57.639 W115 48.750

6.9 Climb steep wash then cross paved road heading north. [11.9]

7.6 Continue straight. [11.2]

7.9 Continue straight where popular "Sand Dam Canyon" goes left [10.9]
04 N32 58.069 W115 49.681

8.5 Stay left. [10.3]

8.8 Cross big wash. Then cross paved road following sign for 196. [10.0]

10.1 Continue straight where difficult "Knock-on-Wood" goes left. [8.7]
05 N32 58.581 W115 51.651

10.8 Stay right and head west, following the more-traveled road. [8.0]

11.3 Follow more-traveled road as it heads south. [7.5]
06 N32 58.609 W115 52.773

11.5 Stay left on 196. [7.3]

12.0 Bear right on 197. (Road 201 goes east along the foothills of the sand dunes.) [6.8]
07 N32 57.961 W115 52.752

14.1 Continue straight following 197. [4.7]

17.6 Turn sharp right. [1.2]

18.8 Return to main camping area near information board where you started. [0.0]

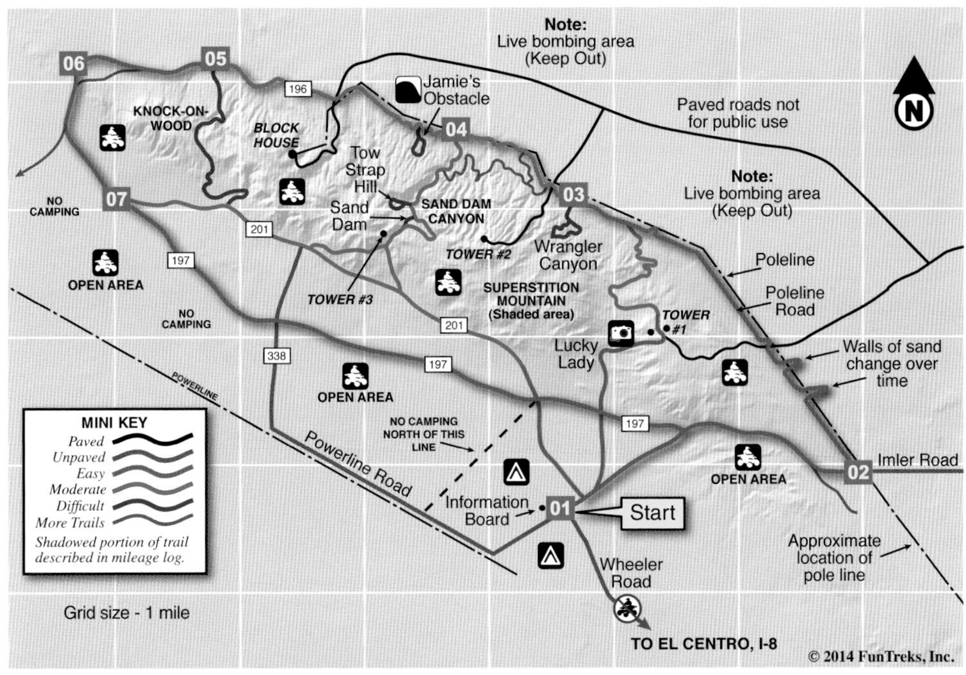

Coming down from Tower #1 on Lucky Lady Trail (see map).

Glamis, Oldsmobile Hill, Sand Highway

AREA 6 map on page 178

Depending on sand conditions, SUVs can often drive up to the top of smaller dunes.

Sand Highway may not have tire tracks to follow.

Historical Highlight: *Only the dunes south of Highway 78 are open to vehicular recreation. A lawsuit led by the Sierra Club in 2000 closed more than half of what used to be open south of Hwy. 78. The lawsuit continues today, but OHV enthusiasts remain hopeful that this "temporary closure" will eventually come to an end. During major winter holiday weekends, the dunes often see more than 150,000 visitors.*

Overview: These two routes serve as an introduction to the Imperial Sand Dunes Recreation Area. **Route A** takes you to Glamis and the north central dunes area, including Oldsmobile Hill. **Route B** traverses the entire western edge of the dunes. Open to licensed and green-sticker vehicles. Fee area, permit required. Safety flags required. Obey all posted regulations. Camping is first-come, first-served. Supplies and gas available at Glamis Beach Store at premium prices.

Rating: Difficult: Conditions vary depending on time of year and wind conditions. Routes shown here are easy to moderate except if you attempt to drive up larger dunes, like Oldsmobile Hill. Use extreme caution on steep slopes. Downwind side of dunes can be extremely soft, where it's easy to get stuck or even roll over. Route-finding can be challenging during the off-season when no tire tracks are present.

Stats: Length: A: 2.8 miles, B: 18.7 miles. Time: A: 30 min, B: About 2 hours. Elevation: 150 to 300 ft. Best time to go: Late October- mid May. Halloween is first big weekend.

Current Conditions: BLM Cahuilla Ranger Station (760) 344-3919, hours vary, mostly open just Fri-Sunday. BLM El Centro Field Office (760) 337-4400. Free BLM maps available on site.

.

Getting There: From intersection of Highways 86 and 78 in Brawley, take Highway 78 east. Go 21.4 miles to Gecko Road on right, or 27.5 miles to Beach Store. **Start A** is ½ mile west of the Beach Store. **Start B** is 6.2 miles south on paved Gecko Road. From Yuma, get off I-8 at Ogilby Road and head north to 78, then west.

START MILEAGE LOG:

0.0 Zero trip odometer **[Rev. Miles]**
OLDSMOBILE HILL START A
Head west across broad, flat area running parallel to Highway 78. No road is defined. **[2.8]**
01 N32 59.595 W115 04.798

0.6 Swing south away from Highway 78 following broad valley. **[2.2]**
02 N32 59.597 W115 05.411

2.8 You reach base of Oldsmobile hill. Depending on sand conditions and type of vehicle, you may be able to drive to top where views are impressive. **[0.0]**
03 N32 57.824 W115 05.924

0.0 Zero trip odometer
SAND HIGHWAY START B
From the south end of paved Gecko Road, continue onto open sand. No signs mark route. Follow sandy ridge south-southeast. Off-season, you may not see tire tracks. When we drove trail, closure area posts helped define the route; however, these may be removed someday. Coachella Canal helps define western boundary. **[18.7]**
04 N32 54.538 W115 06.919

13.3 Markers on left define turn to Patton Valley, a fun side trip when the area is active. **[5.4]**
05 N32 45.972 W114 57.967

16.3 Trail starts to come down off ridge and swings more south. Aim for cell towers about 1.5 miles farther. **[2.4]**

17.8 Trail goes by vault toilets for Dune Buggy Flats Campground. Turn right and cross bridge over canal. **[0.9]**
06 N32 42.836 W114 56.535

18.3 Road becomes paved. **[0.4]**

18.7 Entrance to Interstate 8 on left. This is Gordon's Well Exit #151. **[0.0]**
Note: If you continue west on frontage road past freeway entrance, you'll find Duner's Diner and Gordon's Well RV Park.

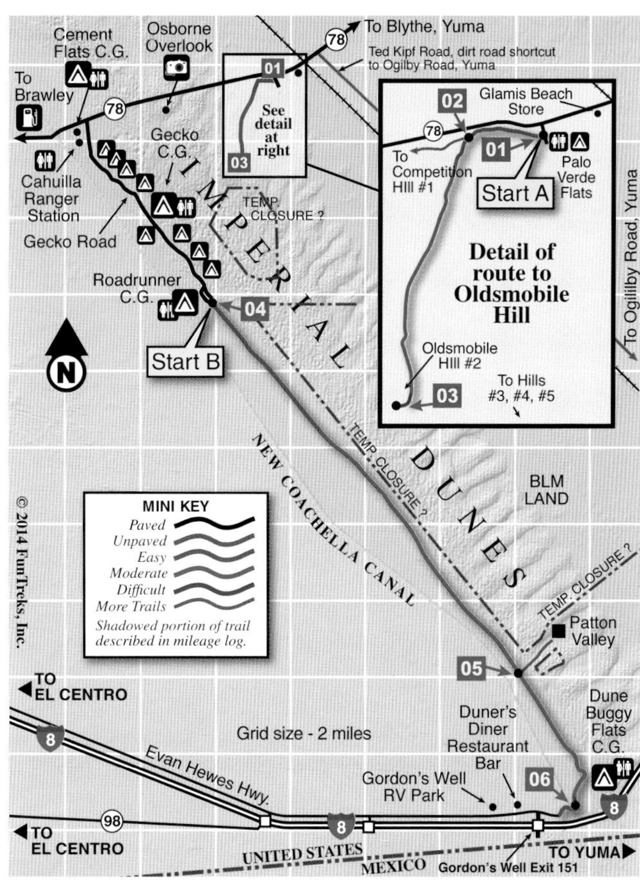

Huge dunes at Patton Valley.

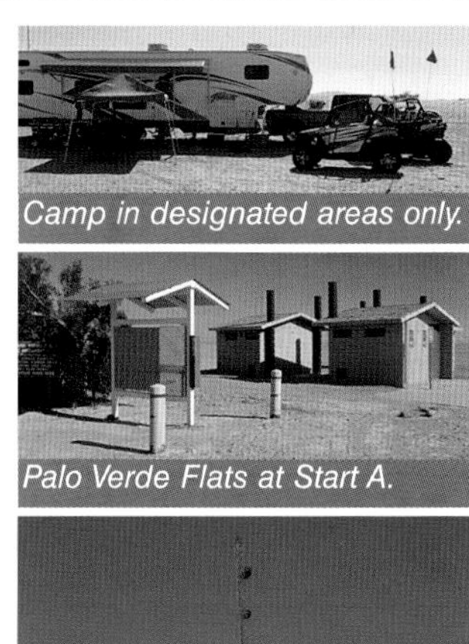
Camp in designated areas only.

Palo Verde Flats at Start A.

Cell towers at end of Sand Hwy.

Green = Easy, Blue = Moderate, Red = Difficult

Pacific Coast, Hollister Hills, Oceano Dunes, Mojave Road

Areas 7, 8 and 9 each contain a minimal number of trails. To simplify, we've chosen to show all three areas on one map.

Area 7 has only one trail, *Lost Coast Beach, Trail #94*. It's a quiet, remote experience. Frequent foggy conditions may give you the feeling you're the only vehicle on the road. At the end of this route, you may wish to head north on Highway 101 to see the giant redwoods in Humboldt Redwoods State Park.

Area 8 contains two popular SVRAs and one scenic coastal route. *Oceano Dunes, Trail #97,* is the only state park where vehicles can drive on the beach.

Area 9 encompasses the entire *Mojave Road*, broken into three parts. It offers no hard-core challenges, but is a good test for stock, high-clearance 4x4 SUVs. We ran the trail from east to west. For more history on the trail, we used and highly recommend the *Mojave Road Guide*, by David Casebier.

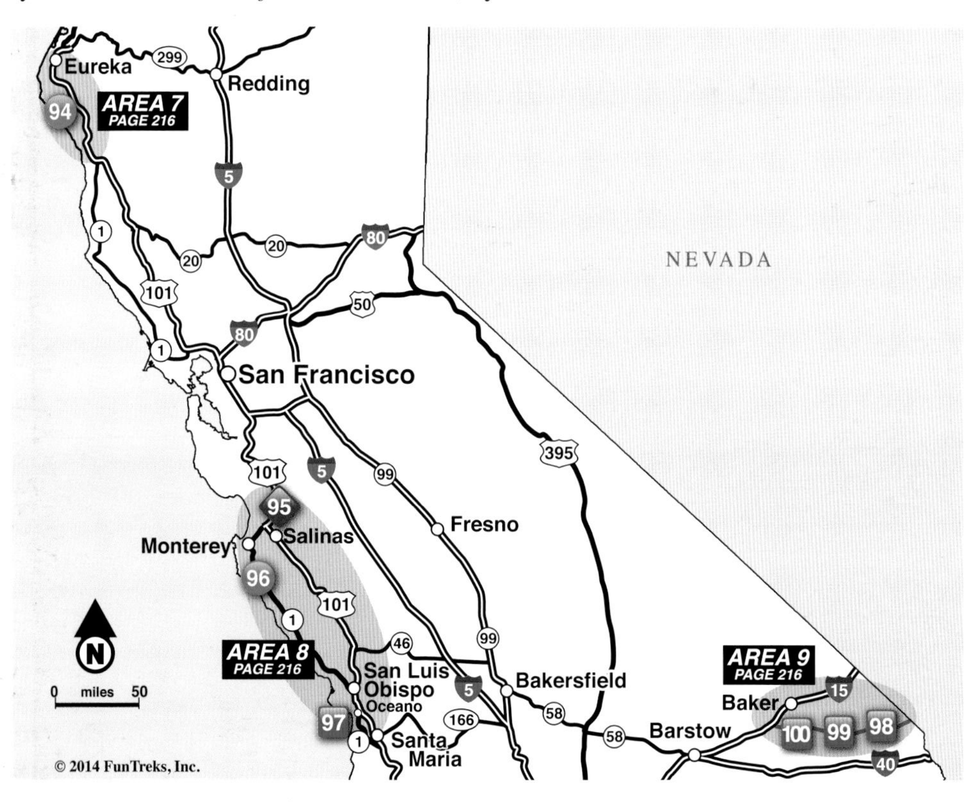

Old Coast Road, Trail #96, rated easy. Trail begins with this great view next to Bixby Bridge.

94 Lost Coast Beach

AREA 7 map on page 216

Beautiful ocean views despite cloud cover.

Typical conditions along the route.

Dry camping spots available at Usal Beach.

Fisherman prepare to hunt for shellfish.

Historical Highlight: *Usal Beach was once a loading point for redwood lumber, which was transported by water to the point of sale. As this business faded away in the 1930s, the area became known as the "Lost Coast." All vestiges of lumber production have long ago been destroyed by fire.*

Overview: Enjoy misty ocean views along a forgotten beach while exploring a remote coastal road. Camp and relax in near seclusion. Swing through Sinkyone Wilderness State Park, where you might get lucky like we did and see an elk or two strolling past the visitor center. When you're done, head north on Highway 101 for a drive through amazing Humbolt Redwoods State Park, where you'll see some of the largest redwood trees in California.

Rating: Easy: Roads are mostly hard-packed dirt but can get muddy after prolonged periods of rainy weather. Road is steep and narrow in a few places.

Stats: Length: 38.7 miles. Time: Route takes 2-3 hours. Extend trip by planning an overnight campout. Elevation: 0 to 2,114 ft. Best time: Mid June-August. Road closed during winter and late fall, the area's wettest time.

Current Conditions: Sinkyone Wilderness State Park, (707) 986-7711.

Getting There: Take Highway 101 north past the tiny town of Leggett where Highway 1 intersects. Turn left on Highway 1 and go southwest 14.7 miles to Mendocino County Road 431 on the right. This turn is near mile marker 90.88.

START MILEAGE LOG:

0.0 Zero trip odometer [Rev. Miles]
Follow narrow dirt road as it slowly climbs heading north. [6.3]
01 N39 46.800 W123 49.826

5.9 Turn left at an information board for Usal Beach. [0.4]
02 N39 50.086 W123 50.614

6.3 Reach Usal Beach. Return to Waypoint 02. [0.0]

0.0 Zero trip odometer from Wpt. 02
Head north over wooden bridge. [22.0]

0.2 Continue straight at what looks like a 4-way. [21.8]

0.7 Continue straight uphill. [21.3]

1.2 Bear left on 431. [20.8]

4.4 Bear right. [17.6]

9.0 Stay left. [13.0]

11.6 Stay left following more-traveled road. [10.4]

18.5 Turn left on narrow dirt road to wilderness area. [3.5]
03 N39 58.385 W123 57.968

22.0 Arrive at Sinkyone Wilderness Visitor Center. Road to Bear Harbor hiking trail was blocked due to damage. It may reopen. Return to Wpt. 03. [0.0]
04 N39 56.561 W123 57.892

0.0 Zero trip odometer from Wpt. 03
Turn left heading north on Usal Road, 431. [6.5]

1.7 Bear left where road is now paved. [4.8]

4.5 Pass two campgrounds on your left. [2.0]

6.5 End trail at Shelter Cove Road. [0.0]
05 N40 02.167 W124 01.548
To reach Shelter Cove: Turn left and follow Shelter Cove Road 5 miles to small remote town.
To reach Humbolt Redwoods State Park: Turn right and follow Shelter Cove Road 5 miles. Take a slight left on Briceland Thorne Road and drive another 12 miles to Redway. From here take Highway 101 and Avenue of the Giants north about 24 miles.

Trail updates & GPS downloads at www.funtreks.com

MINI KEY
Paved
Unpaved
Easy
Moderate
Difficult
More Trails
Shadowed portion of trail described in mileage log.
Grid size - 5 miles

Elk shows no fear of humans as he walks past the visitor center.

Hollister Hills SVRA

AREA 8 map on page 216

Obstacle course is a great place to test vehicles.

Ranger station at main entrance to park.

Lower Ranch, motorcycles and ATVs only.

Historical Highlight: *Hollister Hills State Vehicular Recreation Area was originally a private hunting club. Patrons used Jeeps, motorcycles, and "tote-goats" to get around the trails on the ranch. In 1975, the area became an OHV park.*

Overview: This is one of the most popular and diverse OHV parks in the state. Trails are provided for all vehicle types including stock SUVs, serious modified rigs, ATVs, UTVs and dirt bikes. Entry fees are reasonable. Everyone must check in at the ranger station where you receive a detailed map of each of the OHV areas. We visited the Upper Ranch where the popular Top Truck Challenge is hosted every year. One of the hardest trails in the competition is the Tank Trap, on which only about half the vehicles are able to finish. Dry camp spots for motorhomes and RVs available at various points inside the park. The park is open from sunrise to sunset, 365 days a year. Before you go, visit the California State Parks website at ohv.parks.ca.gov and select Hollister Hills SVRA. There you'll find complete details and downloadable PDF maps.

Rating: Difficult. Easy drive to obstacle course. Fremonita Road is narrow and steep with loose rock. McCray Road is moderate but quite steep and narrow. The Tank Trap is an axle twister in a narrow, high-banked ravine.

Stats: Length: Less than a mile to the obstacle course. Time: You can spend all day at the Upper Ranch. Elevation: 660 to 2,425 ft. Best time: June-September.

Current Conditions: Hollister Hills SVRA. Call (831) 637-3874.

Getting There: Head south through Hollister on San Benito Street. Turn right at T on Union Road, cross bridge, then go left on Cienega Road. Go 1.4 miles and turn right at T where Hospital Road goes left. Go another 3.7 miles and turn right into ranger station. Pay entry fee and get the gate combination for the Upper Ranch. Return to Cienega Road and turn right. Head south to entry gate on right in about a mile. Relock the gate after passing through.

START MILEAGE LOG:

0.0 Zero trip odometer
From entry gate, follow McCray Road west. [0.7]
01 N36 45.500 W121 23.846

0.3 Turn right on Garner Flat Road. [0.4]
02 N36 45.449 W121 24.040

0.4 Bear right towards day-use area. [0.3]

0.7 Arrive at large parking area. Obstacle course is just past restrooms. [0.0]
03 N36 45.496 W121 24.416
The obstacle course is more difficult than most of the roads in the park.

View of Hollister Hills SVRA from Hector Heights.

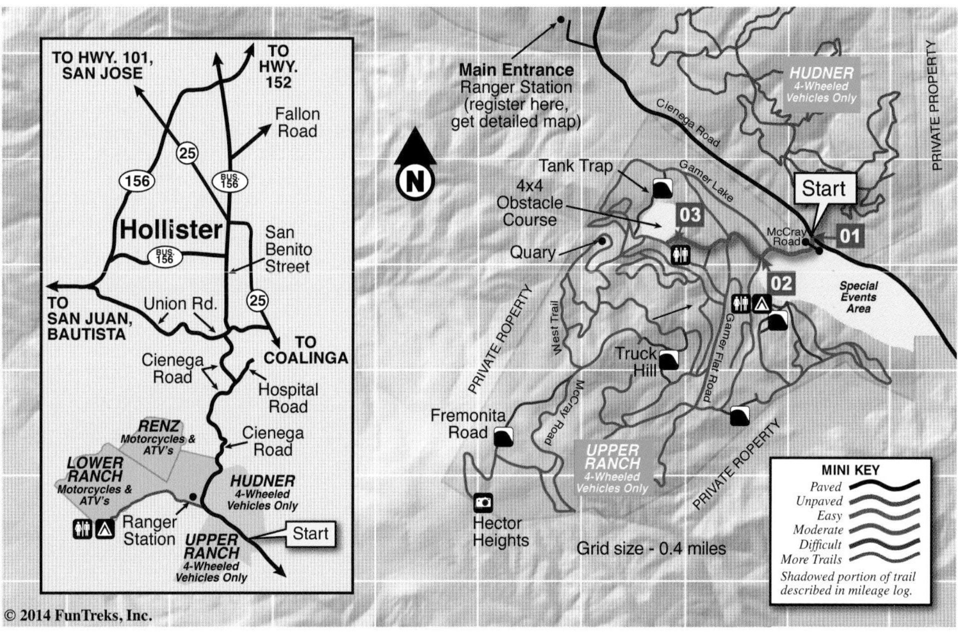

Difficult climb on narrow Fremontia Road.

The Tank Trap.

96 Old Coast Road

AREA 8 map on page 216

Dense forest on northern end of route.

Coastal view where trail starts at Bixby Bridge.

Road, when dry, is suitable for passenger cars.

Historical Highlight: *Towards the end of the trip on a clear day, you can look down and see the Point Sur Lighthouse perched atop a large rock dome along the shore. The lighthouse was a manned facility from 1889 to the early 1960s. Today it is automated and maintained by the U.S. Coast Guard as part of Point Sur State Historic Park. Call (831) 625-4419 for information on guided tours.*

Overview: Winding dirt road meanders downhill through cool wooded valleys with large sycamore and redwood trees, then climbs steeply to scenic rangeland high above the Pacific coastline. Take binoculars to see every detail below, including historic Point Sur Lighthouse. Street-legal vehicles only. Drive road in either direction. No turns to get lost. Great hiking in Andrew Molera State Park at south end.

Rating: Easy: Suitable for passenger cars when dry, but you'll want 4-wheel drive if you get caught in the rain. Road can even be impassable in very wet conditions.

Stats: Length: 10.1 miles one way. Time: 1 to 2 hours plus stop time. Elevation: 86 to 1,146 ft. Best time: Anytime when dry and not too foggy.

Current Conditions: Public road crosses private land. Check general weather forecast to see if rain is expected.

Getting There: Take Hwy. 1 south from Monterey about 17 miles. Turn left immediately before crossing Bixby Bridge. There is an overlook on the right at this point. To start on south end, take Hwy. 1 north from Big Sur about 2.5 miles and turn right opposite the entrance to Andrew Molera State Park.

START **MILEAGE LOG:**

0.0 Zero trip odometer **[Rev. Miles]**
Head east on wide dirt road as it descends along the mountainside into deep canyon. **[10.1]**
01 N36 22.351 W121 54.179

1.0 Cross narrow bridge over Bixby Creek as road winds through woods in bottom of canyon. **[9.1]**

3.7 Road turns right and climbs up hillside out of canyon. **[6.4]**

3.9 Highest point of trip at 1,146 ft. Views of ocean to the west. Begin long descent. **[6.2]**
02 N36 20.594 W121 52.124

5.6 First of two bridges over Little Sur River. Lowest point of trip except at the end. **[4.5]**
03 N36 19.838 W121 51.757

7.6 Another high point. More views. **[2.5]**

9.0 View of historic Point Sur Lighthouse, now a state park. **[1.1]**

10.1 Road ends as it returns to Highway 1 across from entrance to Andrew Molera State Park. **[0.0]**
04 N36 17.318 W121 50.675
Right takes you back to start in about 8 miles. Closest gas is 2.5 miles south at Big Sur.

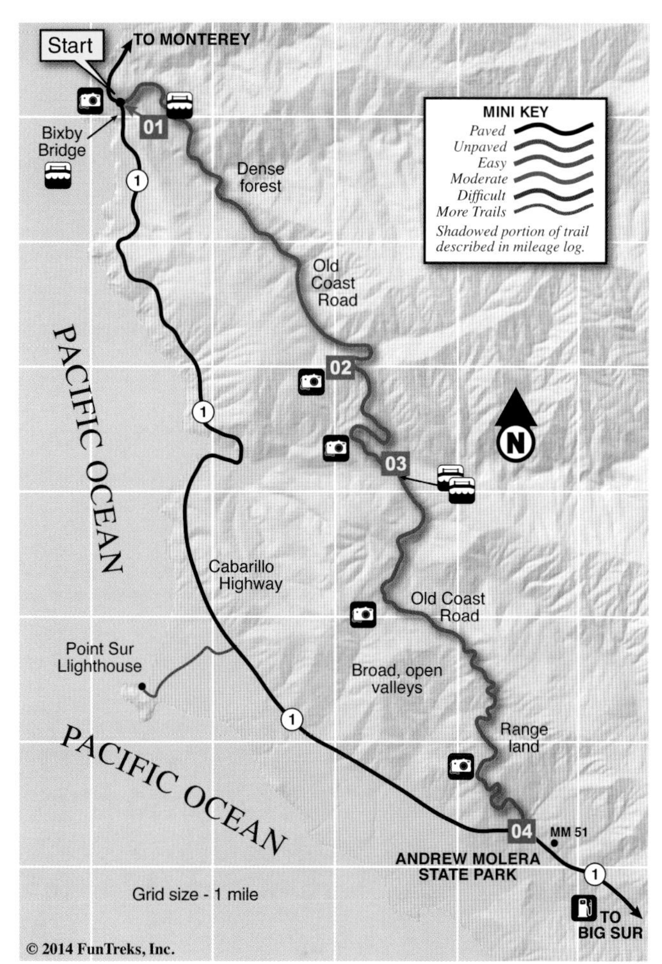

Beautiful pastoral scenes and ocean views from high points along the route if weather is not too foggy.

97 Oceano Dunes SVRA

AREA 8 map on page 216

Lots of camping along the beach.

We had fog all day during our visit.

Follow numbered posts along Sand Highway.

Larger dunes can reach heights of 100 feet.

Historical Highlight: *The OHV open area covers 1500 acres and includes portions of the beach. It took millions of years for the dunes to form. Sand reached the shore carried by rivers and streams, then ocean currents and wind spread it around.*

Overview: The only state park in California where you can ride your OHV on dunes along the beach. Camp in firmer sand in designated areas along shore. Summer mornings are often foggy and cool. Winters can be blustery with deeper water to cross at Arroyo Grande Creek. All vehicles must have safety flags. Get map of area at entrance and follow all regulations. Rental ATVs available from concessionaires.

Rating: Moderate: Flat beach area is easy, but airing down tires may still be necessary. Sand highway is moderate with softer sand. Eastern slopes of large dunes can be difficult to dangerous.

Stats: Length: The direct route we drove was 5 miles one way. Time: Several hours, but plan on spending at least a day. Elevation: 0 to 200 ft. Open all year. Fall may be best. Day-use hours 6 a.m. to 11 p.m. Camping 24 hrs./day, 7 days per week.

Current Conditions: Oceano Dunes District Ranger Station, (805) 473-7220.

Getting There: From the intersection of Highways 1 and 101, approximately 12 miles south of San Luis Obispo, take Highway 1 south about 3.1 miles and turn right on Pier Avenue. Go west 0.4 mile to entrance and pay fee.

START *MILEAGE LOG:*

0.0 Zero trip odometer **[Rev. Miles]**
After entrance station, head south along beach. (Street-legal vehicles only to beach post #2.) **[5.0]**
01 N35 06.338 W120 37.839

0.5 Exit point of Arroyo Grande Creek. Water flows across beach at various points. Can be deep at times. May even be closed at rare times. **[4.5]**

2.1 Bear left to follow Sand Highway. **[2.9]**
02 N35 04.509 W120 37.803

2.7 Trail turns south at post 12 and heads into dunes. Explore open area of dunes. Be careful. Eastern slopes of dunes, called "slip faces," can be extremely steep and soft. **[2.3]**

5.0 General area where dunes end at post 25. We turned around here. **[0.0]**
03 N35 02.310 W120 37.076
As you return to entrance at Pier Avenue, note that there is another 1.2 miles of Pismo Beach to the north, where you can exit at Grand Avenue. This portion of beach is for street-legal vehicles only.

Trail updates & GPS downloads at www.funtreks.com

Our first visit in 2004.

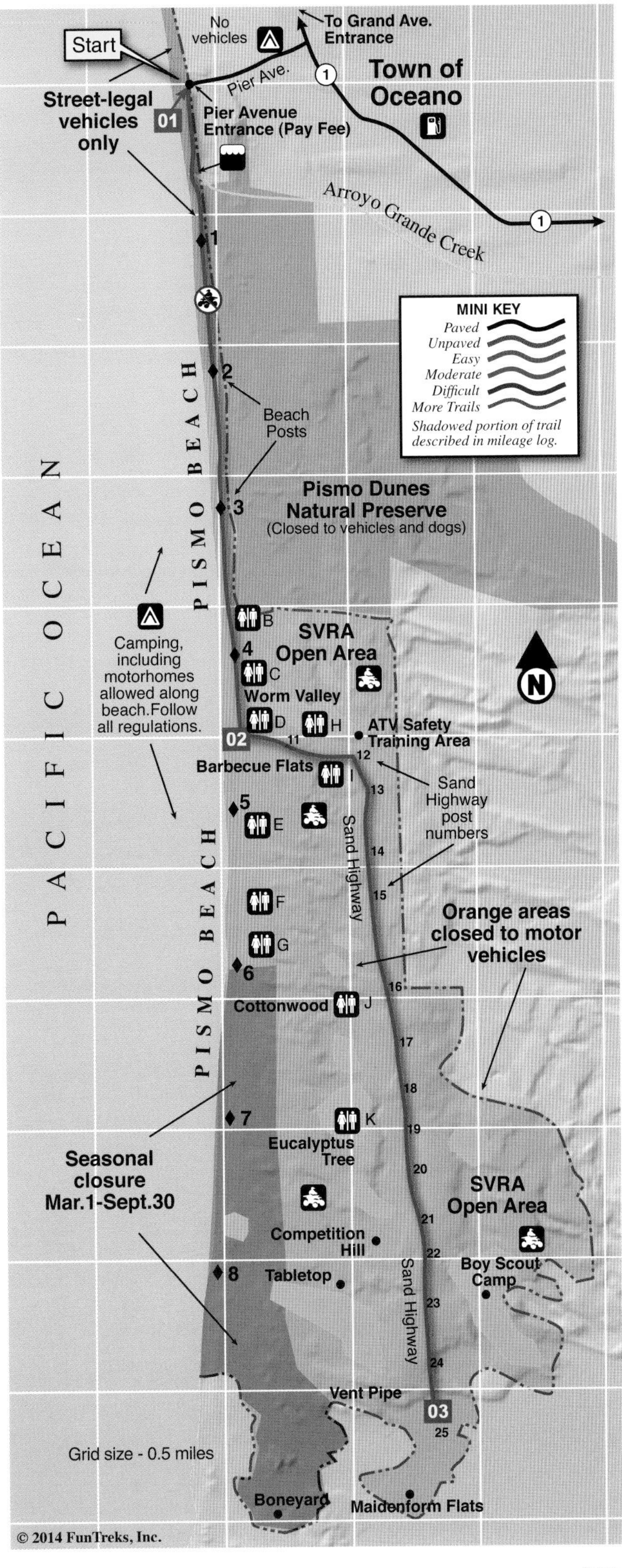

98 Mojave Road, East

AREA 9 map on page 216

Not much, if anything, marks start of trail.

It's easy to get lost. We recommend use of GPS.

Aggressive stock SUVs can manage this trail.

This old school bus is 300 ft. to side of road.

Historical Highlight: *Like many roads in the West, this route started as an Indian foot path and later became an important wagon road servicing mining operations and travelers heading west. The route's many natural springs provided life-sustaining water. In 1981, volunteers formed an organization called "Friends of the Mojave Road." They reopened the road for recreational and historic purposes, and are today committed to its preservation.*

Overview: This portion of the trip starts east of the California/Nevada state line. At first, it's not well marked and takes some patience to stay on the trail. You'll take a fun side trip to historic Fort Piute once you reach the boundary to the Mojave National Preserve. At this point, only street-legal vehicles are allowed to proceed. Dispersed camping is allowed along route unless posted otherwise. Pack out everything.

Rating: Moderate: Most of this route is easy, but several spots are steep, rocky and rutted. OK for aggressive stock 4x4 SUVs. Soft sand and muddy at times. Don't go alone. Carry plenty of water and gas. Flash floods possible. Route-finding is challenging. Follow cairns, which are always on the right. Free GPS waypoints can be downloaded from our website at www.funtreks.com.

Stats: Length: This part measures 38.7 miles. Time: Allow 5 to 7 hours. Elevation: 3,406 to 4074 ft. Open all year. Best time: Mid-September to mid-November, mid-March to mid-May.

Current Conditions: BLM Needles F.O., (760) 326-7030. Mojave National Preserve, Kelso V.C. (760) 252-6108.

Getting There: This trail starts in a dry wash on the west side of Needles Highway, exactly ¾ mile north of the Nevada state line. We found only tiny BLM posts marking the spot. These could easily be washed away. The easiest way to find this point is to follow signs to the Avi Casino located between Bullhead City, AZ, and Needles, CA. Head west from the casino to connect with Needles Highway (see map). Or head north on River Road from I-40.

START *MILEAGE LOG:*

0.0 Zero trip odometer **[Rev. Miles]** Head northwest in sandy wash. **[20.3]**
01 N35 03.102 W114 40.580

0.5 Continue straight past first line of telephone poles. **[19.8]**

1.7 Swing right and follow 2nd line of telephone poles uphill. **[18.6]**
02 N35 03.586 W114 42.150

3.2 Turn hard left away from telephone poles and head downhill. **[17.1]**
03 N35 04.613 W114 42.894

3.5 Bear right and follow wash northwest. Sign says wilderness left. **[16.8]**

5.8 Continue straight under powerline. **[14.5]**

6.8 Bear right at fork. Look for trail marker. **[13.5]**
04 N35 06.241 W114 45.374

8.0 Cross state line into California. Trail swings more westerly. **[12.3]**

8.6 Intersection of 3 marked roads. Continue straight on 9036. Cairn marks Mojave Road. **[11.7]**
05 N35 06.806 W114 47.028

11.3 Gradually descend to U.S. Hwy. 95. Cross pavement and continue west. **[9.0]**
06 N35 06.771 W114 49.740

13.9 Continue west where N045 crosses on an angle. Gets rockier. **[6.4]**

16.9 Steep, rutted section will challenge stock SUVs. Use caution. **[3.4]**

18.5 Continue west under double power lines to take side trip to Fort Piute. You'll return here. **[01.8]**
07 N35 06.739 W114 57.245

19.9 After curving around Jed Smith Butte, go past Turkey Farm. **[00.4]**

20.3 Kiosks explain history of Fort Piute. Road ends ahead. You must turn around. Return to Waypoint 07. **[00.0]**

0.0 Zero trip odometer at Wpt. 07. Head south between powerlines. **[16.6]**

1.4 Turn right away from power lines at cairn. **[15.2]**
08 N35 05.471 W114 57.305

4.8 Road winds uphill to high point with view, then continues west as it flattens out again. **[11.8]**

5.4 Hard right turn. **[11.2]**

5.9 Hard left turn. **[10.7]**
09 N35 05.992 W115 00.839

8.0 Continue west across wide wash. **[8.6]**

10.6 Join wider road, then exit left on other side. **[6.0]**

11.9 School bus on right. **[4.7]**

12.9 Turn right along fence line. **[3.7]**

13.1 Bear left at "T" and continue to follow fence. **[3.5]**
10 N35 07.577 W115 07.757

14.1 Bear right away from fence. **[2.5]**

14.7 Merge with another road, then in 50 ft., leave it to the right. **[1.9]**

15.2 Washed-out spot. **[1.4]**

16.0 Penny Tree on right. For good luck, leave a penny in dangling can. **[0.6]**

16.6 Intersect Ivanpah/Lanfair Road. Cross road and continue west to continue on Part 2 of Mojave Road. Left goes to Goffs and Interstate 40. **[0.0]**
11 N35 08.317 W115 11.212

Remains at Fort Piute.

Traveling with others is best.

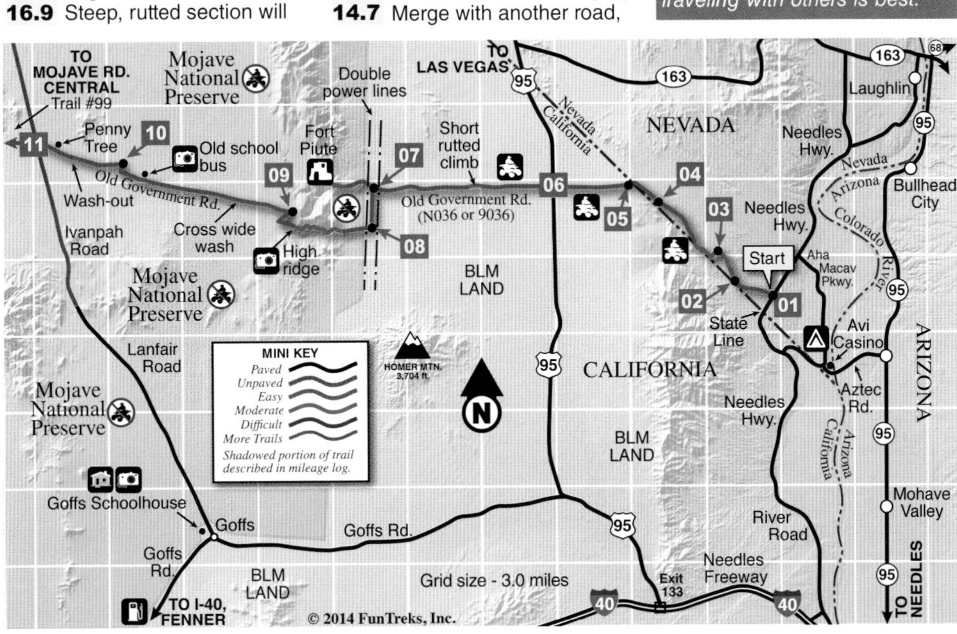

99 Mojave Road, Central

AREA 9 map on page 216

First part of trail is lined with Joshua trees.

Gorgeous sunsets are frequent.

Bert Smith's Rock House. Start of loop hiking trail.

Long stretches of sandy road. Don't go alone.

Windmill marks Government Holes.

Historical Highlight: *Bert Smith built the Rock House in 1929. He came to this desolate place in an attempt to prolong his life after being exposed to poisonous gases in WWI. Although not expected to live long, he lasted another 25 years. You'll see signs for a loop hiking trail by the cabin. We recommend the hike. It leads to photogenic Rock Spring that provided water for the cabin. From 1866 to 1868, Rock Spring was the site of a military outpost.*

Overview: Highlights of Mojave Road Central include stops at the Rock House, Government Holes, Marl Springs and the Mail Box. Entire route is inside the Mojave National Preserve, open to street-legal vehicles only. Trail departs from and rejoins larger Cedar Canyon Road several times.

Rating: Moderate: Mostly easy, but the descent to Watson Wash can be very challenging for stock 4x4 SUVs. This spot will be intimidating to novice drivers. Much of the route is soft sand, which, when dry, can quickly bog down any vehicle. Don't camp in washes where flash floods are possible.

Stats: Length: Almost 44 miles. Time: 6 to 8 hours. Elevation: 2,230 to 5,174 ft. Best time: Mid-September to mid-November, mid-March to mid-May.

Current Conditions: Mojave National Preserve, Kelso V.C. (760) 252-6108.

Getting There: Trail starts on Ivanpah/Lanfair/Goffs Road, where Mojave Road East ends. This point is about 17.2 miles north of Goffs and 0.8 mile north of Cedar Canyon Road.

START **MILEAGE LOG:**

0.0 Zero trip odometer [Rev. Miles] From Ivanpah Road after completing Mojave Road East, head west on sandy single-lane road. [20.6]
01 N35 08.310 W115 11.231

4.0 Continue straight where Caruthers Road crosses. [16.6]

7.0 Continue straight as you join wider Cedar Canyon Road. [13.6]

7.4 Bear left off Cedar Canyon Road at cairn. [13.2]
02 N35 08.850 W115 18.898

7.5 Very rough section as trail drops steeply into Watson Wash. At bottom, turn north in wash. Dangerous flash flood area. [13.1]

8.5 Stay left as you rejoin Cedar Canyon Rd. [12.1]

8.7 Continue straight as New York Mountain Road joins on right. [11.9]

8.8 Turn left off Cedar Canyon Road. (We couldn't find a cairn.) [11.8]

9.0 Turn left to visit Rock House. [11.6]
03 N35 09.329 W115 20.197

9.1 Parking lot. Hike short distance to stone cabin, then return to Wpt. 03, where you turn left to continue heading west-southwest. [11.5]

10.4 Soft left turn. [10.2]

10.7 Bear right at intersection to reach Government Holes at windmill. Continue north past windmill, then stay left until you reach Cedar Cyn. Rd. [9.9]
04 N35 08.834 W115 21.562

11.2 Continue west on Cedar Canyon Road. [9.4]

14.7 Continue straight where Black Canyon Road goes left. [5.9]

18.6 As you descend along wide wash, Cedar Cyn. Rd. becomes paved. [2.0]

20.6 Arrive at Kelso-Cima Rd. after R.R. tracks. [0.0]
05 N35 10.569 W115 30.555

0.0 Zero trip odometer at Wpt. 05 Cross Kelso-Cima Road and continue west past historical marker. Lots of whoop-ti-dos follow. [23.3]

4.7 Continue straight as road joins on left. [18.6]

5.4 Stay left where lesser road goes right. [17.9]

6.3 Terrific camp spot on left with some shade. [17.0]

7.6 Pass under power lines. [15.7]

8.5 Take short side trip left to Marl Springs, then return and continue left. [14.8]
06 N35 10.201 W115 38.813

10.1 Pass under major power lines. [13.2]

11.9 Can't miss the Mail Box on right. Please sign the log book. [11.4]
07 N35 11.123 W115 41.567

16.9 Cross Aiken Mine Road as you circle around the Cinder Cone Lava Beds Wilderness. You pass through Willow Wash where it is easy to get stuck in soft sand. If necessary, use Aiken Mine Road as a bypass. [6.4]

23.3 Intersect Kelbaker Road. If you need gas, right 14 miles is as close as it gets. Last leg of Mojave Road continues on other side of Kelbaker Rd. [0.0]
08 N35 11.938 W115 52.338

Sign-in at the Mail Box.

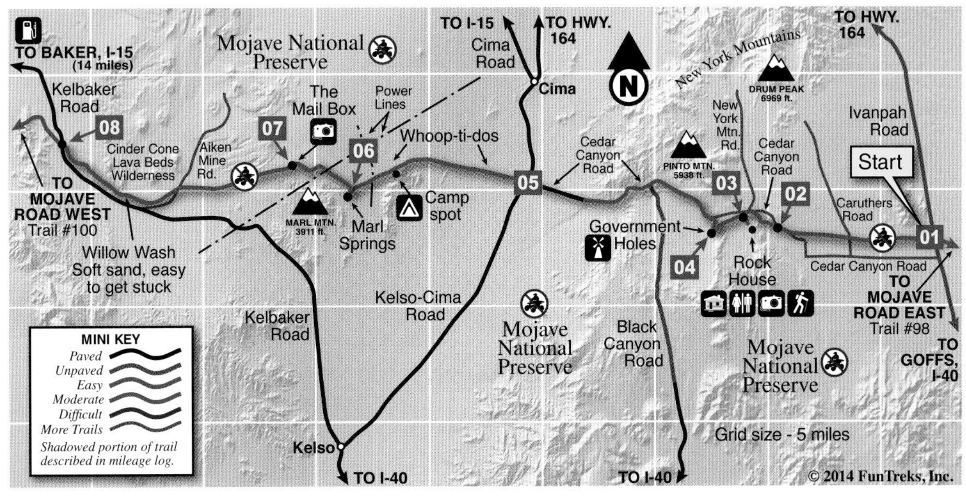

Mojave Road, West

100

AREA 9 map on page 216

Stay on most-traveled route across Soda Lake.

Leaving Mojave National Preserve.

Water often flows through Afton Canyon.

Traveler's Monument. Did you bring a rock?

Historical Highlight: *In the 1860s, Soda Springs was a small military outpost and stage stop. In 1944, the abandoned property was claimed by Dr. Curtis Springer, who developed it into a health resort. He named it Zzyzx as a gimmick to make it easy to find at the end of any alphabetical listing. He was evicted by the BLM in 1974. Concrete buildings and abandoned pools still remain (see map). Today, it's a Desert Studies Center run by California State University under the auspices of the Mojave National Preserve.*

Overview: The first part of the drive is uneventful as you head west from Kelbaker Road. Crossing Soda Lake is fairly routine, too, when the lake is dry. Concerns peak, however, if it has rained recently. You may be forced to take a long detour (described in mileage log). If you can cross the lake, you then enter an area where the trail may be obscured by wind-blown sand, increasing your chance of getting lost. Finally, you pass through Afton Canyon, which includes two crossings of the Mojave River. At rare times, these crossings can be very deep. Only street-legal vehicles are allowed inside Mojave National Preserve. OHV area west of preserve.

Rating: Moderate (when dry): Variable conditions may include: deep mud, soft wind-blown sand and difficult route-finding. Without question, 4-wheel drive is required. GPS is highly recommended.

Stats: Length: 36 miles. Time: 4 to 5 hours if all goes well. Allow more time in case you get lost. Elevation: 2,236 ft. at start to 917 ft. at Soda Lake. Best time: Mid-September to mid-November, mid-March to mid-May.

Current Conditions: BLM Barstow Field Office, (760) 252-6000, Mojave National Preserve, Kelso Depot Visitor Center, (760) 252-6108. Don't go if it is stormy or rained in the last few weeks.

Getting There: If you're driving as a continuation of Mojave Road Central, cross Kelbaker Road and follow sandy road northwest. This point is 14.1 miles southeast of Baker and 20.6 miles northwest of Kelso.

START *MILEAGE LOG:*

0.0 Zero trip odometer **[Rev. Miles]**
From Kelbaker Road, the trail angles northwest across sandy floodplain along foothills. [36.0]
01 N35 11.938 W115 52.338

2.0 Trail curves left around end of foothills and heads southwest. [34.0]

3.9 Continue straight where road crosses. (Paymaster Mine is to the left.) [32.1]

6.2 Continue straight across Kelso Road, often called Jackass Canyon Road. (Jackass Canyon is about 10 miles to left.) [29.8]
02 N35 11.201 W115 57.232

10.1 Bear slightly left. Do not go right. [25.9]

11.4 After very rutted section of road, you reach edge of Soda Lake. [24.6]
03 N35 09.420 W116 01.991
If road is dry, proceed cautiously on marked route only. Space out vehicles, so, if first vehicle gets stuck, others can help. If lake is too wet to cross, head north to Baker, then return to trail via Rasor Road from I-15.

15.4 Traveler's Monument. Did you bring a unique rock to add to the pile? [20.6]
04 N35 07.849 W116 05.718

16.6 Bear right at granite field. Follow markers north, then west, crossing over Zzyzx Road (may not be visible). [19.4]

17.9 Leave Mojave National Preserve. Follow cairns through wind-blown area where trail is often obscured by sand. [18.1]

18.8 Continue straight crossing Rasor Road. [17.2]
05 N35 06.517 W116 08.615

21.3 After crossing Shaw Pass (you may not realize you're going over a pass), bear left downhill. At bottom, head west again. If you can't see trail, drive on a line aimed at the south side of Cave Mountain, about 7 miles in the distance. [14.7]
06 N35 05.492 W116 10.882

29.2 Continue straight across marked Road 8711. [6.8]

30.2 Cross Basin Road at shallow angle heading southwest. Don't go south on Basin Road (may be obscured). [5.8]
07 N35 02.770 W116 18.165

30.8 Follow Mojave Road under Union Pacific trestle into Afton Canyon. Obey all signs. [5.2]

34.3 Turn right and follow improved road close to tracks. Keep moving. [1.7]

34.8 Cross Mojave River alongside trestle. Can be very deep. On other side of river, road goes right under trestle. [1.2]

36.0 You'll cross the river again before arriving at BLM Afton Campground on right. Fee area. [0.0]
08 N35 02.282 W116 23.048
After campground, follow good road uphill to the right 3.5 miles to I-15 at Exit 221. Note: A lesser-used section of Mojave Road continues to left part way up the exit road. This part is described in the "Mojave Road Guide," by Dennis Casebiar.

Trail updates & GPS downloads at www.funtreks.com

First crossing of Mojave River.

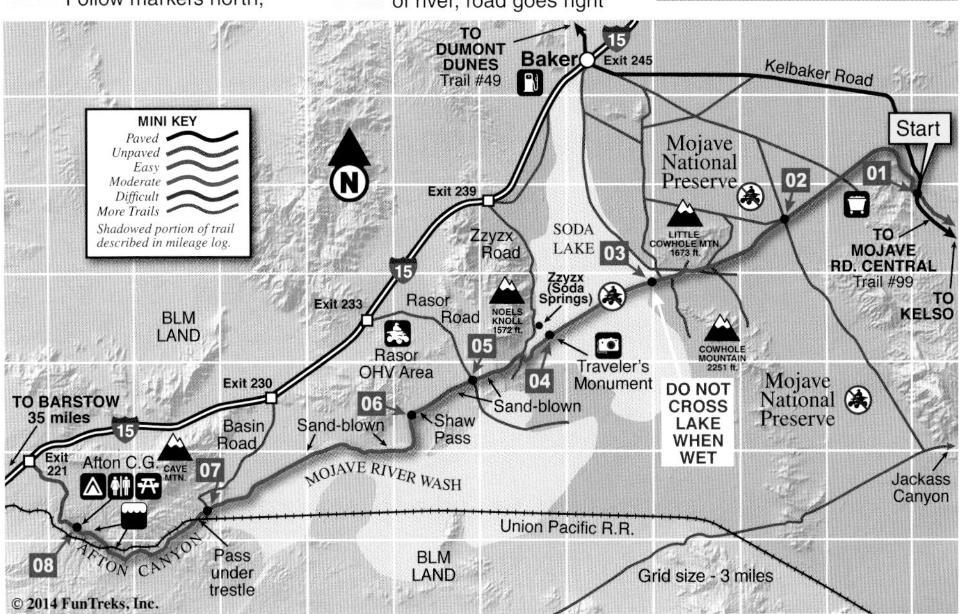

Map Legend

Interstate

Paved Road

Unpaved Road

Easy Trail

Moderate Trail

Difficult Trail

Other Trails

Described in Log

Hiking Trail

Boundaries

Public Toilet

Gas, Service

Parking

Staging

Camping

Mine

Hiking Trail

Mountain Biking

Waterfall

Water Crossing

Bridge

Picnic Table

Scenic Point

Fishing

Cabin

Windmill

Ghost Town

Arch

Rock Art

Ruins

Obstacle

Unlicensed OK

No Unlicensed

Author Bios

Charles (Chuck) Wells bought his first 4-wheel-drive SUV in 1993, and he had no idea how it would change his life. Like most SUV owners in Colorado, he bought the vehicle primarily for winter driving. But one summer day, he saw an intriguing dirt road that headed into the mountains. Off he went on his first real trip beyond the pavement. It was so much fun, he searched for other roads to duplicate the experience. Many more trips followed.

As his confidence grew, he ventured farther and farther into the backcountry. He realized he needed some guidance, so he bought every guidebook and map he could find. Unfortunately, most of the information was vague, incomplete or inaccurate. He continued to get lost, run into places too difficult for his vehicle and waste time on boring roads. This frustration led him to write his first book, Guide to Colorado Backroads & 4-Wheel Drive Trails, in 1998. Sales took off immediately. Within a year, he quit his job and started FunTreks Publishing.

Many years later, Wells has 11 books in print (most in second or third editions). His books include easy and moderate routes for stock SUVs, difficult trails for serious 4-wheelers and trails for unlicensed vehicles (ATVs, UTVs and dirt bikes). Today his books are standard equipment for thousands of motorized adventurers. He strongly promotes responsible use of public lands.

Wells continues to scout most of the trails and spends a great deal of time traveling in his motorhome. His books presently cover Colorado, Utah, Arizona and California. More states are planned.

Wells graduated from Ohio State University in 1969 with a degree in graphic design. After practicing design in Ohio, he moved to Colorado Springs in 1980 and worked 18 years in the printing business. He and his wife, Beverly, have two adult children and 4 grandchildren. They now live in Monument, CO, close to their business.

Matt (PT) Peterson got into 4-wheeling in 2000 after graduating from college. He built several off-road 4x4s starting with bolt parts, and later progressed to custom-built, off-road buggies. Wanting to share his new pastime, he and a few friends started their own 4-wheel-drive club in Michigan and the club is still going strong today. He has always had an interest in exploring less-traveled roads and was overjoyed when he moved to Colorado in 2003.

He worked several years as a graphic designer and computer technician, then joined FunTreks in 2008. He currently manages the office, scouts trails, then helps Wells write and produce the books.

Peterson graduated from Bethel College in 2000 with a degree in graphic design. He met his wife, Cassie, soon after moving to Colorado. Together, they enjoy camping and other outdoor activities in Colorado's enormous backyard.